D1547855

TIME AND A PLACE

MCGILL-QUEEN'S RURAL, WILDLAND, AND RESOURCE STUDIES SERIES

Series editors: Colin A.M. Duncan, James Murton, and R.W. Sandwell

The Rural, Wildland, and Resource Studies Series includes monographs, thematically unified edited collections, and rare out-of-print classics. It is inspired by Canadian Papers in Rural History, Donald H. Akenson's influential occasional papers series, and seeks to catalyze reconsideration of communities and places lying beyond city limits, outside centres of urban political and cultural power, and located at past and present sites of resource procurement and environmental change. Scholarly and popular interest in the environment, climate change, food, and a seemingly deepening divide between city and country, is drawing non-urban places back into the mainstream. The series seeks to present the best environmentally contextualized research on topics such as agriculture, cottage living, fishing, the gathering of wild foods, mining, power generation, and rural commerce, within and beyond Canada's borders.

Time and a Place

An Environmental History of Prince Edward Island

Edited by

EDWARD MACDONALD, JOSHUA MACFADYEN,
AND IRENÉ NOVACZEK

McGill-Queen's University Press
Montreal & Kingston • London • Chicago
and
Island Studies Press at UPEI Charlottetown

BRESCIA UNIVERSITY
COLLEGE LIBRARY

© McGill-Queen's University Press and Island Studies Press 2016

ISBN 978-0-7735-4692-9 (cloth)
ISBN 978-0-7735-4693-6 (paper)
ISBN 978-0-7735-9872-0 (ePDF)
ISBN 978-0-7735-9873-7 (ePUB)

Legal deposit second quarter 2016
Bibliothèque nationale du Québec

Printed in Canada on acid-free paper that is 100% ancient forest free
(100% post-consumer recycled), processed chlorine free

This book has been published with the help of a grant from the Canadian
Federation for the Humanities and Social Sciences, through the Awards to
Scholarly Publications Program, using funds provided by the Social Sciences and
Humanities Research Council of Canada. The publishers gratefully acknowledge
funding support from the Network in Canadian History and Environment.

McGill-Queen's University Press acknowledges the support of the Canada
Council for the Arts for our publishing program. We also acknowledge the
financial support of the Government of Canada through the Canada Book
Fund for our publishing activities.

Library and Archives Canada Cataloguing in Publication

Time and a place: an environmental history of Prince Edward Island / edited
by Edward MacDonald, Joshua MacFadyen and Irené Novaczek.

(McGill-Queen's rural, wildland, and resource studies series; 5)
Co-published by: Island Studies Press at UPEI Charlottetown.
Includes bibliographical references and index.
Issued in print and electronic formats.
ISBN 978-0-7735-4692-9 (hardback). – ISBN 978-0-7735-4693-6 (paperback). –
ISBN 978-0-7735-9872-0 (ePDF). – ISBN 978-0-7735-9873-7 (ePUB)

1. Human ecology – Prince Edward Island – History. 2. Natural history – Prince
Edward Island. 3. Ecology – Prince Edward Island. 4. Prince Edward Island –
Environmental conditions. I. MacDonald, Edward, editor II. Novaczek, Irené,
editor III. MacFadyen, Joshua, 1979–, editor IV. Series: McGill-Queen's rural,
wildland, and resource studies series; 5

GF13.3.C3T54 2016   304.209717   C2016-901340-5
                                           C2016-901341-3

This book was typeset by Interscript in 10.5/13 Sabon.

With great respect, we dedicate this volume to the memory of a much-loved Islander, organic farm entrepreneur, defender of wildlife, and friend of Island Studies, Raymond Loo (1962–2013)

Contents

Acknowledgments

In any large project involving multiple partners over many months, there are too many people, institutions, and organizations to thank in order to do it comprehensively or properly. Among those many, however, we would like to acknowledge (in no particular order) the following: the Social Sciences and Humanities Research Council for funding the Time and a Place conference; the Awards to Scholarly Publications program and the Network in Canadian History and Environment for helping to fund the book that the conference inspired; our colleague Alan MacEachern of Western University, whose fertile brain first hatched the notion that time and place should usefully intersect with environmental history, and who has contributed to the project in many ways; the wonderful Joan Sinclair of Island Studies Press, who somehow kept this project on the rails (even though there is no longer any railway on Prince Edward Island); Mark Abley, our Good Shepherd at McGill-Queen's University Press; our families – especially, Sheila, Colleen, and Ernest – who always end up sacrificing time and place to our projects; and, of course, our authors for their perception, their persistence, and, in the end, their patience.

Figures and Tables

TABLES

TIME AND A PLACE

Promise and Premise:
An Environmental History
for Prince Edward Island

Edward MacDonald, Joshua MacFadyen,
and Irené Novaczek

How odd, when you think of it, that a man rows backwards.
What experiences, deduction and sophistication
There had to be before men dared row backwards
Taking direction from where they'd been
With only quick-snatched glances at where they're going.

Milton Acorn, "The Squall"[1]

Walk anywhere on Prince Edward Island, and you know that it's been walked before. The Island has been home to Canada's First Nations for ten thousand years, to French and British settlers, and now to Canadians. It has experienced intensive settlement and resource use for centuries, and its forests, fisheries, and farmlands bear the wounds of soil and water contamination, urban and shoreline development, and a corrosive erosion that bleeds red soil from the land and coastal cliffs into its rivers, estuaries, and the surrounding Gulf of St Lawrence. Writes historian Alan MacEachern, "The Island is such a cultural artifact that one can be forgiven for thinking that its nature is nothing *but* history, time masquerading as space. And yet what has survived is a place still so pastoral, so beautiful, that it attracts a million visitors every summer."[2] This book is about that place and how its human and natural ecosystems developed together over time. The pastoral landscapes, red sandstone cliffs, and small fishing villages are appealing because they appear timeless, but they are as culturally constructed as they are shaped by the ebb and flow of the tides. Prince Edward Island's long and well-documented history, its small size, its status as a distinct political entity, and its islandness make it a compelling case study of human interactions with a particular landscape over thousands of years and the ways that environmental attitudes and practices have shaped that place's society and ecology.

Why focus on a place so famously disparaged by William Cobbett as "a rascally heap of sand and rock, and swamp?"[3] It began some 285 million years ago as little more than a sandbar, so much sediment washed from the flanks of the Appalachian Mountains in their geological youth, when the Atlantic Ocean was just beginning to open and "Prince Edward Island" rested within five degrees of the equator as part of what geologists call the Maritimes Basin. Time and geology created the brittle layers of sandstone that form the bedrock of today's province. The fine layer of rust – iron oxide – that coats each quartz sand grain gave the formation its name, the Prince Edward Island Redbeds. Continental drift gave it its current location in the southern Gulf of St Lawrence. Shifting ocean currents and climate fluctuations shaped its marine and terrestrial environment. Indeed, it was climate change – rising sea levels from melting glaciers – that made it an island as recently as five thousand years ago (see Keenlyside and Kristmanson, this volume).

Already by then, that landscape had been home to highly adaptive Amerindian peoples for five millennia. The Mi'kmaq people called it Abegweit (loosely translated as "cradled on the waves") and Minagoo, "The Island." In the sixteenth century French voyagers christened it Île Saint-Jean, and by 1720 France had planted a struggling colony there. Most of those Acadian fishers and farmers were deported or fled when the fortunes of war delivered the colony into the hands of the British in 1758, but as with their mainland counterparts, the Acadians' remnant agricultural lands contributed critical resources to early British settlers.[4] By the Treaty of Paris in 1763, Île Saint-Jean became, with a singular lack of imagination, St John's Island. The British era began with a detailed survey by Samuel Holland in 1764–65; a land lottery in 1767, which imposed large-scale, leasehold land tenure; and, somewhat improbably, the grant of colony status in 1769. Three decades later, in 1799, there was one last name change, to honour a lacklustre British prince whose chief accomplishment was to father the future Queen Victoria. Much against Britain's better judgment, Prince Edward Island achieved self-government in 1851 and, much against *its* better judgement, entered Confederation with Canada in 1873.

And what of the place itself? Tucked into the southern basin of the Gulf of St Lawrence, it stretches scarcely 224 kilometres from North Cape to East Point. A narrow strait, anywhere from 13 to 43 kilometres wide, divides it from the rest of Maritime Canada. In places, the little island is narrow enough (4 kilometres) to portage in a few arduous hours, and even at its widest it is no more than 40 kilometres from one deeply indented coast to the other. The island's saltwater borders enclose 5,660 square kilometres of signature-red soil, spread like butter over a soft sandstone base. Much of the interior is rolling hill country, but its topynomy habitually makes mountains of molehills; the highest point is only 142 metres above sea level. The till contained enough cobble for most of the tools of its first peoples and provided a relatively uniform base for the Island's three types of Acadian forest and diverse fauna (see Keenlyside and Kristmanson, Curley, and Sobey, this volume), but the uplands were largely undisturbed by the coastal-based Aboriginal and French Acadian populations. The British settlement period (1763–1855) told a different story. By the late nineteenth century, commercial lumbering and land-clearing for settlement had devastated the Island's forest and cleared two-thirds of its surface for agriculture. As the upland forests fell to settlers, they revealed the best agricultural land in the region. But that valuation is relative. Most of the land is arable, but only some of it is fertile; poorly drained soils alternating with sandy loams are vulnerable to wind and water erosion.

The surrounding sea does much more than define the Island's borders. It complicates its weather, air-conditions its people, and mediates its climate. Winter ice in the Gulf and Northumberland Strait usually ensures a late spring, and even if, as tourism boosters claim, Island shores are washed in summer by the warmest waters north of the Carolinas, the seas stay cool enough for the prevailing westerlies to cut the high heat of July and August. In autumn, the effect is reversed, and the lingering warmth of the shallow, sun-warmed Gulf helps hold winter at bay.

The general consistency of the climate – an annual average of 860 millimetres of rain and 290 centimetres of snow, an average temperature of -7°C in January and 19°C in July – masks its yearly fluctuations. Climatologists and historians have shown the extreme variability of the region's climate, particularly in the nineteenth century. The ice extents halted navigation for around 125 days each year in the early nineteenth century, but the average number of navigable days increased along with average annual temperatures as the century progressed. Still, as Teresa Devor argues, gradual warming did not reduce the sporadic occurrence of cold growing seasons – such as those of 1881, 1884, 1905, and 1921,

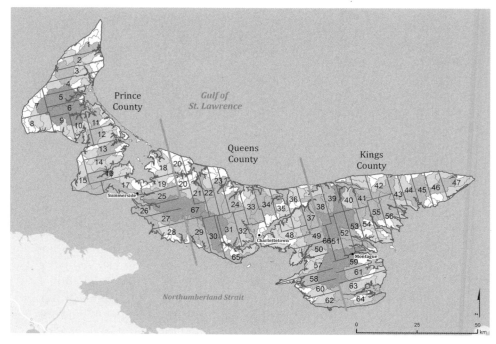

Figure I.1 Prince Edward Island jurisdictions and watersheds.

where the mean temperature was below 14°C – or cold winters – such as
in 1875 and 1920, when the mean January temperature was around
-15°C. Every decade in the nineteenth century (with the exception of the
balmy 1850s) featured at least one winter when harbours were frozen
for over 130 days.[5] With a climate like this, weather has always been a
favourite topic of conversation, forming what Liza Piper calls the region's
"colloquial meteorology."[6]

Over many centuries the Island's sea, soil, and climate have offered
rich habitat for plant and wildlife and valuable resources for First
Nations, fishers, and Irish moss harvesters. However, creating habitat for
the primary vector of nineteenth-century resettlement, the sedentary
farm family, was more challenging, and like many Maritime regions, the
Island attracted a relatively small agricultural population. Both French
and English settlers were reluctant to leave other centres and cross over
to these shores. Condemnations such as William Cobbett's were no help,
but other reasons, such as the Island's distance from its markets and
its troubled management by mainly absentee proprietors, were larger

deterrents. Environmental historians have also noted the early food scarcities created by adverse crop and climate conditions, and MacFadyen (this volume) shows that nineteenth-century farming was a precarious business.[7]

Even now, Prince Edward Island is the smallest, though most densely populated, province (an estimated 145,000 people in 2013) in a vast country, and the only one with (by census definitions) a majority-rural population. Garden tropes litter its descriptive literature, yet most visitors still find it apt rather than hackneyed (and dangerously superficial) to read about the "patchwork quilt" of its pastoral landscape. Viewed from a distance, it seems encouragingly self-contained, an unambiguously bounded, curiously homogenous space, a place where nature has largely been tamed and where time has meshed its people with their environment.

The environmental history of Prince Edward Island is deeply shaped by humans, but as Dolly Jørgensen reminds us, it was "not by human hands" but by technologies that people shaped this island. "To be human is to employ technologies," Jørgensen writes, "including physical objects as well as the processes of design, production, maintenance, and knowledge that go into their making. It is technology that has made humans into a force of nature."[8] As many historians have argued, the relationship between nature and technology is highly complex. Technology drives history and shapes environments, but not without reciprocal forces from human culture and not without influence from other natural organisms. In fact, a place like Prince Edward Island is not "natural" at all. Like other recent environmental historians, we lean toward "environments" rather than nature. The term describes dynamic human and non-human relationships in place, and as we argue in this collection, there is little that resembles wilderness or untouched nature on Prince Edward Island.

On the other hand, technologies are also more "natural" than we often assume. Islanders modified the environment with tools ranging from Mi'kmaq arrowheads, Acadian *aboiteaux*, and British axes, but they also introduced, modified, and constrained a range of plant and animal species. Plants and animals are tools as well, and like all technologies, they demand a certain set of responses and behaviours from us. They also demand valuation. Because so many plants and animals are functional members of our environments, we assign meaning to them mainly in relation to how they behave in these environments.

Thus, non-human species enrich and confound their users, and as active members of an ecosystem they interact with each other in ways that humans both desire and dread.[9] By removing forests and planting single-species crops of grain, early British settlers created an ideal habitat for the "plague mouse," which Douglas Sobey (this volume) argues was the red-backed vole (*Clethrionomys gapperi*). The nineteenth century saw the slow and steady displacement of these and other forest "wildlife" by a population of primarily ruminant livestock. These central members of the Island's agro-ecosystem were joined by an extensive population of silver foxes, famously bred for fur ranching by Charles Dalton and Robert Oulton. Rosemary Curley (this volume) describes how introduced fur animals such as the silver foxes, striped skunks, and raccoons contaminated local genetic stock and habitat and became regarded, along with beavers, as pests in the twentieth century.

The Island was also home to many marine organisms that were either harvested for industry, such as Irish moss (Novaczek), or farmed in bays, such as mussels and oysters. The oyster was an excellent example of an organism that might appear wild but was actually highly manipulated by First Nations (Keenlyside and Kristmanson), nineteenth-century farmers (MacFadyen), and twentieth-century aquaculture officials (MacDonald and Beck). After narrowly escaping destruction by farmers, oysters were protected for aquaculture and then nearly extirpated after 1915 with the introduction of diseased oyster spat from Chesapeake Bay.

These stories of animal misadventures will sound familiar to readers who know about the disruptions of settlement and the experiments of modern states. Prince Edward Island's environmental and technological history – referred to by many as "envirotech" – stands out for at least two reasons. First, it experienced a relatively recent and rapid transition from Cobbett's "rascally swamp" to a measured and manipulated coastal agro-ecosystem. Second, what seemed to many contemporaries like a typical experience of settlement and technological progress actually slowed significantly in the early twentieth century. Just as the technologies employed, and created, in Prince Edward Island blurred the boundaries between human and non-human environments, there was no simple trajectory from basic to advanced technologies. The province has never been a leader in the high-tech sector, but at various points, particularly in its shipbuilding (Sobey) and energy histories (Wynn and Stuart), it attracted early advances and world-class specialists. The Island was serviced by coal-fired steamers by the mid-nineteenth century, gas lights by 1854, one of Canada's first narrow-gauge railways by 1871, and localized electric stations by the mid-1880s. Yet what seemed like technological progress in the late nineteenth century did not benefit all Islanders equally. Rural Islanders were among the last in the country to widely adopt electricity and telephone service in the postwar period, and the province's railway was abandoned in 1989, having never turned a profit.[10]

The misplaced optimism and faith in technology was perhaps most evident in 1929, when Island premier Albert C. Saunders published his article "The Rapid Progress of Prince Edward Island." He highlighted the province's cooperative marketing groups and its agricultural products: dairy, certified seed potatoes, foxes, and "the famous Island oysters," which Saunders admitted "for some time have not been producing." In a special Maritime edition of the Canadian Manufacturers Association's boosterist magazine *Industrial Canada*, Saunders argued that, despite its insignificant manufacturing sector, the Island "is nevertheless sharing in the growth and expansion so much in evidence throughout the entire Dominion."[11] In reality, the Island had a small – and aging – agricultural sector in a period when most wealth was generated by industry and finance. The environmental and technological transformations that began with shipbuilding and agricultural settlement in the nineteenth century had been followed in the twentieth by a period of agricultural stagnation, industrial decline, and out-migration.

Recognizing that change is both constant and contingent brings us back to the basic principle of *Time and a Place*. This book began with an idea: that time and place are inextricably bound when it comes to environmental history, and that larger insights can come from examining environmental change in one well-defined place across the long sweep of time. Most of the authors set out to write a coherent collection of essays at a joint meeting of the Network in Canadian History and Environment (www.niche-canada.org) and the Institute of Island Studies (www.upei.ca/iis); taken together, their essays assemble an environmental mosaic that pieces together the story of interaction between humans and this particular place. Environmental history is a house with many rooms, and the essays in the collection also draw on island studies, natural history, pre-contact archaeology, marine and land geology, environmental law, wildlife management, and environmentalism itself, in addition to environmental history. The contributors thus speak with many voices, but all share a conviction that the way forward leads through the tangled and often contested landscapes of the past. In addition to offering expertise from several disciplines, the authors of this volume have walked the Island's fields and forests, its shores and streets. In the process, they have identified links between its past and present, and broadly considered the Island's future sustainability. The result is not a comprehensive environmental history of the province, and yet it is much more than a beginning.

The goals of *Time and a Place* are thus local and global, pragmatic and theoretical. This place-based exploration of Canada's smallest province should afford policy insights for planners within Prince Edward Island, but it also informs broader questions about the value of islands – these geographically bounded spaces – for the study of environmental history and the crafting of comprehensive plans for global sustainability. And we hope that it will be a useful piece of a larger puzzle, the environmental history of Canada itself. In his comprehensive account of environmental history from the 49th parallel to the Arctic, Graeme Wynn adopts a continentalist approach to human relationships with nature, and recent anthologies have done the same for regions like Atlantic Canada. As Wynn found for a continental overview, the stories of work and other interactions with land and sea are the best way to understand humans in this natural environment, but the broad scope of such a work means that some regions, and smaller provinces such as PEI, escape notice.[12] By down-sampling the continentalist approach and focusing on field, forest, and estuarine ecosystems, we have covered many of the critical environmental issues in one province, over the same time frame. Like Wynn, we begin with a *tabula rasa*, a land scraped by ice and then engulfed by rising seas. Our authors document the arrival of flora, fauna, and humans and the different ways these inhabitants have used and understood this place over time.

Prince Edward Island's small size and rural, resource-based population make it an ideal place for Canada's first provincial environmental history. Thanks in part to its relatively late settlement and history of absentee proprietors in the eighteenth century, reinforced by its late entry into Confederation, it is the only Canadian island endowed with what Godfrey Baldacchino and David Milne call the "gift of jurisdiction."[13] But the very reason for its gift, its islandness, makes *Time and a Place* unique in another way. As two of our contributors (environmental historian Graeme Wynn and nissologist John Gillis) point out, islands have long fascinated us. Boundedness makes an island a place apart. As Claire Campbell writes elsewhere in this volume, it "telescopes our attention, inviting us to delve deeply into the past in one place." It also lends to that place an imaginative power, making an island a metaphor. It can be refuge or prison; a utopia or its dark, dystopic opposite; a museum where the past lingers, or a laboratory for testing theories; a microcosm yielding insights into the larger world, or a world entire unto itself. Of course, islands have no monopoly on boundedness. A mountain valley or a desert oasis constitute geographic islands of a different sort, just as race, culture, demography, or economics can create social "islands" within larger entities. But nowhere are the boundaries "here" and "there," "us" and "them" more precise or more felt than on a body self-consciously surrounded by water, and nowhere else are these physical ecotones so ideally suited to environmental history.

Conceptually and psychologically, islands exist in relation to mainlands, and all islands have been colonized many times from across the waters, first by flora and fauna (as both Curley and Novaczek remind us in this volume), then by people (see Keenlyside and Kristmanson), and as often by ideas. Waves of human ideologies and ideas resulted in social and economic development, often with mixed results for people and their environment – as evidenced by Sobey (with respect to forestry), MacFadyen and Arsenault (agriculture), MacDonald and Beck (fisheries), MacEachern (tourism), and Stuart (energy). When you're island born, as Island poet Milton Acorn observed, you are "native with a habitat,"[14] and negative environmental consequences of development are difficult to ignore.

Both Prince Edward Islanders and their historians have been accused of culpable insularity, a conviction that their province's story is somehow outside the larger currents of history.[15] This stubborn insistence on particularity is arguably linked to Islanders' perception that other Canadians consider the province as inconsequential to any larger narrative. Certainly, the province fitted awkwardly – or not at all – into the grand old theories that dominated Canada's twentieth-century historiography. Frederick Jackson Turner's "frontier thesis" moved the cutting edge of history and democracy ever westward away from the Atlantic shore, and there was scant room for a small producer such as Prince Edward Island in the Laurentian school of Canadian history or its allied "staples theory," although both looked to environmental factors in tracing Canada's economic development.[16] Contrary to these theories, Prince Edward Island population and industry surged in the mid-nineteenth century based not on staple or even primary sector exports, but on a highly manufactured product: sailing ships.[17] Environmental collapse in the forest was one of the main factors for that industry's decline; this decline and the transition to farming and fishing are explored in the chapters by Sobey, MacFadyen, and MacDonald and Beck. The Island then became a hinterland without a metropolis, a food-producing province separated by ice and ocean from its growing but industrially decentralized region, and the trickle of underemployed youth "goin' down the road" to Central Canada and New England in the late nineteenth century became a steady stream by the interwar period.[18]

Perhaps as a result of its unique environmental and economic trajectory, Prince Edward Island historiography has either emphasized the province's intrinsic importance for its own residents or treated it as a convenient case study for larger purposes.[19] This somewhat artificial binary is where comparisons to the continentalist approach break down. As scholars of Northern and Indigenous history now posit, the study of "marginal" regions is only marginal when we insist on understanding one place in relation to another – the colonized in relation to the colonizers, the province as part of the nation, the island as extension of the mainland – rather than understanding it as homeland.[20] The writing of island history is changing, in part as the discipline of history fractures into sub-genres, and in part because of the emerging field of nissology – the study of islands on their own terms. Instead of a tiny province perched on the periphery of a great landmass where power tilts towards the centre, Prince Edward Island can locate itself within an island-centric world view in which islands are the norm rather than an anomaly.[21] In environmental terms, nissology has a particular significance. As scientists are apt to remind us, islands are the canaries in the mine of the world's environment, the places where climate change and ecological dysfunction may first be felt. It is a sobering reminder to read in Keenlyside and Kristmanson's chapter that Prince Edward Island, which began as so much silt,[22] was not even an island five thousand years ago, and many of its most intensively settled sites are now under water.

And then there is environmental history, that multidisciplinary crossroads where so many paths meet: history, natural history, geography, science, nissology, archaeology, folklore, literature, to name a few. As the most recent environmental history of this region shows, the debate over the analytical relevance of bioregions versus geopolitical boundaries subsides into mutual accommodation (physical features, flora, and fauna do not recognize political borders, but the humans who exploit all of them do).[23] Prince Edward Island, which is both a bioregion and a political entity, moves sharply into focus. It is at once case study, exemplar, and model. The Island is not entirely virgin territory in terms of environmental history, although much of the writing about it has come at it aslant, under the guise of conventional history, geography, or biology.[24] Apart from geographer A.H. Clark's monumental *Three Centuries and the Island*, the essential reference point for any new study, environmental history has also tended to be subject specific: for example, Alan MacEachern's studies of the Prince Edward Island Natural Park and the Institute of Man and Resources.[25] And while land has figured largely in Island historiography, especially that concerning the nineteenth century, it has too often been preoccupied with the struggle *for* the land rather than settlers' struggle *with* it. Political issues of land tenure and land use have tended to overshadow any extended exploration of agriculture on environmental terms.[26] Similarly, historians have tended to a narrowly economic approach to the Island's other main resource-based industries, shipbuilding, fishing, and forestry, ignoring questions of environment and sustainability. This collection is the first to approach the entire province from a self-consciously environmental history perspective. Each contribution falls somewhere along the topical spectrum, deftly encapsulated by MacEachern, that defines environmental history: nature itself over time, and how it affects humans, how we use nature, and what we think about it.[27]

Libby Robin reminds us that islands helped define evolutionary theory, island biogeography, and environmental history, but the continentalist and bioregional approaches of environmental history now provide new and more cosmopolitan ways of looking at islands and complexity in a globalizing century.[28] If environmental history is important because place is always bound up in time, islands' environmental histories are important because those places are connected and isolated at different times. In one sense, then, this is a book about connectedness and disconnectedness. For much of its history as an island, the place we call Prince Edward Island was in most years virtually cut off from the mainland from December until April. Island society arguably bears the marks of that solitude. And yet, the southern Gulf of St Lawrence was always also a road, albeit a treacherous one, and a road with different off-ramps from those of the fluvial and upper St Lawrence River. The Mi'kmaq people travelled it seasonally by canoe. European sailing vessels fished its waters and frequented its harbours. As with the Hebrides in the Middle Ages, the sea connected the Island to the world more readily than pre-railroad trails and rivers could penetrate the great plains and mountain fastness of the North American interior. To Islanders, then, the sea was not an end but a beginning. Its saltwater walls defined and delimited, but the walls had wide doors to the ideas and technologies of the Atlantic world. Just as periodic disconnection shaped culture, the routes and means of connection contributed to the Island's sense of place and identity. Navigational charts and technologies connected the first Acadians with Louisbourg. Land surveys, censuses, and urban development connected United Kingdom colonists to Britain. Railroad and ferry services connected (and confederated) all parts of the new province with the Dominion of Canada. The telegraph and then the telephone connected local fisheries officers and politicians to Ottawa. Paved roads connected rural consumers to the city.

During the nineteenth and twentieth centuries, transportation and communication technologies diminished space. In recent decades, as William Cronon has argued in *Nature's Metropolis*,[29] they have obliterated it. Now even time, so connected to distance, seems to contract. What will this mean in environmental and psychological terms for the physical place of Prince Edward Island? According to John Gillis, the tide of human migration is washing back towards our coastlines, even as our cultural relationship with the coast undergoes – pardon the pun – a sea change. As coastal dwellers generally become more detached from nature,[30] Islanders are the only ones who can, as Gillis puts it, walk "the continuous loop" of the ecotone, both in mind and on foot. As North American societies sidle closer and closer to the water, putting pressure on coastal ecosystems and higher value on coastal properties, they too must understand the nature of the coast, its changes over time, and the long human history of life along its shores.

Time and a Place addresses that need. The collection has been organized into four sections (islands, people, industry, and governance) that move the discussion from the conceptual through the actual. But whether exploring the changing habitats of land, shore, and sea or documenting the historical exploitation of landscape and resources and their (mis) management, each essay is haunted by the ecological footprint of human presence. Humans have been drawn to this place for millennia to exploit its resources: to fish and hunt and gather, to plant and harvest, to consume (as tourists do) its visual landscape, to find a space to call their own. In the process they have both transformed and created landscape. As contributor Claire Campbell points out, *Time and a Place* reminds us that environmental histories and environmental futures are bound together. The past helps makes sense of the present, and so, charting Islanders' past impact on the environment – and its consequences – can inform current issues and frame possible outcomes. There is much that both Islanders and global citizens can learn from how we have struggled – and often failed – to manage our mediation of habitats and species. Islands are perhaps the most obvious places to teach the lesson of limits. Environmental sustainability will undoubtedly require, as ecologist Garrett Hardin posits, mutually acceptable levels of coercion, the age-old balance between individual freedom and communal good. Will that be more possible on a small island than a vast continent?

Many people imagine islanders as helpless victims of coastal and environmental change, but in times of unpredictable shifts in the natural world, we are perhaps more fortunate.[31] As Gillis argues elsewhere in this volume, islanders are people who "master margins and exploit multiple environments." Unlike people in the Rockies or on the Great Plains, islanders and coastal dwellers live in a landscape that changes every six hours and steadily over time. The dynamic possibilities of such an environment hold both threat and promise. Milton Acorn, again, on islands: "Growing up on one's good training/For living in a country, on a planet."[32] *Time and a Place* argues that Acorn is right.

I

Imagining Islands: Islands and Environmental History

To be born on an island's to be sure
You are native with a habitat.
Growing up on one's good training
For living in a country, on a planet.

Shall I tell you the soil's red
As a flag? Sand a pink flesh gleam
You could use to tone a precious stone?
All its colours are the colours of dreams.

"I, Milton Acorn," Milton Acorn
First published in *The Island Means Minago*, 1975

Muddying the Waters of Environmental History: Islands as Ecotones

John R. Gillis

Islands are different from all other lands insofar as they are defined by water. "The concept 'island,'" it has been noted, "implies a particular and intense relationship between land and water."[1] No wonder, for the word itself comes from the Old English *igland*, *ig* meaning water. As water-lands, islands have not one but several ecosystems. They are *ecotonal*, that is, places where ecosystems intersect, overlap, and, as the word implies, exist in creative tension with one another. Islands are never the clearly bounded entities we imagine them to be. It was Rachel Carson who rightly insisted that "always the edge of the sea remains an elusive and indefinable boundary."[2] We will never understand island environments until we stop treating them as exclusively territorial, as continents in miniature.[3]

Even though islands have played a key role in generating modern environmental awareness, they have been overshadowed by larger land masses. Early European explorers identified tropical islands as lost paradises, the location of the original Eden. The devastation wrought by invasive species and deforestation on the Madeiras, St Helena, Mauritius, and the sugar islands of the Caribbean in the early modern period produced the world's first environmental awareness. As Richard Grove has noted, "The island easily became, in practical environmental as well as mental terms, an easily conceived allegory of a whole world. Contemporary observations of the ecological demise of islands were easily converted into premonitions of environmental destruction on a more global scale."[4] Even before Charles Darwin's visit to the Galapagos in 1835, islands had been treated as laboratories for the biological sciences. Their purported boundedness and isolation made them ideal sites for religious fantasy as well as scientific speculation. As Grove points out, the island, together with the garden, in their "symbolic (or even totemic) forms seem to have proved central to the task of giving a meaning and an epistemology to the natural world and to western interaction with it."[5]

Biologists treated islands as if they were separate ecosystems. Later, islands would recommend themselves to anthropologists as sites of scientific study of human nature, as if islanders were pure specimens, fossil societies somehow untainted by outside influences or historical change.[6] In recent years, the notion of the insularity of islands has been repeatedly challenged, and evidence continues to accumulate that island histories and geographies are not coterminous with the physical limits of the island itself.[7] Even so, the theory of island biogeography, developed in the 1960s, remains powerful. David Quammen writes in *Song of the Dodo*, "Islands have been especially instructive because their limited area and their inherent isolation combine to make patterns of evolution stand out starkly ... Islands give clarity to evolution."[8] Islands continue to be portrayed socially and politically as bounded, isolated entities, existing outside the flow of time. This isolation makes them ideal sites for projects ranging from penal colonies to utopias.[9] From the beginning, westerners have treated islands as lands rather than waterlands, thinking of them in ways that "emphasize the bounded landscape at the expense of the broader seascape."[10] Environmentalists have followed in this tradition, focusing either on land or on sea, ignoring that which connects them. It is that connectedness that has driven the emergence of fields of study such as "Atlantic history."

For the most part, the environmental sciences have been landlocked disciplines. Oceanography is one of the last born of the modern sciences, always playing catch-up. Even environmental history has sometimes been guilty of ignoring the 70 per cent of our globe's surface covered by water, a biosystem estimated to constitute 98 per cent of our biosphere. Western civilization has largely ignored the sea except as something to pass over, while other societies, notably those of Pacific isles, have felt much more at home with water. The West has consistently defined the sea as "other," exotic. The cartographic tradition of colouring it monotonic blue suggests a vacuity that we rarely attribute to land.

In western pagan and Christian traditions, the sea is a mysterious presence, the "Great Unknown," as Henry Gosse put it. For the Greeks, land stood for order, water for chaos. The Judeo-Christian culture was equally insistent on identifying humanity with soil, locating its origins in an inland Eden, ignoring all evidence of aquatic ancestry. Medieval Europe perpetuated the ancients' notion of the continents as constituting one continuous earth island, Orbis Terrarum, surrounded by a deadly river called Oceanus. It was not until the fifteenth century that the river came to be understood as a series of navigable seas. Yet, these were of interest not for themselves but rather for the access they provided to other lands.

Until the later nineteenth century, western understandings of oceans were one-dimensional. They were perceived as surfaces, without depth or an environmental history of their own.[11] Naval or maritime history might take place on its surface, but the sea itself existed outside of time. Even as land was coming to be seen as a factor shaping human destiny, oceans were refused historical agency. Modern historical writing has been largely continentalist in orientation. For most historians, history begins and ends at the shore. Even maritime history has been largely concerned with what happens *on* rather than *in* the sea. "People who live on continents get in the habit of regarding the ocean as journey's end, the full stop at the end of the trek," writes Jonathan Raban.[12] But islands afford another perspective, one that takes water into account. Again, Raban: for "people who live on islands, especially on small islands, the sea is always the beginning … Islanders also know the sea goes on and on, in a continuous loop of shoreline and life, without a terminus." Unfortunately, island history and geography are too often told in continentalist terms. When European and American imperialists entered the Pacific in the eighteenth century, they set boundaries around islands that made no sense to Indigenous peoples used to seeing the water as connecting rather than dividing their "sea of islands."[13]

Reformulating and revitalizing environmental history means not only going offshore but also following the waters inland. More attention must be given to watersheds and estuaries, to brown as well as blue water. We must follow migratory species, including humans, back and forth across the tide line, for island environmental history must be a history without borders, a history in depth as well as breadth, where earth, wind, and water are in constant motion and interaction and humankind plays a significant role. Of necessity, such a history will be more liquid, but still grounded in the actual experiences of islands and islanders. We need to muddy the waters by bringing earth and water, man and nature together.

ISLANDS AS CO-CONSTRUCTIONS
OF MAN AND NATURE

It is particularly important to understand that island history is a co-construction of humans and nature. Humans have been shaped by islands, but islands also bear the imprint of humans. It has been said that "it is just as interesting to ask how people make islands as how islands make people."[14] Islands appeal to us because they appear to be bounded objects that can easily be grasped by the mind's eye. Of all topographies, they are perhaps the most metaphorically powerful. We use the concept of "island" to describe all kinds of places – mountains, parts of the brain, traffic dividers – when we want to suggest separateness and isolation.[15] But our idea of islands often blinds us to their realities, which are by no means disconnected from the world at large.

How islands are perceived varies from culture to culture, and over time within cultures. Islands in the minds of islanders are very different from those perceived by people who dwell in the interiors of mainlands, but not necessarily so different from those in the minds of coastal people, who have a relationship to the sea similar to that of islanders. In the past, both islanders and coastal people qualified – along with the flora and fauna they depended on – as *edge species*, capable of exploiting the possibilities of the ecotones they occupied. Inlanders can also master margins, taking advantage of multiple environments; however, as industrial agriculture and forestry have become increasingly monocultural, interior ecotones have become rarer.[16] But it is also important to differentiate people who live *on* coasts from those who live *with* them, making their livings by crossing the tide line as fishers, gatherers, or mariners. Today, increasing numbers of people live *on* the shore, but fewer and fewer know how to live *with* the sea in an ecologically sustainable manner.

Environments are not something apart from us but something that we have had a hand in constructing. The scale of an island environment is partly determined by nature, the patterns of winds and waves that impinge on it, but it is also defined by how far its inhabitants range off- and on-shore in search of resources. Newfoundlanders were traditionally expert at hunting and gathering on both sides of the tide line. In summer, they turned their backs on the interior, but in winter they could be found inland, shooting moose, harvesting berries, and felling timber. Where fisheries are involved, the relevant environment is established not just by the migrations of the species being pursued but by the range of the fishers: the operative environment of an oysterman or clammer may be relatively narrow in scope, but a deep sea mariner will engage with several different ecosystems in a single voyage. The whalers of Nantucket, for example, ranged the Atlantic and the Pacific, encountering a remarkable variety of conditions. Living an ecotonal existence, islanders are extraordinarily sensitive and adaptable to the conditions of both land and water, but their relationship to nature is by no means passive. On the contrary, they have been shaping their own environments for millennia.

Islands are notorious shapechangers. Because coasts are fractal rather than linear, the exact dimensions of islands are hard to pin down.[17] They change with every tide, with every major storm and earthquake. Our ancestors were right in thinking of them as moving or floating, as alive, for in the same way as coasts, they are elusive and indefinable. In places of seismic activity, they are known to erupt suddenly from the seabed and disappear just as quickly. Both the Atlantic and Pacific are full of vanished islands, some quite real, others mythical.[18] Mariners are all too familiar with "looming," an atmospheric effect that makes islands appear to rise out of the sea into the air.[19] Islands have a powerful hold on our imaginations. Western Europeans dreamed of Atlantic isles long before they discovered, surveyed, and settled them.[20] Even now that we have global positioning systems, we are still searching for mythical islands and surprised when islands pop up in places they are not supposed to be.

Furthermore, islanders' relationship to their habitat has been extraordinarily variable over time. Prince Edward Island itself offers a particularly dramatic example. Until quite recently, its people approached the sea as a resource, but, seeing it as a place of toil and danger, avoided it in their leisure hours. They built well back from the shore and faced their houses away from the sea. Those who frequented it were described as "chasin' the shore," an eccentric behaviour associated until recently with tourists from the mainland. Mainlanders were also the ones who built close to the sea, orienting their decks and picture windows to it. Of late, however, islanders themselves have been chasing the shore. Even as they have become disengaged from traditional fishing and seafaring occupations, their emotional attachment to the sea has increased exponentially. For David Weale, the shore is a ritual space, "a place of power and revelation … More than one person has told me that when they feel life closing in on them they find a quiet place, close their eyes for a few moments, and imagine that they are once again 'chasin' the shore.'"[21]

PREHISTORIC ISLAND ENVIRONMENTS

Islands and the coasts that define them have been in the making for millions of years. Humans did not begin to have a hand in shaping them until quite recently, when African *Homo sapiens* first came down to the sea about 160,000 years ago and set out to populate the globe around 50,000 BCE. This feat was accomplished in large part by alongshore migration and island-hopping at a time when sea levels were much lower than they are today. Marine hunter-gatherers were able to move all the way to the southern tip of the Americas by 14,000 BCE. Some of the higher elevations on the coastal plains that they visited en route later became nearshore islands when waters began to rise and seas assumed their present shapes around 7000 BCE. By then, humans had accumulated navigational skills that allowed them to reach and populate offshore islands, which early on were prized as places of settlement, both for the safety they offered and the abundance of resources to which they gave access.

Hunter-gatherer existence constitutes 95 per cent of human history, but it has been relegated to the category of "prehistory," treated, at best, as a primitive prelude to civilized existence. Civilization is conventionally thought to begin with the inland agrarian societies, which we moderns designate as our place of origins. The fact that many marine hunter-gatherers enjoyed a cultured and abundant life until well into the early modern period has still to register on the historical profession, which insists on viewing them as peoples without history, fated to extinction. We have systematically ignored their contributions to human development, including agriculture itself. Of all peoples, marine hunter-gatherers have suffered the most from the condescension of retrospect. Among anthropologists and archaeologists, attention has been focused on indigenous inlanders; only recently has the record of marine hunter-gatherers been given its due, especially with regard to coastal migrations and seaboard settlements. Anthropology has been almost as landlocked as history, and, while it has given proper attention to Pacific islanders, it has generally treated them as backward in comparison to inlanders, exotic rather than central to the larger human story.[22]

As long as western culture continues to locate human origins inland, organizing the grand narrative around the myth of the landlocked garden of Eden, the real story of human emergence at the edge of the sea remains inaccessible. It is now a half century since the Berkeley geographer Carl Sauer suggested that the shore was the original home of mankind, "where our evolution turned aside from the common primate by going to the sea. No other setting is as attractive for the beginnings of humanity. The sea, in particular the tidal shore, presented the best opportunity to eat, settle, increase, and learn."[23] Archaeologists have recently confirmed that it was when Africans migrated to the southern cape of Africa and began to harvest shellfish that *Homo sapiens* developed the technical and cognitive talents we associate with modern humans. It seems that the addition to their diet of fish oils containing fatty acids was a key factor in the expansion of the mental faculties beyond those found among their interior ancestors.[24] Curtis Marean, who directed the work at the caves of the Cape's Pinnacle Point, has shown that the first shore dwellers not only fashioned stone knives but practised body painting, the earliest evidence ever found of human symbolic activity. Mastering the art of making a life from the tidal zone required remarkable acuity. Marean speculates that this accomplishment may have involved mastering the lunar calendar, at least as great an accomplishment as deciphering solar systems.[25]

It is only now that serious consideration has been given to the ways in which island and coastal peoples have played a leading role not only in so-called "prehistoric" times but in ancient civilizations of the Mediterranean and right up through the early modern and modern eras. As Wendell Berry reminds us, change, when it comes, comes from the margins.[26] It seems that we need to turn our sense of human evolution inside out, recognizing the degree to which it has come from coasts and islands. Today, as we witness a massive surge to the sea by populations all around the world, it is possible to recover something of the lost significance of waterlands to human evolution. Renewed interest in islands, the most coastal of all landforms, is part of this trend, a welcome sign that humanity is challenging its landlocked fables, looking afresh at its aquatic origins.

The character of islands is the product of millions of years of geological and biological change. Those we call *continental* islands were once a part of larger land masses, now cut off by rising seas and changing earth levels. Their flora and fauna are often quite similar to that of mainlands. Others, so-called *oceanic* islands, emerged from the sea by seismic and volcanic action. Barren at first, they were colonized by plants, birds, insects, and animal species carried there from somewhere else by wind or water. In the Pacific, they arrived first in the carcasses of dead whales, on driftwood, and trapped in pumice mats.[27] Humans came much later, to continental and then to oceanic islands. Some may have arrived by accident, blown off course or carried by powerful currents, but we are now reasonably sure that most Pacific island settlement was intentional, a deliberate choice by both coastal and island peoples to take advantage of even richer environments than those they enjoyed on their own shores. They came in waves, sometimes separated by long periods of time, determined in part by environmental changes.

The colonization of oceanic islands in the Pacific was quite possibly caused by periodic sea rises that drowned some islands and encouraged their inhabitants to move to others. A warming trend accompanied by sea rise, which began in the eastern Pacific around 1330 BCE and lasted about a thousand years, seemed to encourage voyaging. A second round of migration in the western Pacific began around 650 CE and was completed by 1200 CE when New Zealand was settled.[28] It would seem that periods of warming encouraged long-distance voyaging and population growth, but around 1300 CE a different kind of environmental crisis occurred when cooling set in; there was an increase in wet, stormy weather, and sea levels dropped. As Patrick Nunn has shown, tidal habitats were damaged and, without access to shellfish, islanders retreated inland and began to compete for scarce resources, which led to unprecedented levels of warfare. Inter-island voyaging was much reduced, and in many places around the Pacific, populations declined. In the most famous example of this process, Easter Islanders turned in on themselves and lost contact with the sea around them.[29] Elsewhere, including in the Atlantic, changes drove islanders to extend the range of their fishing expeditions and colonize previously uninhabited places.[30]

Climatic changes may also have caused California's Chumash people, who lived along the Santa Barbara coast, to move to the Channel Islands just offshore about 7500 BCE. There they developed much more sophisticated forms of fishing, creating for the first time a relatively complex society that traded with the mainland for whatever the islands themselves could not provide. By 1500 BCE they had developed sophisticated fishing technologies, including plank canoes. The level of cooperation demanded by fishing encouraged the development of complex sedentary societies. Hunter-gatherers settled down, created larger, more hierarchical groups, and developed more sophisticated technologies than their inland neighbors.[31]

Mainlands have colonized islands, but the reverse is also true. Islands have provided platforms from which previously underpopulated mainlands were colonized. Island environments were also transplanted to continents. For example, early agriculture moved from the Levant to the

Aegean isles, and from there to the Greek mainland, where it spread during Neolithic times to northern Europe. In the case of northwestern Europe, coasts and islands played a key role in the Stone Age, as hunter-gatherers moved along its Atlantic edge. They settled in biotically rich estuaries and moved inland along rivers. But it was on islands that western Europeans first took up permanent residence, combining agriculture with fishing and shellfish gathering. As Barry Cunliffe has put it, "It was the sea that set the pace."[32]

Western historiography would have us believe that everything begins inland, but this is certainly not the case. Just to the north of Scotland lie the Orkney Islands, where the winds are so ferocious that the land has never been able to support forests. Yet it is there that we find the oldest permanent settlements in northern Europe. The Neolithic Orkneys are filled with Stone Age burial chambers, rings of standing stones, and the oldest-known European house, the Knap of Howar on the island of Papa Westray. But the most impressive site of all – predating both the pyramids of Egypt and Stonehenge – is Skara Brae, a World Heritage site centred on an intact Stone Age village five thousand years old. The village of Skara Brae was built in two phases, beginning in 3100 BE, and abandoned about 2500 BE. The tight cluster of ten stone houses is visible today on the edge of the Bay of Skaill on the western side of Orkney's largest isle, known as the Mainland. When the village was first built, it was well back from the sea, surrounded by meadows, with access to a freshwater lake. Its inhabitants had brought cattle, pigs, and sheep across the Pentland Firth, and they grew barley and wheat, even as they continued to hunt and gather along the shore in the manner of their ancestors. At first they moved from place to place, leaving behind huge middens of abandoned bones, shells, and other refuse. Later, they settled down and sunk their well-constructed stone dwellings into these mounds, which protected them from the fierce winds.[33]

When archaeologist V. Gordon Childe excavated Skara Brae in 1928, he immediately recognized why the first Orcadians had been attracted to the site. He described it accurately as an ecotone on the margins of a "sandy, sheltered bay with a rich and grassy hinterland ... attractive alike to the fisher, the pastoralist, and the cultivator."[34] In fact, the people of Skara Brae were all three, fishing, herding, and harvesting in a seasonal manner. In time a giant sandstorm would fill in the stone houses, but the way of life continued elsewhere. Until the twentieth century, Orcadians remained fisher-farmers, living in so-called "black houses" identical in layout to the original dwellings at Skara Brae. Like so many other island communities, they pursued an ecotonal economy, demonstrating a remarkable cultural and social continuity that can only be attributed to the abundant resources available at the place where land and water meet.

Had islanders around the world built of stone, there would no doubt be many other World Heritage sites at the edge of the sea. Until recently, most archaeologists were reluctant to get their feet wet, but underwater sites are now revealing just how rich were the civilizations that developed at the shore. While interior monocultures faced periodic famines and inundations, coastal and island peoples were better able to ride out environmental changes simply by moving alongshore and shifting from one side of the tide line to the other.

As late as 1500 CE, 15 per cent of the world's population were still hunter-gatherers, many of them located on islands or coasts. On what is now the Canadian and American northwest coast, there developed a particularly rich coastal culture which turned its back on the interior without becoming wedded to the deep sea. The Haida people occupied a waterland that they called *xhaaydla*, which was neither land nor sea but a different kind of alongshore world, living not only in a different kind of space but on a different kind of time, much more attuned to daily, monthly, and seasonal rhythms of the sea.[35] They not only lived *at* the edge of the sea but knew how to live *with* the sea, in a manner that has been largely lost today. As Rowan Jacobsen has reminded us in his fine study of oyster culture in this region, for most of human history, "we are made for – and made by – that thin world where land meets sea."[36]

LIFE SPENT HALFE ON LAND AND HALFE ON SEA

By the end of the Stone Age, Europe had turned inward and the coasts became less important. For most of the Middle Ages, human protein needs were provided for by freshwater fishing, but when streams and lakes became seriously polluted after 1300, Europeans turned back to the sea with a vengeance. They returned to the coasts and islands of the North Sea and Baltic for herring, and, when these were fished out, began moving ever further offshore in what amounted to a kind of marine transhumance, following fish on a seasonal basis, going further and further out to sea to supply the needs of a European market ravenous for cod and other species. By the sixteenth century, the migratory fishery had brought European fisher-farmers to the New World, where they set up a series of fishing stations, often on islands. Arriving in the spring and leaving before winter set in, Europe's fishers initially "had no intention of being colonists – much less failed ones – but rather were migratory and sojourning members of their home society. They oriented themselves to North American spaces in relation to the needs of their home societies, rather than as spaces for new societies."[37]

True sea people, who spend most of their lives on boats, are quite rare and confined mainly to Asian waters.[38] Europeans were a coasting people and thought of the sea as something to cross over rather than to dwell in. Like most coastal peoples, they combined fishing and farming. Their maritime activities were seasonal and part time. It was said that early modern Swedes had "one boot in the boat and the other in the field," while Shetland farmers were said to be "fishermen with a plough."[39] When Lewes Roberts described the migratory fishermen of early seventeenth century Newfoundland, he noted that "their lives may be compared to the otter, which is spent halfe on land and halfe in sea."[40] It was not until the late nineteenth century that modern mechanized fisheries wrenched land and sea asunder.[41]

On American shores, European fisher-farmers encountered other peoples who also practised maritime transhumance. Native Americans had been fishing and whaling alongshore for centuries, using islands in ways very similar to what Europeans had done. Coastal peoples along America's shores were numerous, and, having learned the secrets of the ecotone, relatively prosperous and powerful. They too exploited both sides of the tide line, moving seasonally to take advantage of runs of anadromous fish – smelt in March, alewives, salmon, and sturgeon in April – and the arrival of cod and other ground fish in May. It is estimated that half of the annual food supply of Maine Native Americans came from such sources; they moved "from one place to another according to the richness of the site and season."[42] They had learned to alter environments by planting clam gardens and burning forests to create "ideal habitats for a host of wildlife species."[43]

Initially, relations between Europeans and Native Americans were amicable, even mutually supportive. As long as the newcomers did not actually settle Native lands, there were more than enough resources to be shared. And, even after European coastal colonies were established, cooperation continued. However, an invisible, deadly enemy against which the locals had no defence was brought by Europeans. Disease, as well as wars and the hunting down of Aboriginal people, soon emptied out the coastal zone, creating an entirely new situation in which Natives became only seasonal visitors to the sea, spending their winters inland hunting and trapping the furs that had become their most valuable trading item. In time, this trade would decimate animal species, remaking interior as well as coastal environments.[44]

WHEN THE WORLD WAS ARCHIPELAGIC

For most of the early modern period, both northwestern Europe and northeastern America were essentially coastal societies in which islands played a role disproportional to their territorial size. In effect, the Atlantic had become a sea of islands, not unlike the Pacific, where plantation economies, inter-island trade, and fisheries all accounted for a vast share of the accumulation of wealth and power. Around the Atlantic rim, a combination of proto-maritime and proto-industrial pursuits wholly altered the environments of both coasts and islands. Islands were neither remote nor isolated but central and integral to the expansion of early modern capitalism.

In the Middle Ages the earth had still been considered one great island, encompassing Africa, Asia, and Europe, surrounded by an impassable sea. In the wake of Columbus and other voyages, it fragmented into many islands, the largest ultimately coming to be called continents. But until the eighteenth century, all were thought of archipelagically, belonging more to the sea than to land. In the age of sail, it was water that connected. The kinds of distinctions we make today between islands and continents did not exist. Not until the mid-nineteenth century did the core of economic and political existence shift to the interiors of continents. At that point, islands came to be seen as remote and marginal. Archipelagic connections dissolved, and islands began to lose population to mainlands.[45]

And it was then that island environments came to be seen as static, even pristine, as if untouched by history, a popular perception that also found resonance in the emerging anthropological and biological sciences. Projected retrospectively to earlier periods, this view tended to obscure the earlier dynamism of island environments. For over three hundred years, islands were arguably the most anthropogenic of all landscapes, altered far more than continents by deforestation, colonized by all manner of alien flora and fauna. This fact was registered in early modern environmental consciousness, but was forgotten in later periods when islands ceased to be centres of intense economic activity.[46] In the nineteenth century, environmentalists' concerns turned inland, but in the 1970s islands again became the focus of the new science of biogeography. Following the lead of the pioneering work of E.O. Wilson and R.H. MacArthur, who treated islands as closed systems to test various theories, scientists tended to fail to see the ways in which islands had earlier been interconnected parts of a much larger ecotone involving water as well as land.[47]

OUT OF THE LOOP: ISLANDS BECOME INSULAR

Of course, the relationship between water and land differs from island to island. Large islands are more like continents, with their own interior ecosystems, less influenced by oceans, very different from smaller islands whose climates, flora, fauna, and human populations are inseparable from the sea around them. Human inhabitants of small islands have always been what ecologists call an *edge species*, moving back and forth across the tide line, simultaneously exploiting land and sea. They have been part of the loop of shoreline and life that Raban talks about, their movements more cyclical than linear as they take advantage of daily, monthly, and seasonal changes to harvest the riches of both land and sea.[48]

Around the globe, the loop has now been broken, and coastal dwellers, insular as well as continental, are no longer true edge species, except for their geography. With rare exceptions, islands have become less ecotonal. Coasts are increasingly armoured and traditional wetlands have disappeared, thereby severing the physical connection between land and sea. And islanders no longer experience the connections between the two as they once did. Except in the underdeveloped world, it is rare for farmers to fish, or fishers to farm. With the industrialization of the world's fisheries, connections between land and sea have been severed. Fishing fleets have become footloose and crews internationalized. Many ships are now registered in foreign lands, some of them landlocked. They no longer have home ports. In the age of container ships and supertankers, fewer people now cross the tide line to make a living.

It is not just that the natural environment of islands has changed: both island and continental populations have altered their attitudes toward land and sea. Islanders, particularly in the Atlantic and Mediterranean, have become more continental in their habits and perspectives, less like otters and more like landlubbers. Their experience of water is more episodic. It is only when hurricanes, tsunamis, and oil spills strike that they are reminded that they live in a watery environment, in what constitute waterlands. In Japan, awareness of living not just *on* but *with* the sea has for hundreds of years been a part of coastal consciousness. In this realm of extreme seismic activity, tsunamis have been frequent and devastating to life and property. For centuries, the Japanese have erected so-called tsunami stones to mark the farthest extent of these inundations and encourage people to build above the danger line. This practice has been periodically successful, but stones are easily ignored, particularly as the desire to build close to the sea has increased. Gigantic seawalls have provided a false sense of security, and, in the recent Japanese tsunami disaster, only those inhabitants who retained a memory of past tsunamis knew to head for higher ground. They survived, even if their villages did not.[49]

Though an ever-growing part of humanity now lives close to the sea, only a diminishing minority have an idea of how to live *with* it. The latest shore-dwellers, who come down to the sea for leisure rather than work, have no notion of how earlier generations coped with the oceans. Many coastal peoples have turned their backs on their own history, opting for technological fixes rather than deploying historical experience to deal with present dangers. Modern societies are blind to their own complicity in what are too frequently called natural disasters. *Tsunami* means "harbour wave" in Japanese, suggesting the ways that the building of channels and basins has funnelled sea surges with ever greater velocity and destructive power. Evidence from the Katrina disaster in New Orleans also suggests how interference with natural waterlands, especially the eliminating of wetland buffers and straightening of rivers, contributes to ever greater destruction in coastal areas. It seems time to recognize that the environment is as much man-made as natural in character.[50]

Today the separation of man and nature is no longer acceptable. Even the sea, which in the nineteenth century came to be seen as the last redoubt of timeless wilderness, has revealed itself to have been affected by humans for many thousands of years. Deforestation changed the ecology of the Mediterranean in ancient times; in the Middle Ages the damming and pollution of streams destroyed freshwater fishing, forcing Europeans to seek protein ever further out to sea. We now know that both Native American and European fisheries had important effects on fish and whale stocks even before industrial-scale fishing was introduced.[51] In the nineteenth century, the burning of massive amounts of fossil fuels increased carbon levels in both sea and air. Oceans became major dumping grounds; and, as fishing became mechanized, virtually every known fish stock came under enormous pressure, leading to today's catastrophic conditions.[52]

Rachel Carson rejected Alexander Pope's notion of man's earthly existence, "His time a Moment, and a Point his space." Instead, she urged us to consider deep time and broad horizons in studying environments, even those as supposedly bounded and static as islands.[53] The challenge to environmental historians is to find the appropriate spatial and temporal frame, to reset the boundaries of the subject so as not to mistake momentary and local phenomena for the large processes that have had such a profound impact on island life. Island environments are affected by air and water pollution, storms and tsunamis, all originating thousands of miles beyond their shores, all subject to influences from the deep past. The diminution of fish stocks does not happen all of a sudden. The trend toward smaller fish which we see today is the result of skimming off the big fish by earlier generations. Pollution builds up over decades, sometimes for centuries, without being noticed by contemporaries; the lack of historical baselines has made it very difficult to measure what is happening to the marine environment.

The Pacific is a good place to start in our revision of island environmental history. Even if European explorers focused almost entirely on the islands' terrestrial features, indigenous people had a much more terraqueous perspective.[54] They were as much at home on the sea as on land. Their swimming and diving skills amazed eighteenth-century European explorers, who were comfortable on but not in the water. The American missionary William Ellis called the Hawaiians "almost a race of amphibious beings."[55] They were accomplished blue-water sailors, but most of their activity was confined to the coastal waters that constituted the richest biotas. It was in coastal waters that they staked out their sea tenures. For them, the boundaries between land and sea were relatively open. Sea was treated like land, as belonging to particular families and groups, whose fishing rights were often contested.[56]

In the modern western tradition, a seascape artist turns his back on land to paint what he sees on the water's surfaces. In the Pacific, seascapes encompass both land and sea, and are understood to extend beneath the surface. This terraqueous view of the world was also common in the early modern Europe; only in the nineteenth and twentieth centuries did land and water come to be conceived of as wholly separate realms in both the arts and sciences. Today, however, there is a growing appreciation of the need to think of the two as a continuum.[57] A new rapprochement with the sea is taking place all around the world, but particularly in the South Pacific where interest in indigenous traditions of seafaring and fishing is highly developed. As climate change asserts its power, small, low-lying islands are beginning to recall some of the building and planning techniques that allowed them to survive earlier periods of sea level rise.

Those who come down to the sea today experience it in a way entirely different from the island and coastal populations of the past. Typical tourists, observes John Stilgoe, "want to *watch*, not do."[58] For inlanders, the seascape is one dimensional, something to see, but not to be experienced in the ways that were once a normal part of the lives of those who made their living from the ecotone. In contrast to our other senses, sight distances us from nature.[59] In many places, the sea is fenced or walled off. Fishermen in Japan complained even before the disastrous tsunami of 2011 that gigantic seawalls prevented them from observing the behaviour of the water, picking up early warning signs of the surge to come.[60] By and large, islanders and coastal people are far more alienated from the sea than they once were. In the past, they had known the sea by touch, sound, and feel. When the Pacific Marshall islanders went to sea, they left their stick charts behind, preferring to wayfind by reference to the stars, the sun, clouds, birds, waves, and a host of other features, including their own naked bodies.[61]

Now we are so reliant on cartography for wayfinding that we see lines in nature when none exist. "The stranger who walks or drives to the shore ... always sees divisions," notes Cape Codder Paul Theroux, while "the local does not distinguish between land and water, and keeps going, actually or mentally seeing shoals and eddies and sunken ships and rocks that are exposed only at low tide – not barriers but features."[62] To those who cross the tide line to make their living, Cape Cod has no real limits. It is much bigger than it looks to the tourist, for it encompasses a seascape of almost infinite extent. And its environment is equally unbounded, something that makes it different from the interior. And what is true of the Cape is even more true of islands: their true extent is always greater than their territorial edges. Their smallness (and islands are almost always described as "small") is in the eye of the beholder, especially when that viewer is a landlubber with no connection to the sea. Wrote Henry David Thoreau, "The question is not what you look at, but what you see."[63]

Island edges have hardened of late, literally and figuratively. Now islanders build to the very edge of the sea and, in the face of rising sea levels, armour the shores, building sea walls ever higher. But this is but a short-term solution, encouraging ever greater beach erosion. In the long run the only sensible solution is accept the sea and its dangers, to build well back from the shore, to beat a strategic retreat – something that property owners, and the governments dependent on shore property for taxes, have been reluctant to do. Yet there is really no option if we are to adapt successfully to the climate changes that are already upon us.[64]

LEARNING TO LIVE IN A TERRAQUEOUS WORLD

It is now more than a decade that Martin Lewis and Karen Wigen explored the myth of the continents.[65] A parallel challenge to the myth of islands has also been going on for some years, though it appears not to have affected scientific and popular conceptions of island isolation as much as might be expected.[66] Global history has caused us to be wary of reifying political borders, and we must be prepared to treat natural boundaries as equally liquid. As we have seen, land and water constitute an ecological continuum. So-called "blue-water history" has vastly exaggerated the importance of the deep seas at the expense of nearshore waters, where most of the world's fishing and shipping has always taken place. Perhaps it is time to focus on what might be called "brown-water history" in order to better understand those ecotonal spaces where sea and land are inseparable. Once we have grasped the nature of these worlds, we will be in a better position to comprehend island environments past and present. In this era of ecological crisis, it is vital that we understand those places made of both land and water. We must learn to live *with* islands, not just *on* them. Our survival, and theirs, depends on it.

Museums, Laboratories, Showcases: Prince Edward and Other Islands in Environmental History

Graeme Wynn

ISLANDS OF UNDERSTANDING

Islands have long been thought of as museums and laboratories; more recently, they have also been compared to novels, for many of the same reasons. They are bounded spaces, "self-contained worlds, populated by a manageable cast of characters"; past and present are often closely intertwined in these places, as their histories and ongoing "narratives hinge on a series of incidents, accidents, coincidences, births and deaths"; colonists, curators, experimenters and protagonists appear by various means, and by "luck or accident"; early arrivals are able to "claim ecological niches and put down roots," to break through to new (intellectual) territories and burnish their prospects; over time, some flourish and others struggle, but in these "limited spaces, existence is tenuous" and seemingly small perturbations can "change the trajectory of the whole" story.[1] In much the same vein, Rachel Carson observed sixty years ago that there was no "more delicately balanced relationship than that of island life to its environment," and marvelled at the ways in which "islands have always fascinated the human mind."[2] Indeed.

Prince Edward Island has fascinated human minds the world over since the publication of Lucy Maud Montgomery's novel *Anne of Green Gables* in 1908. In a foreword to a centennial edition of this much-loved work, Kevin Sullivan, producer of a television miniseries based on the book, remarked on the "often mystical insights" by which Montgomery "transform[ed] the pastoral landscape of turn-of-the-century Prince Edward Island into an idyllic fantasy land, ripe with 'scope for the imagination.'"[3] The adventures of an exuberant, red-headed Anne Shirley, in this and subsequent stories, as well as the novelist's evocative descriptions of Lover's Lane, the Birch Path, the Haunted Wood, and the White Way of Delight have transported untold millions of readers to a mythic pre-modern, pre-industrial place of mind. They have also spawned an important tourism industry, led to the creation of a national park, and encouraged a reworking of the landscape of Cavendish, "according to the interpretation of features described in ... the ... literary works of Lucy Maud Montgomery," that has sought to remove "twentieth-century interferences" even as areas surrounding the park have been developed by private interests, exploiting literary associations in ways that many find offensive, in order to attract mass tourism.[4] It is no exaggeration, then, to say that the appeal of Montgomery's conservative vision has had significant material consequences, freezing Avonlea in time and inspiring a range of commercial enterprises that have turned this part of the island at once into a museum and an ongoing experiment in capitalist development.

Similar themes echo in other registers. From the perspective of literary criticism, the delicate balance between island life and island nature is central to Montgomery's oeuvre. Human circumstances are illuminated by metaphors drawn from nature. So the brook that began in the woods of the old Cuthbert place was "intricate, headlong ... with dark secrets of pool and cascade" in its upper reaches, but "by the time it reached Lynde's Hollow it was a quiet, well-conducted little stream, for not even a brook could run past Mrs. Rachel Lynde's door without due regard for decency and decorum."[5] So, comments Elizabeth Rollins Epperly, it is "the brook against Rachel Lynde, just as it will soon be Anne Shirley against unimaginativeness."[6] But Island nature is more than a convenient and evocative source of images and similes in Montgomery's writing. It is a strong shaping influence, central in quite different ways to the lives of Montgomery's two best-known characters, Anne Shirley and Emily Byrd Starr, protagonist of Montgomery's *Emily of New Moon* books. Emily – the "elfkin," with "little ears that were pointed just a wee bit" – is a child of nature, born in a house that appeared "as if it had never been built like other houses but had grown up there like a big, brown mushroom." She finds her companions in an anthropomorphized nature, in the "tall and misty" Wind Woman who "was always around," and the "trees-Adam-and-Eve, and the Rooster Pine and all the friendly lady-birches." For Emily, nature is "a place where magic was made" and dreams grew. It is something akin to a museum or *Kunstkamera*, a cabinet of curiosities, capable of provoking wordless rapture but ultimately and most basically a storehouse of knowledge, inspiration, and empowerment. For Anne Shirley of Green Gables, by contrast, nature serves as a tool, a means of escape from the difficulties of everyday existence or, as Irene Gammel has suggested in identifying the embodied qualities of Anne's multi-sensorial engagement with nature, an instrument for the construction of her developing identity. Thus the ecological universe of the island becomes a training ground or laboratory for the experiment of growing to maturity.[7]

Islands have also fascinated scientists and social scientists who have likewise come to think of these places as laboratories or museums,[8] time-worn tropes that have been invoked worldwide. Early in the nineteenth century, James Cowles Prichard, author of *Researches into the Physical History of Man*, considered the South Sea islands of great interest to the natural historian of mankind because their diversity and location in a variety of climates offered a natural laboratory in which to observe "whatever influence physical causes may be supposed to exert over our species."[9] Half a century or so later, Lewis Henry Morgan, a leading American ethnographer of his day, likened the islands of the Pacific to "so many cages in which their insulated occupants were shut in from external influences, as well as denied knowledge of the uses of flocks and herds and of the principal cereals."[10]

Certainly, many oceanic islands supported distinctive species and unique ecosystems, developed through millennia of relative isolation, before they were incorporated into ever denser networks of global interconnection, leading at least one scholar to lament that islands were not treated "as precious possessions, as natural museums filled with beautiful and curious works of creation, valuable beyond price."[11] But the line between museum and laboratory is not always clear. It was in the natural museum of the Galapagos Archipelago that Charles Darwin learned, as a later commentary has it, to think of islands as test tubes.[12] Darwin's visit to the Galapagos aboard the *Beagle* in 1835 brought him to question the stability of species, not least because the birds and tortoises of those islands presented evidence of a long-running experiment in the workings of natural selection and evolution. And even as Darwin was formulating his arguments for *On the Origin of Species* (1859), Alfred Russell Wallace was concluding, on the basis of work in Indonesia and the Philippines, that the reduced diversity of species on islands meant that they could be regarded as natural laboratories in which evolutionary processes were simpler and easier to sort out than on continental land masses.[13]

Elsewhere and in parallel, as environmental historian Richard Grove has observed, small, tropical islands were emerging as important seedbeds for ideas about environmental conservation.[14] In Grove's telling, the impacts of human activity upon the soils, the biota, and (it seemed) the climate of a handful of oceanic islands, precipitated by the expansion of European shipping and commerce across the globe, produced a new awareness of humankind's role in environmental degradation. In the eighteenth century, colonial administrators began to interpret the evident transformation of small islands – such as St Helena by the introduction of browsing animals, or St Vincent by the clearing of forests for plantation agriculture – through contemporary intellectuals' developing interest in economics, agriculture, botany, forestry, and the workings of nature and the state. Joseph Banks averred in 1771 that the colonists of St Helena had made "a desert out of paradise";[15] deforestation was connected with desiccation and erosion, to encourage tree-planting efforts and early initiatives in forest conservation.

Islands became metaphors "of global vulnerability to human economic demands." Islandness imposed limits; and limits sharpened perceptions. Islanders quickly came to understand that the consequences of squandering nature's bounty could rarely be avoided in situ: moving on meant moving off. Islands were, in effect, living laboratories in which the adventitious combination of European colonization, the dictates of the market, and spendthrift attitudes toward the natural world constituted a novel experiment, the results of which sparked the formulation of new ideas about the relations between forests and rainfall and human-environment interactions. Indeed, these insights were fundamental to the development of George Perkins Marsh's powerful arguments for forest protection in his landmark *Man and Nature* (1864), in which he marshalled seventeenth and nineteenth century accounts of Malta, St Helena, Gran Canaria, and the Cape Verde islands to demonstrate the scope and severity of human environmental impacts.[16]

Building on all of these developments to extend the prevailing cultural evolutionist paradigm in British anthropology, late nineteenth-century ethnographers began studies of small island communities, hoping to understand patterns and processes of human cultural variation in much the same way as their scientific colleagues had found in island populations the key to plant and animal evolution. Following the lead of A.C.

Haddon, who took a multidisciplinary expedition to Torres Strait in 1898 (and whose initial training as a zoologist likely introduced him to the ideas of evolutionary biology), Alfred R. Radcliffe-Brown conducted fieldwork in the Andaman Islands, and Bronislaw Malinowski began his celebrated investigations in the Trobriand Islands.[17] Central to all of this work was the conviction that island societies formed "bounded, self-contained and easily manageable units."[18] Even as the material artifacts of island life were being collected and transported from their remote locations for display in western museums, the islands themselves became research laboratories peopled, in the view of most of those working in the structuralist-functionalist tradition, by societies "isolated in space and frozen in time, simpler and hence more amenable to holistic understanding than populations elsewhere."[19]

By the 1920s, when the American anthropologist Margaret Mead began her work in Samoa with the biological laboratory and the importance of hypothesis testing under strictly controlled conditions firmly in mind, the notion that island cultures were "isolated, closed aggregates in the backwaters of history" with important lessons to teach had gained firm hold of the social scientific imagination. Whether "isolated on small Pacific islands, in dense African jungles or Asiatic wastes," wrote Mead, pushing back against psychoanalysis and asserting the importance of nurture over nature, "it is still possible to find untouched societies which have chosen solutions of life's problems different from our own, which can give us precious evidence on the malleability of human nature."[20] Three decades or so on, the scholarly utility of islands seemed all but self-evident. For the great geographer and historian of the Pacific Oskar Spate, writing in 1963, the great ocean was "all the better as a laboratory for including "a whole congeries of little universes, point-economies, ready-made isolates for study," whose "small" populations and "short" written histories "spared" those who studied them consideration of "a whole host of variables which confuse the ecology of the great landmasses."[21] And for ecologists Andrew Vayda and Roy Rappoport, writing in the same volume, islands provided "special opportunities for studying cultural development with a clarity lacking under mainland conditions."[22]

Against this sketch of the place of islands in the stream of western thought about humans and their environments, we turn now to explore three incidents in the history of Prince Edward Island since the Second World War. At base, these episodes used the island as a place for experiment and display, but they differed markedly in focus and form; all fell short of their initial objectives, and none can be counted an unqualified success. The first involved a scholar's explicit attempt to use Prince Edward Island as a laboratory during the 1950s; the second turned upon the largely independent and essentially idiosyncratic ventures of an indeterminate (but never very large) number of people who experimented with the dream of living simpler lives in the Island in the 1960s and early 1970s; and the third centred on a pair of coupled energy initiatives that sought to make of Prince Edward Island a model for Canada, if not the world, in the 1970s and 1980s. These cases considered, we turn in conclusion to reflect upon their larger, if perhaps unintended significance for understanding Prince Edward Island, ourselves, and the future.

MAPS AS MICROSCOPES: STUDYING CULTURAL TRANSFER IN PRINCE EDWARD ISLAND

For many geographers and Canadian historians, Andrew H. Clark's *Three Centuries and the Island* (1959) is a classic (albeit flawed) work.[23] As the first, and for five years the only, English-language monograph in Canadian historical geography written by a Canadian, it holds an important place in the development of the discipline, and it remains the only book-length study of Prince Edward Island by a geographer. Yet it is a profoundly enigmatic work, not least for the way in which it approaches the task of understanding this island territory.

In a preface to the book, Clark confessed "a deep and affectionate interest in the island and its people." Though Manitoba was the province of his birth, both of his parents and three of his grandparents were Prince Edward Island born, and he spent many happy childhood summers there. While conducting research for the book, he wandered the island's highways and byways, feeling "his roots ... deeply set in its red soil"; he counted many happy memories of spending days with fishermen "digging clams in the sandy mud of ... [island] estuaries," watching harness races, and tucking in to the "luscious fare of 'strawberry festivals.'"

Beyond the preface, however, this personal attachment to place is almost completely obscured by a tight-drawn veil of "objectivity." The book is built around maps, over 150 of them, most showing patterns of settlement and agricultural activity in the island during the nineteenth and twentieth centuries. Clark uses these maps to scrutinize the past. Through the first sixty-five pages of the book, maps and other sources are combined in four chapters that provide geographical accounts of settlement and agriculture at approximate half-century intervals, between the mid-seventeenth and early nineteenth centuries. Thereafter, reflecting the quantity of census data available, maps become even more prominent, to the point that they essentially frame and define detailed chapter-length treatments, occupying some 125 pages focused on "The Island One Century Ago" (ca. 1850); "Decline and Adjustment" in Island farming since Confederation; and "The Last Century of Agricultural Change" (effectively, 1871 to 1951). A twenty-page review then proffers several conclusions, the most substantive of which is that there were marked regional differences in culture (or more accurately, in agricultural practice, reflected in different mixes of stock and crops, and by such indicators as sheep to swine ratios) across the thin, curved space of an island that was generally thought of as rather uniform. So, the regional (ethnic, cultural, or homeland) origins of those who settled Prince Edward Island are identified as crucial determinants of land use patterns, even into the twentieth century.

Clark made it quite clear in his preface that he conceived of this work as part of a larger project, concerned with the geographical "study of the transfer of people from northwestern Europe to new homes overseas in the seventeenth, eighteenth and nineteenth centuries." Moreover, he was explicit in describing the book as a "pilot study," an experiment, and a "model." Despite his professions of personal affection for the island, he announced that his real interest in the Maritime Provinces lay in Nova Scotia. But it was hard to disaggregate the ecological and historical complexities of that place, to discern "what significance cultural origin had for the character of ... farming." So Prince Edward Island – described (Clark noted) by the prominent Canadian agricultural economist J.E. Lattimer as "no doubt the best laboratory for studying agriculture of any place in the Dominion," because of the relative uniformity of landforms and soils (as well as climate and pre-European vegetation) there – became a "control area" for resolving the vexing problem posed by Nova Scotia.

In his conclusion, Clark hinted that his book had another larger purpose, which was to exemplify the possibilities of historical geographical scholarship. I have explored this dimension of *Three Centuries* elsewhere, concluding that it was "as much a methodological tract as a study of Prince Edward Island."[24] This is not the place to reprise the details of this argument; suffice it to say that an enormously influential attempt to define the field of geography, Richard Hartshorne's *The Nature of Geography* (1939), had set time and space, history and geography, apart.[25] In that view, geographers studied "spatial arrangement[s] on the surface of the earth"; areal differentiation was their concern, and time, central to the work of historians, stepped into the background. Clark took issue with this conception of the field, arguing that geographies were ever-changing and that it was important to study "the past circumstances of, or … changes in phenomena of concern to geography." His *Three Centuries* sought to show how this could be done, proclaiming its geographical pedigree in the hundred or so maps that represented instantaneous cross-sections of area and provided "skeletonized frameworks upon which various geographies of various times" were erected, but complementing these with maps showing patterns of change and pointing to the processes that made geographies "dynamic rather than static entities."[26] How successful all of this was as "history" remains open to debate (it seems to me to offer at best a limited and stilted approach, largely descriptive of outcomes rather than engaged with the vital historical tasks of explaining the contexts and telling the stories of people struggling with their circumstances). Within geography, however, it opened space for just the kind of work Clark had accomplished. In the same year as his Prince Edward Island book was published, Hartshorne, author of the 1939 creed, conceded that the differences between history and geography were not absolute and that that the difficulties of dealing with change over space and time together might be met by studying "a relatively small region of restricted variation in area and affected by a limited number of factors producing historical change."[27]

Rereading *Three Centuries*, and thinking about the larger agendas self-consciously proclaimed by its author, I am struck by the extent to which Clark's work on Prince Edward Island appears as a product of its times, and not simply as a contribution to a debate among geographers. Interest in evolutionary anthropology increased markedly from the 1940s. Julian Steward's work (widely noticed with the publication of his *Theory of Culture Change* in 1955, and perhaps especially influential for its embrace of "multi-linear evolution") focused attention on the ways in which history and ecology – the very complexities that Clark sought to clarify through his pilot study in PEI – influenced cultural change. Likewise, the study of culture areas and cultural diffusion, which was at the core of Clark's "transfer of people from northwestern Europe" agenda, was much in the air in the 1950s. The culture area concept, found in the work of Boas and Kroeber but often more strongly associated with Clark Wissler, who identified distinct groupings of Native Americans based on their shared cultural traits, was widely accepted in American anthropology in the decade or so after the Second World War.

BRESCIA UNIVERSITY COLLEGE LIBRARY

A little earlier, it had been introduced, in slightly different form, to American geography by Carl Sauer – under whose supervision Andrew Clark completed his doctoral research in 1944, and whose influence he acknowledges in *Three Centuries*'s preface. Sauer, combining ideas drawn from the European Kulturkreise school with those of his Berkeley colleagues in anthropology, Alfred Kroeber and Robert Lowie, identified the diffusion of ideas and practices from a few "cultural hearths" as a driving force in human history; this emphasis on the diffusion (and persistence or decline) of cultural traits shaped Clark's first book on New Zealand, just as it later informed the work of several of his University of Wisconsin graduate students.[28]

The immediate antecedents of Clark's use of the islands-as-laboratories trope (which echoes through the preface of *Three Centuries*) are harder to pin down. In a probing review of the development of island archeology, a field that garnered considerable attention from the 1960s onward, Matthew Spriggs has demonstrated that this idea "came of age with a heady mix of new developments in genetics, archaeology, cultural evolutionary anthropology, and historical linguistics during the early- to mid-1950s,"[29] and that it was substantially codified by three papers in the *Journal of the Polynesian Society* for 1957. Offering a brief commentary on articles by Ward Goodenough, Marshall Sahlins, and Irving Goldman, Margaret Mead captured their theme in her title "Introduction to Polynesia as a Laboratory for the Development of Models in the Study of Cultural Evolution." The papers were quite different from one another, but all rested on the conviction that the islands of Polynesia promised heightened understanding of cultural change, because their isolation made patterns of cultural difference much clearer than in mainland or continental areas – where, as Goodenough had it, the elements of cultures were prone to "blend and reblend in the course of migrations, conquests and trade."[30] Islands were good to think with precisely because they simplified the intractable complexities of human cultural adaptation and evolution characteristic of most (larger) areas of the world.

Three Centuries makes no reference, general or specific, to any of this discussion. The book lacks a consolidated bibliography, and Clark's footnotes are characteristically local and specific, focused resolutely on the Island and the primary sources germane to his preoccupation with settlement and land-use patterns. We know that he began his work on PEI early in the 1950s – he presented the framework of the book in lectures at the University of London in 1954 – and that he began to think about insularity as a category of analysis even earlier. However, his 1947 comparison of New Zealand's South Island with Prince Edward Island was more methodical than insightful and concluded with a timid call for wariness in using the expression "insularity" because "generalizations which are not almost self-evident truths would seem to be highly speculative."[31]

The most that can be said is that Clark found in PEI a location he considered "almost ideal for an assessment of the significance of cultural origin to farming practice by a comparative study of changing patterns." In broad terms, his approach – treating the Island as a control area or laboratory from which to derive a better understanding of processes that were difficult to analyze elsewhere – strongly resembled the research strategies advocated and adopted by a significant and influential group of anthropologists working around the same time on islands in the Pacific. Whether Clark knew of, or drew from, this increasingly vigorous body of scholarship is unclear.[32] Even as the anthropological work of the 1950s was brought together in a series of essays (including those by Spate and Vayda and Rappoport, mentioned above) published in 1963, given a fillip by the development of the theory of island biogeography (1967), and reinterpreted by the British archeologist J.D. Evans in 1973 to provide the platform for the emergence of a vigorous school of island archaeology, Clark pulled back from the wider implications of his work.[33] A prudent, even excessively cautious scholar and thoroughgoing empiricist, he never formulated any larger insights from, or distilled the results of, his PEI pilot study into anything more than the welter of detail presented in the book. The achievement of *Three Centuries*, he concluded, was to bring us a little closer to "understanding what we are" by offering "a clearer view of what we have been." The promised study of Nova Scotia (said to be nearing completion in 1959), for which the island essay was to clarify some conundrums, was never finished.

DREAMS OF ESCAPE: BACK TO THE FUTURE IN PRINCE EDWARD ISLAND

In 1977, McClelland & Stewart, the Canadian publisher, released a new edition of *The Master's Wife*, Sir Andrew Macphail's semi-autobiographical account of life in late nineteenth-century Prince Edward Island. There were many reasons for the rerelease – the book is a remarkable literary achievement; it offers a superb evocation of time and place; its original publication, posthumously at the beginning of the Second World War, had failed to garner much attention; and historian Ian Ross

Robertson was a strong advocate for such an initiative. The timing was also propitious. Central to Macphail's celebration of island life was his strong commitment to traditional rural patterns of existence. Indeed, Macphail's biographer invokes the concept of "Catonism," developed by the sociologist and historian Barrington Moore, Jr, to clarify this aspect of Macphail's thinking. According to Moore, Catonism extols "the peasant as the backbone of society" and advocates a way of life that "somehow proved its validity in the past." Further, this "way of life is supposed to be an organic whole and ... being connected with the soil is essential to making it organic ... The organic life of the country-side is supposedly superior to the atomized and disintegrating world of modern urban civilization."[34] Substitute "farmer" for "peasant," says Robertson, and "Macphail emerges as the closest there is to an English Canadian Catonist."[35]

The reissue of Macphail's *chef d'oeuvre* came after almost a decade of growing disillusionment with the corporate dominance and materialistic, militaristic course of contemporary western and particularly North American society. Just as at the end of the nineteenth century some people seemed to find "themselves at an intellectual precipice – their old convictions challenged ... unsure of where to turn and ... searching for a new synthesis," so in the 1960s significant numbers of North Americans were disaffected with the state of their world, questioned its fundamental premises, and sought alternatives.[36] Many disengaged from the so-called rat-race of modern urban society, giving rise to what Theodore Roszak christened the counterculture. Eschewing rampant consumerism and the validation of lives by their material possessions, members of this emergent group espoused the "good" life over the "goods" life. They abandoned the dress codes of corporate North America, grew their hair, and adopted a new "uniform" of casual attire signalled most evidently by the unisex style of jeans, t-shirts, and love beads. Ostentatiously open to new experiences, many experimented with illicit drugs and flaunted the rules of middle-class morality, often advocating communal living and "free love." Hoping to simplify their lives and find more "authentic" modes of existence, many of them joined a continent-wide movement back to the land.[37]

By some estimates, over a million North Americans followed this course in the late 1960s and '70s, trading technologically dependent convenience for lives close to nature. Such was the groundswell of enthusiasm for this strategy that in 1968 Stewart Brand and friends began to publish the *Whole Earth Catalog*, identifying tools to assist those who wished to live this way; a couple of years later John and Jane Shuttleworth's *Mother Earth News* magazine began to carry how-to articles and stories of interest for would-be homesteaders and those who sought greater control over their lives.[38]

The origins of this impulse are commonly traced back to Thomas Jefferson's agrarianism and Henry David Thoreau's retreat to Walden Pond, but it tapped a broader vein of sentiment – exemplified by Macphail's insistence that "for the man who would live a quiet, interesting, reasonable and useful life ... no ... occupation [but farming] ... affords so favorable an opportunity." More directly, it fed upon unease about the course of the contemporary world.[39] In *The Unsettling of America*, published in 1977 but foreshadowed in earlier essays, Wendell Berry, a guru for many of those who sought to reconnect with nature, articulated a trenchant critique of agri-business and the farm consolidation that had proceeded apace since 1945. Labour-saving machines robbed people of opportunities for "good" work with the earth, and ravaged nature; chemical fertilizers damaged ecologies; new farming systems increased soil erosion. Society's obsession with "the future" was a "utopian fantasy" driven by blind belief in technological solutions; as people lost touch with the natural world and an appreciation that everything was connected, nature was being reduced to scenery and the world was being impoverished.[40] This was a crisis of character and culture as well as agriculture, because "the health of the land is inseparably bound up with the health of the community, the body, and the spirit."[41]

There was, in short, a good deal of Catonism in this impulse. Indeed, Berry later reflected that "when going back makes sense, you are going ahead" – and some very basic considerations shaped its geographical patterns.[42] Back-to-the-landers, most of them young, generally sought relative isolation, along with available land at low prices – abandoned farms or small parcels of raw land. (See MacFadyen's chapter for the background of farm abandonment.) For their new beginnings, they chose remote and declining rural regions across the continent – from the Appalachians to the Ozarks, from Maine to Oregon, from the Kickapoo Valley of Wisconsin to the Slocan Valley of British Columbia, from the shield-fringe of Ontario to Powell Lake back of Lund on the Pacific Coast of the continent.[43] However, they favoured islands, both literal and figurative. Thus the revealing focus of one recent study of the phenomenon in Canada considers Cape Breton in Nova Scotia alongside Denman, Hornby, and Lasqueti islands in British Columbia as sites of encounter between back-to-the-landers and older-established residents.[44]

Prince Edward Island was one among these many destinations. By the mid-1970s, several hundred people had come from various parts of the continent and various stations in life, by plan or by chance, to settle "into a society that had, in many ways, never left the land, that was itself trying to join modernity but still seemed closer to the 19th century than the 21st."[45] Many Island farmers still worked their fields with horses, milked their cows by hand, and pieced together a modest competence from the proceeds of a rather traditional form of mixed husbandry that depended upon family labour. Here more than most places in North America, "the organic life of the countryside" seemed to be within reach.

In 2008–09, Ryan O'Connor and Alan MacEachern, historians and Islanders both, combined to investigate the back-to-the-land movement on Prince Edward Island. Their valuable website includes audio recordings of sixteen interviews, fifteen to forty-five minutes in length, conducted by O'Connor with twenty-one people who came to the Island as back-to-the-landers and, for the most part, stayed.[46] The website also features a summary narrative by MacEachern, making use of the interview material. Together, these pieces constitute a rich source of insight into the motivations, tribulations, achievements, and reflections of this particular group for whom things, by and large and in retrospect, turned out well. Although some, like Steve Knechtel, who grew tired of his airline job in Toronto, found themselves on the island because "it just seemed like the thing to do at the time," MacEachern notes "a thread of great satisfaction, even joy, running through the back-to-the-landers' interviews, when they talk about what work they found themselves able to accomplish." There were challenges – moving from modern suburbs to French River or Bonshaw was one thing in theory, living without electricity or running water and adjusting to Charlottetown after Chicago could be quite another in practice. For those interviewed, MacEachern concludes, "PEI was a grand adventure, but one that offered no escape from reality – just a different, often more difficult, reality." Indeed he would argue that many, perhaps most, of the back-to-the-landers were "not so much escaping as experimenting, seeing whether living small, simply, and self-sufficiently would be as fulfilling ... as it sounded."[47]

In the end, many of those who came to the Island – whether they experimented with escape or escaped to experiment – would likely have agreed with Laurel Smyth, an "out-and-out hippie" whose Island homes included an old school bus and a teepee on Panmure Island, that "it's really hard ... unless you're extremely competent and have a very wide-ranging sphere of activities to support yourself back on the land … If you don't have electricity, then you're going to either buy a lot of candles or you're going to be making them or you're going to have lanterns – then you have to buy the kerosene for them. So everything, you have to spend money, no matter what. There's no getting away from the money economy without very, very serious group application to achieving that goal."[48] For all its scenic beauty and attractive summers, Prince Edward Island was also a hard place in which to live without the comforts of modern conveniences, especially with young children: "Surviving winter alone, and mud season, that was enough of a harsh reality" (Smyth again). So, observes MacEachern, the arrival of "kids often precipitated not just the arrival of modern conveniences but the eventual abandonment of the back-to-the-land way-of-life altogether."[49] Most Prince Edward Island back-to-the-landers lived a precarious existence in which the desire for simple, self-sufficient lives spent in the company of interesting like-minded people was continually undercut by the ubiquitous power of the market and the lure of technological comforts.

What to make of this moment of Island history? On the evidence of the O'Connor-MacEachern interviews, the story is a positive one, not to be judged by mere numbers or by the extent to which the pattern of living simply on the land was emulated, or by whether and how long people sustained their back-to-the-land ventures. It is to be measured instead by what individuals gained from their experience: "Some found what they were looking for in that life, some didn't, and some found it the source of other opportunities."[50] Like many of those who rushed for gold, a significant number came looking for one thing and found another: themselves.

Looked at from afar, however, the back-to-the-land episode stands as an intriguing, albeit perhaps largely fruitless, effort to find hope in the past, or to envisage and shape a different future by travelling back along what promoters of living history museums call the "tunnel of time." The ultimate question posed by these initiatives of the 1960s and '70s was, and remains (as Jeffery Jacob has recognized in his book about "new pioneers" in the American Pacific Northwest and British Columbia) whether those isolated farms and small holdings, laboratories for a range of experiments in alternative ways of living, offered sufficient evidence that "a fulfilling, happy existence on this planet is possible without recourse to the high-consumption habits that jeopardize a sustainable future."[51] The answer remains ambiguous.

BEYOND OIL: PRINCE EDWARD ISLAND AS A MODEL
FOR THE WORLD

In 1973, world oil prices surged to levels not seen in almost a century. Driven upwards by the financial instability associated with the collapse of the Bretton Woods agreement in 1971, the price of oil quadrupled in nominal dollars (and rose from less than $20 to approximately $50 a barrel in constant 2008 dollars) when the Organization of Petroleum Exporting Countries (OPEC) curbed exports in retaliation for American support of Israel in the Yom Kippur War. As the western world scrambled to adjust, the words of English economist E.F. Schumacher in *Small Is Beautiful* (1973) seemed eerily prescient: the "rich" he claimed, were "in the process of stripping the world of its once-for-all endowment of relatively cheap and simple fuels," which "could easily become dear and scarce" in the face of continuing "ever more exorbitant demands." It was time to recognize that the "expansionist success" and economic prosperity of the West were "propelled by a frenzy of greed and ... an orgy of envy" and to ask whether these forces "carry within themselves the seeds of destruction."[52]

As a significant oil producer, Canada was less exposed to the dramatic implications of OPEC export restrictions than some other countries. But by 1970 oil and gas accounted for almost three-quarters of Canadian energy consumption. Domestic producers enjoyed a protected market west of the Ottawa River and exported approximately half their oil and gas production to the United States. Meanwhile, Quebec and the Atlantic Provinces depended upon imported oil. In response to the world oil-price shock of 1973, the Canadian government acted in what it took to be the national interest by freezing domestic Canadian oil prices, and taxing exports to offset some of the additional costs of oil imported into the eastern provinces. Alberta producers were outraged. And in PEI, which had the country's highest energy costs, prices of heating oil, gasoline, and electricity (from oil-fired generating stations) continued to rise.

The situation was soon exacerbated by another major jump in oil prices, associated with the revolution in Iran, and by the serious political frictions generated by the federal government's National Energy Policy. But out of crisis came opportunity, and PEI responded with remarkable alacrity to opportunity's call. Premier Alex B. Campbell's government had concluded a fifteen-year federal-provincial agreement in 1969 to modernize, or, as the Comprehensive Development Plan had it, to produce "social and economic advancement" in Prince Edward Island. By the mid-1970s the premier was envisaging a future somewhat different from that outlined in this modernist manifesto. In place of industrial expansion and incorporation into an increasingly interconnected and thus ultimately somewhat undifferentiated global economy, he came to advocate a far more decentralized, diversified, and pluralistic society with self-reliant, engaged citizens rather than a population of passive consumers. The time had come to question the holy capitalist grail of continuing growth and to worry about social justice. Nailing a new flag to the mast, he declared himself to be "one who believes that small is not only beautiful but in the long run more practicable."[53]

The Schumacher effect is obvious, but it was not the only source of this intellectual shift. MacEachern has traced, revealingly, the far-spread roots from which Campbell's conversion drew substance, from the influence of his executive secretary Andy Wells through to the Club of Rome's ideas about "the limits to growth" and beyond to Lewis Mumford's critique of western society's slavish devotion to the power of machines, and Amory Lovin's call for soft energy paths, conservation, and the use of renewable energy sources. By 1975 the pieces had aligned to the point that the premier could once again promote the island as a laboratory for social change. Announcing the establishment of the Institute of Man and Resources – its mandate to engage in "the analysis, invention, adaptation and application of appropriate energy, food and crop production and living and shelter systems which are socially desirable and ecologically sustainable, and the assessment of probable impacts of such system" – he claimed that Prince Edward Island was the only place in Canada seriously investing in renewable energy. The institute, he envisaged, would provide leadership locally, nationally, and internationally. Small, beautiful Prince Edward Island stood fair to become a model for the planet.[54]

A concurrent initiative, the product of collaboration among Wells, John Todd of the New England-based New Alchemists Institute ("To Restore the Lands, Protect the Seas, and Inform the Earth's Stewards"), and the federal government's Urban Affairs department in its role as coordinator of the 1976 UN Conference on Human Settlements, led to the development of "The Ark" bioshelter on Prince Edward Island. "Designed to be self-sufficient like the biblical ark," according to one account, "it will illustrate how food, shelter and power needs of urban and rural families can be supplied in a single building."[55] In the spring of 1976, when the provincial legislature held a heavily publicized four-day hearing considering the energy situation and future prospects for the island, there was scepticism as well as excitement in the air. But it was clear, as MacEachern has noted, that expert witnesses from "away" (including Lovins, Schumacher's associate George McRobie, and Todd) "envisioned the tight island community as a perfect petri dish for the application of a small-is-beautiful philosophy."[56]

At the opening of the Ark in summer 1976, Prime Minister Pierre Trudeau recognized it as a model for "living lightly on the earth." Todd reflected that the island location heightened a "sense of what we have and our own limits." He went further, to suggest the importance of history, geography, and nature in offering a template for the future: "Perhaps it's through the sense of place and past that we can begin to design and create for the 21st century."[57] Soon the experiment was garnering favourable attention from national and international media. Reporters waxed eloquent about the satisfactions of "working with the wind and the weather ... instead of depending on anonymous utilities" to create a "comfortable micro-environment"; one floated the notion that "As the Ark is to PEI, so PEI can be to Canada, so Canada can be to the rest of the world."[58] Meanwhile the institute shaped its agenda, recognizing the benefits of energy conservation through efforts to reduce energy demands and facilitate the development of low energy communities and reflecting its commitment to alternative energy paths by formulating plans for research into and the development of wood, wind, solar, and small-scale hydroelectricity energy sources. Working across such a broad front, with a limited budget and a strong sense of the need to disseminate information and encourage public support of its goals, the institute allocated time and money to these projects unevenly, and approximately in the order in which they are listed. It quickly became "a player in the alternatives [energy] scene." [59]

In the end, however, neither the institute nor the Ark fulfilled the hopes attached to them. As MacEachern has shown (perhaps in echo of Donald Creighton's dictum that "history is the record of an encounter between character and circumstance"), politic(ian)s, personalities, and the ever-changing times undermined the aspirations, agendas, and operations of these initiatives. At one level the story was straightforward. In 1981 oil prices began to fall from a level around $100 a barrel, hovering around $30 a barrel in 1986. Concerns about energy shortages and the need for renewable sources declined in lockstep. But there was more to it: even before oil prices began to fall, the Island's alternative energy experiments were faltering. It turned out the Ark drew power from the Island's electricity grid, and the bioshelter's occupants were increasingly irascible in the face of continuing public interest in the project. Even as it supported the Institute of Man and Resources, the PEI government contracted to buy (oil- and coal-generated) electricity from New Brunswick. Despite its success in raising Prince Edward Islanders' awareness of energy matters "well above the national average" by 1980, the institute ran into rough water created by changed economic circumstances and shifting political agendas. As the Canadian economy entered a recession, government funding for energy alternatives dried up; such resources as there were went, through other channels, to energy conservation initiatives.[60] The institute limped through the early 1980s, but by the end of the decade it, like the Ark, had essentially slipped from sight. Only archives and memories recalled the dream of energy self-sufficiency achieved with simple technologies.

ISLAND FABLES AND ENVIRONMENTAL FOIBLES

What then do these three Prince Edward Island episodes, and the place of islands in the stream of intellectual endeavour more generally, tell us? First: although islands may be good to think with, research on, and live in, they do not necessarily provide the answers one seeks. Nor do they lead automatically to conclusions of larger interpretive significance or foster experiments that change the world. Second, and despite the enthusiasm for island archaeology that followed J.D. Evans's suggestion that islands be considered "laboratories" for the study of sociocultural processes, interest has waned in viewing islands through a positivist lens, as places in which "variables" can be controlled and the outcomes of particular actions, policies, or strategies can be calibrated.[61] Reflecting the critical perspectives on traditional ethnography articulated by James Clifford, George Marcus, and Michael Taussig, among others, as well as wider trends in scholarship, many researchers are now uncomfortable with the premises that underpinned such work.[62] Critics have taken issue with the implicit assumption that islands are isolated – are islands islands? – to insist that they are as much social constructs as geographical entities, "insofar as they reflect feelings of isolation, separateness, distinctiveness and otherness."[63] Some argue that ideas drawn from the scientific study of island biogeography are inappropriate for understanding human societies because they fragment knowledge and tend to underplay "the unique adaptive strategies of *Homo culturalis*."[64] Others characterize island archaeology narrowly as predicated on the idea "that the manifestations of human behaviour on islands show persuasive structural similarities and are essentially divergent from those of main-lands," to call the foundations of that field into question.[65] Although Evans was clearly interested in processes affecting all societies and regarded islands as ideal settings in which to study these processes, because (as Clark believed) there were fewer variables to consider and these were more easily defined than in less clearly bounded continental areas, it is no longer much in vogue to treat islands as "accident[s] of geography which provided a magnetic metaphor for separation and boundedness."[66] The pendulum of scholarly interest has swung from isolation to interaction – reflected in appeals to move from the study of island laboratories to the investigation and understanding of "seascapes in their own right" – and single islands have lost their cachet as ideal units for analysis.[67]

A third lesson, an important and perhaps somewhat contradictory one, to be drawn from the foregoing discussion is that islands often serve as showcases, revealing patterns and processes that are harder to discern elsewhere, provoking reflection and providing insight into the human condition. These islands need not be geographical, and their revelations may not be definitive. Counterculture Catonism found space to grow in an archipelago of remote locations across the continent. The few scores of people congregated here, the few hundreds gathered there, all seeking to instantiate the organic life of the countryside, gave sharper point to a wider groundswell of unease at the tendencies of modern urban society. The forms taken by these social islets, the frictions they generated, and the lives they changed differed from place to place.[68] Those who went back to the land did so for innumerable, often inchoate reasons, and it is correspondingly dangerous to generalize about motivations, experiences, and outcomes. But each instance gives us cause to reflect, and larger questions emerge from the cacophony of particular stories. What impelled so many (young) people to become disillusioned with and disengaged from mainstream society? When did dreams seem to come within reach of realization? How were aspirations turned to action? Who joined the movement? Why did they choose to live life this way? Was this a serious effort to break free of modes of living that placed excessive demands on people and places, individuals and environments? Or was it merely a self-indulgent denial of expectations and the abrogation of larger societal responsibilities? More broadly, if Prince Edward Island's back-to-the-landers were harbingers of things to come, prescient futurists who anticipated the need for more locally centred, ecologically sensitive, sustainable modes of living (about which we hear so much today), what do their limited numbers, their failure to generate a spirit of emulation among the larger populace, and the continuing sense of otherness or exoticism attached to the counterculture of the 1960s and '70s tell us about environmental anxieties and the prospects of the environmental movement?

Similar questions are raised more pointedly by the falterings and eventual failures of the Ark and the Institute of Man and Resources. In the mid to late 1970s, the fossil-fuelled foundations of western industrial society were shaky; the times could not, it seemed, have been more auspicious for the development of alternative energy sources and fuel conservation strategies. The small size and particular vulnerability of Prince Edward Island, coupled with its relatively low concentration of industry and a favourable alignment of political interests and personalities, encouraged the establishment of the institute and the Ark and brought the Island international attention as a showcase for "carefully planned and well-structured efforts at energy and self-sufficiency."[69] Yet for all that (and personal failings and political antagonisms that were also part of the story aside), this moment of high promise soon passed. As oil prices fell, public interest in alternative energy sources – that "airy-fairy stuff on top of roofs, windmills and what have you," as one critic characterized it – dissipated.[70] Without short-term pain (expensive oil), there was little societal interest in long-term gain (sustainable energy sources). Economics trumped ecology as the world returned to the status quo.

The fourth lesson in all of this, therefore, is about the difficulties of changing public attitudes and of forwarding environmentalism's agenda. Canadians had seen this before, in the failure of the Commission of Conservation, spawned in 1909 from anxiety about resource depletion in the heady days of the North American conservation movement but disbanded in 1921.[71] As public concern about another environmental and fossil-fuel related problem – global climate change – focuses early twenty-first-century minds on ecological footprints, hundred-mile diets, and the need to tread more lightly on the earth, we should be mindful that the core elements of these concerns inspired counterculture Catonism and undergirded the goals of Prince Edward Island's IMR and its Ark.[72] Ecological and environmental arguments, and even more broadly based ideas about the quality of lives lived and society's responsibilities to generations yet unborn, are unlikely to change a world in which the market is the measure of things, and wallets rule hearts and minds.

Fifth, and finally, then, this discussion reminds us that we are almost inescapably products of our times. Most of us find it difficult to withstand the stream of tendency and diverge from long-established and widely accepted patterns of behaviour.[73] Thus, some of those concerned to advance the current sustainability agenda ponder whether meaningful change in societal values can be realized incrementally or whether a more radical, revolutionary shift is necessary to achieve lasting modification of attitudes and actions.[74] But if we believe it possible to learn at least something of the "probabilities of the future from what we know of the past," then perhaps the short stories of Prince Edward and other islands told here can help us to reason from experience, to understand what "we see going on around us," and to strive for a more promising future.[75]

II

Shaping Abegweit:
People and Environmental History

The Palaeo-Environment and the Peopling of Prince Edward Island: An Archaeological Perspective

David Keenlyside and Helen Kristmanson

PALAEOGEOGRAPHY

As part of global climatic trends, the northwestern Atlantic was subject to dramatic changes during the late Pleistocene epoch and subsequent after-effects due to global warming, isostatic land rebound, and changing sea levels. From about 25,000 BP to 15,000 BP,[1] glacial ice, referred to as the Laurentide ice mass, covered much of the land from Labrador to southern New England. Most of the northern part of the continent at this time was largely sparse in terms of vegetation, animal life, and people – but not for long! With the melting of the glacial ice masses beginning after 15,000 years ago, plant and animal life rapidly returned to these areas, followed by Aboriginal people who exploited the southern ice margins that were gradually receding northward, creating resource-rich, peri-glacial[2] environments good for hunting and gathering (figure 3.1).

The Atlantic seaboard today is very different from how it first appeared to the earliest Aboriginal inhabitants. Marine geologists, employing coring methods and underwater sonar mapping coupled with computer modelling, have been able to reconstruct in detail this evolving landscape for the past 25,000 years. In addition, through dating of marine mollusks, they can also reconstruct the changing patterns of sea currents and water temperatures.[3] For example, as late as 14,000 years ago, glacial ice blocked the Strait of Belle Isle channel between Newfoundland

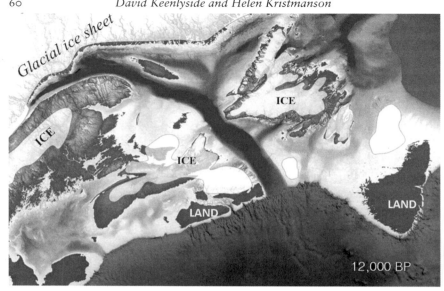

Figure 3.1 Atlantic Canada, ca. 12,000 years before present.

and Labrador, cutting off water flow to the Gulf of St Lawrence. Clearly, these changes would have had a profound effect on marine and coastal ecosystems. Much of our palaeo-ecological data comes from neighbouring Nova Scotia where, at the end of the glacial period, bogs were formed on the deglaciated landscape and soils began to develop.[4] These areas supported rapid vegetation growth along the retreating frontal ice lobes. Typically, these peri-glacial conditions first supported an herbaceous tundra dominated by sedges, grasses, and herbs, with willow shrubs present in some areas.[5] A significant climatic shift and cold interval about 12,800–12,000 years ago, known as the Younger Dryas, saw significant drops in temperature resulting in the re-establishment of ice sheets in Atlantic Canada. This cooling period lasted for over a thousand years. Data indicate that as recently as 10,500 years ago, remnant glacial ice persisted in upland areas of the Maritimes and Northumberland Strait, Prince Edward Island, and adjacent areas of the Gulf of St Lawrence shelf.[6] Even so, conditions in this area did not preclude the presence of wildlife or, for that matter, people. We know from dated settlements at Debert near Truro, Nova Scotia, that people were present there at least 12,000–13,000 years ago; on Prince Edward Island, a contemporaneous site is located near Tryon in Prince County.[7]

The earliest Prince Edward Island vegetation data reflect tundra conditions of about 10,000 years ago.[8] Pollen studies record the earliest vegetation as "tundra-like with non-arboreal birch, willow, Artemisia, and upland grasses and sedges."[9] A pollen core from the Summerside area dating to 9900 BP appears to be in agreement with the earliest dates from eastern areas of the Island. The forest cover was by no means static. By 8,000 years ago, pine dominated the forest. Hemlock became established about 7,000 years ago, giving rise to a mixed hemlock/pine forest lasting until about 4,500 years ago. Beech is first recorded in Island pollen profiles about 3,400 years ago, gradually giving rise to the establishment of the "Acadian Forest" that European settlers would encounter three centuries ago. It was characterized up until modern times by part of a hemlock-beech-birch association. The effects of European settlement and land clearing are reflected in pollen assemblages by sharp increases in the presence of grasses and declines in hemlock, birch, and beech.[10]

As climate change transformed plant life on Prince Edward Island, so did it shape the landform. Interpretations of late glacial events on Prince Edward Island, taking into consideration factors such as post-glacial uplift and subsidence, present a complex picture. Our current understanding of coastline elevations comes from recent bathymetry studies undertaken by the Bedford Institute of Oceanography in St Peter's Bay and offshore between Prince Edward Island and the Magdalen Islands. By 10,000 years ago, glacial ice had mostly melted from southern regions, including Prince Edward Island. Isostatic rebound, as the earth's crust was released from the crushing weight of the glacier ice, caused sea levels to drop dramatically in our region. The emergent offshore banks formed coastal lowlands fronted by sandy barrier beaches and lagoons. It is even possible that people inhabited these offshore islands (figure 3.2). A large area around the Magdalen Islands was dry land, and only a short distance separated it from the mainland. Prince Edward Island at this time was part of the mainland, forming an ancient landscape referred to as Northumbria.[11]

Well-preserved fluvial landscapes have been identified in the Northumberland Strait area under the present-day path of the Confederation Bridge, revealing a rare glimpse of ancient Northumbria. This ancient landscape emerged about 10,000 years ago and lasted about 5,000 years. These lowlands supported faunal, floral, and human populations. Research first published in the 1970s by Kranck (1972) and more

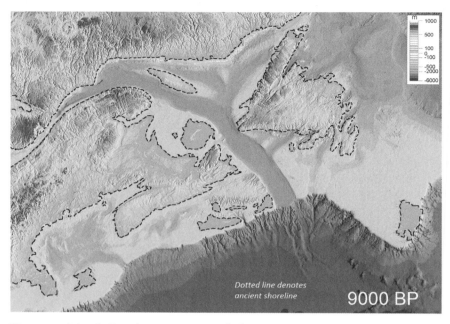

Figure 3.2 Atlantic Canada, ca. 9,000 years before present.

recently by Shaw (2011), initially employing side-scan and then multi-beam sonar methods, clearly identify a well-preserved river system with the principal river draining towards the east, fed by tributaries from both Prince Edward Island and the mainland. Geologist John Shaw describes this ancient landscape as "irregular, with numerous closed basins, so that many small lakes existed, in addition to those connected by the principal river … the maximum emergence in the region occurred at 9000 years BP when the river mouth was probably located offshore from the modern coast of Cape Breton Island."[12] These ancient environs must have supported a resource-rich ecosystem with abundant fresh-water fish, waterfowl, and terrestrial mammals. As sea levels began to rise, these river systems became saltwater estuaries, probably not unlike today's Hillsborough River ecosystem.

By about 5,000 years ago, Northumbria was breached by rising waters, forming what is now Northumberland Strait and eventually creating the Prince Edward Island we know today. Over the past several thousand years, the rate of sea-level rise in northern Prince Edward Island has decelerated and is now just over 0.3 m/century.[13] Northern regions, however, such as the shore of Labrador and parts of Newfoundland, are still rebounding, and the shoreline is actually emerging.

The early post-glacial faunal history of Prince Edward Island, in terms of the fossil and archaeological record, is not well known, although reconstructed environments and vegetation provide some indication of the kinds of animals that might have been present. According to R.F. Miller, "Most species that likely inhabited the Maritimes during the late glacial and post-glacial times still exist, although they may no longer exist in this region."[14] Large mammals or megafauna typically associated with the late Pleistocene, such as mastodons, mammoths, and giant beavers, may not have survived the Wisconsin glaciations. However, Miller continues, "Caribou were certainly present on the landscape and grizzly bears may have inhabited the Maritimes also, although when they arrived is uncertain. Small mammals, reptiles and amphibians eventually populated the region as the climate and vegetation suited their requirements, however the timing of first appearance of species is generally unknown. In the oceans, an arctic fauna of marine mammals including narwhal, beluga and walrus were probably common as soon as conditions allowed, along with whales whose range still includes this region."[15] Throughout this period of evolving ecosystems, the Island's first peoples depended upon these fauna for their food and raw materials for clothing, tools, and other material culture.

THE ARCHAEOLOGICAL RECORD

The archaeological record tells us that Aboriginal people have lived in New England and Canada's Maritime provinces for at least the past 13,000 years, in southern Labrador for over 9,000 years, and on the Island of Newfoundland for 6,000–7,000 years and possibly longer. Archaeology can provide only a glimpse into the ancient people's daily lives as seen through the material manifestations of their culture and features on the landscape. Our sample is drawn from those few preserved archaeological sites – and those we have been lucky enough to identify. These places are far from evenly distributed across the Island, which is a function of the relatively short period of archaeological study and the few researchers who have pursued Island archaeology. Moreover, it is a reflection of human behaviour and habit – where people lived and travelled and the changing population and social organizations over the millennia. In this brief summary we highlight the major time sequence and key elements in defining the nature of this human legacy over more than five hundred generations of human settlement. This archaeological construct of the human occupation of Prince Edward Island can be framed within the conventional archaeological record for Northeastern

North America spanning 12,000–13,000 years. Evidence is known only for the period following the last glacial event. Archaeologists have roughly divided this time frame into four periods in years before present: (1) Palaeo-Indian, 13,000–10,000 BP, (2) Archaic, 10,000–3000 BP, (3) Maritime Woodland, 3000 BP to AD 1500, and (4) post-European contact, AD 1500 to the present.

THE PALAEO-INDIAN PERIOD
(13,000–10,000 YEARS AGO)

The Palaeo-Indian presence in the southern Gulf of St Lawrence/northern New England region has been well established for several decades. The primary chronological reference point for earliest human presence in Atlantic Canada comes from the Debert site in north-central Nova Scotia, radiocarbon dated to 10,600 radiocarbon years ago or 12,000 to 13,000 calendar years.[16] This antiquity is further substantiated by closely comparable dates from the Vail site in western Maine and the Whipple site in New Hampshire.[17] All of these sites are interpreted as hunting camps for the caribou that once roamed in great numbers in this tundra environment, similar to today's subarctic Canada. The strategic location of sites and the kinds of hunting and processing tools discovered point to a herd-hunting economy – at least for part of the year. In broad cultural terms, most Palaeo-Indian research supports George MacDonald's assignment of these components to a "middle period" Clovis horizon, dating between 12,000 and 13,000 years ago.[18] No other archaeological sites in the northeast offer the same chronological control with associated large tool assemblages. Only stone tools and tool production waste flakes have been preserved; missing are the wood, bone, and hide perishable tools that would surely make up a large portion of any material culture. Distinctive fluted point finds from New Brunswick, Nova Scotia, Maine, and Prince Edward Island, although lacking temporal control, convincingly demonstrate on stylistic grounds the widespread distribution of Palaeo-Indian peoples throughout the Maritimes region.[19] The single Island-based example of this type of fluted point, which is fashioned of the same Bay of Fundy chalcedony that is typical of the Debert finds, was surface-collected by local resident Aage Sorensen in the late 1930s from an inland location near Tryon, in the south central part of Prince Edward Island (figure 3.3). A more recent examination by archaeologists of the find area at Tryon did not reveal any additional palaeo-archaeological evidence.

Figure 3.3 Palaeo-Indian spear point.

For decades, archaeologists and Pleistocene geologists have attempted to reconcile the late Wisconsin glacial picture with human occupations, because during the Paleo-Indian period much of Prince Edward Island was covered by ice. Although this state would appear to preclude a human presence, recent discoveries from northern British Columbia and the southern Yukon Territory confirm that people travelled and hunted on glacial ice sheets in pursuit of caribou.[20] The very proximity of the Maritime sites to ice suggests that the peri-glacial conditions and access to ice hunting areas were part of the resource strategy of early hunter-gatherers.

PRINCE EDWARD ISLAND STONE
TOOL INDUSTRIES

Since much of what we know of the Island's pre-contact cultures derives from surviving artifacts fashioned from stone, it is worth discussing the nature of that resource. It is a generally held belief that little stone material exists on the Island for making tools. In fact, many of the tools found in surface collections come from locally obtained sources. Most are cobbles originating from glacial tills deposited during the melting of the last ice advance of the Wisconsinan glaciation, around 15,000 years ago. These well-worn, fist-size quartzite cobbles can be found along many Prince Edward Island beaches, particularly in inland waterways and estuaries. In the same context and also common are pebbles of white quartz. These are difficult materials to work; however, when heated and flaked, they produce sharp cutting edges. Other types of glacially derived stone include rhyolites and colourful agates, which were also desirable for fashioning into spear points, blades, and an assortment of scraping and cutting implements. Other rock types were sourced from mainland quarries or brought to the Island from elsewhere. One such source, Ingonish Island, is described later in this chapter. In more recent Island assemblages, after about AD 600, multicoloured cherts from Bay of Fundy sources become quite popular, possibly brought over and used by visiting mainland people. Another off-Island source, appearing about 1,000 years ago, comes from a well-documented quarry over 1,500 kilometres distant at Ramah Bay, northern Labrador. This material was likely traded by palaeo-Eskimo or ancient Innu peoples either directly or indirectly to people in the Gulf of St Lawrence – a significant example of an extensive ancient trade network with which Prince Edward Island was associated.

ARCHAIC PERIOD
(10,000–3,000 YEARS AGO)

Until relatively recently, there was little evidence in Atlantic Canada regarding the fate of peoples during the Paleo-Indian period – or even evidence that might relate to the occupations of their descendants. However, recent archaeological investigations on the Labrador coast now shed some light on this question. Between 9,000 and 10,000 years ago, archaeological evidence from the Gulf of St Lawrence region indicates, people were heavily dependent on a marine economy for at least part of the year. Migrating sea mammals, in particular harp seal and walrus, which whelp in the southern Gulf of St Lawrence every spring in great numbers, served as a major draw to Aboriginal Islanders and likely populations on the mainland, quite possibly from New England and settlements along the St Lawrence estuary. Clusters of sites along the Quebec/Labrador coastline and the Magdalen Islands are interpreted as marine late Palaeo–early Archaic mammal hunting camps, notably for walrus and seal.[21] This seasonal pattern of reliance on migrating sea mammals continued throughout the region until historic times. The high density of archaeological sites along Prince Edward Island's north shore reflects this resource dependence.

Excavated initially in 1983, the Jones site is a multi-component, stratified deposit found near the entrance to St Peters Bay (figure 3.4). This is a shoreline camp with deposits comprising water-laid and windblown sands. Much of the accumulated deposits come from nearby wind-deflated dunes early in the twentieth century. As it is a submerging coastline, the weathering of the low-lying shoreline banks has been extensive, so that artifacts are continually being weathered on the beach in front of the site. The site has six horizons or habitation zones – two historic (one European, one Mi'kmaq) and four pre-contact. Large surface collections covering each of these six horizons come from the beach collection. The lowest habitation zone lies about eighty centimetres below the surface. A triangular spear point was excavated and has been attributed to a late Palaeo-Indian occupation. The absence of any organic material has precluded any firm dating; however, the deep stratigraphic position of this find indicates considerable antiquity.

Approximately one hundred specimens of this distinctive type have been found in Prince Edward Island from North Lake in the east to Cascumpec Bay in the west.[22] They have the same basic triangular form with the characteristic indented base to facilitate hafting. Fluting, technically speaking, is not present; rather there is channel flaking and basal thinning. Specimens often are characterized by an asymmetric form creating a protruding barb. Typically, but not exclusively, the rock material used is a medium-grained rhyolite, black or grey to buff depending on the degree of weathering.

The closest and only known source for this rock is Ingonish Island on Nova Scotia's Cape Breton Island. These Ordovician-age geological deposits are exposed as laminated bedrock outcrops along the shores of Ingonish Island where, during excavations in the late 1970s, archaeologist Ron Nash documented indications of quarry use. The preference for

Figure 3.4 Jones archaeological site excavation, 1983, St Peters Bay, PEI.

this raw material probably lies in its desirable fracturing qualities. The fracture plane tends to follow the natural laminations, allowing for easy extraction at the source and in the flint-knapping process, which removes large and small flakes to prepare the final tool form. Ingonish rhyolite is important for the story of Prince Edward Island's pre-contact history as it is found in many archaeological sites across the province. From sites at Miminegash in the west to South Lake along the northeast shore, Ingonish rhyolite appears in varying amounts. Some of the earliest sites identified suggest that Ingonish rhyolite end blades were used for sea mammal hunting. In later assemblages, such as those found at St Peters and Rustico, rhyolite is widely used for cutting knives and spear blades.

Accessing Ingonish Island from Prince Edward Island was certainly no easy task. "As the crow flies," the island lies roughly 130 kilometres east of East Point, Prince Edward Island. Boats from the South Lake area would cross Northumberland Strait to the east coast of Cape Breton, with Margaree, Cheticamp, or Mabou Harbour areas as logical landing points. Canoeing around the Cape Breton coast, although possible, seems less likely, given the more open water and potentially difficult weather conditions; the arduous task of traversing Cape Breton carrying heavy stones would likely favour the shortest route. These obstacles may have resulted in the choice of a southern route to link into the Bras d'Or lakes system. In the end, we can only speculate, as archaeological evidence is virtually absent throughout central Cape Breton.

Other mainland lithic sources were also important to Island Aboriginal peoples through the ages. Of particular importance from earliest times were volcanic basalt deposits from the Bay of Fundy in Nova Scotia, especially near Cape Blomidon, Parrsboro, and Scots Bay, where rich Jurassic-age volcanic basalt flows have created layers of crystalline rocks. Their vitreous and colourful glass-like consistency is ideal for flaking and shaping very sharp-edged tools.

A hallmark of the material culture of Archaic period is the development of ground stone tools, which appeared for the first time roughly 8,000 years ago.[23] Although woodworking would appear to be the main area benefiting from this technology, ground slate spears and multifunctional blades such as semi-lunar knives have also been found. In the following millennia, across the Maritimes, we see this technology developed to a high degree of specialization and workmanship – tools and ornaments of ground slate, bone, and ivory (figures 3.5; 3.6).

Such technology would facilitate the making of dugout canoes and cutting poles for shelters, fish weirs, and domestic articles. Hand spears and atlatls (throwing spears) would have been the primary hunting weapons. Bows and arrows do not appear to have been developed until two or three thousand years ago.

THE MARITIME WOODLAND PERIOD (3,000 YEARS AGO: AD 1500)

The end of the Archaic period is marked notably by the introduction and development of a ceramic making industry – the hallmark of the Maritime Woodland or Ceramic Period. Most pre-contact sites discovered on the Island are attributed to this time period – although their seemingly high proportion is likely due to preservation rather than convincing evidence of greater numbers. Coastal submergence and erosion on the Island have undoubtedly been responsible for the loss of much of the early archaeological record.

The earliest ceramic technologies in the New World first appear in the archaeological record in South and Central America about 5,000–6,000 years ago. Ceramics tend to appear later in the archaeological record as the technology was gradually transmitted northward, reaching the

Length 19 cm

Figure 3.5 Ground slate knife recovered from scallop dragger, north shore, P E I, ca. 6,000 years old.

Figure 3.6 Decorated stone plummet as net or line weight recovered from scallop drag near Sea Cow Head, P E I, ca. 5,000–7,000 years old.

Maritimes about 2,500–3,000 years ago.[24] On Prince Edward Island, the oldest known ceramics date from about 2,200 years ago, and pottery continued to be manufactured and used (at least) until first contact in the fifteenth and sixteenth centuries (figure 3.7).[25]

At most archeological sites, only the most durable of materials such as stone, ceramic, and some charred organics escape decomposition. These materials, while of considerable interpretive value, reflect only a small percentage of past Aboriginal cultures, societies, and identities, which were also expressed through media and actions that have disappeared. However, archaeological material culture gives archaeologists enough of a window into pre-contact society to see evidence for continuity as well as change during the Maritime Woodland period. This is seen, for instance, in the various types of archaeological sites and changing forms and functions in Middle Woodland period technologies such as ceramic making, flint-knapping, and even transportation. Aboriginal people are believed to have possessed the technology to construct watercraft from earliest pre-contact times in the Atlantic region. The dugout canoe, which is recorded historically, is possibly the oldest form of Aboriginal water transportation. It is the antecedent of the birchbark canoe, which is believed to have been developed during the early Maritime Woodland period. The Mi'kmaq are well known ethnographically for their distinctive river-adapted birchbark canoe and also a larger ocean-water canoe. Moose and caribou hide-skin watercraft, probably precursors to the birchbark canoe, were also used into the twentieth century. The birchbark and skin-covered canoes were lightweight and portable and increased mobility and transporting capacity on the network of rivers and lakes that were key to people moving across the landscape in all seasons. During the winter, the same watercourses, now frozen, provided the easiest and the only practical means of accessing parts of the Island and mainland interiors. Trails, portages, and trade routes became well established over generations; many of our transportation routes today are based on early established routes.

We do not have an accurate picture of pre-contact dwellings, but a two-thousand-year-old semi-subterranean winter structure is known archaeologically from southern New Brunswick, and a later dwelling was seen at the Sutherland site on St Peters Bay where soil imprints of a number of circular structures are interpreted as house patterns and date from about 1,200 years ago.[26] The earliest descriptions we have of Mi'kmaq dwellings come from New Brunswick in the form of the seventeenth-century documents of the agent and merchant Nicolas Denys.[27] For the Mi'kmaq of southern New Brunswick, Denys describes two types of wigwams: a round structure, holding ten to twelve people, and the long wigwam, holding twice as many – probably summer and winter dwellings, respectively. The round type of wigwam was supported by poles and covered with sheets of birchbark. These were moveable structures, easily dismantled and rolled up for transport. Historic photographs and drawings from the late nineteenth and early twentieth

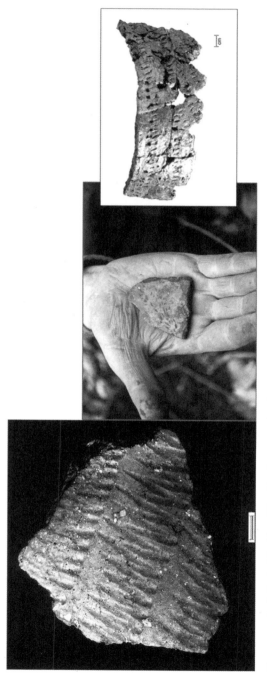

Figure 3.7 *Left*: Early Maritime Woodland ceramic sherd, Savage Harbour, PEI, Jones collection; *centre*: late pre-contact ceramic vessel sherd, Pitawelkek shell midden site, Malpeque Bay, PEI; *right*: late pre-contact decorated ceramic vessel rim, South Lake, PEI.

centuries illustrate examples and typically show small groupings of a few wigwams located along the shore. Some Mi'kmaq continued to make use of wigwams on Prince Edward Island as late as the early 1950s.

One of the characteristics of these later period settlements is the shell midden site, an accumulation of discarded shellfish, animal bones, and other food waste, along with various refuse left over from daily human life. On Prince Edward Island and across the coastal areas of the Maritimes, shell middens underline the importance of the intertidal zone for food gathering sources. While shellfish constituted an important part of the Aboriginal diet, archaeologists have also been able to reconstruct dietary preferences through the analysis of preserved faunal remains recovered at various sites across the province. Most of this evidence is associated with human food waste deposits in shell midden contexts where the rich carbonate soils have preserved the organic matter. Notable pre-contact terrestrial remains from the past two thousand years include bear, caribou, rabbit, beaver, muskrat, various smaller vertebrates, and waterfowl.[28] Marine mammal remains of walrus and harp and grey seal have been found as well, along with a wide variety of fish species, including the Great White shark (figure 3.8).

Indeed, the many pre-contact sites found in estuaries and bays of the north shore likely relate to marine mammal hunting. Vast numbers of walrus are well documented historically from Newfoundland to New England. European hunters killed hundreds of thousands of them in the 1600s and 1700s, driving the species to the point of extirpation in the region around 1800. Another of the great Island attractions was the migrating herds of harp seal that frequented the Island's north shore in late winter and spring. Aboriginal peoples were also drawn to the shore by Prince Edward Island's great abundance of migratory birds and waterfowl, a very important part of the historic Mi'kmaq seasonal resource cycle and likely in the more distant past as well. Archaeological evidence for the walrus hunt has also been recovered at the Pitawelkek site on Georges Island in western Prince Edward Island. The artifact assemblage from Pitawelkek includes a range of pre-contact and historic materials typical for this region, including faunal remains, earthenware ceramic sherds, stone tools, fire-cracked rock from campfires, and an eighteenth-century metal trade axe along with decorated bowl fragments from a historic, European-manufactured, clay smoking pipe.

The paragraphs above have broadly outlined the climate and geography of Prince Edward Island and the northwestern Atlantic for most of the post glacial-period. Our knowledge of the palaeo-cultural-

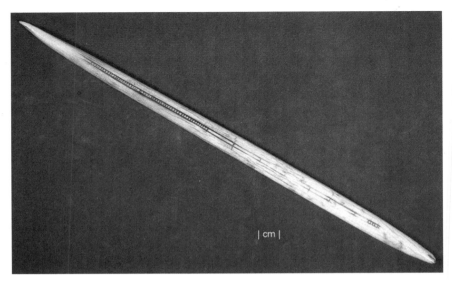

Figure 3.8 Decorated walrus ivory implement. Malpeque Bay, PEI, ca. 600–700 years old.

environment is based on archaeological data, coring methods, and underwater sonar mapping, which, together with computer modelling, have allowed us to reconstruct in detail the evolving landscape for the past 25,000 years.

This long period of constant adaptation between humans and eco-systems was disrupted about five hundred years ago with the arrival of a human population whose perceptions of environment and nature were unfamiliar to Aboriginal people.

HISTORIC PERIOD: AD 1500 – PRESENT

The end of the Maritime Woodland period is marked by the arrival and permanent settlement of Europeans in the Northeast. As early as the late fifteenth century, the seasonal appearance of European fishers and trad-ers began to destabilize the human-ecosystem relationship that Aborigi-nal people had developed over hundreds of generations. By AD 1615, contact between Europeans and the Mi'kmaq changed from sporadic to regular events, resulting in a wave of epidemics that devastated Aboriginal populations in the Northeast.[29] Population collapse was compounded by changes to traditional rounds that hinged on the exploi-tation and preparation of seasonally available resources at various locations. Opportunities for trade kept the Mi'kmaq to the coast, away from their usual subsistence routines. Subsequent changes to the Mi'kmaq diet and overall health, in addition to exposure to foreign pathogens, resulted in a reduced quality of life and life expectancy.[30] The ability of the Mi'kmaq to function as a hunter-gatherer society was permanently altered.

Some effects of cross-cultural interaction were already in evidence in the early seventeenth century when Mi'kmaq informants notified French chroniclers of their declining numbers. In Nova Scotia, for example, Membertou, grand chief of the Souriquois,[31] recalled that during his youth, ca. AD 1525, his people were as "thickly planted ... as the hairs on his head." Membertou attributed the decline of this population to the arrival of the French. Although we do not know the true size of the pre-contact population in the Maritime provinces, Hoffman speculated that about six thousand was not out of the question.[32]

For an indeterminate period during this transitional time, the ancestral Mi'kmaq continued to produce a material culture relevant to a hunter-gatherer society. Archaeologically, this is represented by artifacts such as small corner- and side-notched projectile points, earthenware ceramics, stone scrapers, faunal material, shell, and fire-cracked rock. The Mi'kmaq economy, however, was also infused with select European goods such as glass beads, firearms, iron tools, and copper kettles. Copper "kettles," which are actually large cauldrons, may have been attractive to the Mi'kmaq for their apparent utility, but there is also a possibility that they bore significant cultural value based on their red sheen. For Aboriginal peoples in northeastern North America, the colour conveyed "animation, emotion, intense experience ... fire, heat, and blood."[33] Possession of a red object conferred similar qualities to its owner, and when ritually consecrated, provided an "insurance and assurance of ... physical, spiritual and social well-being."[34] The presence of native copper in archaeological sites for as many as 2,500 years suggests an enduring cultural and ceremonial importance to Aboriginal people in the Maritime provinces.[35]

From this perspective, it is not difficult to understand why copper kettles obtained from European traders were not purely utilitarian items, as we might expect, but came to be refashioned into Aboriginal forms, such as small tools or rolled cones or beads. These transformed objects may have been used as ceremonial or grave goods or for other culturally significant purposes such as decoration on clothing, which also sometimes served as a protective device for the living.[36] Another use for the copper kettles was to bury the dead. As many as twelve copper kettle burial sites have been identified in the Maritime provinces, most of them in New Brunswick and Nova Scotia, with at least one identified in Prince Edward Island. None have been identified in Newfoundland and Labrador. These burial sites, which include a combination of Aboriginal and European grave goods, point to a period of transformation in Aboriginal mortuary practice among a portion of the Aboriginal population in this region in the late sixteenth and early seventeenth centuries and help illustrate the complexities of the archaeological record during this transitional period.[37]

In Prince Edward Island, permanent European settlement took place later than in other parts of the Maritime provinces, beginning with the French establishment of Port La Joie in 1720 followed by numerous Acadian settlements throughout the Island. Between 1720 and the Acadian Deportation in 1758, the Island Mi'kmaq and Acadian populations, each with their own way of interacting with the land, managed a "middle ground" existence. This type of social contract allowed for mutual subsistence in shared ecosystems without major conflict.[38] An example of this generally amicable coexistence is seen at the Pointe-aux-Vieux site, located on the west shore of southern Malpeque Bay within view of the Pitawelkek site. Among the remaining material culture at this pre-deportation site were found numerous glass beads, likely intended for trade with the local Mi'kmaq.[39]

But the spread of European settlement, and the concurrent development of the Indian Act and related social policy, eventually forced the Mi'kmaq, like Aboriginal peoples across Canada, to discontinue Aboriginal cultural practices as well as subsistence and settlement patterns integral to their hunter-gatherer existence. This took a toll on many aspects of pre-contact culture (including stone tool and ceramic technologies) which, aside from the production of marketable baskets, toys, and other craftworks, lost application in a colonial setting.

Following the deportation of the Acadians and the assertion of British sovereignty in the mid-eighteenth century, the Island was carved into sixty-seven lots, which were assigned to British owners. With this geopolitical shift began a transformation of the landscape that in turn transformed the Aboriginal-ecosystem relationship. The Mi'kmaq were no longer able to move freely between seasonally available resources, as most were now located on the property of British landowners.[40]

A rare archaeological example of Mi'kmaq life during these most difficult times is found at the Red Bank site on the Hillsborough River at Mount Stewart. Here, in the late eighteenth and the nineteenth centuries, an unknown number of Mi'kmaq families lived on the Pigot family farm. The story was brought to our attention by landowner Bruce Pigot, who has, through surface collection at the site, amassed a large artifact assemblage ranging from the pre-contact to historic periods. With Mr Pigot's assistance, systematic testing at the site by archaeologist Pat Allen revealed two late eighteenth–early nineteenth century wigwam features, both of them containing an array of typical historic materials, such as ceramic, glass, clay pipes, gun flints, buttons, and beads, as well as distinctively Mi'kmaq artifacts such as stone smoking pipes and chipped and ground stones.[41] There is also evidence that the Mi'kmaq at Red Bank recycled European objects for Aboriginal use. At Red Bank, 162 sherds of glass were recovered, including fragments of lantern globes, bottles, other vessels, and pane glass. Twenty-one of these show that the Mi'kmaq sometimes made expedient use of discarded glass fragments which, with their sharp edges, offered ready-made tools. Close inspection also showed that at other times the Mi'kmaq called upon traditional technology to reshape and sharpen the glass sherds, using a method analogous to flint-knapping, to create a secondary tool.[42]

The Red Bank site, located on settler land and comprised of traditional Mi'kmaq dwellings and a combination of European and Mi'kmaq material culture, offers a rare glimpse of the Island Mi'kmaq during this "period of extreme hardship."[43] The syncretism of the familiar and unknown as observed archaeologically is indicative of the human capacity to adapt to environmental, economic, political, and other changes visited upon them (figure 3.9).

ENVIRONMENT, HUMAN ADAPTATION, AND POPULATION SIZE

As we have seen, the arrival of newcomers to the eastern shores of Canada in the late fifteenth century set important changes in motion that changed the course of Aboriginal society. But how had Aboriginal peoples sustained life in an often harsh and changing environment for so many generations prior? Environmental historian William Cronon has offered one way of looking at hunter-gatherer subsistence strategies. Focusing on hunter-gatherer and agricultural Aboriginal societies in northern and southern New England, Cronon explored subsistence strategies in terms of the ecological principle known as Liebig's law. This states that "biological populations are limited not by the total annual resources available to them but by the minimum amount that can be

Figure 3.9 Mi'kmaq man and wigwam, PEI, photo taken
mid-1800s.

found at the scarcest time of the year."[44] By keeping population densities
low, Aboriginal people are thought to have exerted less pressure on the
food scarcities of winter, assuring the abundance of spring and a general
stability of human-ecosystem relationships. The strategic exploitation of
resources where and when they were most abundant meant that no source
was exhausted at any time. That Aboriginal people were conversant with
the rhythms of their environment is supported by ethnographic accounts
that record an Aboriginal preference for diverse eco-zones and deliberate
avoidance of areas where overuse had reduced ecological diversity.[45]

Attempts have been made to estimate the population of hunter-
gatherers in the Gulf of St Lawrence region since the seventeenth century. From Port Royal in the early 1600s, Jesuit priest Pierre Biard
emphasized the smallness of the population: "The [Indigenous] are not
numerous. The Etheminqui number less than a thousand, the Algonquins
and the Montagnais together would not amount to much more, the
Souriquois [ancestral Mi'kmaq] would not amount to two thousand.

Thus four thousand Indians at most roam through, rather than occupy, these vast stretches of inland territory and sea-shore. For they are a nomadic people, living in the forests and scattered over wide spaces, as is natural for those who live by hunting and fishing only."[46]

A number of researchers have since tackled population estimates for Aboriginal people in the Gulf of St Lawrence, the most noteworthy examples flowing from twentieth-century scholarship. But none have been able to agree on a plausible population size for the Mi'kmaq, and few analyses have sufficiently differentiated between pre-contact and post-contact populations.[47] In 1928, American ethnographer James Mooney made an estimate of about 3,500 for the Mi'kmaq population in the Maritime provinces region for AD 1600.[48] Subsequent scholars widely accepted this figure, with the exception of anthropologists Wilson D. Wallis and Ruth Sawtell Wallis and ethnographer Bernard Hoffman, who noted extensive changes to Aboriginal populations in the Maritimes between the seventeenth and eighteenth centuries.[49] Several decades later, anthropologist Virginia Miller reviewed the evidence for the Mi'kmaq population.[50] Based on the density of archaeological sites in Nova Scotia and a prediction of one person for about every 3.37 square kilometres, Miller estimated a total Mi'kmaq population of 35,000, presumably in reference to the pre-contact population. Her estimate contrasts sharply with Bock and Snow's estimates for the pre-epidemic Mi'kmaq population of 4,500 and 12,000, respectively.[51]

Cronon more recently applied Snow's population estimate formula to Aboriginal Maine (approximately 12–29 people per 100 km²) to calculate the hunter-gatherer population of New England.[52] His example provides a reasonable point of comparison for the Prince Edward Island Mi'kmaq, who in the pre-contact period lived in comparable eco-systems, relied on a similar resource base, and practised similar subsistence and settlement strategies. Applying Snow's New England formula to Prince Edward Island, we see that the Island could sustain a hunter-gatherer population of approximately nine hundred individuals.[53] This is consistent with Hoffman's estimate for the historic Mi'kmaq population when we adjust for the fact that his calculations were not specific to Prince Edward Island.[54] However, as Hoffman, Miller and the Wallises cautioned, extrapolation of this formula beyond a pre-contact application must be properly historicized to take into account the impact of the colonial era on the Aboriginal population.

Early records indicate that by the seventeenth century the effects of cross-cultural relations had damaged the human-ecosystem relationship maintained by the Mi'kmaq for so long. French sources point to disruptions in the Mi'kmaq subsistence pattern and the hardship they experienced during winter, which may have originated with and resulted in an increased reliance on European trade goods. The fur trade is identified as a major source of Mi'kmaq hardship because it reduced access to fauna and also created a preference for a winter beaver hunt, which oriented the Mi'kmaq away from their regular winter hunting patterns and exploitation of diverse winter coastal resources.[55] In the summer, the Mi'kmaq tended to linger at the shore to take advantage of trading opportunities; as a result they were distracted from the summer fishery and the time they normally spent in making provisions for winter. And so, with the arrival of Europeans, the Aboriginal-ecosystem relationship was permanently disrupted within the space of a few generations.

Cronon's application of Liebig's law provides a reasonable starting point for understanding how Aboriginal people in the northeast may have maintained a successful relationship with dynamic eco-systems for approximately twelve thousand years. Through generations of adaptation and knowledge-building, they developed key strategies that may have involved population control and resource conservation. Fundamental to their success was the intergenerational transmission of ecological knowledge, achieved through the use of expressive place names and information-rich oral histories. This means of information-sharing lost some of its application with the arrival of Europeans and the subsequent disruption to Aboriginal subsistence and settlement systems.

In the present day, it is often assumed that the Mi'kmaq were only summer residents of Prince Edward Island who wintered on the mainland. Yet there is no reason to believe that the mainland offered access to a significantly different resource base at any time of the year. However, this notion may have historical relevance if it can be demonstrated that the Mi'kmaq were forced to leave the Island during the winter due to pressures that the settler population placed on game animals.

Archaeological evidence for seasonality is to date known from only a few sites in Prince Edward Island, such as the Pitawelkek and Sutherland sites. In those instances, we see that pre-contact Aboriginal people exploited a wide variety of species, including birds, fish, and terrestrial and marine mammals. Some species were available only seasonally, while others were available year round, leaving open the question of whether Aboriginal people were year-round residents. Avoiding an environmentally deterministic approach, consideration must also be given to the social and cultural factors that may have provided incentives for temporarily leaving the Island.

The idea that the Mi'kmaq were only summer residents of Prince Edward Island has not been subject to scholarly examination nor is it substantiated by archaeological evidence and must not be uncritically accepted as a generalization for historic or pre-contact settlement and subsistence patterns. Until such time that the matter is given scholarly attention, the question of whether the Mi'kmaq wintered on the Island remains unresolved.

CONCLUSION

In this chapter, we have reviewed the palaeo-environment and outlined the human history of Prince Edward Island for a period of approximately twelve thousand years. It is virtually impossible to present a complete story of the Island's earliest inhabitants, and archaeology can only provide a narrow glimpse into ancient peoples' daily lives as witnessed through the material remains of their culture and existing features of the landscape. Our current understanding is drawn from environmental data and those few preserved archaeological sites that are distributed across all regions of the Island, though much of the Island's archaeological evidence has undoubtedly been washed away in whole or in part due to coastal erosion. The distribution and number of remaining sites are a function of the amount of archaeological field research conducted to date but are also a function of human behaviour and choices.

We have also reflected on the changing but enduring relationship between Aboriginal people and the eco-systems they inhabited for millennia. We have considered the interrelationship of population density and resource exploitation to help us understand how the Mi'kmaq and their ancestors adapted to changing environmental circumstances. Scientific and historic evidence demonstrates that hundreds of generations of successful adaptation and adjustment were rapidly undone with the arrival of newcomers on the east coast. The effects of this legacy in Prince Edward Island are at present most vividly expressed at the Red Bank site, where the hardship of the Prince Edward Island Mi'kmaq is evident from the archaeological record. While today the Mi'kmaq are proudly regarded as the Island's original inhabitants, they have never fully recovered from the impact of colonization and the fundamentally different way of interacting with the land that was brought to the Island centuries ago.

4

The Forests of Prince Edward Island, 1720–1900

Douglas Sobey

When the first European settlers arrived on Prince Edward Island in 1720, they found an island entirely covered by an old-growth forest that had been developing ever since the retreat of the glaciers some twelve thousand years before. By 1900 over two-thirds of that forest had been destroyed to create farmland, while the area still remaining under trees had been drastically altered by continual cutting and the action of forest fires.[1] For seventy years, from about 1810 to 1880, the forests played a significant role in the economy of the Island, a role, however, that was not appreciated at the time and was forgotten soon afterwards. Until recently, the story of the exploitation and destruction of the Island's forests has been largely untold. This chapter aims to rectify this deficiency by providing an overview of recent research carried out on both the nature of the present-day and pre-settlement forests and the history of their exploitation and destruction. I hope that, as a result, a first step will have been made in appreciating the economic and cultural importance of the forests in the history of the Island.

THE PRESENT-DAY FORESTS

Lying within the Acadian Forest Region, and part of the so-called boreal-broadleaf ecotone (or boundary zone),[2] the forests of Prince Edward Island contain tree species and communities characteristic of both the "northern hardwood forest" and the more northerly "boreal coniferous forest."[3] A recent study of the present-day forests has resulted in their classification into five forest types (table 4.1).[4] Three of these are

Table 4.1
A classification of the present-day forests of Prince Edward Island, based on 1990 PEI Biomass Inventory.

Forest-Type	% of Plots [% of 1127 plots]	Five Leading Canopy Trees [mean % contribution to woody biomass]	Soil Drainage [% of plots in each of four drainage classes]	Soil Chemistry [mean in the humus layer]	Topography [mean, as read from maps]
Upland Hardwood Forest	38	rM – 33; bF – 19; sM – 10; wB – 9 wS – 7.	Well/moderate – 98 Imperfect/poor – 2	pH – 4.3 %C – 14 C/N – 20 Ca – 810	Elevation – 44m Slope – 3.3%
Wet Rich Woodland	14	rM – 25; wS – 18; bF – 14; Po – 8; Ta – 7.	Well/moderate – 42 Imperfect/poor – 58	pH – 5.4 %C – 22 C/N – 17 Ca – 5120	Elevation – 20m Slope – 0.84%
Black Spruce Forest	7	bS – 53; rS – 17; Ta – 9; wS – 7 bF – 7.	Well/moderate – 34 Imperfect/poor – 66	pH – 3.9 %C – 31 C/N – 32 Ca – 900	Elevation – 19m Slope – 0.76%
White Spruce Woods	12	wS – 62; bF – 8; Po – 5; rM – 5; rS – 5.	Well/moderate – 99 Imperfect/poor – 1	pH – 4.2 %C – 14 C/N – 22 Ca – 650	Elevation – 36m Slope – 3.5%
Disturbed Forest	25	bF – 25; rM – 19; wS – 17; bS – 10; Po – 7.	Well/moderate – 84 Imperfect/poor – 16	pH – 4.1 %C – 22 C/N – 23 Ca – 1020	Elevation – 25m Slope – 2.4%

Trees: bF – balsam fir; bS – black spruce; rS – red spruce; wS – white spruce; Ta – tamarack; Po – poplar species (almost all is trembling aspen); wB – white birch; rM – red maple; sM – sugar maple.

Chemical properties: %C – % of total carbon; C/N – ratio of total carbon to total nitrogen; Ca – available calcium (ppm).

recognizable as descendants (though greatly altered) of pre-settlement forest types: Upland Hardwood Forest, which occurs (as it did in the past) on well-drained or "upland" soils; Wet Rich Woodland, a wet "swamp-type" forest, which is both species rich (in its ground and shrub flora) and base rich (i.e., with a higher calcium content and pH); and Black Spruce Forest, a nutrient-poor and acid coniferous forest type in which black spruce (*Picea mariana*) and tamarack (*Larix laricina*) are dominant. The two other forest types are even more heavily affected by human activity than these first three – in fact, the White Spruce Woods is entirely a "secondary" forest type that has developed on abandoned farmland, largely in the twentieth century, while the highly coniferous Disturbed Forest has over a long period been heavily disturbed and cut over.

Two environmental factors are particularly significant in determining the distribution of these present-day forest types on Prince Edward Island, as well as their tree composition: the soil moisture content (or soil drainage) and the amount of human disturbance. Given the limited range in soil parent materials (i.e., the materials from which the soils are formed – most are glacial deposits derived from sandstone and similar rocks) and of climatic variation,[5] the principal factor responsible for the distribution of the three pre-settlement-related forest types is differences in soil drainage. Drainage in turn is determined by the interaction between topographic factors (especially elevation and slope) and the properties of the soil parent materials, especially the soil texture (i.e., the proportion of sand, silt, and clay particles). In addition, in the areas with poor drainage, there is then the important distinction between the more acid, base-poorer soils with high carbon-to-nitrogen ratios (i.e., their nitrogen levels are low relative to the carbon content) supporting Black Spruce Forest, and the less acid, more base-rich soils with lower c / n ratios (and thus a higher relative nitrogen level) supporting the Wet Rich Woodland, a swamp-type forest in which deciduous trees predominate – nowadays red maple (*Acer rubrum*) is especially prominent, but also occurring in a few places are black ash (*Fraxinus nigra*), white cedar (*Thuja occidentalis*), and white elm (*Ulmus americana*) (though the elm has been devastated in the past twenty-five years by Dutch elm disease).

However, affecting the tree composition of all of these present-day forest types, and playing a role especially in determining the presence of the White Spruce Woods and the Disturbed Forest, are the effects of almost three centuries of human interference. This has involved the initial forest clearance for the creation of farmland (which reached its maximum in the early twentieth century) and the continual exploitation of the remaining forest stands for timber and firewood. Since the early twentieth century especially, much of the poorer farmland has been abandoned, resulting in its recolonization by trees, especially white spruce.

THE PRE-SETTLEMENT FORESTS

But what were the forests like before European settlement? Study of less-disturbed remnants, where they still occur, as well as equivalent forest types elsewhere in the Acadian Forest Region is useful, but especially valuable are the many early written accounts containing descriptions and comments on the forest.[6] These accounts range from private letters to published handbooks for immigrants; tree and forest descriptions are also recorded on many of the manuscript maps and in the surveyors' field-books housed in the Public Archives.[7] Such records reveal that, though the tree composition of the pre-settlement forest was very different from that of today (as is evident from a comparison of figures 4.1 and 4.2), we can recognize in the descriptions and comments of nineteenth-century recorders the pre-settlement ancestors of the forest types that are still present today in a degraded form. In rudimentary forest classifications, a standard approach was to divide the Island's forests into three broad types: areas under a normal forest cover, usually subdivided by the surveyors and cartographers into "hardwood forest," "softwood forest," and "mixed forest"; and the areas that they termed the "barrens" and the "swamps." Generally these latter two also had a tree cover. A synthesis of material from many different forest descriptions enables us to get a useful picture of each.

Many recorders refer to a forest type that can be recognized as the equivalent of the present-day Upland Hardwood Forest, consisting of the shade-tolerant climax hardwood trees occurring on soils with good drainage. In fact, in most parts of colonial North America the presence of such forest was taken as an indicator of land suitable for farmland.[8] Three species were usually listed as its principal trees: "Beech" (*Fagus grandifolia*), "Black Birch" (i.e., yellow birch, *Betula alleghaniensis*), and "Maple," probably mostly sugar maple (*Acer saccharum*), though there may also have been some red (*A. rubrum*). From the descriptions and comments, the three evidently could occur together in any proportion, ranging from a mixture of all three to stands comprising just one of them. Of the three, however, beech was clearly the leading tree. Not only is it mentioned more frequently than the other two in the records (figure 4.2)[9] but there are also many explicit comments indicating its dominance.[10] Which of the three was present at a site was thought to depend upon the drainage properties of the soil, with yellow birch being the most demanding in terms of soil moisture and beech the least. Two other broad-leaved trees, red oak (*Quercus rubra*) and white ash (*Fraxinus americana*), could also contribute to the hardwood forest, though both were considered uncommon. There was also frequently a minority conifer element, comprising any of three species: "Pine" (undoubtedly white pine, *Pinus strobus*), "Spruce" (presumably mostly red spruce, *Picea rubens*), and "Hemlock" (*Tsuga canadensis*). These conifers could occur as scattered individuals (especially the pine) or in small clusters. Where they were the dominants over an extensive area, as in the "hollows"

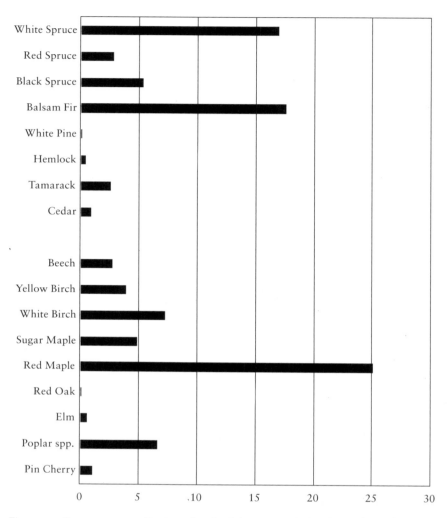

Figure 4.1 Percentage contribution of each of the tree species to the total woody biomass in the 1,200 plots assessed in the 1990 Forest Biomass Inventory.

within the hardwood forest, or in low-lying areas along brooks, it is questionable whether the forest of that specific area could still be called hardwood forest.[11]

"Softwood forest" was the term used, especially by surveyors, to describe areas where the predominant tree cover was any of pine, spruce, fir, tamarack, hemlock, or cedar, present as single-species stands or sometimes in different combinations. In fact, rather than using the

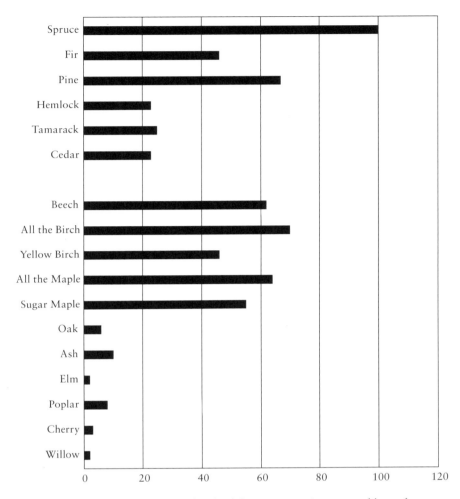

Figure 4.2 Total tally of mentions of each of the tree genera in an assemblage of 172 historical documents for the British period on Prince Edward Island (excluding mentions in "lists" of trees). The explicit references to white birch and red maple have then been subtracted from the "Birch" and "Maple" totals so as to give the maximum possible scores attainable by the two climax species, yellow birch and sugar maple.

term "softwood," surveyors often recorded the direct designation of the forest type by the name of the predominant conifer, as, for example, the use in western Prince County of the terms "spruce land" and "cedar land."[12] It is also evident that the boundaries (both conceptually, and physically on the ground) between the softwood forest type and what were called the barrens and the swamps were not always sharply defined, for these two habitat types usually also had a high conifer component comprising some of these same species. The factor responsible for the presence of softwood forest was considered to be higher soil-moisture levels and/or lower soil fertility, and so the presence of conifers on their own was taken as an indicator of soils either less suited for agriculture or totally unsuited.[13]

The name "barrens," or "barren land," was used – as the name implies – for an unproductive land type considered to be of no use for agriculture and also of little value for its trees.[14] Though some recorders seem to reserve the term for vegetation that had more the appearance of scrub than forest, many record the presence of a tree cover. The principal tree of the barrens was spruce (undoubtedly black spruce, as specified by one recorder). Some even used the term "spruce barren" as a land-type name, and stressed that it was quite different from "spruce land" with its larger, more valuable trees. Tamarack and balsam fir (*Abies balsamea*) were also found on particular barrens. Whatever the species, these trees were frequently small in size and of little value, except sometimes for fencing poles.[15] The barrens in general were perceived to be underlain at least in part by a white sandy soil, but their drainage could actually vary considerably.[16] They were also considered susceptible to fire, and once burned, recolonization by trees was long and slow. Such barren lands were thought to make up only a small part of the Island's land surface, though they were especially prominent in west Prince County.

The word "swamp" was apparently used mostly as a synonym for wet woodland, as is indicated by the tree names used to describe these areas: "red spruce swamp," "black spruce swamp," "ash swamp," "cedar swamp," "juniper swamp" (i.e., tamarack), and "alder swamp" – and there may have been other types that have not entered the records.[17] For example, red maple is described as "generally found growing in swamps," though the term "maple swamp" is not recorded. The swamps were viewed by some as being potentially convertible to "meadow" or "pasture" rather than to cultivated arable land, but, like the barrens, they were thought to cover only a limited land area. Clearly, they are the pre-settlement equivalent, at least in part, of the Wet Rich Woodland.

There are comments in the historical records on various aspects of the ecology of the pre-settlement forest, including the large size of the trees, especially in the upland hardwood forest: the three dominant hardwoods were commonly three to five feet in diameter, with the associated pine and hemlock trees being even larger.[18] Also drawing comment was the absence of a shrub layer in the hardwood forest,[19] the prevalence in old-growth forest of "cradle-hills" with their hummock and hollow pattern,[20] the presence in particular forest types of fallen trees in large numbers,[21] and the distinctive nature of the coastal spruce woods.[22] Many recorders also noted a relationship between the distribution of the forest types and soil fertility and moisture levels, and the handbooks written for prospective settlers placed much stress on the use of the natural forest trees as an indicator of soil quality.[23] The occasional large-scale damage to the forest due to hurricanes and wind-storms was also recorded,[24] as was the phenomenon of forest succession after forest fire, timber-cutting, and farm abandonment[25] and the food-chain interrelationships between the various forest animals.[26]

The early records include few general comments on the *geographical* distribution of these forest types.[27] However, by making use of the soil drainage characteristics of their present-day equivalents, it is possible to map tentatively the pre-settlement distributions of the upland hardwood forest and of the two wet forest types combined (figure 4.3A).[28] Such a mapping suggests that much of the Island's land area was covered by upland hardwood forest, which occupied most of the central part, with smaller but significant blocks in the western and eastern parts. By contrast, the two wetter forest types (the pre-settlement precursors of the Black Spruce Forest, including the barrens, and of the Wet Rich Woodland, or swamp forest), predominated at lower elevations in specific areas in the west and in a more general mosaic pattern in the east. It is thus on these low-lying sites that the boreal element of the Island's forests, in the form of black spruce and tamarack, would have occurred. Such a division of the landscape, based on soil drainage, between the "northern hardwood forest" and the "boreal forest" is characteristic of the boreal-broadleaf ecotone in eastern Canada.[29] This distinctive geographical pattern has had important effects on the settlement patterns of Europeans within the Island as well on their utilization of the forest, as will become apparent.

THE NEW IMMIGRANTS AND THE FOREST

These pre-settlement forests developed largely undisturbed by human activity over a period of some ten thousand years.[30] The Aboriginal Mi'kmaq, being hunter-gatherers, and also crossing over to the Island only during the summer (at least in the immediate pre-settlement period), made use of its forest resources in a limited way, which, as far as we can

Figure 4.3A Conjectured distribution of pre-settlement Upland Hardwood Forest (*upper*) and Wet Rich Woodland and Black Spruce Forest combined (*lower*). The upper map is based on the combined distribution of well-drained soils (as mapped by the 1988 Soil Survey of Prince Edward Island) and stands of Upland Hardwood Forest in 1990; the lower, on the combined distribution of imperfectly and poorly drained soils (excluding the stream complexes), and the distribution of stands of Black Spruce Forest and Wet Rich Woodland in 1990.

determine, did not have any long-term effects.[31] But the new immigrants from Europe were to have an immediate and major impact on the forests. These immigrants can be divided into two groups: farmer-settlers, who arrived with the intention of clearing land to establish a farm on which to raise a family (most fell into this category); and a minority who arrived with the intention of exploiting the timber resources they knew the Island to possess.[32] In the course of time, the distinction between the two would become blurred, and farmer-settlers began to participate increasingly in the commercial exploitation of the forest.

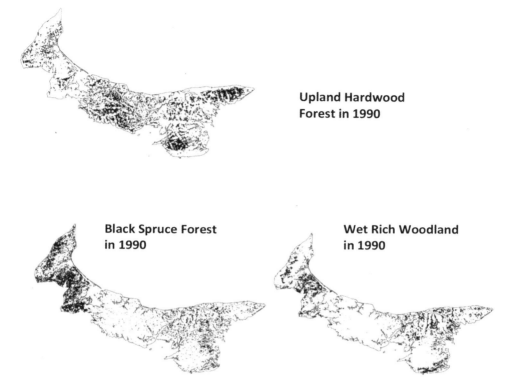

Upland Hardwood
Forest in 1990

Black Spruce Forest
in 1990

Wet Rich Woodland
in 1990

Figure 4.3B Distributions of the three forest types, Prince Edward Island Forest Inventory 1990.

Those who arrived with the intention of farming, whether they came from northern and western France in 1720 or from widely scattered parts of the British Isles from 1770 onwards,[33] were coming from lands where woodland was highly valued on account of its scarcity and because of its useful products.[34] They were transferring their abode to a land where, in contrast, there was such an abundance of woodland that it presented a great obstacle to settlement – in fact, before any settlement could take place, this woodland had to be destroyed. And in terms of their encounter with this forested landscape, these new farmer-settlers were in effect travelling back in time by several millennia to the period when the first farmers in Western Europe had faced the similar task of making farmland out of primeval forest.

Those who came wholly or partly on account of the timber resources came especially from the British Isles and from the late eighteenth century onwards. Usually they were persons who, already having experience in working with wood and timber in the Old World, saw an opportunity to transfer that experience to exploiting the New World's wood resources. The Island's timber was certainly an important element in the enterprises of a few of the landed proprietors in the eighteenth century, though most would lose a great deal of money in their ventures.[35] By contrast, many of the timber entrepreneurs who arrived after the changed economic opportunities brought about by the Napoleonic Wars had no prior holdings in the form of large grants of land, yet would thrive in the timber business and in its offshoot, shipbuilding.[36] The Island's wood also drew a larger group lower on the social scale, comprising craftsmen such as shipwrights and carpenters, either brought out by the entrepreneurs or arriving independently. Many of these in the course of time would cross over into the farmer-settler category.[37]

Whether arriving as farmer-settlers or as timber exploiters, these new "Islanders," as a result of their experience with the forest, would acquire a range of new attitudes to the forest to add to those they had brought with them from Europe.[38] The predominant attitude of both groups was of course utilitarian: the forest was viewed as the source of many useful materials. For the farmer-settler, these were especially firewood, fencing wood, and building materials, either for use on the farm or through its sale or barter, providing a means of paying the rent or the local storekeeper. For the timber merchant and his employees, it was the merchantable timber that was suitable for export or for building ships.

Despite this utilitarian outlook, paradoxically, farmer-settlers would soon acquire an extreme antagonism towards the forest,[39] fuelled by several factors. Especially important was the fact that it took a major part of a family's human energy and financial resources to convert the forest into farmland, a process that took more than one generation. The forest was also perceived to be the home of a number of troublesome and destructive animals, ranging from the bear and the lynx (both predators of livestock) and a "plague mouse" that periodically irrupted from the forest to destroy the crops in a pioneer settlement,[40] to the mosquitoes and blackflies that were a major nuisance throughout the summer. In addition, the forest made travel and communication difficult, especially in the pioneer period before roads, or even blazed trails, had penetrated the interior, thus contributing to the social isolation felt by the pioneer settler.

Given the utilitarian attitude that prevailed, it is not surprising that there was considerable conflict over the ownership of the useful materials that the forest contained. Even where the legal ownership of the wood on a particular township or piece of ground was not in dispute, theft of timber was common, with questions rarely being asked by the timber merchants; it is likely that much of the best timber was not harvested by its lawful owners.[41] Also, despite the prevailing utilitarian attitude, and despite the fact that it was the forest that drove the Island's export economy in the first half of the nineteenth century (in the form, first, of the timber trade, and later, shipbuilding), it was not until near the end of the century, by which time the forest had been virtually destroyed, that anyone voiced a concern about the *conservation* of the timber resources remaining (from the point of view of harvesting them in a sustainable fashion).[42] However, the idea of the *preservation* of examples of the pre-settlement forest was a concept alien to the period. It was in fact the view of some recorders that eventually the entire forest would be replaced by cleared farmland.[43] Such an outcome was not viewed unfavourably, even by the timber-exploiters themselves, although most people made an allowance for the retention of small woodlots on each farm to act as a renewable source of firewood and fence poles.

There were some Islanders (as well as visitors), however, who have left on record a positive appreciation of the forests, an appreciation unconnected with the utilitarian. Such persons were very much in a minority, and they usually belonged to the leisured and educated classes. They also tended to be "post-pioneer." Among them were those who have recorded an "aesthetic" appreciation of individual tree species, of the forest itself, or of the forest as an element adding variety to the landscape.[44] And, in line with contemporary fashions in literature, some expressed a "romantic" attitude to the forest, viewing it, for example, as a place for novelty and adventure,[45] for contemplation and self-discovery,[46] or for recreation and pleasure,[47] though equally there were those who expressed what might be termed an "anti-romantic" attitude to the forest, viewing it as a place of temptation and sin.[48]

FOREST CLEARANCE FOR AGRICULTURE

Given the prevailing utilitarian and antagonistic attitudes towards the forest, it was soon facing assault from many different activities. The most destructive, especially for the old-growth hardwood forest, was its clearing to make way for farmland, for, unlike the effects of forest fire or timber harvesting, clearance resulted in the total destruction of the forest on the land being cleared. The historical records provide numerous descriptions of the methods used: it was principally by the direct felling of the trees using an axe, and the burning of the surplus wood within the same year; "stumping," the removal of the stumps, took place five or more years later.[49]

The census records, combined with other data, give some idea of the overall pattern of clearance. Beginning in the 1770s near the shoreline and estuaries in specific townships, it slowly spread in the next half century along most of the coasts and waterways (wherever the land was suitable), pushing inland from the coast as well. From the 1820s on, the new lines laid out for government roads in the interior attracted settlement, such that by 1860 most of the land suitable for agriculture had been subdivided into farms, the peak in land clearance occurring shortly after 1900 (see figure 4.4). On each individual farm, clearing began in the narrow front that faced the water or road,[50] with the cleared area being pushed into the back end of the farm only gradually. However, because of the need to retain an area under woodland on each farm as a source of firewood and fence rails, the forest was not totally removed, even in areas where all of the land would have been suitable.[51] The overall result was that in most of the hardwood areas a large body of uncleared woodland (initially old-growth) was retained, comprising the contiguous back ends of adjacent farms, which would run into the back woodlots of the farms on the next roughly parallel road. During the course of the nineteenth century these large areas of uncleared forest gradually became the "islands" of forest that are still with us today. However, in the areas of boreal forest in the east and the west, there was far less clearance; it came later, and was also brief, for it was soon realized that these soils would not support farming.

FOREST FIRES

Another major factor in forest change in the settlement period was fire. Most fires, if not all, were a by-product of land clearance operations. Because fire was the principal tool used to get rid of the great amount of surplus wood resulting from clearing, there was always the risk of it spreading into the woodland.[52] This was especially so because such burning usually took place in the spring and early summer, when the forest was more flammable.[53] Once a fire had taken hold in the woods, it could "kill the timber for many miles."[54] Before long, the various problems due to such fires[55] came to be widely recognized: the loss of "so much valuable timber,"[56] as well as wood for firewood and

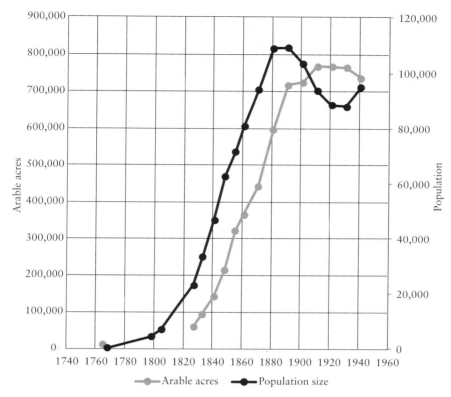

Figure 4.4 Population size and amount of arable land cleared of forest on Prince Edward Island between 1765 and 1941, as recorded in official censuses.

fencing;[57] the problems arising for subsequent land clearance operations on the burned-over sites;[58] the loss of soil fertility;[59] the ugly burned forest that blotted the landscape for more than a generation;[60] and the potential losses to human life and property.[61] The effects on the native fauna in the burned areas must also have been severe.[62] As a result, those responsible for the governance of the Island made at least four attempts through legislation and proclamation to exert some control on the damage caused by fires, though without much effect.[63]

Lack of documentation makes it now impossible to distinguish between the relative loss of the pre-settlement forest to fire and to land clearance, either in terms of the area affected or of the volume of timber destroyed. In the early years of the British period, however, runaway fires likely affected a far greater acreage than that destroyed by land

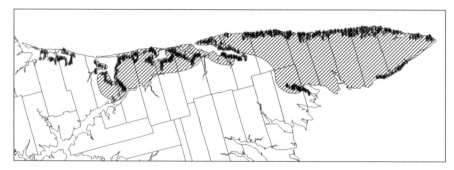

Figure 4.5 Hypothetical reconstruction of the bounds of the area in the northeast of Prince Edward Island burned over by two fires during the French period (1736 and 1742), based on the descriptions of the woods in each township as contained in the table attached to the 1765 map of Samuel Holland, plus his general comments on the location of the burned area in two letters (4 March and 8 October 1765). Superimposed on this area are symbols representing burnt trees drawn on the original Holland map.

clearance. This was certainly so in the French period, during which there occurred (in 1736 and 1742) two of the most destructive and best documented of any of the fires.[64] Taken together, they affected an area in the northeast stretching from Rustico Bay to East Point (figure 4.5), which as mapped constitutes some 12 per cent of the Island's land surface.[65] The effects of these two fires were evident for well over a century, and there was speculation among later British residents about the type of forest that had been burnt. John Stewart in 1806 reasoned from the "old pine trees and stumps still remaining" that the land had been "covered chiefly with pine and other resinous woods."[66] His reasoning receives support from Samuel Holland's comment during his 1765 survey that "in many places ... the burnt timber looks at a distance like lofty pillars or columns," a description that would especially fit the growth-form of large pine trees.[67] We might expect that such coniferous forests, as well as any mixed forest with a high conifer component, or even small patches of conifers within the hardwood forest, would have been more susceptible to fire than pure hardwood forest, but there is contemporary evidence that the hardwood forests were not immune.[68]

In general terms, the agent directly involved in the destruction of the various forest types may have differed. Areas under coniferous forest, less suitable for agriculture and so less likely to be selected for clearance, were more likely to succumb to runaway forest fires; the broad-leaved forests, less susceptible to fire and containing as they did the trees indicative of good soil, were more likely to be "grubbed out" to create farmland. In some districts, the two agents may have acted in succession; some areas burnt over by runaway fires would have been subsequently subject to land clearance operations.[69] And there must also have been some areas that were subjected to repeated fires at intervals.[70] However, fire, unlike land clearance, does not actually *destroy* a forest, for even though all of the living trees may be killed, within a year the processes of natural succession will have been set in motion, acting to re-establish the forest.[71]

THE DOMESTIC USE OF THE FOREST

That part of the forest not destroyed by clearance or by fire continued to be a source of many useful products to the pioneer settler. Some of these were required in relatively large amounts on each farm, such as the spruce or pine trees needed to build the first log house – followed a few years later, for most settlers, by a frame house as well as buildings housing livestock. Then there were the continuing annual requirements for firewood and fencing wood, which meant that a wooded area capable of supplying them needed to be maintained within the farm bounds. A method of sustaining such an annual supply likely was developed empirically on many farms, though there is no comment on this in the written records. Tentative efforts have been made at estimating some of the quantities involved. For example, the amount of wood required to build the 11,241 log-houses likely to have been built on the Island before 1861 works out at 126,000 tons (a ton is forty cubic feet), made up of some 922,000 spruce or pine trees of about eight inches diameter.[72] The annual fencing requirement for the "snake" fences on a typical Island farm in the late nineteenth century works out at between 720 and 900 spruce and fir rails, and between 180 and 225 bracing poles, with these values being reduced by two-thirds if cedar was used.[73]

In addition there were many other specialist requirements for particular wood types in the small-scale and localized wood-based industries that developed all over the Island, such as the manufacture of carriages and sleighs, household furniture, barrels, mill-machinery, household and farming utensils, and the ancillary equipment used on ships. Then there were the non-wood materials which came from the forest (some of them also sustaining local industries): hemlock bark used in tanning, birch bark for waterproofing buildings, and wood ash for making lye. The woodland was also a source of maple sugar, several medicinal and therapeutic plants, fruits and nuts used for food, plants used as green manures for fertilizing farmland, and trees used in land-scaping. It was also the habitat for birds and mammals hunted as game or for their furs.[74]

Another important function of the forest, especially during the pioneer period, was the provision of sustenance for the farm livestock in the form of "wood pasture," for it was the practice to turn cattle, sheep, and pigs out to range freely in the woods.[75] This was necessary because of the scarcity of pasture on pioneer farms, especially those distant from coastal marshes and dunes. In fact, on a pioneer farm the principal function of the fencing was to *exclude* the animals from the cleared arable land rather than to fence them in.[76] Undoubtedly, there must have been effects on the forests around settlements, though there are no comments in the literature on any of these. One effect would have been damage to the ground vegetation from overgrazing and trampling as well as local manuring effects; the dung of livestock would also have introduced seeds of European weeds into the woodland. Native herbivores would have faced increased competition from introduced mammals, especially for the important beech mast resource. Moreover, the free-range pasturing in the woods of livestock made them more susceptible to woodland predators, especially the bear and the lynx, raising the level of antipathy towards these animals and leading to the institution of bounties which contributed to their extirpation.[77]

THE COMMERCIAL EXPLOITATION OF THE FOREST

A forest disturbance of even greater significance – in quantitative terms – than the domestic harvest was its exploitation for commercial purposes. The two major industries dependent upon the forest were the timber export industry and shipbuilding. The possibility of exporting the Island's timber was first explored shortly after the establishment of the first French settlement. Two separate efforts were made in the 1720s to investigate the suitability of the Island's pines for masts for use by the French navy.[78] Both ventures involved red pine, considered by the French to be more suitable than the white; both extracted it from an area at the top of the Hillsborough River along the portage to Savage Harbour. Both ended in disappointment: the two different samples of logs sent to France failed to meet the high standards of the French naval inspectors. Otherwise, in the French period, the surviving records report the shipment to France of only a few planks and boards in the 1720s.

THE TIMBER EXPORT TRADE

The first real commercial exploitation of the forest began only after the transfer of the Island to British rule in 1763. As in the French period, the Island's pines as a potential source of masts were the initial focus of attention. In October 1765 a London vessel, the *Diadem*, was seized at Three Rivers by two Royal Navy sloops for illegally "lading" masts, all presumably of pine.[79] Three years later Gamaliel Smethurst, the "Deputy Surveyor of Woods" for Nova Scotia (to which the Island was then administratively attached), reported what he considered to be the illegal felling of some twelve hundred white pine trees, also at Three Rivers.[80] We may presume that, like the trees laded by the *Diadem*, these pines too were being felled for export to Britain, the larger ones cut for masts.

By July 1767 the ownership of almost all land on the Island, including the forests, had been transferred to about one hundred proprietors in parcels of 10,000 to 20,000 acres, in the infamous "land lottery." In this transfer, the authorities, unusually, failed to reserve any of the timber to the Crown, including pine for masts – unlike, for example, in neighbouring New Brunswick.[81] Thus, it was private landowners who would henceforth be the main agents in exploiting the timber, and the principal market for the Island's wood products in the nineteenth century would be the British domestic market, driven by the Industrial Revolution. In that market there was a much greater demand for North American softwoods than hardwoods, and among the softwoods it was pine, and especially white pine, in the form of "square-timber" or "ton-timber" (i.e., axe-hewn baulks of at least eleven inches square),[82] that was especially in demand.[83]

Though efforts were made in the late eighteenth century by some of the more enterprising proprietors or their agents to export the Island's timber resources, all were small-scale ventures, none seemingly turning a profit.[84] Such efforts laboured under a major disadvantage, namely, the cost of freighting the timber across the Atlantic, in comparison with the cost of importing wood to Britain from the Baltic Sea area, the traditional source of softwood timber for the British Isles. However, in 1807, as a result of his military campaigns, Napoleon was able to close most of the Baltic ports to British shipping. Britain's timber imports from the area consequently dropped dramatically, and timber prices rose sharply in the British market. British wood importers turned to British North America, and the colonial timber trade was born. The few entrepreneurs already on the Island were quick in getting in on the action: customs

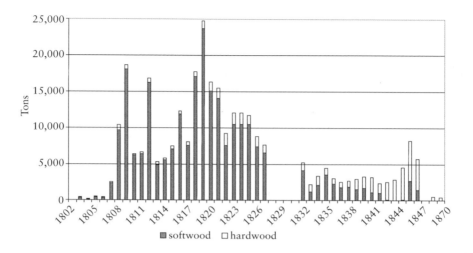

softwood □ hardwood

Pine: percentage contribution to timber exports

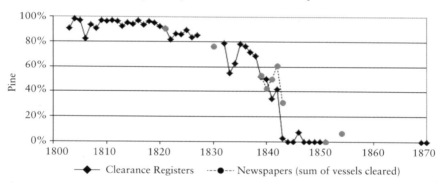

Clearance Registers   ···●··· Newspapers (sum of vessels cleared)

Figure 4.6 Annual shipments of ton-timber from PEI and the percentage contribution of pine, as determined from Ships' Clearance Registers or from contemporary newspaper summaries of the annual customs reports. (Data missing for 1828–31.)

records indicate that exports to the United Kingdom rose from only 375 tons of pine timber in 1806 to 18,268 tons in 1809 (see figure 4.6).[85]

Although the wartime timber shortage sparked the trade, it was the subsequent action of the British government that was to sustain it for the next thirty years. In response to lobbying by timber importers and shipowners in Britain reluctant to risk investment in a short-term war-induced trade, the government raised the import duties on Baltic ton-timber in 1810 from 20 shillings per load (a load is fifty cubic feet) to 27s 4d, and then in 1811 to 54s 6d, compared with 4s on North

American timber, a differential in favour of colonial timber that greatly exceeded the added cost of the transatlantic voyage. Similar tariffs were placed on sawn deals and other wood.[86] This advantageous tariff structure, in place from 1810 to 1842, enabled the Island's timber to compete successfully in the British market. Between 1811 and 1820 the amount of pine ton timber exported each year to the United Kingdom, as recorded by customs officials, ranged from 4,867 to 23,776 tons (figure 4.6).[87] The latter figure comes from the peak export year of 1819, after which there was a steady fall in both the total amount exported and in the contribution of pine to those exports, the pine falling from 96 per cent in 1819 to less than 3 per cent by 1843 (as can be seen in figure 4.6). Since export figures from New Brunswick and the Canadas show that the demand for pine ton-timber in Britain had not decreased,[88] the decline on the Island can only be because the forest was no longer able to provide sufficient pine to meet the demand; there is ample contemporary comment in support of this.[89] However, the scarcity of pine did not bring an immediate end to the Island's transatlantic trade. Timber merchants turned instead to yellow birch, tamarack, and spruce, but as figure 4.6 indicates, the total amount of wood exported continued to decline.[90] Although the reliability of the Island's customs data has been questioned, a computation based on them reveals that some 324,000 tons of ton-timber were exported between 1803 and 1847 – which is considerably more than the 126,000 tons required to build all of the pioneer log-houses.[91]

SHIPBUILDING AND THE FOREST

Early on, the timber trade gave birth to a second major export industry based on the forest: the building of wooden ships for sale in the British market. In economic terms this was a more advanced industry, going beyond the simple export of a natural forest product.[92] Instead, shipbuilding utilized and financially rewarded Island entrepreneurship and craftsmanship. By converting wood into a more valuable product, it brought in an even greater income, some of which worked its way down to the farmers who cut and sold wood from their land to the shipbuilders. Figure 4.7 shows a steady increase in the number and total tonnage of ships built in the nineteenth century. From a low of 57 vessels totalling 4,450 tons in the first decade, production rose to 913 vessels comprising 236,000 tons by the 1860s.[93] However, the 1870s brought a downturn in output, with the industry collapsing suddenly and terminally in 1878.

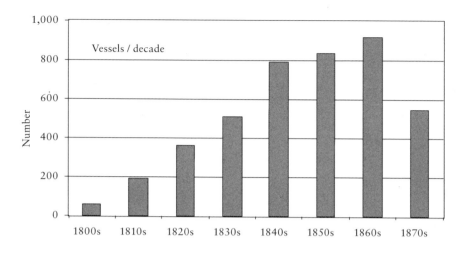

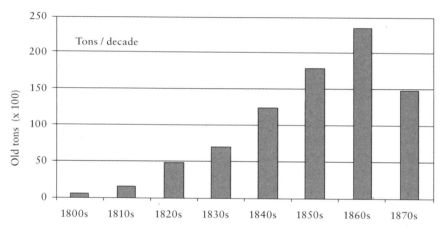

Figure 4.7 Total number and total tonnage (in "old tons") of vessels built and registered in each decade on Prince Edward Island between 1801 and 1880. (Each decade runs from the "01" year to the "10" year.)

What is especially evident is that the demands of shipbuilding on the forest were substantially greater in the later decades: in fact, 68 per cent of the Island's ship-tonnage was produced in the three decades from 1850 to 1880. And this increased demand for wood was occurring at a time when there were also other rising *internal* demands on the forests associated with the substantially increased human population (figure 4.4), demands which, on account of forest clearance for agriculture, had to be met by a decreasing forest area.

Although the relationship between a ship's tonnage and the amount of wood built into its hull is not a linear one, the tonnage values of figure 4.7 should provide an index of the amount of wood used by the Island's shipbuilding industry. Using the only value I have come across in the literature on the amount of wood required per registered ton to build a vessel,[94] I calculate that 515,000 tons of wood were incorporated into the hulls of vessels between 1834 and 1880.[95] This figure is at least of the same order of magnitude as the 324,000 tons of "ton-timber" that customs officials recorded as exported between 1803 and 1847.

This demand was directed towards a narrow range of trees.[96] Between the 1830s and 1870s the principal woods used in the hulls of ships (in the order of their frequency of recording on the survey forms of Lloyd's Register) were spruce, yellow birch, tamarack, beech and pine, the two hardwoods being used primarily below the water-line and the three soft-woods above. However, the years saw notable changes: a fall in the use of yellow birch, beech, and pine; a rise and then a fall in the use of tama-rack; and a rise in the use of spruce. From the 1840s onwards, ships fell into three distinct types in terms of the principal woods used in their hulls: ships built of a mixture of hardwoods and softwoods (though always with a high contribution of yellow birch); ships built of tamarack (the so-called "juniper ships"); and ships built of spruce. The building of each of these has its own chronological pattern (figure 4.8B). Mixed-wood ships are the norm from the 1830s into the 1850s. Juniper ships appear in the 1830s, begin to increase in the late 1840s, reach a peak in the 1860s, and decline to almost nil in the early 1870s. Spruce ships appear in the early 1860s and rise dramatically to dominate shipbuilding in the 1870s until the collapse of the industry late in the decade. Further analysis reveals that these chronological patterns are the result of the interaction between two factors: the year-class assigned by Lloyd's Register of Shipping to each of the woods when used in the different structural components of a vessel, and the availability of each of the woods in the forest.[97] Thus, the shift towards tamarack and spruce wood can be attributed to the gradual increase in the ratings of these woods from the 1840s onwards, causing shipbuilders to make greater use of them in order to achieve a higher classification for their ships and a greater profit when they were sold.

In addition, mapping the place of construction of the different ship types (figure 4.8A) reveals a significant finding: juniper and spruce ships were built almost entirely east of the Hillsborough River (especially in the northeast), or from the Bedeque-Malpeque isthmus westward. This

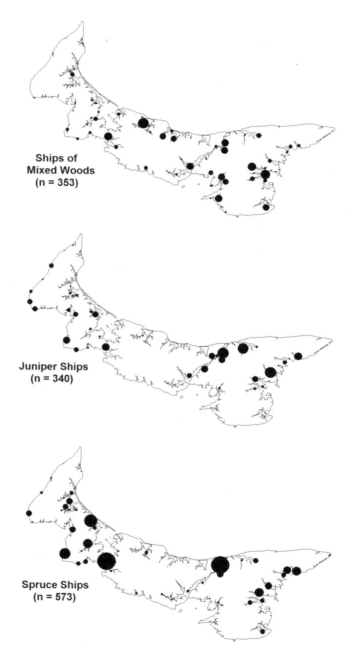

Figure 4.8A Geographical distribution of the sites at which three different types of vessel (in terms of their principal woods) were built between 1856 and 1880, based on the names of the shipbuilding sites as given on the surveyors' forms of Lloyd's Register. The areas of the circle are proportional to the number of vessels built at each site.

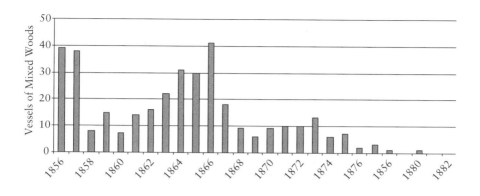

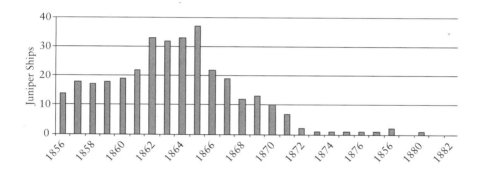

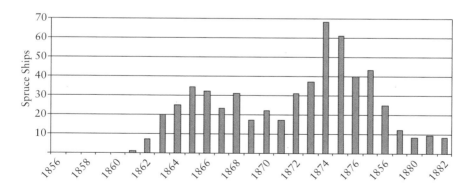

Figure 4.8B The chronology of the building of the three types of vessel between 1856 and 1882. (Lloyd's survey data for PEI vessels only becomes available from 1856 with the appointment in that year of a surveyor based at Charlottetown.)

pattern reflects the fact that the Island's boreal forest, the main repository of the black spruce and tamarack resource, was to be found in these
regions (figure 4.3). Also, the ability of Island shipbuilders to turn out
these two ship types in such high numbers in the 1860s and '70s suggests
that this forest had only been lightly exploited up to that time. By contrast, the building of mixed-wood ships was concentrated in the area
between the Bedeque-Malpeque isthmus and the Hillsborough River, an
area deficient in tamarack and spruce, as well as in the southeast of the
Island, where these two trees must also have been deficient, probably as
a result of earlier forest fires.

The chronological patterns thus suggest that, as the years went by, the
particular woods required for shipbuilding were becoming depleted. Pine
is evidently in decline from the 1840s (figure 4.6), while by 1870 tamarack of a size and quality suitable for shipbuilding had been used up to
the point where it could no longer contribute to the industry, not even in
the small quantities that would have served to add an extra year to
spruce ships under the Lloyd's "mixed materials" rule.[98] It also appears
that by the 1870s the timber resources of the central part of the Island
had become so depleted as to preclude the building of even mixed-wood
ships there. Evidence given to the 1875 Land Commission suggests that
the spruce in the west had largely been "lumbered" by then, so that, had
not external factors brought about the industry's sudden demise, it would
have soon collapsed on account of the wood having run out.[99]

THE EFFECT OF THE COMMERCIAL HARVEST
ON THE FOREST

The selection of timber for export and for shipbuilding (as also, presumably, for domestic use) involved the felling of the better and larger specimens of whatever tree was the object of the lumbering. In the early
decades of the nineteenth century, this was white pine, a tree that tended
to occur either in "groves" or as scattered trees within the hardwood
forest. We may presume that the pine occurring in groves would have
been particularly vulnerable to being systematically "destroyed" (to use
Smethurst's word for the process at Three Rivers;[100] "clear-cutting" is
the modern word), whereas in the hardwood forest, pine trees would
have been selectively removed. Later on, when lumbermen began to turn
to spruce and tamarack, the small area of the Island's boreal forest,
mostly on land unsuitable for agriculture in the eastern and western
regions, would have borne the brunt of the assault, and it would seem,

as noted above, that by the 1870s most of these forests had been "lumbered over."

Of course, such a harvesting method (the modern term for it is "high-grading") did not result in the destruction of the forest. However, it did lead to its gradual degradation, as first the larger trees were removed, especially those large enough to yield the minimum sizes for making ton-timber, and then the smaller trees. Over a period of some fifty or sixty years (1800–1860) such harvesting would have brought about a great change in the age structure of the forest trees as well as in the species makeup, with pine especially being greatly reduced and even eliminated from many parts of the hardwood forest. The effect on other commercial species would have been similar: yellow birch (harvested for both export and shipbuilding), tamarack (highly sought after for shipbuilding, but also in the 1840s for the export of both ships' knees and railway sleepers), and spruce of any of the three species (for shipbuilding, especially in the 1860s and 1870s). The end result was the degraded forest we have today. It should thus come as no surprise that early successional trees now make up 75 per cent of the forest's woody biomass (as is evident in figure 4.1).[101]

CONCLUSIONS

The heterogeneity in the geographical distribution of the Island's forest types noted at the beginning of this chapter has had important effects on the patterns of forest use by Islanders. In the hardwood areas covering most of the Island's area, the principal factor affecting the forest was clearance, primarily for farmland but also for roads and other minor land-uses. By the peak of agricultural settlement in 1910, some 77 per cent of the pre-settlement forest had been cleared and destroyed. But the hardwood forest was also a source of several highly valued commercial woods: white pine and yellow birch for export, and yellow birch, beech, white pine, and red spruce for shipbuilding. After the end of the commercial era in the 1870s, what remained of the hardwood forest was subjected to continuing degradation by annual harvesting of firewood and fencing wood. The result was the gradual conversion of a climax forest of shade-tolerant species (beech, sugar maple, and yellow birch) to the woodlots of today with their smaller, early-successional trees, such as red maple, white birch, and trembling aspen.

By contrast, the land under coniferous forest, especially in the boreal areas of the east and west, was subjected to a different set of factors. Fire was certainly a major one, but also, on account of these areas being the major repository of the Island's spruce and tamarack resource, another was intensive exploitation by the shipbuilding industry, especially from the 1840s to the 1870s. Also, much of this inferior land (from the point of view of agriculture) was by the 1860s being subdivided into farms, and so was subject to some clearance. The presence of the highly valued tamarack and spruce was possibly an additional incentive for settlement of these more marginal lands – additional, that is, to the fact that by the 1860s all of the good hardwood land had been occupied.

A full analysis of the Island's customs records will likely show that for much of the first half of the nineteenth century the combined timber export trade and shipbuilding were as important, if not more so, than agriculture in the Island's balance of trade.[102] It thus is surprising to learn that in the nineteenth century not one person placed a high economic value on the forests per se. Instead, during the years they were being destroyed to make way for agriculture, they were viewed as a temporary resource to be exploited for financial gain but not as capable of yielding a sustainable product; nor was it considered desirable that they be so. Given such an attitude, it is not surprising that few people placed any importance on their conservation. Not until the first decade of the twentieth century was a reasoned case made for the protection of what forests remained: in 1902 A.E. Burke argued that the Island's forests should be protected so that they would continue to serve as a source of wood and firewood as well as giving protection to water catchment areas.[103] It appears that Burke's advocacy led to the creation of an advisory Forestry Commission in 1903, although it would be another fifty years before any of his proposals began to be put into effect, with the formation of the first provincial Forestry Division in 1951.[104] In the event, the nature of the Island's forests in the first half of the twentieth century was to be largely determined by attitudes and actions in the century that preceded it.[105]

5

Wildlife Matters:
A Historical Overview of Public
Consciousness of Habitat and Wildlife
Loss on Prince Edward Island

Rosemary Curley

Environmental history takes as its starting point humans' relationship with nature.[1] The given perspective varies along a spectrum that may view humans as *apart from* that nature or as *a part of* nature. It may even consider "nature" as essentially a human construct rather than an objective reality. Whatever the perceived "nature of nature," our view is, for obvious reasons, generally human centred, even though it is subtly shaped by the nature of the physical environment. In imaginative terms, so the cultural trope goes, Canada's harsh climate and vast landscape have dominated Canadians.[2] But things are different on small islands. While the sea might intimidate islanders, the terrestrial landscape tends to be both less psychologically overwhelming and more vulnerable to human intervention. If the need or desire is present, it is much easier for people to subdue nature on an island, especially one such as Prince Edward Island, with its highly accessible, gently rolling terrain. As a result, the Island's wildlife populations are highly susceptible to the stresses of habitat loss and unregulated hunting.

This chapter presents a sketch of the history of wildlife on Prince Edward Island and explores how people both destroyed and sought to conserve wildlife and wild habitats. People are central to this story, of course, as principal agents of change, but the spotlight remains on the wildlife, which is both victim and actor in this drama. It is a familiar story, not dissimilar to the litany of human destruction and the duty of stewardship propounded by George Perkins Marsh so long ago in his classic treatise *Man and Nature*[3] – but it is compounded by islandness.

The narrative arc follows two loose, simple trends. First, as human populations and their technological capacity increased, so their effect on wildlife accelerated. Habitat was destroyed or fundamentally altered by processes such as forest cutting and clearing, farming practices, settlement patterns, and transportation infrastructure. Within the close confines of the Island, populations of existing species were reduced and, sometimes, driven to extinction, even as new ones were introduced – both deliberately and by accident – with dysfunctional consequences. Second, as pressures on wildlife have mounted, conservationist and, later, preservationist tendencies slowly increased. Over the past fifty years, individual preservation efforts have fused into non-governmental agencies and meshed with state-led initiatives that have groped towards a more comprehensive approach to wildlife management, conservation, and preservation.[4] Slow progress is not merely a question of lack of will, education, or resources. On an island where the high percentage of arable land has made it a critical but limited resource, there will inevitably be conflicts over who uses it and what it is used for. Wildlife preservation is only one voice among many. It is now heard; it is unclear how much it will be heeded.

Definitions here become important. In this chapter a broad view of wildlife is taken consistent with the Wildlife Policy for Canada,[5] which defines wildlife as "all wild organisms and their habitats – including wild plants, invertebrates and micro-organisms, as well as fishes, amphibians, reptiles, and the birds and mammals traditionally regarded as wildlife," always bearing in mind that "without habitat, there is no wildlife."[6]

PREHISTORIC POPULATIONS

The earliest relationship between wildlife and humans was the most basic: wildlife fed and clothed human populations. The geological history of glaciations and post-glacial colonization of the Maritime provinces by plants, animals, and Aboriginal people is described elsewhere in this volume (Keenlyside and Kristmanson). The current view is that the entire Atlantic region was covered with ice at the glacial maximum.[7] However, some authors still believe that there were local areas in the region that were free of ice, where certain mosses and insects survived through the glaciations.[8] Even without such refugia, wild species could have repopulated Prince Edward Island as spores (i.e., fungi, mosses, and ferns) or windblown seeds. Birds, bats, and many insects could have flown in, and birds undoubtedly transported seeds in their feathers, feet, and digestive tracts. Many species arriving from the edge of the icefields, being cold hardy and excellent dispersers, would have invaded across the Northumbria land bridge or on seasonal ice. The same routes would have been available to people, although probably much later.

It is generally thought that the number of people affecting wildlife was quite low until Europeans arrived in the Gulf of St Lawrence and began commercial exploitation of wildlife. A variety of artifacts of differing ages have been found that provide clues about human use of wildlife, although the picture is fragmentary and incomplete. A stone tool known as an ulu that was recovered off East Point, PEI,[9] is estimated to be between five thousand and six thousand years old; it would have been used for cutting and scraping, perhaps for butchering seals on the ice. Likewise, a stone plummet carved in the shape of a whelk, found in Northumberland Strait near Seacow Head in 2001, reflects the Archaic period 6,000 to 3,500 years ago.[10] The plummet would have been used to weight a fishing net or line. Near Basin Head 2,000 years ago, Mi'kmaq people used a variety of stone tools made from local gravels; however, the nature of Mi'kmaq interaction with wildlife is not known, as animal remains were not preserved at the site.[11] By AD 500, Mi'kmaq people had a small living space on Rustico Island and remained there for some time, judging from the thick deposits of shell; around AD 1480 the same site was temporarily in use as a harvest station for shellfish, Atlantic walrus, and possibly harp seals.[12] This site also retained the foreleg of a caribou and an ivory spear point, more evidence of early wildlife and their uses. Beaver incisors modified for use as tools were found in the AD 1480 level of excavation.[13] At East Point, meanwhile, between AD 800 and 1000, people hunted and fished, leaving in their garbage the remains of shellfish, seals, beaver, otter, fox, turtle, and caribou, and also flounder and salmon.[14] (Turtles are not considered native to Prince Edward Island today.) David Keenlyside has also documented a Malpeque Bay hand-working tool made from ivory (likely from walrus) dating to seven hundred years ago (AD 1300).[15] These are merely glimpses into the past; much archaeological work is needed, and there are many sites awaiting excavation.

Unlike other First Nations groups who altered the New England forests, Prairie grasslands, and North Pacific mollusc beds, the Mi'kmaq were relatively few in number and do not appear to have greatly altered habitats for wildlife.[16] They relied on fish and both marine and terrestrial mammals as mainstays in their diet and were masters at capturing sturgeon and eels from their birchbark canoes.[17] Lean meats, such as caribou, would necessarily need to be supplemented with a source of fat, such as bear, eels, or seals, and smelts and eels could also be caught through the ice in winter. The Mi'kmaq likely had little effect on their resources; it is said they killed only what was needed.[18]

COMMERCIAL EXPLOITATION

The real catalyst for wildlife disturbance in Atlantic Canada was the arrival of European traders, hunters, and settlers. As described elsewhere in this volume (MacDonald and Beck), commercial fisheries in Atlantic Canada began in the 1400s on the Grand Banks of Newfoundland. By 1534, when Jacques Cartier sailed the Gulf of St Lawrence,[19] fur trading was already underway wherever companies or individuals had set up camp to fish and preserve cod.[20] Individual fishers made many small purchases from Native peoples for the fancy fur trade and marketed these goods independently, with fishing vessels transporting them to market. When a demand arose in the mid-1500s for water-resistant felt hats made from beaver underfur, beaver became the mainstay of the trade. It would remain so until about 1840, when silk hats became more desirable. By 1580, the fur trade was no longer tied to the fishery, and not enough beavers were left on the Atlantic coast to supply market demand, forcing fur traders to seek new areas or to trade for furs with more distant Native suppliers.[21]

In the written historical records of Prince Edward Island mammals, there is no plausible first-hand account of beavers being resident.[22] Sparse archaeological evidence[23] suggests that beavers may have been present, but if so they must have been extirpated sometime after AD 1000–1500. If this possibility can be verified, it would represent the first known extirpation of wildlife on Prince Edward Island due to human activity.

While Prince Edward Island was certainly not central to the beaver fur trade, it appears to have felt the impact of trade in other fur-bearing species. In 1654, a French merchant named Nicholas Denys had a land grant that included Prince Edward Island by which he "over all others shall enjoy the … right to make the fur trade with the said Indians." The grant expressly prohibited others from trading for furs or engaging in the fishery.[24] Historian D.C. Harvey dismissed the possibility that any serious fur trade took place in Prince Edward Island in Denys's time, but

Harvey did allow that the Island Mi'kmaq likely pooled their furs with those of their people on the mainland, and also that travel there was easy.[25] Some sort of Native fur trade no doubt continued well into the European settlement period, but documentary evidence is sparse. For example, there is documentation that the Mi'kmaq of 1757 took pelts to sell at Louisbourg (on Cape Breton Island), and in the 1830s they sold furs to a Charlottetown merchant.[26]

Island natives were not the only ones hunting and trapping. Douglas Sobey reports records of trapping between 1791 and 1802 and also cites customs export records.[27] In his famous *Account of Prince Edward Island*, published in 1806, John Stewart mentions the prices paid for various furs, including bear, lynx, otter, and marten, and notes methods of capture. Foxes were also taken, though the price had fallen in favour of bear.[28] Scottish writer Walter Johnstone took instruction as a fur-buyer in the winter of 1821, probably working to supply a merchant in Charlottetown,[29] while John McGregor in 1828 reported the continued value on the Island of prime bear skins as well as marten and less esteemed lynx pelts.[30] Yet, no one was getting rich on fur; it was a small part of the economy in a colony where subsistence was the norm.

The pressures of trapping and European settlement in the first half of the nineteenth century had a perhaps predictable result. Several species became extinct in the colony. Woodland caribou, last reported by Surveyor-General Samuel Holland in 1765, disappeared late in the century.[31] The reasons are unclear, although caribou were the only large game animal in the colony. Governments observed and occasionally abetted the trend towards local extinction. Generally speaking, legislation in the first half of the nineteenth century sought either to regulate hunting or to encourage it in an effort to rid the colony of unwanted species. Later, an element of conservation crept in. The words "protect" and "preservation" increasingly cropped up in the titles of acts. Legislation in 1879[32] that forbade trapping of muskrat, otter, and marten between 1 May and 1 November came on the heels of a period of intensive forest removal to support shipbuilding.[33] By 1900, the Island forest was reduced to only 30 per cent of its original area,[34] and many stream banks were denuded of trees. The half-hearted effort to preserve furbearers for hunting and trapping by specifying closed hunting seasons came too late. Indeed, low reproductive rates and a reduction in forest cover may have had as much to do with the disappearance of otter and marten as overhunting.[35] In 1937, protection for the marten was removed, an admission that the species was no longer extant.[36]

As the fate of the Island's river otters demonstrates, even the remaining woodland was likely suboptimal habitat. River otters are somewhat limited by the availability of forest den sites.[37] In seventeenth and eighteenth century forests, otters would have established dens in hollow logs or the hollowed base of standing trees, or in cover provided by uprooted trees. A second-growth forest arising after cutting and burning virgin forests would have supported far fewer den sites. Though the species has a widespread distribution in North and South America today, showing some adaptability to varying environmental conditions and to the proximity to human populations, there is good evidence that disturbed landscapes are not adequate habitats.[38] The lack of beaver in the 1800s likely affected prospects for the otter as well. Beaver houses are favourite denning sites for otters, and their absence probably accentuated the shortage of otter den sites.[39] And so, while naturalist Francis Bain considered the otter to be present in 1890, there are no records after that.[40] Nevertheless, the province continues to this day to protect otter with a limited hunting season, in the event that any show up.[41]

The omnivorous black bear should have thrived in the second-generation woodlands of Prince Edward Island in the mid-1800s, but the elimination in 1855 of the bounty that had been paid for bears since the 1790s signalled that all was not well with *Ursus americanus*.[42] It is unlikely that shortage of food was the cause. Profuse wild berry crops from the many flowering shrubs and on fire barrens would have been bounteous alternatives to the dwindling supplies of beech mast reported by Douglas Sobey.[43] As well, there were sheep, calves, and other livestock, honey hives, and oat crops for the taking.[44] (Or perhaps that was the problem!) Local conservationist Stan Vass concluded that "changing land use crowded the bears into ever-decreasing areas of habitat and increased hunters' access to them."[45] Given the degree of habitat change and settlers' less than friendly attitudes towards bears, it is amazing that they hung on until 1927, when the last known black bear was shot in a forest near the Souris Line Road. The determination that characterized the hunting of the last bear leaves little doubt that human intolerance had a lot to do with the animal's demise.[46] As folk memory repeatedly attests, the black bear was not only a threat to farmers' resources: it was feared. The adamant consensus among Islanders that bears had no place among them contrasts with the unintentional loss of the marten and otter through habitat destruction. Vass judged the outcome as "another example of man's preoccupation with his needs and wants, resulting in the loss of other creatures."[47] Today, there is no plan to reintroduce the species.

PUSHING LIMITS

As the local extinction of the black bear illustrates, European settlers' needs and customs largely dictated their relationship with wildlife on Prince Edward Island. Those needs included commerce, recreation, and, especially during the settlement period, food. Game was indiscriminately hunted by many colonists and was a regular feature of the dinner table until livestock multiplied.[48] Writing in 1806, John Stewart commented on geese being at first very poor returning from the North, then becoming fat and fine, referring no doubt to their edibility.[49] Small birds were fair game, following the practice in Europe; the Snow Bird (i.e., snow bunting), Stewart said, was "very delicate in flavour."[50] A generation later, in 1840, land proprietor Horatio Mann described some of the wild fare he sampled. He picked mushrooms, donating them to Government House for a stew, and lunched on oysters over a foot long. At the governor's table he was treated to a five-course meal, of which the third was game: partridges, wild duck, snipes, and plovers, with sauces.[51]

As settlement progressed, hunting for survival became less important. At the turn of the nineteenth century, Stewart wrote that partridges were protected by law during the breeding season (April 1 to September 1); otherwise everyone could shoot wherever or whenever they pleased, and indeed, most things could be shot.[52] This situation remained true in 1828.[53] Not until 1873 were seasons set on the shooting of ducks, snipe, woodcock, and bittern, but even then any number could be taken.[54] Though we know settlers relied on game and wild fruits to some degree, what is not known is the frequency and extent of that dependence. Instead we have only a series of glimpses, but it would seem that the 1879 game law was trying belatedly to limit some of the effects of wildlife use, including species extinctions.

Part of the pressure on wildlife came from commercial exploitation. The original trade in fish and furs extended naturally into trade in wild birds. In the 1800s market hunting was quite prevalent almost everywhere in settled Eastern North America. Game birds, especially waterfowl and shorebirds, were shot without thought given to sporting tactics or the eventual disappearance of species. Partridges were sold in the Charlottetown market, and geese and brant were shot "by the thousands, put in barrels with ice and shipped to Boston." [55]

William Jenkins of Lot 50 was only one of many hunting the passenger pigeon, claiming to have "shot 15 a shot."[56] Extinction of the millions of passenger pigeons was due to hunting but also to habitat destruction. The breeding population seems to have disappeared from Prince Edward Island by 1858.[57] Likewise, the Eskimo curlew no longer flew in Prince Edward Island skies, as it had been successfully decoyed for flock shooting during both spring and fall migration. When Robie Tufts, a migratory bird officer in Nova Scotia from 1919 to 1947,[58] wrote *The Birds of Nova Scotia* in 1961, he noted that the Eskimo curlew[59] was extinct or on the verge of extinction due to "uncontrolled slaughter inspired by human greed."[60]

The migration patterns of such birds meant that, whether coming or going, they were taken by hungry citizens, sportsmen, and market hunters in settlements from Patagonia to the high Arctic. Tufts identified other shorebirds, also occurring in Prince Edward Island, which had been reduced to remnant populations. The golden plover[61] and the black-bellied plover were "marked for early extinction," and even after the Migratory Birds Convention Act came into effect in 1916, they were being legally hunted up until 1925. Similarly, the knot (now known as the red knot), a great table bird, had become exceedingly rare by 1961.[62] In another example, the willet, a local breeder, survived north of Virginia only in southwest Nova Scotia by 1916, although it is now relatively common on Prince Edward Island salt marshes.[63] All these large shorebirds, excepting the willet, flew to decoys in tight flocks, providing easy targets. They also took up more room on a plate, and sold accordingly.

In contrast, the fate of the cormorants was motivated by disdain for a bird that competed with fishermen. The double-crested cormorant was reduced by hunting to very low numbers by 1900. While the great cormorant was thought to be extirpated, a few apparently survived on Anticosti Island.[64] The latter species, which is confined to the east coast in Canada, remained rare for many years.[65] Biologist Geoff Hogan found only six colonies in Prince Edward Island in the 1970s and reported that the birds were persecuted at the mixed colonies at Cape Tryon and Durrell Point, though protected by provincial law since 1966.[66]

The double-crested cormorant was also among those birds affected by mid-twentieth century use of DDT.[67] Its numbers began to climb in the 1980s, and an open season on the species was declared on the Island in 1992, mainly in response to demands from fishermen convinced the birds were depleting trout stocks.[68] As the great cormorant migrates later and the two species are hard to distinguish, the unintended result was a reduction of the great cormorant nest count from 1,389 to 779 by the time the season was closed in 1994. While the double-crested cormorant nest count continued to increase, the great cormorant nest count has continued to decrease and was only 222 in 2010. The decline has perhaps also been influenced by other factors such as suspected bald eagle predation on young. Meanwhile 11,074 nests of double-crested cormorant were tallied in 2010, up from 4,679 in 1992.[69] There is as yet little sympathy for these birds among commercial and sport fishers, and they are still persecuted through unregulated shooting.

The attitude towards the cormorant reflects an historical truism that applied on Prince Edward Island as it did elsewhere. Specific species were historically judged according to whether they helped or harmed human endeavours. Although aesthetics were seldom a factor, negative views sometimes seemed almost totemic in nature. It has been suggested, for instance, that there may have been a general prejudice among legislators against black birds of all kinds.[70] The Migratory Birds Act of 1917 neglected to protect most black birds in Canada (i.e., crows, ravens, cormorants, and most species of blackbirds). But that may have had more to do with their depredations than their colour.

The Migratory Birds Act also failed to protect those birds that ate fish (such as ospreys and kingfishers) or birds of prey that might take barnyard chickens. When P.A. Taverner wrote *Birds of Eastern Canada*, he used evidence from a quick look at stomach contents to confirm whether a bird was "bad" or "good." He also pleaded for the birds based on an economic argument.[71] This argument for conserving nature is still widely used,[72] echoing the human-oriented approach to wildlife that continues to permeate our society.

By 1900, species lost from Prince Edward Island included walrus (extirpated before 1800) as well as species reliant on mature forest, such as caribou, lynx, marten, otters, passenger pigeons, and pileated woodpeckers. The degree to which plant species have been lost is not known, but some species would surely have wilted away with removal of forest canopy. In contrast, the plants that arrived with settlers are relatively well understood, and today, augmented by more recent arrivals, make up 34 per cent of the provincial plant list.[73] It is one of the tenets of island biogeography[74] that species richness on islands is greatly influenced by immigration and extinction events. It is difficult for terrestrial species to colonize an island, and difficult for these species to be replaced when island populations are stressed by major habitat alterations. In recent decades the province has regained productive habitat through forest regrowth, and some species have flourished as a result. It is a hopeful sign that bald eagles now outnumber piping plovers. On the other hand, pileated woodpeckers have merely returned and need more areas of older forest if the recovering population is to increase to viable levels.

FROM RIVERS TO MILL PONDS

Human activity also transformed the Island's waterways. When European settlement commenced, there were very few natural lakes or ponds, but damming of streams to operate mills had a major impact on the local environment. It was akin to clear-cutting the forest, in that most dams separated smelts, alewives, Atlantic salmon, and brook trout from their spawning grounds. Some streams were dammed soon after the arrival of Acadian settlers – for example, the Acadian settlers of Malpeque had water-powered grist mills for flour production at modern-day Tyne Valley and Birch Hill.[75] Colonel Franquet indicated a sawmill on the Hillsborough River in 1751, while the Sieur de la Roque enumerated four grist mills and two sawmills the following year.[76]

As populations increased, water-powered sawmills producing wood for local use or export became widespread.[77] In 1879 the fisheries inspector John Hunter Duvar described two hundred sawmills and 150 shingle mills, and in 1886 three hundred to four hundred sawmills.[78] The cadastral maps in the *Illustrated Historical Atlas of the Province Prince Edward Island*[79] show 259 dams in 1880, many supporting more than one mill – for example, saw and shingle mills, carding and grist mills, woollen, cloth, and fulling mills, and different combinations thereof. The atlas illustrates two separate spillways from the millpond at Tyne Valley, one with a sawmill and the other with a grist mill.[80] In other instances, two ponds were built in quick succession, each outlet powering a mill. The environmental effects would have included blocking fish migrations, covering fish habitat with sawdust and wood, and depleting oxygen, leaving, according to Duvar, "the poison of vegetable decay."[81] While sportsmen might have decried this destruction of habitat, their lobby was considerably less influential than the economic argument for dams as coveted sources of energy for milling.[82]

These dams were earthen; some were cribbed with hemlock, and the earliest ones had wooden weirs (concrete was eventually used). The plans for a mill for the Earl of Selkirk in 1803 described a dam thirteen feet high, one hundred yards long, ten feet wide at the top, and sloping to a base thirty feet wide.[83] Some dams were likely fortified with layers of brush, and all were constantly tested by flowing water. Breaching in spring freshets was no doubt common, such as occurred in the Dunk

River salmon hatchery pond in 1886.[84] Considerable volumes of soil must have entered the water during these events, covering fish spawning areas and suffocating eggs and fry. While some early millponds may have been only temporarily maintained for sawing wood, a surprising number of the 1880 era dams persisted in the same locations 130 years later, long after milling operations had ceased.[85]

WILDLIFE IN A FARMSCAPE

In 1889, J. Hunter Duvar, then the federal inspector of fisheries for Prince Edward Island, confided to Charles H. Tupper, the minister of marine and fisheries for Canada, that fishing was the main recreation of Prince Edward Islanders.[86] But as early as 1882, Duvar had already compiled a list of the many things that were wrong with the streams bearing these much-appreciated fish. "Trout do not thrive comfortably unless in pure water, not more than 70 degrees Celsius. Now as the rivers run for miles at a heightened temperature between banks, denuded of trees, exposed to the sun, shoaled by the tricklings from farms, muddied by the washings from roads, paved with sunken water-sodden sticks … it is not to be complained of that the quantity of trout and salmon have fallen away."[87]

Duvar's report coincided with the close of the settlement period and the point when the Island shipbuilding industry came to an abrupt halt, in part for lack of lumber, after an intense twenty-five year period of dedicated timber clearing.[88] Thus, by 1896 the siltation of waterways by sawdust and other wood waste from sawmills[89] had been augmented by soil washed from riverside farms and the Island's mud roads. Predictably, the supplies of trout and salmon were greatly reduced.[90]

Twentieth-century developments did not help matters. In 1931, game inspector Albert Morrison reported to the Prince Edward Island House of the Assembly that the clearing of land and bushes was causing erosion leading to the destruction of the best trout streams.[91] Only a year earlier, in a study of brook trout in Prince Edward Island, H.C. White of the Biological Board of Canada noted that water that percolated through the porous soils carried fertilizer from repeated applications by farmers. He thought this runoff probably contributed to the fertility of ponds and streams and to trout abundance.[92] However, excessive use of fertilizers has led to the recent realization that Island streams and estuaries are over-enriched, causing adverse health effects for both wildlife and humans.[93]

The modernization of farming practice also promoted the use of chemicals to eliminate fungi and voracious insects on cereals and potatoes, as well as to curb competition from weeds. The chemicals had inevitable consequences for Island wildlife. Copper sulphate was an early pesticide used for control of potato late blight, but dithane (that is, mancozeb) became the fungicide of choice after 1946.[94] Insecticides of the postwar period included persistent organochlorides such as aldrin, endrin, heptachlor, and thiodan (endosulfan, still used today), and the wide-spectrum killer toxaphene. Other less persistent insecticides, such as malathion and rotenone, were also part of the arsenal to increase food production. DDT, the cure for potato beetles and barn flies, came into use in 1946, replacing inorganic metal-based compounds. DDT and related organochlorides widely affected bird populations by reducing eggshell thickness and hatching success, especially among top predators such as osprey and falcons.[95] The effects of farm insecticides on such bird populations were not documented locally but were probably significant, though difficult to separate from the effects of indiscriminate shooting. In any case, only ten osprey nests and one bald eagle territory were known on Prince Edward Island in 1975.[96]

Island farmers did not know about the insidious effects of DDT,[97] so it was not the case that bird mortalities were seen as an acceptable cost of growing food. However, until very recently, national regulators ignored wide-scale bird losses from modern insecticides (organophosphates and carbamates) that have proven exceptionally toxic to birds. The insecticide carbofuran provides an instructive example. In granular form it was widely applied to crops, including rutabagas and potatoes. Lethal effects on birds that ingested the granules (which resembled seeds) eventually led to its being withdrawn from use in Canada. Carbofuran sprays are also lethal. As one research scientist notes, with the spray, "bird species are also exposed through their skin and eyes; they ingest residues when they preen their feathers, and inhale small droplets and pesticide vapours when they enter treated fields or spend time in field borders."[98] Yet the liquid formulation continued to be used and in 2006 was still one of two main choices for beetle control on potatoes. Its voluntary withdrawal from the Island marketplace by its manufacturer after 2006 was most likely sparked by concerns for human health and economic reality rather than its impact on bird populations.[99] In 2009 the United States established zero tolerance for carbofuran residues on food, and since 2010 its use is gradually being phased out by Health Canada.[100] As of 2012, it was still registered for some uses.

The "wholesale destruction of trout" from poison entering streams was noted in the 1950s,[101] and newspaper articles a decade later indicated that fish kills were an annual event.[102] The documentation of the effects of misplaced endosulfan and the like eventually resulted in a provincial Pesticides Control Act, but this did not stop the periodic and catastrophic losses of fish. There have been over sixty recorded fish kills on the Island since the 1960s. In the industrialized farmscape of the new millennium, wildlife remains vulnerable to choices that prioritize short-term economic pressures over environmental threats.

NATURAL HISTORIES

The popular indifference to the harmful effects of agricultural chemicals on Island wildlife reflects human priorities, but it also reflects a lack of knowledge about the natural environment and, in many cases, a tentative relationship with it. Of course, "knowing" nature is not a prerequisite for having an opinion about it, but it does shape attitudes towards it. Ecologist Daniel Botkin[103] has postulated three distinct appreciations of nature held by European settlers. First is the "divinely ordered nature," with a lasting constancy and stability. Second is the notion of "nature as organic," a creature working independently of humans. Third, with advances in science in the 1600s, is a mechanistic view of the earth "operating like clockwork," stable and returning to a steady state after it is disturbed. Little such appreciation of nature can be found in early accounts from Prince Edward Island. Whether getting rich or living a hardscrabble existence, settlers were engaged in using wildlife for their own ends, though they may have taken the biblical view that God provides "dominion over the fish of the sea, and over the fowl of the air, and over the cattle, and over all the earth, and over every creeping thing that creepeth upon the earth" (Genesis 1:26).

Of course, none of this was true of the province's earliest inhabitants, whose cosmology predicated a contract between humans and wildlife: game allowed itself to be killed so long as certain rituals and proper respect were maintained.[104] While there are only sparse historical records about Mi'kmaq use of wildlife, these are now being augmented by archeological studies (see Kristmanson and Keenlyside, this volume) and ethnographic surveys. When it comes to Islanders of European descent, the sparseness of documentation is more suggestive. We know of some Island species that disappeared with the arrival of European settlers, but other wildlife losses remain obscure because of gaps in historical records. Little was written before 1900 about Island wildlife and about how people perceived the wildlife around them. Available records reveal how bears menaced or killed people[105] and lynx stole their sheep, but there are few indications that people spent hours watching birds or hunting for pleasure. Douglas Sobey managed to compile a scant six pages of original notes about wildlife in the French period (1534–1758)[106] and twenty-five pages of summary and analysis pertaining to bird and mammal records from 1758 to 1900.[107]

In colonial times, records were made by the privileged minority who could write, not necessarily those with much personal experience of wildlife. The letters and documents compiled by Sobey stretch over 350 years but provide little sense of change over time. All are biased by the European upbringing of the writers, who tended to make note of mammals and birds with circumpolar distribution but to ignore indigenous species. The majority of their comments related to the utility of flora and fauna, but even in this respect detail is lacking. We are left with a series of isolated facts: people hunted for food, sport, and profit; there were fur trappers and berry pickers; and up to forty wardens were hired to patrol rivers in the 1880s to protect salmon from poachers.[108]

John Stewart, the Island's first "historian," made many authentic observations of nature's bounty on Prince Edward Island. In 1806 he described a range of Island flora, and in the 1820s, John MacGregor wrote about the aesthetic value of various wildlife species, particularly the butterflies and the frog chorus.[109] However, most species were ignored, just as most plants, insects, frogs, and small birds are often overlooked today. Plants came in for special treatment in the 1840s and '50s when a lady of means, Ann Elizabeth Grubb Haviland, hobby-collected and preserved thirty-three specimens for posterity.[110]

By 1889 there was evidence of a change in public sensibilities when the Natural History Society of Prince Edward Island formed in Charlottetown.[111] In the Victorian tradition of the inspired amateur, the society was intellectual in nature and facilitated learning, publications, and information exchange about science and nature. It had many small successes but failed in its major goal of seeing its natural collections lodged in a natural history museum. Around this time Francis Bain wrote *The Natural History of Prince Edward Island* (1890), which became a primary school textbook, and *Birds of Prince Edward Island* (1891). But this spurt of intellectual activity with reference to wildlife was brief. The first incarnation of the society faded away in 1908,[112] and it would be 1969 before another formed. That organization remains active today (2014), holding regular meetings, producing a newsletter (*The Island*

Naturalist), and consistently demanding a provincial museum to properly house natural history collections.[113]

More successful from the outset was the Prince Edward Island Fish and Game Protection Association (PEIFGPA), incorporated in 1906, whose members were appointed as wardens under the provincial Fish and Game Protection Act. [114] The PEIFGPA advocated responsible fish and game management. Today, renamed the Prince Edward Island Wildlife Federation, it continues to work on behalf of wildlife, hunters, and fishers, especially through stream enhancement programs.

The scientific record – or lack of it – is similarly telling. According to Austin Cameron,[115] who reviewed the literature in the 1950s, Bain's *The Natural History of Prince Edward Island* (1890), though recording useful notes on mammals, was not a scientific work, and there were no other extant texts of any great value. It may be that by the early twentieth century, when many more people could read and write, the opportunity for exceptional familiarity with wildlife had passed.

As for the Island flora, *The Natural History of Prince Edward Island* included a list of only forty plants. It seems likely that local plant enthusiasts had limited access to scientific expertise and publishing venues. Other research escaped local attention for decades. When botanist David Erskine reviewed the limited gains in knowledge about plants over the half century leading up to his 1950s study, he discovered that the famous Harvard botanist M.L. Fernald, with others, had collected plants in Prince Edward Island in 1912 and 1914, their work upping a 1907 list by John MacSwain from 407 species to 713.[116] More recently, our knowledge of native and introduced European plants common on farms during the French colonial period is being enhanced through archaeological excavation of Acadian farm wells.[117]

As the Harvard example shows, for much of the twentieth century, outside expertise was critical in documenting the province's natural history. Studies of Prince Edward Island wildlife by the National Museum of Canada in the 1950s and 1960s provided rather complete lists of birds,[118] mammals,[119] plants,[120] and amphibians and reptiles.[121] Nevertheless, gaps exist in our understanding of the distribution and ecology of most wild species, especially since Prince Edward Island is the only province without a natural history museum. It is still possible to record native vertebrates for the first time. Northern long-eared bats,[122] pickerel frogs,[123] and slimy sculpins[124] were all discovered in the past twenty-five years. Entomologist Christopher Majka, noting the Prince

Edward Island insect fauna as the most poorly documented of any Canadian province, was able to add, with the assistance of Prince Edward Island colleagues, 608 new species of beetles to a 1991 list of 341. Such information, he reflected, "is indispensable in determining and tracking human impact on the province's environment. If we want to ascertain the effects of pollution, acid rain, the use of biocides … clear cutting of forests, climate change and other impacts of human civilization on the natural world, we first need to know what species are present, and where, and in what numbers."[125]

The 1997 establishment of the Atlantic Canada Conservation Data Centre in Sackville, New Brunswick, and a similar national program ranking the risk of extinction for various species (www.wildspecies.ca) has addressed some information gaps, but the educational and scientific role of a natural history museum goes unfulfilled and continues to be poorly appreciated by government despite persistent lobbying by some interest groups.[126]

GAME CHANGERS

Those who most appreciated wildlife in the twentieth century were often hunters and fishermen, many of them members of the Prince Edward Island Fish and Game Protection Association (PEIFGPA). Not only were they anxious to conserve certain desirable species but they often advocated the importation of non-native game animals. Though the introduction of exotic species is not acceptable today in most jurisdictions in North America, it was an exciting part of game management in the twentieth century.

Considering the history of wildlife manipulation, it is not surprising that when Island sportsmen wanted white-tailed deer, they simply imported some from the mainland between 1949 and 1951. The first pair were presented to the premier of the day, Walter Jones. Thereafter, sportsmen, likely including members of the PEIFGPA, brought deer over as they felt necessary for a successful introduction. The deer became a nuisance to farmers in Queens County, and so were rounded up and removed to Kings County; a large herd was also known to winter in the cedar stands of Poplar Grove and Black Banks in Prince County. Farmers protecting their crops and those epicures who wanted a taste of venison helped themselves. By 1954, the success of the introduction was in doubt, and deer were gone by the time that Austin Cameron published his report on mammals in 1958.[127]

Introduced game birds fared somewhat better. The PEIFGPA success-fully introduced ten pairs of gray partridge in 1927, and another fifty-nine pairs were set out by the provincial government between 1929 and 1931. Partridge numbers expanded rapidly, and an estimated 200,000 partridges were available for the first open hunting season in 1939. Said to be most abundant in 1948, they thereafter slowly declined and today are centred in the farmlands of central and southern Queens County, where they can still be hunted.

The gaudy and extremely tasty ring-necked pheasant was first released in 1917. Many small introductions followed, but it was 1950 before an open season on ring-necked pheasant could be declared. Despite contin-ued augmentation, hunting of pheasants had to be suspended in 1963. Chukar partridge, prairie chickens, and several other species were also released, but failed to survive.[128] The PEIFGPA was the main interest group involved in the introduction of such exotic species, and when the pheasants failed, the PEIFGPA demanded a study to find out why. That study, by J.D. Heyland, encouraged a "put and take" pheasant hunt,[129] later established as the Earnscliffe Pheasant Preserve. In all of such endeavours, the overriding intent was to promote game animals for hunting (and fish species for angling) with an eye to both local demand and tourism potential (as a wealth of promotional literature from 1880 to 1960 confirms). Nevertheless, the sportsmen introducing the game birds and animals were usually also the greatest proponents of protect-ing wildlife and wildlife habitats.

FUR RANCHING

Attempts to manage the Island's wildlife were actually preceded by efforts to farm it. And if sportsmen were mainly motivated by the pleasures of the hunt, others manipulating wildlife populations were driven by the prospect of profit. One of the province's most romanticized experiments in animal husbandry was the domestication of the black and silver phases of the red fox. Charles Dalton and Robert Oulton, who first bred silver foxes in cap-tivity in 1883, were widely heralded as pioneers. At the time, dark-phase foxes were in high demand, and as fox populations were said to be trapped out over large areas, fur farming was judged an appropriate option for reducing pressure on local fox populations.[130] At least six different red fox subspecies were imported to Prince Edward Island, some of which no doubt escaped and contaminated the local genetic stock,[131] something that would not be sanctioned by the 1992 Biodiversity Convention.[132]

During the fox farming boom just prior to the First World War, the prices paid for breeding stock reached dizzy heights, as much as $25,000 per pair.[133] When the cost of breeding stock fell, average Islanders invested so that from a base of 3,130 foxes in Prince Edward Island ranches in 1913, the industry grew to 32,831 ranched foxes in 1929. About 50 per cent of the original stock were silvers; many were actually red phase foxes,[134] some of which originated from dens in the wild.

As fox ranching developed into a new livestock industry, authorities moved to standardize fox farming practices. In 1913, J. Walter Jones (later the premier of Prince Edward Island) produced a standard treatise, *Fur-Farming in Canada*, which was quickly reprinted.[135] Diseases among farmed animals were also of concern to the early ranchers and regulatory authorities. In 1914, mangy foxes on several Island ranches were destroyed, and sanitary measures taken to prevent the mange mite from spreading to other fur farms or to the wild.[136]

As the Great Depression pushed more and more pelts into the marketplace, the number of farm foxes peaked at 56,697 in 1937. The practice in the 1920s and 1930s of feeding brook trout and salmon to ranched foxes and mink (a reflection of the depressed price for pelts) was outlawed in the 1937 edition of the Fish and Game Protection Act, but the protection soon became unnecessary.[137] Oversupply, the Depression, and the Second World War all combined to depress fur markets. By 1959, only 636 foxes remained on Island ranches.[138] When long-haired fur prices rose in the late 1960s, there was renewed interest in fur farms, and many ranched foxes were sourced from the wild. In 1976, for example, 11 per cent of fifty-three fox dens examined were found to be destroyed and the foxes gone. Thus was the line blurred between wildlife and livestock.[139]

The quick wealth associated with furs led to two non-native furbearers being imported and eventually released (around 1916–17): the striped skunk[140] and the raccoon.[141] These multiplied rapidly and today are widely regarded as pests. Around the same time, beaver were brought in by private individuals and released to produce fur. The process has been repeated several times; the temptation to trap beavers was high and ended with more being taken than intended.[142] Since the 1970s, beaver management programs have managed populations more successfully, even as disagreement continues about how many beavers are optimal. In contrast, Islanders were slow to warm up to mink as a semi-domesticated fur-bearing animal. First ranched successfully in New England between 1860 and 1880,[143] ranched mink was a minor item in 1950, being present on only fifteen of 127 farms.[144]

MANAGING HABITATS

Introduced species inevitably affected wildlife habitats, though not as drastically as settler practices. Neither impact was systematic or particularly intentional. In the twentieth century, however, the state took a more deliberate hand in shaping habitat. In the post–Second World War era, provincial authorities adopted management ideas from the rest of Canada, including a popular wildlife bounty paid for removal of under-appreciated wildlife (owls, skunks, foxes, raccoons, and crows) from 1932 to 1963. This boosted revenues in poverty-stricken rural households but had little detectable impact on the target populations. The program paid out $19,182 in 1963,[145] after which the bounty system was discarded.

At the same time as government authorities tried to manage wildlife, they began more consciously to manage habitat. In the Fish and Game Protection Act of 1951, section 21 allowed six ponds to be created, maintained, or restored, using public funds in order to allow angling of a public resource (fish) on private lands. The act also allowed private ponds to be stocked for fishing, free of charge, provided the fishing was open to all anglers[146] – an approach that is still followed. Later, the federal Agricultural Rehabilitation and Development Act (ARDA) of 1962, which was administered by the provincial Department of Agriculture, supported pond construction for water conservation projects, including stock watering. It enabled many small dams to be built in the "barrier bypass"[147] or "runaround" style, at least until 1965.[148] Quite a few of the "ARDA ponds" remain today. The ability of fish to move past these dams varied according to the steepness and water velocity in the bypass. Most would have allowed trout and salmon upstream, probably some gaspereau, and possibly some smelt.

The popular dam-building program proved to be a silver lining obscuring a cloud of habitat degradation. In the late 1960s, dam-building stopped, and an inventory was undertaken by the federal Department of Regional Economic Expansion. The inventory counted 443 dams that "had been placed indiscriminately on streams and were having an adverse effect on fish ... causing siltation of streams, playing havoc with water tables and drainage."[149] Although there were no standards for controlling siltation during construction, the last claim was likely false.

Since 1969, fish ladders meeting Department of Fisheries and Oceans standards have been built into many dams to restore passage for trout and salmon, chiefly by Ducks Unlimited Canada and the province. However, there are still obstructions that do not allow smelts and alewives to go upstream to spawn. Meanwhile, some new dams have been built and then removed in response to demonstrably warm temperatures detrimental to salmonids. Today, the province looks after fifty-three ponds, nineteen of which are bypass ponds. Ducks Unlimited maintains thirty-two, and another thirty are operated jointly.[150] There are also many privately owned ponds. Meanwhile, pond numbers have been augmented by beaver dams since the successful re-establishment of beavers across the Island.[151] It is frequently stated that there are eight hundred man-made dams on the Island, but there is no documentation to support this claim.

Such manipulations of habitat were increasingly entrusted to a professional bureaucracy. In the postwar era, the PEIFGPA had lobbied for the hiring of professional biologists and game wardens. Thus, waterfowl biologist Charlie Bartlett was hired in 1964, and two additional biologists were hired in 1965. When the Island government revised the Fish and Game Protection Act in 1966, it established the Fish and Wildlife Division to "look after" wildlife, regulating wildlife harvests and managing populations so as to increase recreational and economic opportunities for fishermen, hunters, and trappers. Bartlett, a graduate of the University of Wisconsin's wildlife science and ecology program, was named director. Three conservation officers were added the same year.[152] In 1969, a fisheries biologist, a waterfowl and furbearer biologist, and an upland game biologist were monitoring both harvestable wildlife and the harvesters. More enforcement staff were also hired, reflecting a general societal trend toward state intervention and management that was supported by an increasing provincial budget and bureaucracy. It might also be argued that the general growth in staffing reflected popular support for a more scientific approach to management of the Island's wildlife. [153]

With the hiring of a permanent fisheries biologist in 1969, the province was finally able to assess the condition of rivers and document the widespread problem of silt in fish spawning areas. The Prince Edward Island Royal Commission on Land Ownership and Land Use[154] of 1972 heard about "streams, bays and estuaries running red in the spring of the year" as a consequence of agricultural practices associated with potato monoculture. The Dunk River Interdisciplinary Study of the mid-1970s, led from the University of Prince Edward Island, was another attempt to get a handle on silt and its watershed effects. One participant was inspired to write the book *Watershed Red: The Life of the Dunk River, Prince Edward Island*, making it clear that misplaced soil was detrimental to river and estuary, fish and oysters.[155]

The Dunk River studies discovered much about the extent of soil losses and pathways of silt to water, but potato farmers and other local residents were not adequately engaged during the process or afterward to discuss results. Potato farming and the sports fisheries were opposite forces that seemed to prevent local people from agreeing on common goals. Nevertheless, the fall 1975 issue of the *Prince Edward Island Environeer* suggested the range of PEI Fish and Wildlife Division activity: it was actively banding waterfowl, addressing beaver flooding of roads, operating a pheasant preserve, conducting stream improvements, studying cormorant and ruffed grouse populations, providing a replacement osprey nest for one that had toppled, and giving input to policy discussions regarding aerial spraying of pesticides, spruce budworm control, and mosquitoes.[156] Clearly, there was much to learn and do.

Prince Edward Island took a radical step forward in 1987, when it produced the first provincial conservation strategy in Canada.[157] The strategy spoke only briefly and with little insight about wildlife and used the economic argument to justify keeping wildlife on the landscape. Its recommendations to conserve wildlife habitats were, however, exemplary, if somewhat fish-centric. The document noted that "stream degradation is the most important problem now confronting the maintenance of existing stocks of fish and wildlife in the province," and called for stream rehabilitation and funding for farmers to practice soil conservation. The strategy envisioned stable funding from a conservation fund that would allow volunteer groups to employ a large labour force in stream restoration, planting of greenbelts to stabilize stream edges, and development of watershed management plans. In addition, there would be more fish enhancement measures, including semi-natural rearing of Atlantic salmon. In the process, siltation and over-enrichment of estuaries would be addressed, significant wetlands and natural areas would be designated for protection, policies to stem the loss of wetlands would be developed, and ecological reserves would be set in place. The strategy also recommended protection for the endangered piping plover and called for government to determine what numbers of cormorants people could live with. (The latter was a guarded response to complaints from commercial fishermen, fish farmers, and anglers.) The strategy also proposed designation of Malpeque Bay as a Ramsar Wetland of International Importance. Major developments were to be subject to environmental assessment and review, both in municipalities and in rural areas.

Many of the recommendations in the Conservation Strategy were processed in short order by the government of the day; others stimulated

progress over a longer time frame. The Conservation Strategy was followed in 1995 by a Wildlife Policy for Prince Edward Island. Its guiding
principles include the statement: "the maintenance of viable natural
populations of wildlife and ecological functions always take precedence
over any human use of wildlife."[158] The importance of wildlife to Prince
Edward Island culture and the stewardship responsibility of the populace for wildlife were affirmed. The precedence thus given to conservation of native wildlife represented a major change from the narrowly
utilitarian view of nature held by previous generations (see MacIntyre,
appendix A in this volume). A modern, inclusive definition of wildlife
was part of a new Wildlife Conservation Act in 1998, when provision
was made to list endangered species provincially.

One of the Conservation Strategy's recommendations concerned the
establishment of greenbelts around watercourses as buffers against agricultural contaminants and siltation from runoff. In 2000, the recommended greenbelt legislation was passed. There was also progress on
other fronts. The Agricultural Crop Rotation Act was passed in 2001 to
reduce soil erosion, and in 2004, a game-changing wetland policy[159] was
accepted by government, ensuring no net loss of wetlands, a ten-metre
buffer zone between streams and fields, and compensation for destroyed
wetland habitats.[160]

Despite the incremental progress over many decades, soil erosion and
siltation of watercourses remain profound environmental problems on
Prince Edward Island today. The entry of fertilizers into watercourses
promotes eutrophication of rivers and estuaries, and water-borne pesticides are still killing trout and other organisms, as they were fifty years
ago,[161] illustrating the complexity of an issue that involves multiple
departments with overlapping and sometimes conflicting interests and
mandates, working in the context of a powerful industry in a heavily
populated landscape.

CITIZEN ENGAGEMENT

As the foregoing shows, the state is only one player, albeit a key one,
in the process of conservation. Conservation requires the confluence of
public and private interest, science and practical knowledge, paid
workers and volunteers, self-interest and the greater good. To cite one
illustration, the Prince Edward Island Conservation Strategy envisaged
a cadre of local people, with leadership from local communities, practising stream restoration. It has been widely acknowledged that a

concerned public is integral to conservation, and the work to buffer Prince Edward Island wildlife habitat from the ubiquitous stressor – agriculture – is ongoing, thanks to the flowering of watershed associations pursuing stream enhancement and cooperative programs with agricultural producers.

Back in the 1970s, Fisheries biologist Arthur Smith (retired), with input from other concerned wildlife managers and using student labour, began experimenting with in-stream gabions to deflect silt. At one point the Ford Motor Company supplied vans to haul crews to their riverine work sites. One example of such a project took place on the Valleyfield River in 1975.[162] To release silt, crews removed accumulated debris and log jams from the river and deepened the channel to enable fish passage. This project was probably one of the first to successfully encourage a farmer to confine his cattle to about fifteen metres of stream rather than allowing trampling of it along the total length of his pasture. Some cooperation with other agencies allowed several sources of silt to be corrected, all with an eye to increasing the sports fishery potential in the river. Coincidentally, a group of private citizens along the Morell River had formed the Morell and Area Land Use Steering Committee with the goal of limiting the entry of silt to the river by maintaining the forested edge. They contacted landowners along a considerable length of the system, and even though not everyone was in favour, the minister of municipal affairs went ahead and in 1975 established the Morell River Conservation Zone under the Subdivision and Development Regulations of the Planning Act.[163] The Land Use Steering Committee evolved into the Morell River Management Co-operative, and this became a model for many other grassroots watershed management associations.

A decade later, as stream enhancement groups continued to plod up and down sediment-laden watercourses, the Montague Watershed Project[164] was conceived with funding from Wildlife Habitat Canada, which had been established to develop waterfowl-habitat conservation projects with funds collected from migratory bird hunters. A five-year co-operative land use management plan was designed "to demonstrate to landowners and land use agencies the multiple benefits of co-operative land use management." Using a watershed approach to management, the project attempted abatement of sedimentation from forestry and farming practices and the highway system, and improved forest management to correct the problems of high-graded and neglected woodlands, again with the goal of improved trout fishing. Cooperative relationships were established among twenty-four parties, including government agencies and resource interests that had previously conversed very little. Support from 40 per cent of local landowners was obtained, and eventually the Montague Watershed Co-operative was formed. Being very well funded and having a known time horizon, the project staff were able to monitor progress on many fronts.

Improved relations among government agencies was another major accomplishment in a province where departments sometimes worked at cross purposes. For example, when poor farming practices were documented on land leased to farmers by the provincial Land Development Corporation, the government instituted a policy to correct erosion problems on leased farmlands and went so far as to use rent money to fund installation of erosion control structures.

THE PROTECTED AREAS MOVEMENT

Historically, wilderness preservation was never an urgent concern on Prince Edward Island, but in recent decades, identifying and protecting both rare and representative natural areas has become more of a priority. Natural Areas, National Parks, and Provincial Parks are examples of lands set aside (in a province that had almost no public land) for the benefit of wildlife. The idea of protected areas on the Island was revolutionary and met with resistance.[165] Not only was the concept foreign to most Islanders, but the issue was compounded by the very boundedness of the Island, which sharpened competition over land use. The nature of the landscape was also a factor, where the remaining "wilderness" – that is, altered natural habitat – generally abutted the backs of farms.

Arguably, the first such protected area in Prince Edward Island was Victoria Park, Charlottetown, officially recognized in 1873. Reminiscent of the orderly parks of London, it was laid out in geometric patterns, with a cricket field and a proposed lake.[166] Clearly, it was a park designed with people foremost in mind; preservation of wildlife and its habitat was secondary, if considered at all. Even when national parks began to be established in the mountains of western Canada, preservation of wilderness was not at the root of the movement; rather, it was parks' usefulness to people. The idea that parks should be splendid, preferably with mountains, slowed proposals for new parks in the east, and when they were established, their development and management was primarily as tourist attractions.[167] Preservation was not totally ignored, but it took a few decades to appreciate what should be preserved.

Figure 5.1 Aerial view of the proposed Deroche Point National Wildlife Area, looking westward to Tracadie Bay.

Prince Edward Island National Park (PEINP) was eventually established in 1937. The National Parks Act of 1930 iterated that Parks were for the benefit, education, and enjoyment of the people, but that they "should be maintained and made use of so as to leave them unimpaired for the enjoyment of future generations."[168] By the 1960s, tiny PEINP was the second most-visited National Park in Canada,[169] but it also had a mandate to preserve the outstanding ecological feature of coastal dunes, which comprise less than 1 per cent of the province.

While Parks Canada inched towards a conservation ethic, other agencies, private organizations, and individuals were implementing their own ideas for protected areas for varying purposes. The federal Canadian Wildlife Service (CWS) established a 130-hectare Migratory Bird Sanctuary at Black Pond in 1936 with the cooperation of local landowners who agreed to suspend hunting of waterfowl on their properties.[170] Likewise, Harvey Moore's ponds at Milltown Cross, developed in 1949, became Moore's Bird Sanctuary by an order-in-council in 1956. Moore, a fisherman, trapper, and farmer, had dreamed of making such a refuge for waterfowl and acquired a property specifically for that purpose. There he built two ponds and scattered grain to lure ducks and geese.[171] Without so much as a net or trap, he banded thousands of black ducks at the sanctuary and also

Figure 5.2 Rolling duneland has been stabilized to some extent by a vegetative cover of bayberry, beach grass, and false heather.

established a breeding population of Canada geese before his untimely death in 1960.[172] The Wildlife Service abandoned Moore's Bird Sanctuary in 1974, perhaps because of the burden of feeding the waterfowl. In response to local consternation at the loss of the sanctuary, the province agreed to maintain protection for the area under the Prince Edward Island Fish and Game Protection Act. It then became Moore's Wildlife Management Area, and the restrictions previously applied to Moore's sanctuary were transferred into provincial regulation.

The Canadian Wildlife Service was also establishing National Wildlife Areas across Canada in the postwar period, acquiring some of the best marshes under government ownership and permitting public hunting within them. A 1968 proposal to launch the Deroche Point National Wildlife Area (figure 5.1) noted that there were few natural areas remaining in the province and the area was under threat of development.[173] The proposal had the support of local wildlife officials, but when plans for land expropriation leaked out, together with a false rumour that hunting would be abolished, local opinion turned against the plan. Expropriation was front page news in the *Evening Patriot* of 27 May 1969[174] and in the *Guardian* the next day.[175] The project was scuttled. Had Deroche Point National Wildlife Area become a reality, it would have been a step forward in actually protecting habitat for wildlife.

Although the concept of sanctuaries for wildlife species had public appeal, enhanced hunting opportunities beyond the perimeter of "the sanctuary" played into this attraction. By the late 1960s, ecologists were thinking more about ecosystem preservation. Under the International Biological Program (IBP), organized to document representative ecosystems, learn about them, and examine how human activities were affecting them, funds finally became available in 1971 to do fieldwork in the Maritimes. Through this program, the national parks inventoried their flora and fauna and zoned parks accordingly, providing "maximum public use while preserving wilderness recreation values."[176] At this time national parks made up less than 1 per cent of the land area of Canada, and the IBP would add at best only one-tenth of that area. In Prince Edward Island, fourteen sites totalling 7,855 acres were identified for protection, including five sand dune ecosystems, a bog (since mined for peat), seven sites of rare and representative forest, and bird nesting islands.[177] Half of these sites are now protected.

The province was itself slow to take action on the study and preservation of ecosystems. In the late 1970s the PEI government appointed a Natural Areas Advisory Committee, chaired by Daryl Guignion of the University of Prince Edward Island (UPEI), but then disbanded it. Nevertheless, a nucleus of concerned academics and like-minded people, including IBP co-chair Ian MacQuarrie, continued to push the province to do more to preserve natural habitats for wildlife. A plan to develop a resort hotel near Deroche Pond and the sand dunes of Blooming Point was a catalyst for action. Public meetings were held and the plan was scrapped. In the aftermath, the Island Nature Trust was incorporated in 1979 as the first private provincially based nature trust in Canada. The trust intended that public and private lands at Deroche Pond and elsewhere should be protected. Fortunately, the province stepped in and acquired the land from the developers, then turned it over to the Island Nature Trust for management through a fifty-year lease.

Over the next decade, progress in conserving habitats for species accelerated. In 1982, UPEI's biology department presented the Prince Edward Island Natural Areas Survey[178] for the consideration of government, listing thirty-nine areas of note. The recommendations were not immediately accepted, but in ten short years the survey report became the basis of significant lobbying that resulted in progress. A watershed moment came in 1988 when the Island Nature Trust, with a war chest of $100,000, stood between a New York developer and the desecration of the ecologically sensitive Greenwich dunes.[179] The ensuing controversy rallied public support on either side of the issue, pitting economic

Figure 5.3 Diane Griffin (*right*) of the Island Nature Trust, led the hard-fought battle to save the sand dunes at Greenwich from cottage developers. Greenwich, near St Peters Bay, PEI, became part of the national park system in July 1996. In this 1988 photo, Griffin explains the sand dune system to Land Use Commission members, *left to right*, Claude Matheson, Ron McKinnon, Maurice Fitzpatrick, and Anne McPhee. Courtesy *Charlottetown Guardian*, PEI.

development against the preservation of a rare ecosystem and important archeological site. The lands were later acquired by the province through trading in 1995 and conveyed to the Prince Edward Island National Park in 1998. The Island Nature Trust had hired its first executive director in 1984 – Diane Griffin, a graduate of the International Biological Program survey ten years earlier and an incorrigible optimist with a knack for finding ways to get things done (figure 5.3). Griffin preferred good planning to confrontation and legal challenges, but she admitted the trust did not always have the luxury of diplomacy: "Our coastline is the only thing we have that approaches wilderness in this province. We don't have a lot of options left."[180]

There were other landmark cases. On Boughton Island in Cardigan Bay, a cottage subdivision approved by the Prince Edward Island government in 1988 was challenged by three private litigants and the Natural History Society of Prince Edward Island, which feared the loss of a

Figure 5.4 Gilbert Clements, Prince Edward
Island minister of environment, 1974–78 and
1989–93.

nesting colony of great blue herons. The appeal was denied, but additional restrictions on the subdivison were applied by the Prince Edward
Island Land Use Commission to conserve the herons.[181] In August 1991,
the second of two appeals was brought to the Land Use Commission by
the Eastern Kings Community Improvement Corporation, protesting the
plan by a private landowner to establish a camp on his land, which was
part of the barrier dune across the mouth of Basin Head lagoon. The
local municipality had included the dune within a Special Planning Area
and Conservation Zone as early as 1981 due to its status as an IBP site.
Both of these appeals were successful.

A critical factor in the success of conservation advocates was a
champion within government. Gilbert Clements, Prince Edward Island

minister of environment from 1974 to 1978 and 1989 to 1993 (figure 5.4), cared deeply for the environment, an appreciation honed while he was chair of the Canadian Council of Environment Ministers, culminating with his participation in the Earth Summit of 1992.[182] In 1988, he pushed through the Natural Areas Protection Act and used it a year later to designate one privately owned and ten publicly owned sites in response to the World Wildlife Fund 1989 Endangered Spaces campaign to protect 12 per cent of the country.[183]

Local, national, and international conservation trends continued to feed off one another in the late twentieth century. In 1992, the Canadian environment, parks, and wildlife ministers signed a revolutionary Statement of Commitment to Complete Canada's Networks of Protected Areas by the Year 2000.[184] In deference to the 90 per cent private ownership of the island, the province set a more pragmatic goal of protecting 7 per cent of the land, with assistance from private citizens and the Island Nature Trust. That same year government approved a list of areas for protection, and designations proceeded at a rapid clip with 2.2 per cent of the province protected by 1995.[185] Despite a recipe for success presented by then Deputy Minister Griffin, progress soon slowed, and the 2011 tally was only 3.2 per cent, well below the 7 per cent target set twenty years earlier.

The 1986 North American Waterfowl Management Plan[186] also enabled a measure of protection for natural habitat on the Island. Through the Eastern Habitat Joint Venture, and support from Ducks Unlimited, wetlands were acquired and incorporated with other lands into eight new Wildlife Management Areas, totalling nearly twelve thousand acres.[187] Later, other parcels were designated as Natural Areas.[188]

When lands are protected, they still require management because people want to use them. A balance must be found. In 1988 the National Parks Act was amended to require that the ecological integrity of parks be the first consideration in managing visitors. Consistently ranking high in visitation numbers, Prince Edward Island National Park was one park in which stresses from within and without were considered major and severe, respectively.[189] Since then, many recommendations have been acted upon, including better ecosystem research, a distinct mandate for conservation, and decision-making processes permitting better scientific input. At the same time, after many years of educational messages, the public may be more understanding of the National Park's efforts to conserve nature. Tourism associations, for instance, no longer lobby to keep nesting areas of the endangered piping plover open to beachgoers and their dogs.

AN ISLAND IN A WORLD OF CRISES

Wildlife is now in an accelerated age of extinction globally. Political will and resources are needed to counteract the five pillars of destruction of biodiversity outlined by renowned biologist E.O. Wilson: habitat loss, invasive species, pollution, human population effects, and overharvesting.[190] Changing climate causes changing habitats, and up to 30 per cent of mammals, birds, and amphibians may be threatened with extinction in this century due to climate change.[191] Prince Edward Island is, of course, not excepted from change. Many indigenous species appear to be coping, and despite our island-fastness, some new species are actually arriving, most notably the coyote.[192] Others, such as the bald eagle and the pileated woodpecker, are making a comeback. But still others are gone or going; the cliff swallow[193] no longer nests here, and the Gulf of St Lawrence aster teeters on the edge of extinction.[194] As easy as it is to find grim tales about dwindling species, it is also easy to find complacency. The predicted extinction of the southern Gulf of St Lawrence Atlantic cod stock[195] has excited little concern thus far, and the official response to scientists' recent determination (in Charlottetown) that the Atlantic bluefin tuna is endangered has been denial.[196]

Ecological awareness on Prince Edward Island is growing, but awareness must translate into a biodiversity strategy to assess how Island wildlife will cope with climate change and the biodiversity crisis. One of the lessons of time in this place is that we cannot live in this world without affecting nature; indeed, the fate of wildlife species and habitats is a signpost of where our own future lies.

The Mermaid's Tresses:
Seaplants in the Culture and Economy
of Prince Edward Island

Irené Novaczek

ANCIENT DENIZENS

Mermaid's tresses, sea colander, hog's bristle, oyster thief – we have many names for the ancient life forms commonly known as seaweeds or seaplants. Far older than any land plant or animal, multi-cellular algae appear in the fossil records starting from about 1,500 million years ago. Fossils resembling modern seaplants date back 600–635 million years.[1]

Throughout the 4,500-million-year history of the planet, plate tectonics have forced continents to drift back and forth across the earth's surface, sometimes colliding to form larger masses, and sometimes splitting apart, while the watery spaces between and around them, which we call oceans, appeared and disappeared accordingly.[2] The movements of continents and transitions of oceans encouraged development of new species within geographic areas that were in some way distinct or disconnected from others.[3] The marine plants that appear today in the waters around Prince Edward Island therefore reflect the sum of all these changes in the availability, connectivity, and quality of shallow marine habitats around the fringes of continents and islands. As will be shown below, an understanding of this history and of the physiological requirements of marine plants provides explanations for their present-day distributions across geographic space and vertically down shores and into various depths of water. This in turn helps us to understand the consequences of interactions between ancient marine plants and our relatively recently evolved keystone species – human beings – in recent centuries. These human influences are sometimes accidental, often deliberate, and usually connected to economic pursuits that have much more visible impacts on land.

Shallow water is necessary to support seaplants because, with few exceptions, they grow attached to the bottom of the sea and always require sufficient light for photosynthesis. Light penetrating water diminishes with depth, and the colour or wavelength of that light also changes, shifting from white through green to blue, providing a variety of light environments. Some marine plants require not only particular colours of light but also particular day lengths and combinations of day length, colour, and temperature to stimulate reproduction.[4] This light sensitivity limits the latitudes and depths in which each can flourish. Each species also has high and low temperature limits for survival.[5] Some thrive in brackish waters near the mouths of rivers, while others require full salinity. Nutrient requirements also vary from species to species. Some plants grow quickly and can take advantage of openings in disturbed bottom, while others grow slowly and need to be on hard substrates that are undisturbed from one year to the next. Some tolerate periodic exposure to air, as occurs in the intertidal zone of beaches, whereas others must be continuously submerged. In short, each species has a particular niche or suite of conditions to which it is suited, which must be maintained to ensure its long-term survival.

As a result of these requirements, the assemblage of species present in any given location differs from one ocean basin to another and according to latitude (temperature and day length), depth of water (light environment), substrate (mud, sand, cobble, soft rock, hard rock), degree of wave exposure, tidal range, and salinity. The presence of a species may also depend upon the density of herbivores or intensity of competition from other species of seaweeds and sessile animals. The cumulative impact of interacting physical factors explains in large part why the marine plant flora of Prince Edward Island in the relatively warm and sandy Gulf of St Lawrence (figure 6.1) differs somewhat from that of the exposed and rocky outer Atlantic Coast of Nova Scotia, and also why the nearby Bay of Fundy, with its huge tides and distinctive sea temperature regime, has its own distinctive combination of species.[6]

As fascinating as this interplay of geological, meteorological, and biological forces is, it is not enough to fully account for the presence of all

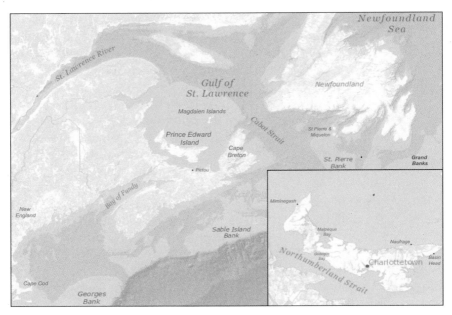

Figure 6.1 The Atlantic provinces and south to Cape Cod, showing the locations of Prince Edward Island in the Southern Gulf of St Lawrence, the Bay of Fundy, New England, and Cape Cod, the Magdalen Islands belonging to Quebec, and the St Pierre and Miquelon Islands belonging to France. Inset map shows locations of PEI's Malpeque Bay, Bedeque Bay, the Northumberland Strait, and Miminegash, the "Irish Moss Capital of the World."

the seaplants in PEI waters. In this chapter, we explore how a more recent force – human intervention – has also helped to shape the Island's unique assemblage of macro-algae (large seaplants); and how seaplants have shaped the Island's human culture and economy. Over time, the interplay of marine plants and human communities has seen the seaplant resource shift from being a subsistence food and medicine to a commercial opportunity, to a global commodity. In a scenario worthy of Hardin's epithet "the tragedy of the commons,"[7] some seaplant resources have, in the process, been driven to the verge of commercial extinction, reducing a once-thriving rural industry to a cultural anachronism. The arc of this slice of environmental history traverses issues of gender, accentuates the plurality of rural livelihoods, reveals links between globalization, technological change, social justice, and environmental sustainability, and questions the role of government in marine environmental management.

ON MALPEQUE BAY

We begin our exploration in a body of water where the traces of post-glacial geological, climatic and anthropogenic changes are particularly apparent: Malpeque Bay. In the context of Prince Edward Island, Malpeque Bay is a significant body of water that threatens to bisect the western end of the island (figure 6.1 inset). Only a slender strip of sandstone separates it from Bedeque Bay and the Northumberland Strait to the south. One of Malpeque Bay's claims to fame is its status as a Ramsar Convention Site, recognized as an ecosystem of global significance for the waterfowl that rest and feed on its shallow mudflats and marshes during their seasonal migrations. This bay, like other sheltered waters of the Southern Gulf, has the warmest summer water temperatures north of Cape Cod.

Imagine a warm August day on the shore of Malpeque Bay, with barely a breath of wind, the water calm and glassy. Slip on a mask and snorkel and lower your body into the welcoming embrace of the bay, and you enter a world where north meets south in unexpected ways. This is the domain of fishes and lobsters, eelgrass beds and oyster reefs, but you will also see other significant features: marine plants that logically should not be here at all at this northerly latitude, because their native home lies far to the south.

Dasya baillouviana is the most stunning of these exotic southern algae, and adds a particular value to any snorkelling experience. Viewed in its natural habitat, attached to a small rock or shell by a small pad of tissue, the pink, finely branching stems of *Dasya*, covered in fine short hairs, gleam and shimmer with iridescent light. Reach out to touch this plant, which may be more than a metre in height, and it is barely there, just a soft whisper at your fingertips. Pull it from its watery domain, and it collapses into a slippery pink puddle. But spread it on heavy paper, carefully teasing out the intricate branches with a fine brush, and you will have an elegant specimen that, if pressed, dried and framed, makes a work of art.

Griffithsia globifera is distinguished by rosy, branching filaments made up of cells so large that you can count them with the naked eye – a source of wonder for adults and small children alike. This plant is exceedingly soft and fine, but without surface hairs, much less luxuriantly branched than *Dasya*, and most often less than 20 cm tall.

Gracilaria tikvahiae,[8] also a red alga, may reach a metre in length and is relatively coarse and well branched. Slender, purplish red, and rubbery

Figure 6.2 Harvesting *Gracilaria* from a river bank.

when growing in sheltered depths, it can form a hefty, brittle, dark-red mat when growing on the bank of a tidal river (figure 6.2). This species is edible, makes delicious pickles and jellies, and has potential commercial importance as a source of agar. Separated from its closest relatives to the south for thousands of years, it has developed genetic attributes that make it part of a distinctive northern variant of *Gracilaria*.[9] Surveys conducted in 1974 found an estimated 330 tons in Malpeque Bay and twice as much in the neighbouring Cascumpec Bay system,[10] but a commercial harvest has never been attempted.

All of these species are part of a small cluster of warm temperate to tropical marine plants and animals that are not found on the open Atlantic coast anywhere north of Cape Cod. They persist in Malpeque Bay and other sheltered, shallow waters of the Gulf of St Lawrence only because, for a few fleeting weeks in summer, temperatures reach higher than 20°C, often to 25°C or more. There are just enough warm days to allow them to reproduce before the plunging temperatures of late summer and autumn trigger disintegration. Through the long, dark winter months, the small pads or filaments that have developed from reproductive spores and minute embryos, or in some cases, the fragments and basal pads of disintegrated mother plants, shelter under the ice in crevices of shell and sandstone. Then the rays of summer sun reawaken them for another frantic burst of growth and reproduction. But how did these plants, which represent a significant food, biodiversity, and touristic resource to the people of Prince Edward Island, get into the Southern Gulf, so far from their native geographic range? The answer lies in geological history.

ORIGINS

The North Atlantic Ocean came into existence over the period of time from 145 to 65 million years ago.[11] As what is now Eastern Canada split from what is now Europe, the North Atlantic basin opened up gradually (with various fits and starts[12]) from south to north. Marine plants and animals from the southern Pacific and Atlantic Oceans and from the ancient Tethys Ocean to the east[13] moved in to occupy the newly available habitats. Once the opening at the north of the Atlantic Ocean basin was complete, marine plants and animals from more northerly waters gained access to the North Atlantic; later there were additional opportunities for the trans-polar migration of species from the North Pacific into the North Atlantic via the Arctic Ocean.[14]

These immigrants could have occupied suitable habitats on eastern and/or western Atlantic shores. Subsequently, during ice ages, glaciers scoured plants and animals from shallow marine habitats, with the damage being more severe along some shores than on others. For example, during the most recent ice age, glaciers covering eastern North America reached further south than the parallel glaciations of Europe.

Species unable to survive in deep, dark waters along the outer edges of the ice perished. Survivors would have been squeezed south onto the inhospitable sandy shores of southeastern North America, with the result that some went locally extinct. In contrast, on European shores glaciers did not reach as far south, and there were more rocky ice-free areas where seaweeds could persist.[15] From those rocky refugia, a greater variety of marine plants and animals advanced northwards to reoccupy the shores of Europe as the glaciers retreated; some proceeded to island-hop across the northern Atlantic to North America.

This difference in glacial impacts, together with the difficulty many species have in coping with the wider temperature fluctuations of the western Atlantic, explains why the marine flora of Atlantic Canada today is less diverse than that of Europe.[16] The absence of certain European species from the shores of Eastern Canada has had impacts not only on economic development related to marine plant resources but also on the culture of seaplants as food. A comparison of food culture in Prince Edward Island (where many families have Irish ancestry) with that of Ireland quickly reveals that the Irish seaplant cuisine is strongly culturally embedded and involves a more diverse range of species and recipes.[17]

Yet as we know from our foray into the underwater world of Malpeque Bay, PEI's marine biodiversity is unexpectedly rich, with species whose native habitats lie far to the south. This is because of the history of post-glacial climatic changes. Along the eastern shores of North America between 9,000 and 4,500 years ago, the continental shelf rebounded, released from the weight of glaciers that were melting under the influence of a warming climate. The near-shore waters surrounding emergent land masses were relatively shallow and warm.[18] As long as the post-glacial coastal waters of Nova Scotia, Newfoundland, and the Gulf of St Lawrence were shallow, they were under the influence of the warm Gulf Stream from the south, which swept southern species into eastern Canadian waters. The cold, deep current that flowed along the Labrador coast from the northern ice caps was deflected east by the Grand Banks of Newfoundland. But, as the saying goes, what goes up must come down, and so it is with isostatic rebound – the process of recovery after a heavy ice sheet retreats from part of the earth's crust. The rebound or uplift proceeds to a certain point, and then the earth's crust begins to settle back down. This is what is happening in many parts of Eastern Canada, including Prince Edward Island, at the present time. Malpeque Bay is sinking at a rate of 30 cm per century.[19]

As the offshore banks and islands subsided under the waters of the Atlantic, the Labrador Current came across the Grand Banks and Scotian Shelf, pushing the Gulf Stream eastward towards Europe. Inshore waters became deeper and colder; plants and animals had to retreat, adapt, or perish. Many of the southerly species that required warm temperatures for growth and reproduction were replaced by sub-Arctic and cold temperate species migrating in from the north. However, in the relatively shallow waters of the southern Gulf of St Lawrence surrounding Prince Edward Island, a few of the southern species were able to adapt to the ice-covered winter conditions and survive in sheltered embayments, because here, summer water temperatures permitted growth and reproduction. As a result, present-day inhabitants of Prince Edward Island benefit from a unique blend of sub-Arctic, cold temperate, and warm temperate marine plant and animal species.[20]

ABORIGINAL USE OF MARINE PLANTS

The literature concerning how Aboriginal peoples used marine plants over their 10,000 years of pre-colonial history in the southern Gulf of St Lawrence is extremely sparse.[21] In South America, archeological evidence of indigenous use of seaweeds for food and medicine dates back more than 14,000 years,[22] but Aboriginal archaeological sites on Prince Edward Island lack such artifacts. However, Mi'kmaq elders interviewed by a researcher from the Institute of Island Studies in 2008[23] recounted how their ancestors used kelp to help strengthen and straighten babies' legs – just as Aboriginal people of southern Chile (whom she also interviewed) use a related kelp to heal broken bones. The common sea lettuce was known to one Mi'kmaq elder as a remedy to clear the complexion, sooth jellyfish stings, and remove warts, while various other seaplants were used to ease sore throats and treat burns and bruises.

We have no evidence that Aboriginal peoples disturbed the abundance or diversity of marine plant life around Prince Edward Island, but the next wave of seaweed consumers – European settlers wielding industrial technologies – certainly did.

MARINE PLANT INVADERS

When sailing ships carried seekers of better fortune from Europe to the New World in the 1700s and 1800s, the boats had to be laden with heavy ballast, because the human cargo was too light to keep the ships stable in rough seas. The common custom was to fill the hold with rocks collected from harbour shores. Upon reaching Canada, where a load of migrants would be replaced by a load of much heavier timber, the excess ballast rocks would be tossed out. In some cases, they landed in shallow water with fragments of living seaweeds still attached. And in some cases, because of the relative poverty of the marine flora of the western Atlantic, these were seaplants hitherto unknown in the Canadian ports where they were deposited. In this way, two prominent seaweed species, *Fucus serratus* and *Furcellaria lumbricalis*, were introduced from Europe into the Gulf of St Lawrence. We know of these introductions because of their absence or single-site occurrence in extensive collections of plants and animals made between 1816 and 1887.[24] Their spread from initial sites of occupation was subsequently confirmed.[25]

Fucus serratus, commonly known as rockweed or serrated wrack, is one of a family of seaplants that occupy rocky habitats throughout the North Atlantic. Considering its wide distribution in Europe, it seems strange that *Fucus serratus* was not part of the native flora of eastern Canada. Perhaps it became extinct in North America during some past ice age, or perhaps it evolved in Europe after the Atlantic Ocean Basin had formed, and failed to find its way to western Atlantic shores until helpful *Homo sapiens* provided ships for transport. Genetic studies have established the locations of glacial refugia of the species in Europe, and the European origins of populations transported at various times to Iceland, the Faeroe Islands, and Nova Scotia.[26] First recorded in 1869 at Pictou, it was common throughout the Northumberland Strait by 1887 and reached the outer shores of Nova Scotia by 1903.[27] *Fucus serratus* has potential commercial value as a source of medicinal and industrial extracts such as alginate and fucoidan, and as livestock feed, fertilizer, and soil amendment, but has been overlooked in favour of its larger native relative, *Ascophyllum nodosum*, which is commercially harvested in Nova Scotia and New Brunswick.[28]

Furcellaria lumbricalis also caught a ride on the early settler ships. This plant was historically harvested in the Baltic Sea as a source of furcellaran, a carbohydrate having industrial applications in food processing. It was first recorded by de la Pylaie[29] as being exclusive to the shores of the French islands of St Pierre and Miquelon near the eastern entrance to the Gulf of St Lawrence. Like *Fucus serratus, Furcellaria* subsequently spread around the shores of the Southern Gulf and eventually broke out onto the shores of the open Atlantic.[30] Although well studied[31] because of its potential commercial importance, it has always been only a minor by-catch in Prince Edward Island's seaweed industry (see below). A cold-water alga, *Furcellaria* tolerates only brief periods of exposure to water that is over 20°C, and so its foothold in the Southern Gulf in this era of climate change and rising seawater temperatures is tenuous.

Let's return to Malpeque Bay, don our mask and snorkel, and have another look. It will not take long to encounter a large green seaplant, *Codium fragile ssp. tomentosoides*, that also does not belong in the bay. This exotic invader hails from Japan and was initially introduced into the waters of northeastern United States in the late 1950s, possibly along with shellfish that were imported for aquaculture purposes.[32] It gradually moved north, reaching the coast of Nova Scotia in the 1980s and the Gulf of St Lawrence in 1996.[33] In Malpeque Bay, warm sheltered water was only one of the attractions.[34] The common name for this seaweed is "oyster thief," and Malpeque Bay, a world-renowned source of Malpeque oysters,[35] provides ample opportunities for thievery. *Codium* is extraordinary, being made up of a mass of entangled filaments and resembling cotton wool in texture. Its branching fingers, reaching 30 cm long, puff up with oxygen generated by photosynthesis during daylight hours. The plant most often grows attached to small rocks and shells in shallow, sheltered bays and so, when it is puffed up and buoyant, a current or wave can easily dislodge it from the bottom. It can then be tossed by waves – together with the stone, mussel or oyster to which it is attached – onto shore. After a major storm, shore-cast oysters attached to oyster thief plants can amount to a million-dollar loss for PEI's shellfish industry.[36]

Although serious, the impact of the oyster thief pales in comparison with that of animal species introduced to the Island's marine waters since 2000. Currently (2014) Prince Edward Island is afflicted with eleven known species of exotic marine invertebrates believed to have been accidentally introduced in ballast waters or on the hulls of ships. Some of these invaders cause serious damage to shellfish industries,[37] and their wider ecological impacts are poorly understood, if at all.

THE IRISH MOSS CAPITAL OF THE WORLD

The most famous of Prince Edward Island's seaplants is Irish moss (*Chondrus crispus*), also known as carrageen, a cold temperate species found throughout the North Atlantic. The ancestor of Irish moss is believed to have originated in the North Pacific and entered the Atlantic via the Arctic Ocean between 80 million and 40 million years ago.[38] Prince Edward Islanders of French and British origins may have had grandmothers who cooked Irish moss pudding[39] or prepared a soothing carrageenan jelly to treat cold, flu, bronchitis, and sore throat. Modern science has confirmed that carrageenan is not only antiviral but also can reduce blood cholesterol and guard against the effects of diabetes.[40] The use of seaweeds containing carrageenan as food and medicine in Europe and among Amerindian tribes dates back thousands of years. In the Caribbean Islands such plants – known generally as "Irish moss," even though they are in fact different species – are touted as aphrodisiacs and form the basis of drinks that are very popular among young men – but not so much among the women they hope to impress ...

Irish moss has been harvested commercially on Prince Edward Island since 1941, when World War II interfered with the supplies of European carrageenan traditionally sourced by American factories. Canada, as part of its war effort, ramped up what had been a minor harvesting effort since the 1920s[41] and developed a new industry to serve the American market.[42] Development of a harvesting industry was greatly aided by the research efforts of Dr Constance Ida MacFarlane, a pioneering female scientist born in Charlottetown in 1904.[43] In the postwar era, up to its peak in the 1960s and 1970s and even beyond, moss harvesting was an important component of many a fishing household's "survival strategy."[44]

Around Prince Edward Island, Irish moss grows on rocks from the intertidal to depths of about ten metres, but because of winter ice that scours the shallows,[45] dense beds are confined to depths greater than two metres – not easily reachable by a person on foot. Initially the moss was harvested from beaches where plants torn from the sea floor by storms drifted ashore and piled up, providing a source of "good easy money"[46] that was free for the picking. No licences were required, and no catch limits or other regulations were imposed until 1977.[47] Men, women, children, and farm horses dragging baskets through the surf laboured together to capture, haul, spread, pick over, dry, and sell moss to international markets. The image of a large work horse in the surf hauling a moss bag, often guided by a child perched on its back, entered the tourist iconography and remains to this day a potent reminder of traditional Island culture.

At first, shoreside racks were built where moss could be spread and dried away from sand and dirt (figure 6.3).[48] Later, people would simply spread the moss on the side of the road. In the 1960s moss buyers invested in fuel-fired dryers, allowing harvesters to sell wet moss directly. But in those families that had the labour force and wanted a higher price, women and children continued to clean and rake over the harvest until dried. This back-breaking work represented one of the few rural occupations where women could earn their own cash, and later, when Unemployment Insurance was made available, women's "moss stamps" also brought a small income into the household in the winter season. As with the Irish fisherwomen of Newfoundland,[49] even such a slender

Figure 6.3 Gilbert Gillis of Point Prim, PEI, demonstrates traditional mossing equipment.

thread of economic independence can be critical to rural women's development of power and agency within families and rural communities.

The coastal village of Miminegash in western Prince Edward Island proudly declared itself the "Irish Moss Capital of the World," but harvesting of storm-tossed moss was practised in other communities along the western and northern shores. Several local companies as well as satellites of larger corporations were established to receive, dry, bale, and export the moss to foreign factories where the carrageenan was extracted.[50] At its peak harvested volume in 1975, the industry contributed more than a million dollars to the province's rural economy.[51] By the late 1980s, landed value of moss on PEI reached $2.7 million. For several decades, mossing was the sole support of about one hundred families on the Island and a source of partial income to at least five hundred more,[52] but for various reasons this was not sustainable.

Because shore-cast moss was not in sufficient volume to feed the global demand, lobster fishing boats were fitted out with metal rakes to drag moss from deep-water beds, starting in the 1950s. Despite attempts to develop rakes that could pluck the fronds without disturbing the bottom,[53] intensive raking during and after the all-too-brief "bonanza period"[54] (1965–75) took its toll both on the moss beds and on juvenile lobsters and other creatures smashed by the rakes.[55] Beds were heavily damaged, allowing other species (such as the relative newcomer *Furcellaria*)[56] to become established, reducing the efficiency and profitability of the fishery.[57] Irish moss harvests on PEI declined from their peak of 24,000 tons in 1975 to 7,000 wet tons in 2004.[58] The harvest of shore-cast "mixture" containing Irish moss and *Furcellaria* also declined after the high point in 1970–71 of 10,000 tons per year. In 1998, a survey of fishing families in the Naufrage area of PEI revealed that only one in ten were still harvesting Irish moss from the shore.[59]

The industry suffered from the lack of value-added processing on the Island, but an attempt by the Prince Edward Island Marine Plants Co-op to establish a carrageenan extraction plant in the years 1969–72 failed, leaving harvesters very much at the mercy of a handful of multinational buyers.[60] The overfishing of moss was in part driven by the low shore price paid by these buyers to harvesters who were barely surviving financially. In the 1940s moss buyers paid 1–2 cents per wet pound, equivalent to 5–10 cents per pound dried,[61] and this price prevailed into the 1950s. By 1980, the price to harvesters had reached 30 cents per dry pound, but this dropped to 17 cents in 1982, precipitating the first harvesters' strike.[62] At that time, 61 per cent of PEI fishing families had incomes less than $10,000/yr, and 20 per cent of this income was derived from Unemployment Insurance.[63] The costs of living and of running a boat were steadily increasing, while the price set by international buyers of Irish moss on PEI remained low, sparking further strikes in 1984 and 1989. Perhaps the most remarkable aspect of this local revolt against globalized capitalism was the leadership role played by female harvesters working under the banner of Women in Support of Fishing of Miminegash.[64] As one participant commented, moss could still be seen drying "in most yards" in Miminegash and nearby villages of St Edward and Pleasant View at that time – evidence of women's work. It was mainly the women who "cared to attend" the strike organizing meetings.[65] In 1989 the price paid for moss on PEI was only 25 cents per pound, and globalized buyers were exploring even cheaper alternatives available from Southeast Asia and South America.

Because the price failed to provide adequate compensation for labour and expenses, some enterprising harvesters tossed rocks and sand into the moss to increase the weight on the buyers' scales (Novaczek, pers. obs.). In spite of being a source of very high-quality carrageenan, Irish moss from Prince Edward Island lost favour in the global market, because dirt in the product ruined expensive extraction machinery in processing plants located in the United States and Europe.[66] The processors – powerful, vertically integrated global corporations linked to pharmaceutical, food processing, and chemical industries – also discovered that a small amount of high-quality carrageenan from Irish moss could be blended with large quantities of lower-cost, poorer-quality carrageenans derived from tropical seaweeds. By the late 1980s, with Southeast Asian seaweed cultivation firmly established and feeding the global food processing industry, companies felt free not only to ignore strikes but also to abandon the Island's seaweed harvesting communities entirely.

Direct harvesting from moss beds, which involved as many as 160 boats in the years 1975–90, was reduced to eighty boats by 1994, and twenty to thirty boats by 2004.[67] When several corporations withdrew their buyers in the 1990s, the Island lost a critical economic resource for rural communities and in particular, for the women and children in the rural labour force.[68] The mossing culture of intergenerational collective shore work also began to fade away.

The cultural history of Irish moss on Prince Edward Island cannot be complete without mention of the Island's first, and to date only, marine protected area, established at Basin Head in 2005, by the federal Department of Fisheries and Oceans. Situated near the northeastern tip of the Island, Basin Head was protected as an example of a coastal lagoon ecosystem, but also because it contains a unique strain of Irish moss, popularly known as "giant moss." These plants are not attached to hard substrate by a holdfast but are held down by byssal threads of mussels. Beginning life as clonal fragments of mother plants, they grow to the size of large dinner plates edged with frilly protrusions – much different in shape and size from the modest clumps of Irish moss fronds attached to coastal rocks (figure 6.4).

In 1970, Basin Head giant moss was taken to be cultivated and studied at a National Research Council laboratory in Nova Scotia[69] and was later acquired by Acadian Seaplants Inc. as the basis for development of various edible seaplant products.[70] Meanwhile, in its native habitat, the

Figure 6.4 A small frond of typical outer coast Irish moss (*bottom left*) contrasts with a much larger specimen collected from a tidal river.

plant was hard pressed to survive deteriorating conditions. Smothering by sea lettuce (*Ulva lactuca*), a rise in water temperatures, and damages from storms and invasive species steadily depleted the population[71] to the point where giant moss may now be on the road to extinction.

The smothering of the bottom at Basin Head by sea lettuce is a consequence of eutrophication – the overloading of a marine ecosystem with nitrogen that comes from agricultural fertilizers, manures, and sewage leaking or dumped into waterways. Thus, the cultural history of Irish moss is linked to the saga of exploitation and (mis)management of agricultural land and surface waters on PEI (see MacFadyen, Arsenault, and

Curley, this volume). Nitrogen stimulates fast-growing "weedy" seaplant species such as sea lettuce. Every summer, sea lettuce rapidly forms massive mats in many Prince Edward Island estuaries. These mats die, sink to the bottom, and rot, stripping oxygen from the water, smothering eel grass and shellfish, and causing fish kills in as many as twenty-one different estuaries.[72] Experimental sea lettuce harvests were undertaken in 2011. Unfortunately, a single harvesting effort made little impact, the cost of harvesting was high, and the harvested seaweed, although potentially an excellent organic fertilizer, was not well received by the farmers who applied it to their lands on an experimental basis.[73]

AN ALTERNATIVE SEAPLANT INDUSTRY

As Irish moss buyers were abandoning western Prince Edward Island in the early 1990s, the federal government had already all but closed down the research station in Miminegash that had been central to marine plant research supporting the Irish moss industry. Women in Support of Fishing, led by Helen Deagle of Miminegash, and with ACOA funding,[74] explored the potential for a low-volume, high-value-added processing effort that could turn Island seaweeds into products for health food markets. They investigated the edible seaweed industry in Maine and the health food markets in urban Canada. Solar dryers were constructed, a line of hand-harvested seaplant products based on a variety of edible and medicinal species were developed, and the village of Miminegash donated an under-utilized building to house the fledgling initiative.[75]

Unfortunately, these women – the same group that had led the strike for fair prices for moss harvesters – were ahead of their time. The health food seaweed market, now a significant, rapidly growing sector, was still in its infancy. The goal of Women in Support of Fishing was dignified seasonal employment that would allow them to make a modest living while also taking care of children, elders, church, school, and other commitments during the winter. Their apparent lack of financial ambition as well as their vision of a grassroots co-op selling locally developed health foods was seen as some sort of idealistic aberration. Funders refused to support them further unless they shifted their target to tourism, which was considered a safer bet. In the end, Women in Support of Fishing developed a small Irish moss interpretive centre dedicated to a dying industry, and the Seaweed Pie Café. The enterprise provided seaweed pie and other edible delights to adventuresome tourists who made it off the well-beaten path to Green Gables.[76] However, tourism in western PEI is marginal, and after almost twenty years in operation, the café did not open for business in the summer of 2013.

The Constance MacFarlane Seaplant Symposium, convened by the Institute of Island Studies in September 2008, brought together regional and international scientists and entrepreneurs interested in exploring the potential for growing and diversifying Atlantic Canada's seaweed industry.[77] On the Island, efforts had already been started to use various rockweeds, kelps, and storm-cast mixtures in compost and livestock feeds. Several entrepreneurs had developed seaweed-based health and beauty products.[78] One couple had piloted a touristic experience called "Seaweed Secrets," including a trip to the shore and a meal featuring seaweed pie. These new small businesses, rooted in the Island's moss harvesting tradition, provide dignified employment and deliver products to the marketplace that are positive contributions to quality of life. They appear to be much more carefully managed to ensure sustainability, and operate at a more appropriate scale, compared to the previous efforts in industrial harvesting for global commodity markets.

A CLOUDED CRYSTAL BALL

Rates of coastal erosion around Prince Edward Island have doubled in the past decade, as a result of climate changes. Deposition of eroded sediments can smother seaweed beds,[79] while rising ocean temperatures compromise growth and reproduction of important sub-Arctic and cold temperate species.[80] Increasing acidity of the sea resulting from the absorption of carbon dioxide will dissolve calcium carbonate from both shellfish and coralline seaweeds. Trends of deoxygenation and acidification apparent in the world's oceans are much more advanced in the Gulf of St Lawrence with its limited flushing and heavy inputs of land-washed pollutants, and this deterioration is reflected in profound, ongoing changes in the gulf's food webs.[81] Scientific data gaps abound, and our understanding of the ecosystem is very limited.

We started this exploration of seaplants in Malpeque Bay, always a highly significant site in the culture and livelihood of the Island's Aboriginal people. In future the bay has the potential to provide dignified livelihoods for Islanders of all sorts, whether native, settler, or newcomer. The seaplants of the bay, if their value is recognized, can play their part beside the eels and waterfowl, oysters and lobsters, in nourishing and supporting future generations. But the future of seaweeds as an economic resource is bound up with many complex issues: climate change, unsustainable land use practices, destructive harvesting technologies, the need for fair returns for harvesters, the roles of women in the Island's social economy, protection of inshore marine ecosystems, and adoption of new forms of sustainable enterprise. Seaplants and other limited but renewable Island resources could be the basis for rural development that is coherent with local values and skills and enhances quality of life – but only if the resources and their supporting ecosystems are carefully restored and conserved, and then exploited only at the scale appropriate to a small island.

III

Harvesting Land and Sea: Development and the Environment on Prince Edward Island

Rankle-hearted jay, why are you scolding
Me working in my own field?
Perhaps you think the land's not mine?
Maybe she isn't, it's been in the family
For generations I'd count if I took the time;
On some occasions been well peopled
With other sweaty men, mostly neighbours
And just now much of this machinery
Isn't mine. It's borrowed. Or will be lent
Since we must take care of each other
Whilst counting every dollar made or spent.

Milton Acorn, "Island Farm," *Dig Up My Heart*

7

The Fertile Crescent:
Agricultural Land Use on Prince Edward Island, 1861–1971

Joshua MacFadyen

This chapter is an environmental historian's reading of a period commonly understood as the "golden age" – and subsequent decline – of agriculture in PEI. The primary sector has been the rudder of the Island's economy, and the potato its most famous crop, but seeing Island agriculture through the eyes of the potato is myopic. Potatoes have been grown successfully on PEI since the first British settlement, providing an excellent food source and a valuable trade good. Historians have long called it the Island's most important cash crop, and governments and environmentalists have tried to mitigate its effect on the Island's soil and habitat; but for most of the Island, and most of the Island's history, the potato has not had a significant effect on land use.

The crop did eventually encourage mechanization, capitalization, and large-scale farming, but this process occurred mainly in certain areas and relatively late compared to other agricultural regions. In the second half of the twentieth century, the Island became a mosaic of small livestock and dairy farms juxtaposed with large potato farms, and visitors took notice. The countryside was a commodified tourist landscape, and many postwar visitors, from back-to-the-landers to tourists to agricultural economists, styled the island as a museum preserving a simpler time, punctuated by eye-pleasing and wealth-generating pockets of deep red potato fields (see MacEachern, this volume).[1] The emphasis on potatoes and mechanization detracts from a sector that was far more important to the Island's agroecosystems, economy, and way of life: a mixed husbandry characterized by horses, cattle, pigs, and sheep, and the systems required to feed them. These animals were partners, unequal but essential, and the origins of the current landscape stems as much from these systems as any other in the Anthropocene. One of those systems was a calcareous soil treatment called "mussel mud," which helped Island farmers produce some of the country's highest per-capita crops of hay and oats.[2] This chapter examines PEI land use (and sea use) through the eyes of its livestock, moving beyond the tuber to the more significant, arguably less glamorous, determinants of ruminant metabolism and river mud.

PEI has been called the "garden of the Gulf," a phrase coined in 1871 and used to market the new seed potato industry in the 1920s, but for most of its history it was the region's pasture.[3] Social and economic histories of other colonies point to a variety of agricultural crises in the nineteenth century.[4] Prince Edward Island's was similar in that it experienced rapid growth on limited land, but a physiological difference in the Island's geology exacerbated the problem. PEI soil has a medium to low level of natural fertility, as well as excessive acidity, erodibility, and drainage.[5] Its light sandy soil makes it excellent for row crops and relatively poor for cereals. But in the nineteenth century, grains and other grasses were considered the path to high farming, in part as cash crops but primarily as fodder crops for livestock. In this way, hay was an indirect cash crop, converting the product of the land into a more valuable product through the ruminant metabolism of cattle and sheep. As one environmental historian phrased it, raising livestock made plants "incarnate."[6] Before mechanization, Island farmers did not have the means to harvest and handle much more than a few acres of potatoes per farm; otherwise they might have specialized in the crop over a century before the arrival of Cavendish Farms and other large processors. Instead, early Island farmers focused their efforts on a crop that did not grow particularly well without soil treatment: hay. In New England the products of meadows "underlay the entire colonial agricultural system," and as Brian Donahue's environmental history of colonial Concord argues, "fundamentally, the amount of hay that could be cut determined the number of cattle that could be kept, and cattle were the key to both subsistence and wealth."[7] The same was true in PEI of cattle, and to a lesser degree sheep, although, like Alan Olmstead and Paul Rhode, we see that animal husbandry and the relationship between animals and their feed crops were constantly in flux.[8]

Most discussions of nineteenth-century PEI have been shaped by the "Land Question," the debates surrounding the Island's early land distribution system of leaseholding and absentee landownership. However, few scholars have considered the effect of the Land Question on the land.[9] The general assumption is that the tenant farmer had no interest in stewardship and soil management and preferred, as the 1860 Land Commission stated, "to take all that he can get out of the land while the opportunity continues." As Douglas Sobey cautions, the commissions were one-sided documents interested in underestimating the value of tenant land.[10] Historians who compare Island agriculture with other places operating under freehold systems might find, as Catherine Wilson's recent study does, that tenancy was a viable strategy in its own right and the improvements made by tenants and even squatters were protected by centuries-old legal systems.[11] Tenancy had no obvious effect on Island farmers' likelihood to use soil treatments in the 1860s. The period under focus (1861–1971) spans a long run of Island history falling between the Land Question and the 1969 Comprehensive Development Plan. The patterns of land use from that eulogized golden age through the period of readjustment and what some Island historians call "the break" were in fact relatively stable and less constrained by these terminal events.

EXPANSION: THE MILLION-ACRE FEEDLOT

As in most new agricultural settlements, PEI farmers expanded their enterprises slowly in the early nineteenth century. Sparse population and nascent transportation, communication, and capital infrastructure exacerbated the normal limitations of farming under the organic, or the pre-industrial, farm regime. Farm production was always limited by the amount of material and energy inputs required to clear farms, erect buildings, fence pastures, feed animals, plant crops, and replenish soil nutrients. These inputs came from a variety of sources – the farm household, the local community, external society, and recycled internal sources – and production was impossible without them. Farmers understood the balancing act this required, and they made livestock a key part of farm-making. They understood the old adage "More crops, more animals; more animals, more manure; more manure, more crops."[12] By the mid-nineteenth century the Island farm economy was expanding rapidly in population, acres of cropland, and numbers of livestock. Figure 7.1 shows the relative importance of each livestock type, and particularly

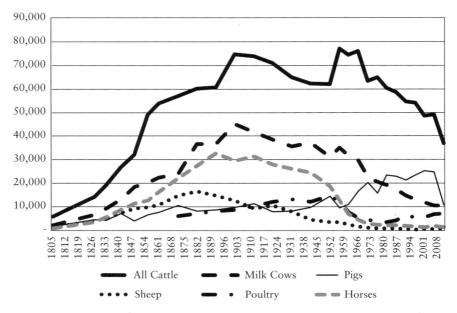

Figure 7.1 Livestock units in Prince Edward Island, 1805–2011 (in units of 500 kg).

the dramatic rise of beef cattle in the 1850s. Cattle represented over 60 per cent of the total weight of livestock units in this period.[13]

The first period examined in detail in this chapter (1861–1921) is usually portrayed as a harmony of pre-industrial agriculture, egalitarianism, plentiful subsistence, and community cohesion. In Nova Scotia the same period has been called a golden age of agriculture.[14] For over a century, according to Errol Sharpe, "the farmers of P.E.I. lived in communities barely touched by the outside world,"[15] and Lorne Callbeck maintained that in the mid-nineteenth century Islanders experienced "years of plenty."[16] Although the period was one of economic growth bolstered by the shipbuilding industry, it did not directly benefit all farmers, and large shortages, inequalities, and geographic disparities existed. Most townships remained predominantly in forest by 1861, while others experienced rapid clearing. Economic stratification was also visible socially. The rise of agricultural societies at mid-century reflected the affluence of gentlemen farmers around Charlottetown more than the general adoption of high-farming methods such as intensive rotations and soil treatment, and Marian Bruce and Elizabeth Cran argue that their decline in the 1850s was because "the club ... lost touch with the ordinary farmer."[17] Although some areas might have relied primarily on subsistence farming, others were actively exporting potatoes to Quebec and hay to Nova Scotia and trading widely in local markets. However, affluence was a matter of scale, not scope, and in many places dramatic shortages existed.[18]

The most important source of animal fodder in the early British resettlement period was marsh hay (*Spartina patens*).[19] This grew naturally in all of the Island's salt marshes and on dyked wetland, but the amounts were small and the demand for beef and draft animals quickly outpaced the capacity of the marsh hay harvest. In the 1850s and early 1860s, Island farms experienced a serious shortage in the amount of hay and other feed for livestock. Contemporary experts argued that the average cow required one ton of hay and plenty of straw to survive the winter. Sheep ate considerably less, but horses could eat more than twice as much fodder, depending on their size and activity. In the early nineteenth century the average hay-fed animal (horses, cattle, and sheep) survived on 700 pounds of hay, a small quantity of oats, and whatever they could forage through the snow, but by 1861, the amount of hay available per animal dropped precipitously by more than half.[20]

One of the soil's distinctive signatures was well known to anyone who attempted to farm it. The Island's soils are "sour" or highly acidic, producing poor grains and worse hay without pH treatment. Matthew Hatvany shows how the price for hay in the mid-nineteenth century shot up over 330 per cent in the spring as supplies dwindled, and farmers who could not feed their animals sold them off.[21] He argues that this cycle exacerbated the already significant economic stratification among Island farmers. Figure 7.2 demonstrates that the size of livestock herds fluctuated significantly by geographic location, but the diversity of livestock units was remarkably consistent across the province. Only the Royalties and a few other townships had an abnormally high or low share of one livestock type, probably because the urban areas required more cattle, and because some townships, like Lot 53 near Cardigan and Lot 63 near Murray River, reported almost no pigs. The most striking pattern visible in the 1871 data was the widespread caloric shortage in each township's hay crop. The average township produced only 58 per cent of the annual feed demand on local farms, and only five townships and Charlottetown Royalty produced a surplus. Most townships simply did not produce enough hay to sustain their livestock through the winter.[22]

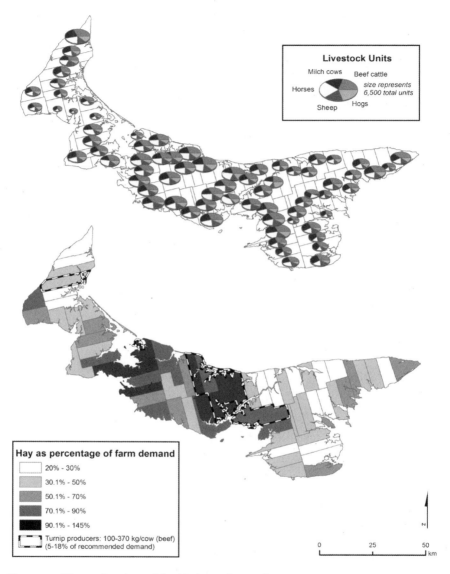

Figure 7.2 Livestock units and feed balance (hay and roots), 1871.

Most of the animals surrounding the Island's capital and its second-largest town, Summerside, were adequately fed on the local supplies of hay, but just barely. Many townships with large herds produced less than 70 per cent of the fodder required to feed them, and many more areas produced even less. Turnips and oats were used to supplement the fodder, but the high-value oat crop was usually exported or reserved for working draft animal (horses and oxen) and human nutrition.[23] In fact, farmers faced a substantial feed deficit at the same time that Island ports exported large amounts of grain and root crops to other colonies. The exports of feed and livestock products surged ahead in the mid-nineteenth century, making PEI the only Atlantic province with agricultural surpluses.[24] The most important export was oats, which had increased from 47,000 bushels in 1829 to 322,000 at mid-century. By 1855, the Island exported over half a million bushels, and the largest shipments (43 per cent of the Island's oat exports) were sent out of the port of Charlottetown. The ports of Georgetown and Bedeque (Summerside) followed at 10 and 9 per cent, respectively. By 1865, the geography of the grain trade was similar, with oat exports even slightly more concentrated in these ports, but the amount exported had tripled. Charlottetown shipped 795,000 bushels (46 per cent), and Bedeque and Georgetown between them shipped another 373,000 bushels.[25] The residues from these oats were almost certainly added to the local bedding and feed demand. Turnips were commonly recommended for fattening beef cattle in the nineteenth-century agricultural literature, and figure 7.2 indicates that some of the townships with the largest hay crops were also notable turnip producers.[26] However, the turnips reported in 1871 were modest, up to 15 per cent of the root crop was exported, and the remaining produce usually provided less than a tenth of the recommended feeding rates.

The majority of the Island's livestock were starved for fodder in this period, and it is no wonder that most farmers turned the animals into the forest in a process known as "wood pasturing." Douglas Sobey finds it "hard to believe that cattle, as well as sheep, would have been able to sustain themselves from the ground vegetation … especially [in] the upland hardwood forest with its comparatively sparse ground cover." He suggests that increased vegetation from forest fires, felled trees, and wet forest types would have improved the available sustenance.[27] The 1871 data support this conjecture and suggest that wood pasturing remained an important practice, especially in the wet softwood forests (see Sobey, this volume).

Many references to the practice of wood pasturing were made in the early nineteenth century, including Walter Johnstone's notes on the general paucity of fodder. Islanders, he said, "have no green feeding for their cattle in winter … and the swine are so poorly fed, that if they get hold of a fowl they will eat it alive ... From the poor way in which their cattle are fed during the winter, some of them die in weakness, or when driven out to the woods in this state, they are more in danger of getting mired, as well as falling prey to the wild beasts."[28] Wood pasturing was also recorded by farmer-diarists like George E. Meggison whose "five head of cattle came home from the woods" in Lot 5 in November 1817. Meggison also "turned out the pigs" late in the following winter, which was such a common practice that some became feral and had to be hunted, according to an 1876 questionnaire.[29] Agricultural societies called the wood-pastured bovines "half-starved, stunted, thriftless cattle, unfit alike for milk or beef," and demanded legislation to limit free-range livestock. Butchered animals were so small that Elinor Vass argued it was common to see farmers coming from the market carrying two entire carcasses of veal, one under each arm.[30] By 1871, the hay crop had increased significantly, but many cattle would have still starved in the forest if they were not sold, and a large proportion of the sheep must have been butchered young. For most of the province, these were not yet years of plenty.

One of the many problems of turning 200,000 animals out into the woods was the loss of most of their nitrogen-rich manure. Throughout the mid-nineteenth century, agricultural experts chided Island farmers for their unscientific use of fertilizers and lime. In 1871 the census enumerator for Lot 66 found the local "tillage system very inferior, and manure making, if possible worse."[31] Most farmers were thus unable to collect fertilizer or afford lime. PEI has no significant limestone deposits, and importing lime to increase soil alkalinity was expensive and unpopular. There were three other solutions to the fodder shortage: farmers could raise their production of grains, clear new land, or treat the soil with calcium carbonate.

The first solution, to produce more grains, generally entailed growing oats and barley in short rotation. Oats, especially black oats, had always been the main feed for horses and draft animals, and they yielded well on both new land and established rotations.[32] Islanders considered barley "too hot" or too high in energy for horses, so it was not grown much until the mid-twentieth century, usually as a feed for hogs. Oats were also important to the livestock economy because they were the best source of bedding and the straw absorbed more moisture than barley or wheat. Both twentieth-century geographers, such as Andrew H. Clark, and the nineteenth-century experts noticed a trend in the "poor-farming" townships. Agricultural society members frequently complained about farmers planting oats every year without proper rotation, and, according to Clark, the census of 1891 showed peculiar concentrations of cropping in newly settled areas. He believed that "the smaller units of improved land were tilled with a surprisingly marked intensity to squeeze out subsistence crops of potatoes, oats and hay," but a consideration of the fodder shortages in these areas seems to suggest that these farmers were maximizing the productivity of new soil to feed their expanding herds.[33]

The second solution – clearing new land – was effective in both high-farming and newly established areas. In 1861, the average Island farmer lived on properties that were only about 38 per cent "arable," or cleared to the extent they could be cropped. If all lands, including the 30 per cent of the colony not yet in farms, were taken into consideration, then only about a quarter of the Island had actually been deforested.[34] However, farmers were busily clearing their land to provide crops and pasture for the livestock economy, and younger generations were beginning to acquire and clear new farms. The felled trees also supplied an immediate need for lumber, fencing, and fuel. John MacEachern of Rice Point hauled loads of cord wood for urban consumers across the frozen Charlottetown Harbour in the winter months. His diary noted that he was clearing a small patch of land in the back half of his property "across the brook," and presumably much of this wood went directly to his own hearths and fences and to urban markets.[35]

The amount of cleared land on PEI doubled between 1861 and 1891, and at its highest point (1911), all but a third of the Island had been deforested.[36] The impact of this period on the Island's forests, watersheds, rivers, and estuaries was enormous (see Sobey and Curley chapters, this volume). Like many farmers who immigrated to Prince Edward Island in the early nineteenth century, MacEachern had mature children who wanted land of their own, and the pressure on the forest was directly linked to the colony's rapid population growth.[37] Agricultural clearing expanded equally as fast to keep up with the mid-century rural population growth. After 1861, this growth stagnated in Queens and Kings and started to decrease in the townships east of the capital. Any real population growth in this period was concentrated in Charlottetown, Summerside, and the new farmland in West Prince.[38] Although the new land on Prince Edward Island had more soil nutrients, it was still highly acidic, and clearing did not obviate the need for lime. All of this new land had to be treated for acidity in some way.

Thus, the third solution was to treat the soil with fertilizers to replenish its nitrogen and with calcium carbonate to raise its pH.[39] During the

1860s, farmers did just this, treating about 49,000 acres of acidic soil. Almost 16,000 acres of farmland had been limed by 1871, and the number of lime kilns more than doubled in that decade.[40] Lime applications were effective, but importing lime was expensive, and a seemingly more sustainable alternative existed in the mud just offshore. Known as "mussel mud," this alternative soil treatment actually consisted mainly of oyster shells. As the shells broke down over time, they released calcium carbonate into the soil and increased its pH level. The region's shell mud contained 4.5 per cent calcium carbonate, although this varied widely depending on the concentration of oyster shells in the mud.[41] The 1871 census also shows that over 1,400 digging machines dotted the landscape, and ten townships along the Island's central estuaries had coated over 15 per cent of their cleared land with the mud.

Coastal farmers have used crushed or burnt oyster shells as a lime substitute for centuries,[42] but the amounts were small and required a fishery (see MacDonald and Beck chapter). As early as 1815, farmers like Meggison harvested "canoe loads of mussel shells for the land." They also used seaweed and even live lobsters as manure, but in 1832 a surprisingly proactive conservation law prohibited PEI farmers from burning live oysters (see appendix) and may have unintentionally saved some of the Island's archaeological shell middens, such as the Fewkes site on Robinsons Island.[43] Burning oysters was now illegal, but still, farmers and geologists knew that hundreds of acres of ancient decomposing shell beds lay at their doorstep, providing a reservoir of seemingly free, limitless, and long-lasting soil treatment.[44]

The simple barrier that stood between farmers and these shell beds was the nature of the coast. For half of the day, sea waters covered the shell beds with strong tides and dangerous currents, and when the tide went out, the beds were separated from shore by a buffer of impassible muck. As a result, crop yields languished in the acidic soil, livestock suffered through the long winter on a few hundred pounds of hay each, and observers like John MacGregor wondered "how many of the settlers raise enough to support their families."[45] In 1860, the Land Commission evaluated farms on a number of criteria, including distance from sea manure, and noted that farmers found it "impossible to preserve land in this Island in a state of fertility, for any length of time, without the application of lime, or some other good substitute such as mussel mud, which but few can procure."[46] Then, according to David Weale, an innovative Island resident developed a mechanical digger in the early 1860s (figure 7.3) that allowed operators to harvest the mud through the ice and haul it to their farms by sleigh.[47]

Figure 7.3 Mud diggers on Bedeque Bay.

Digging mussel mud became a PEI winter tradition and a unique part of the province's folklore. The extraction of close to a billion tons of shells, mud, mollusks, and crustaceans for soil treatment also substantially increased the rural quality of life in the late nineteenth century. The brackish rivers of the southern Gulf of St Lawrence, the world's largest estuary, were ideal sites for extracting mussel mud for three reasons: they formed one of the planet's best habitats for *Ostrea*; the watersheds drained some of the region's best habitat for farmers; and the northern climate allowed one to reach the other through holes in the ice.

Most Island histories suggested that mussel-mud digging in Prince Edward Island was ubiquitous, but new data from the relatively unexplored *1871 Census of Prince Edward Island* demonstrate that only eleven of the sixty-seven townships in Prince Edward Island had treated over a thousand acres of land with mud by 1871 (figure 7.4). The highly uneven picture of soil treatment is even more nuanced when we use historical Geographical Information Systems (GIS) to show which lands were most likely the first recipients of mud. Figure 7.4 shows the proportion that could have been treated within a two-mile (3.2 kilometre) distance from the shores of popular mud sites (bays and rivers) in 1900.[48] In Lots 25 and 26, farmers treated about 15 per cent of cropland in the townships, but the land furthest from Bedeque Bay would have received

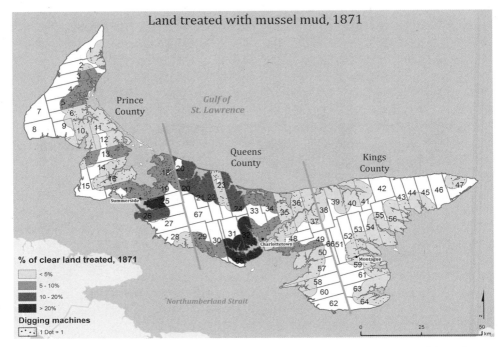

Figure 7.4 Distribution of mussel-mud digging machines, and the proportion of cleared land treated in a two-mile radius from the coast, 1871.

less or no mud. By considering only cleared land within two miles of the bay, we see that cropland was treated at a much higher rate (30 per cent).

Almost immediately, this new form of soil treatment took on features that we commonly associate with industrial farming. Many, and probably most, of the diggers were commercial operators, initially selling mud to farmers for eight to ten cents per load.[49] The principles of supply and demand shaped the industry from there. Only the wealthiest and most established areas of the Island had any significant amount of mud on their farms in 1871. No one in the 1870s would have considered this "traditional" farming; this was a new technology, and tradition meant hungrier animals and poorer farmers. Profiting from the new technology also came with unique risks. Vernon McCarvill hauled mussel mud purchased from diggers in Bedeque Bay, "this side of Holman's Island." Some diggers charged twenty-five cents a load, no matter what the size of the sled. One man put a special box on the sled to maximize the load size, and it sank into a crevice in the ice and came out from under the box, which was then left perched over the crack. McCarvill described this fellow's attempts to empty the two tons of mud, mount the box again on the sleigh, and fill it again by hand as part greed and part ingenuity: "He was on dangerous ground, you see ... he took a chance of losing his team of horses, himself, and everything."[50]

As the Prince Edward Island Railway snaked across the province in the 1870s, it changed the landscape of basic soil treatment and opened the market to farmers unable to haul from central mud sites like Bedeque Bay. Several different boosters proposed to build spur lines to the water's edge, and north to Malpeque Bay in the late nineteenth century, but these did not materialize.[51] Still, the railway moved from 1,000 to 2,500 car loads per year on flatcars like the "Mud Special" in figure 7.5.

One reason people specialized in operating commercial diggers was because knowledge of the river (both its surface and bottom) was so critical. Ice conditions fluctuated quickly, and it was difficult for farmers to anticipate how much they would be able to haul, let alone dig on their own. Basil McNeill bought mud by the load from various outfits in the Alberton area, referring to his suppliers simply by their first names, Warren and Jess. For the better part of two months, when he wasn't socializing with friends or "drunk and scrapping" at local parties, McNeill was hauling mud. According to his diary, an early thaw and soft roads in March 1912 made him conclude, "the hauling is over for this year," but the mild spell and freshets were only temporary and a cold "Nor West Wind" mobilized the diggers for another two weeks. In the first week of April, thanks to weather that was "cold for the time of year," McNeill recorded one of his neighbours was "hauling mud yet."[52]

The mid-nineteenth century yield problem was solved by an enormous outflow of time and capital, and the most dramatic effect of increasing soil pH was the aforementioned increase in hay production. Fodder supplies were still scarce in 1871, but conditions had actually improved by this point. John MacEachern noted in his diary in April 1870 that "hay was plenty and cheaper than for 15 or 20 years past."[53] April was the time of year when those farmers who could afford to save a haystack sold it for a small fortune.[54] By 1875, farmers like William Whitehead argued that without "mussel-mud we would starve on the farms – both man and beast. We could not grow hay enough to feed one horse." Alexander Blue also testified that he "couldn't keep one horse if not for mud." John McLeod claimed he was barely making a living from his farm before mud was introduced, and the soil treatment "increased the crop of hay 10 times."[55] Hay yields per acre varied widely depending on

Figure 7.5 Mud Special (from the oyster beds) on the Prince Edward Island Railway.

the soil, soil treatment, and type of hay in production.[56] Farmers inter-viewed in the 1980s recalled that an excellent crop could yield three tons per acre, but the late nineteenth century provincial average was usually less than one ton per acre.[57] Farming improvements such as mussel mud helped increase the productivity of the soil, but they did not eliminate hunger. Farmers like Bob MacRae, of Pownal, would always remember the greatest challenge of livestock husbandry as "bringing the cows through the winter alive."[58]

The account books of Roderick Munn of Marshfield reveal his soil treatment strategy and how it may have affected yields. The document spans the years 1876 to 1912, including resettlement from Wood Islands to Marshfield in 1880, and a steady period of mud hauling from 1881 to 1888. Based on the timing of his move to Marshfield, the rich shell beds less than five kilometres from his home on the Hillsborough River were a major incentive to buy there. His mud-hauling days produced almost 1,400 loads of mud for his land, requiring hundreds of trips down the "mud road" to the river each winter.[59]

Munn also kept meticulous records of the crops he seeded, harvested, threshed, and sold, and he recorded the amount of hay harvested each year. An examination of crop production between 1877 and 1892 does not reveal any significant increase in the yield per bushel sown of wheat, barley, or potatoes; in fact, they trail down slightly at the end of the period. Figure 7.6 does show a large increase in hay production, around two or three times the 1882 crop.[60] Once the upland hay had received the maximum effect of the mud, the residual effect would help to fertilize subsequent rotations. Munn was an elite farmer who could afford to experiment with different crops and fertilizers,[61] but the mud hauling and hay harvests were staples in his annual production. Not only did he

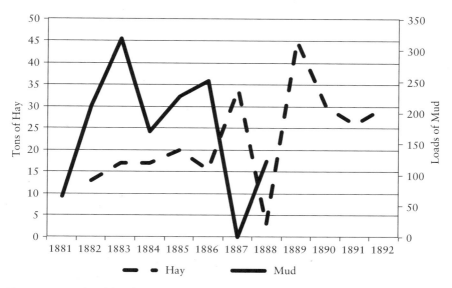

Figure 7.6 Mud and hay harvested by Roderick Munn, 1881–1891.

relocate to have better access to mussel mud but he expended a great deal of time and energy each winter to improve his hay crop.

Between Confederation and the First World War, as Island farmers slowly turned their attention away from the forest, they directed it primarily to the sector's first specialization, hay and pasture land. This use supported the growing beef and lamb industry and provided fodder for the expansion of dairy, the industry that made PEI "the Denmark of Canada" in the 1890s.[62] The increase in the Island's hay crop was impressive. Yields rose 219 per cent in the 1860s, with another 212 per cent increase in the 1870s, followed by a steady increase in the crop's acreage until 1930, despite declines in other land use. A.H. Clark apparently did not have the 1871 census, and so he did not notice the initial increase. He did, however, notice the specialization occurring between 1891 and 1921, and he called "the decrease of cropland as a proportion of improved land an island-wide phenomenon."[63] In other words, this final period of farm expansion primarily about expanding the pasture for livestock.

The land tenure system was often considered the main cause of inequality in PEI, but Hatvany points to several other causes, including environmental limits.[64] He argues that winter hay shortages led to a cycle of poor farmers selling a portion of their herd each winter to those who could afford the fodder. The 1871 census supports this claim. There was a strong correlation between soil treatments and the amount of hay available for each horse, cow, and sheep in the townships. Townships with the largest herds were the most likely to expand their holdings and treat their land with mussel mud in the 1860s. Despite the widely held belief that freeholders were the most likely to consider soil improvements, there was no correlation between the proportion of land treated with mussel mud and the proportion of farmland still held by fee simple (freehold) in 1871.

Mussel mud digging might seem like a troublesome way to coax a plant out of the stubborn soil, and it was. So was clearing a forest. But it was not enough to simply remove the trees, stumps, and stones from the soil; the uplands were relatively barren compared to the productive salt-marshes and almost immediately required pH treatment and nitrogenous fertilizers. This stage required a massive disturbance of estuarine ecosystems and effectively transformed the uplands into extensions of the saltmarsh. Mussel mud was a large part of a metabolic shift in the food systems of nineteenth-century Prince Edward Island. Island crops were oriented toward livestock raising and dairying, not potatoes or other cash crops, and the mussel mud industry was oriented toward hay. The ecological footprint of eating meat in the Maritimes extended deep into the estuaries.

READJUSTMENT AND REVERSION

Following the period of expansion, agriculture in the interwar period was marked by outmigration and farm abandonment in some townships and new livestock and soil management systems in others. Addressing the problem of expansion through improved soil treatments suited the economy and environment of PEI at that time for a variety of reasons, many of which have been outlined by David Weale. The labour of sons was becoming more available as children matured, population grew, and the rate of clearing slowly decreased. The railroad transformed a limited coastal resource into something available to the entire Island; by the end of the century most of its population lived within eight miles of the PEI Railway.[65] This story occurred in time as well as in a place, and the ebb and flow of expansion fits well with settlement trends in other parts of North America. However, unlike New England and central Canada, the Maritime region lacked an urban manufacturing sector to employ its youth, and its best land was now gone. The nadir of the Island's forest also marked the peak of its livestock economy. As the forest all but disappeared from the oldest farms, clearing declined, and outmigration occurred practically uniformly across rural PEI.[66]

In the late nineteenth and early twentieth centuries, PEI farmers experienced a relatively long period known for outmigration and agricultural stagnation. This pattern is usually thought of as the defining economic and cultural story of the Maritimes. It seemed everyone was "goin' down the road," either to work at factories in central Canada and New England, or to visit someone who had. Of those who went south, the overwhelming majority went to Boston and its satellite communities.[67] The Maritime region's early twentieth century "Era of Industrial Ascendancy" was short lived, according to Graeme Wynn. Over half of its factory jobs and about half of the value of its manufactured goods had disappeared by the end of the 1920s.[68] Most historians have focused on the important issue of industry and the relationships with the federal government, usually perceived as working for central Canada's best interests. These historians focused on regional questions, including the linkages between federalism and freight rates and the overall causes of economic decline and outmigration.[69] Julian Gwyn argues that what seemed like growth in the region's farm sector was actually expansion onto non-arable land.[70]

From the early twentieth century, some rural people, tired of living in poverty, were leaving the countryside and leaving the Island. As outmigration continued, many pastures and some entire farms were abandoned. After only a few years without cultivation or intensive grazing, fields began the process of natural reforestation or reversion. When George Perkins Marsh and other New England writers began to notice this trend in the 1850s, they argued that "too much land had been cleared in the first place, much of it marginal for agriculture."[71] In a 1902 address to the Canadian Forestry Association, Father A.E. Burke warned of the complete and imminent destruction of the province's forest due to unrestricted clearing: "Whole settlements may be visited where the farm buildings stand out bleak, bare and storm-beaten, without a single tree to protect, beautify or endear – not one along the roadside, the line fence, the out-places; possibly a bit of coppice on the rear ... to sustain the kitchen stove in hard weather."[72] One of the many problems caused by of the depletion of forests in livestock areas was scarcity of wood for fence posts and rails. The 1931 census argued that "the importance that the woodlot holds in the eastern section of Canada" could not be overstated, and it identified an active trade in fencing from the cedar forests of Prince County to the livestock areas in Queens County.[73] Although Burke's claim sounds apocalyptic, similarly denuded landscapes were common in Canada's other densely settled areas; however, whereas many of these landscapes stabilized, PEI's began to revert to forest.

During the interwar period, cultivated land decreased and the forest experienced a general expansion, from 32 per cent in 1935 to 49 per cent of the area of the province by 1990. The white spruce (*Picea glauca*) was the first species to capitalize on new habitat in the Maritimes, and in PEI reversion appeared predominantly in the steeper highlands of Kings County and the poorly drained soils of west Prince (figure 7.7).[74] The spruce usually self-seeded from the hedgerows of abandoned fields, but L.M. Montgomery in *Jane of Lantern Hill* also framed the language of reversion as a land-use decision. Observed Jane, on returning to Prince Edward Island, "Nothing had changed really, though there were surface changes ... Big Donald had repainted his house ... the calves of last summer had grown up ... Little Donald was letting his hill pasture go spruce. It was good to be home."[75] C.W. Raymond and J.A. Rayburn studied the province's reverting land in aerial photos and divided the Island into three categories: abandoned pasture, "scrub" or reverting pasture, and spruce forests on old fields. Prince Edward Island forest inventories show that "going spruce" was only one part of a complex suite of land cover and land use changes taking place in the twentieth century.[76]

While the predominant trend was reversion, it is clear from figure 7.7 and from Raymond and Rayburn's research that it occurred unevenly across the province. Some areas experienced modest increases in farming, particularly for potatoes, in eastern Prince and central Queens. Islanders had been selling potatoes to Canadian markets since the early nineteenth century, but the most famous tubers to leave the Island were Irish Cobbler seed potatoes, shipped to Leamington, Ontario, from Lot 16 by W.H. McGregor.[77] A vibrant seed potato industry was sparked in the interwar period, including the establishment of a Potato Growers' Association in 1920, but the average farm's land use changed very little.[78] Clark pointed to "a great expansion" of cropland in the 1920s, but actually what he noticed was a modest, and temporary, increase in potatoes roughly equal to the decadal increase in hay.[79]

Part of what made the 1920s "expansion" seem unique was the overall decline of cropland as a proportion of each township in the previous three decades. Clark noted that in many parts of the Island, including the high-farming areas, cropland declined from 40 to 75 per cent of the total

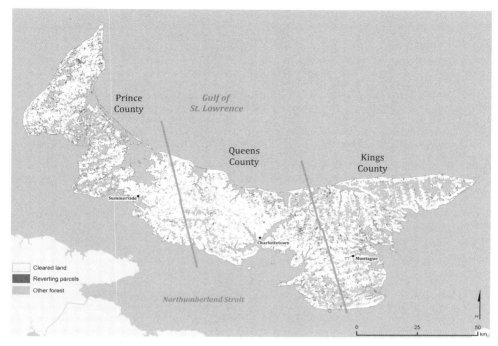

Figure 7.7 Land use and forest reversion, 1935.

area in 1891 to 30 to 50 per cent in 1921.[80] Clark included hay and oats along with crops in all of his calculations, but from a metabolic perspective they should be considered in the same category as pasture. These "crops" were not for feeding people directly but rather for fuelling the Island's work engines and its primary commodity: meat. Table 7.1 shows that by removing hay from cropland and adding it to pasture, Island agriculture of the early twentieth century was primarily about the prolonged development of the fodder and livestock economy. The six townships in this table include selections from each of the Island's three counties and all of the woodland types presented by Sobey (this volume). The results show that the Island's herd was becoming more concentrated in Queen's county, echoing Clark's suggestion that the Charlottetown hinterland was becoming the province's "great cattle region."[81]

If there was a trend toward monoculture across PEI, it was an increasing specialization in cattle, oats, hay, and pasture between 1890 and 1921, at the expense of all the roots (potatoes and turnips) and other

grains (wheat, barley, and mixed grains). It should be noted that, ecologically, hay and pasture are the least destructive specializations, because
they build topsoil, reduce erosion, trap carbon, fix nitrogen, and spread
manures. This raises two points. First, fodder is not the kind of villain-
ous monoculture that critics had in mind when they imagined the end of
a golden age of agriculture. And, second, even ecologically sound land-
use could do little to stem the long-run weakening of the Island economy, the poor quality of life in the countryside compared to other areas,
and the eventual depopulation and loss of services in rural communities. These phenomena occurred gradually and were all in place before
the Comprehensive Development Plan, the rise of large-scale potato
monoculture, and "the break" in Island community history.

At some point during the interwar period, these specialized farmers
switched their soil treatments from mussel mud to imported fertilizers
and lime. As MacDonald argues, "the transition from agriculture as a
way of life to agriculture as industry was gradual, and the mileposts
along that road were degrees of specialization."[82] The 1921 Census of
Agriculture also shows that in the early twentieth century, farmers spent
less than $15 each on fertilizers annually. Ten years later that amount
increased to $74 and remained steady into the 1940s.[83] The standard
explanation has been that potatoes developed harmless but unsightly
scabs from contact with mussel mud, and since potatoes grew well in
slightly acidic soil anyway, the new potato economy allowed farmers to
avoid mud digging by the 1930s. However, just as the Land Question
was an over-simplified solution to social and economic problems on
Prince Edward Island in the nineteenth century,[84] the potato scab is an
inadequate explanation for the decline in mud digging, a practice that
had become such a community-building and value-adding exercise by all
accounts. The potato crop was just too small and localized, and the hay
and fodder crops too important to Island agriculture, to account for the
change in practice. A better explanation will muddy the waters of PEI's
coastal agriculture, and, like most solutions, it will involve a variety of
complex factors.

Rather than hinging on a single crop, this land-use decision reflected the
changing face of agriculture in general and certain environmental problems in particular. Since most of the mud was extracted from three or
four central estuaries at first, reports of exhausted shell beds appeared
in smaller rivers as early as 1875. By 1893, the Federal Department of
Fisheries intervened to identify and protect live oyster beds, and department agents drew lines in the ice that became flashpoints of confrontation

in a predominately agricultural province. Island farmers pushed back by sending petitions to Ottawa and simply ignoring the fisheries agents. In 1901, however, a farmer was successfully charged with digging in a protected area on the North River, and a precedent had been set. After two decades of attempting to manage farmers and fishers, Ottawa handed the problem over to the province, which began to dig mussel mud at St Peter's Bay and distribute it to farmers by rail.[85]

More generally, this was a period of intense outmigration, followed by a sharp reduction in the amount of cleared farmland and a gradual decline in the number of farms. Outmigration caused a labour shortage, which affected both the ability to grow large crops of hay and the ability to dig large quantities of mud. Who would want to dig mud for hay land when the pasture was "going spruce?" Although still preferable to intensive cropping, animal husbandry was labour intensive and a "rugged way of life," according to Arthur Hughes, a mixed farmer in Bedford.[86] In the 1930s, federal officials discouraged the use of sea manures, and the combination of environmental and economic factors led to the decline of mud digging. "The practice of 'muddin' is dying out," federal scientists Frank T. Shutt and L.E. Wright reported, because scientific agriculture had made it more economical to use "commercial fertilizers."[87] By the postwar period, the provincial Department of Agriculture helped farmers to import lime, and applying sea manure seemed archaic in the period of "modern" fertilizers and fossil-fuel based agriculture.[88] Clark himself hardly mentioned the practice of mudding in 1959.

Livestock became even more important as farmers aged; keeping resources on the hoof was a labour solution and an exit strategy. Lands no longer cropped in the early twentieth century became pasture in the mid-twentieth century, partly because of the aging population and declining labour pool.[89] Then, in the 1950s, the geographic disparities visible in table 7.1 became more deeply entrenched. Many small farms tired of maintaining the herd let the pasture "go spruce" and either sold the property or rented the best land to neighbouring farmers. A certain group of those neighbours addressed the labour shortage by investing in tractors, and a smaller subsection, especially in southeast Prince, began specializing in potatoes and investing in the requisite equipment. The decline in the number of farms has always reflected the loss of small operators more than larger ones. Historians Wayne MacKinnon and Elinor Vass noted that large commercial farms dominated the sector in the 1980s, and Arsenault (this volume) shows how the ongoing decline in the number of farms is almost exclusively in the smallest revenue class

($10,000-$99,000).[90] This phenomenon was somewhat exacerbated by census definitions. The definition of "farm" changed in 1961 and eliminated almost two whole townships' worth of agricultural land belonging to "non-commercial" farms.[91]

Despite the rapidly dropping number of farms, the interwar and early postwar period was as much about stability as it was about decline. Clark presented the problem from the context of historical geography. In his opinion, the Island was a "million-acre farm" at the time of Confederation, and it remained so at the time of his writing; rural outmigration continued in 1959 as it had for decades previously, but still "the island's farms produce more of real value than they even [had] in the past."[92] John McClellan argued that although the number of farms dropped rapidly after 1941, the rural population did not: "In many cases the population remains; all that has changed is the census status, from farm to non-farm, as farmers shift to part-time farming and then to no farming at all."[93] Raymond and Rayburn suggested that new programs like employment insurance and universal old-age pension plans were convenient ways to stop what one hadn't been doing anyway.[94]

Although the period from 1861 to 1971 witnessed environmental, social, and demographic upheavals, this chapter argues that land use was also surprisingly stable and strategic, especially in livestock and fodder production. Land use regimes rise and fall, and PEI's cash crops rose and fell more often than its fodder and pasture. Rather than calling this "the break" in a tradition of agriculture, it may help to think of it as an acceleration of pre-existing land use patterns and specialties, all in an attempt to adapt to larger demographic and economic trends.

RESEARCH AND UNDERDEVELOPMENT

The salient feature of agricultural change in the early postwar period (1945–71) was more in degree than in kind. The number of farms was dropping rapidly, in part because of the way the census defined a farm but mostly because rural people continued to abandon marginal farmland and pursue other forms of employment. The average size of a farm was increasing steadily in order to remain competitive, but the overall proportion of total land cleared was decreasing in all but a few townships. New crops such as potatoes for restaurants and barley for hogs increased, but so also did the importance of livestock. Figure 7.1 suggests that trucks and tractors displaced the Island's horses, and a declining dairy herd produced its milk quota, but otherwise the total livestock units increased steadily between 1951 and 2006. Thus the postwar period represented the consolidation and intensification of farms in a few areas and the continued readjustment and "redefinition" of farms in others. One highly visible change in this period was the onslaught of federal and provincial civil servants testing new methods, promoting new crops, and surveying farmers from the land and from the air. As Canada approached its centenary, the country experienced its most prosperous period in history, and many felt that Islanders too should enjoy modernity.

Raymond and Rayburn, two of the social scientists who focused on PEI, claimed that the main cause of farm abandonment was the "inevitable" increase in farm size and the subsequent marginalization of farmers who did not mechanize.[95] Similarly, William Janssen argued that mechanization freed the farmer and family from back-breaking work, but reduced the margin of profit. The number of tractors on the Island increased from 49 in 1921 to 577 in 1941 and to 5,713 in 1961. However, the geography of mechanization was uneven, and not everyone bought in. At mid-century nearly half of the tractor fleet was located in Queens, and even there, only thirty-two out of one hundred farmers owned one. In Kings County only 21 per cent of farms had a tractor.[96] One can hardly blame those farmers for wanting tractors. Mechanization was widely touted as the solution to the very labour shortages PEI's aging farm population had faced for decades. According to Janssen, the farmer had to expand or get out.[97] However, federal research in the postwar period shows that many farmers had already gotten out, in the sense that they relied mainly on forms of income other than the sale of farm products.

Horses were quickly disappearing with the advent of tractors, trucks, and auto transport, but after the Second World War the number of ruminant livestock per farm increased in all six of the study townships, from a pre-war average of ten or fifteen head in most years to over twenty head per farm by 1971 (table 7.1). Along with the abandonment of farms and pastures came a general drop in the Island's farm land – hay, pasture, and otherwise – but on the farms that remained there was a rapid net increase of hay and pasture land. Tractors gradually replaced horses, but motive force was not the only problem faced by the aging population of farmers. Figure 7.8 shows the large labour force required for harvesting time-sensitive crops such as hay. Postwar mechanization reflected the net increase in hay production as well as the declining pool of field hands (see figure 7.9). The intensification of agriculture that

Table 7.1
Land use and livestock in six townships, 1871–1971

Lot	1871	1881	1921	1951	1971
		NUMBER OF FARMS			
15	244	252	248	179	45
25	150	132	166	131	73
30	240	226	231	156	67
34	216	208	243	168	102
43	183	173	200	127	34
59	238	251	193	110	47
		AVERAGE SIZE OF FARM (AC)			
15	72	85	88	111	207
25	113	129	109	126	207
30	75	81	86	103	149
34	94	101	85	103	143
43	61	78	76	105	173
59	68	73	95	136	188
		PROPORTION OF TOWNSHIP IMPROVED			
15	22.8%	32.6%	45.3%	38.8%	18.6%
25	58.4%	69.2%	82.6%	66.0%	72.3%
30	26.3%	43.1%	56.7%	40.4%	26.3%
34	58.7%	64.9%	67.5%	49.0%	45.9%
43	18.2%	26.6%	38.0%	29.6%	17.5%
59	32.2%	48.0%	59.8%	37.5%	24.6%
		ACRES OF FODDER (HAY + PASTURE)			
15	1,728	2,059	6,207	5,474	1,539
25	4,912	6,282	9,867	6,346	4,999
30	2,261	3,976	8,138	5,966	3,366
34	6,785	7,202	8,506	6,549	5,538
43	1,371	1,709	3,943	3,384	1,570
59	5,778	8,227	7,394	3,939	2,141
		ACRES OF POTATOES			
15		562	438	305	481
25		480	499	1,207	2,915
30		658	575	448	170
34		827	526	541	749
43		404	362	400	614
59		217	565	260	192
		HAY-FED LIVESTOCK PER FARM			
15	13.9	13.0	12.0	17.3	25.6
25	27.4	27.2	19.1	22.8	34.9
30	15.0	12.9	10.4	14.3	24.3
34	23.9	18.9	13.9	14.8	25.5
43	13.4	12.5	7.6	14.8	19.0
59	15.9	10.2	10.0	12.0	24.3

Figure 7.8 Haymaking.

occurred in the postwar period was more about steak than potatoes, generally, and not about potatoes at all in the marginal farm areas.

Stompin' Tom Connors's hit single "Bud the Spud" raced to Toronto and to the top of the charts in 1969, but PEI's transition to a commercial potato province was slower and perhaps less significant than is commonly believed. At mid-century, potatoes were by far the most valuable crop, but only 16 per cent of farm revenues came from potatoes, fully half of it from Prince County. Livestock and dairy products generated almost four times as much revenue as did potatoes.[98] A decade later, a joint federal-provincial study of 288 randomly sampled farms revealed that potatoes appeared on only three-quarters of Island farms and occupied only 2 per cent of land on small-scale and part-time farms. "Commercial" farms grew substantially larger acreages, but still devoted only 7 per cent of their land to the tuber. By contrast, oats and other grains occupied 26 per cent of those farms, and hay and pasture were paramount with 35 and 29 per cent of improved land, respectively. The relative importance of potatoes was higher in 1961 than it had been in 1951, but still 60 per cent of farm income came from livestock and dairy products, compared to 30 per cent from potatoes and 6 per cent from other crops.[99] The study found that there was slightly more land idle and reverting to forest than there was in potatoes in 1959.[100]

Figure 7.9 Loading hay mechanically, 1940s.

What were these small farmers doing with barely an acre of potatoes in mixed operations? Just as they had before the war, they harvested them by hand and ate most of the crop through the winter. Baskets, bags, and barrels transported the smaller crops to the house where mounds of fresh spuds could fill an entire cellar. Children were taken out of school each fall for the harvest (figure 7.10), just as they had been for decades.[101] Potatoes were one of the best crops to guarantee food that required very little processing. In contrast, grain had to be stored in vermin-proof containers, and then milled and processed before hungry farm children could eat it. Pork and beef were luxuries, and it must have been the rare occasion that a choice cut of meat was reserved for dinner rather than exchanged for much needed cash from the packers.

Postwar agriculture is perhaps best known for the farmers who increased their potato holdings, but equally as important to the Island's land use history are the people who downsized or dropped farming altogether. Between 1941 and 1961 more people were getting out of potatoes and grain than getting in. Only twenty farms out of the sample of 288 increased the size of their potato crop, and even fewer expanded

Figure 7.10 Potato harvest, Albany, PEI, ca. 1930.

their grain fields. Mechanization was thus initially about expanding the mixed economy, not potato monoculture. The study concluded that Islanders were more likely to adjust their "cash crop" (and by that it meant potatoes) than their livestock feed chain.[102] This seems sensible. The herd was a grazing bank account, multiplying every year or so and providing dairy and other by-products with less labour than intensive cropping. At mid-century, the value of Island livestock was $11 million in Queens, $8 million in Prince, and $4 million in Kings. Livestock represented about a quarter of the value of the average farm.[103] As well, there were serious logistical constraints that came with producing any more than a few acres of potatoes in a largely unmechanized and family-based business.[104] Small crops of potatoes were a versatile source of nutrition and cash for many Island farm families into the postwar period, and they could be adjusted to suit the fluctuating supply of labour.

Between the end of the Second World War and the inauguration of the Comprehensive Development Plan in 1969,[105] Island farmers must have grown weary of the coterie of itinerant agricultural economists surveying their families and imagining ways to increase the productivity of their farms. Agricultural economists and other social scientists extensively researched Prince Edward Island farms and farmers in the 1950s and 1960s, presumably to improve the quality of life and agriculture there but also undoubtedly as a way to test new socio-economic research methods. Graeme Wynn (this volume) addresses the scholarly research on islands and Prince Edward Island, and he notes that the well-known Canadian economist J.E. Lattimer considered PEI the best "laboratory for studying agriculture" in Canada.[106] Accordingly, the federal Department of Agriculture performed a variety of studies as part of its interest in new methods and new ways of classifying the land.

Building on studies from 1943 and 1944, the Whiteside soil survey was published in 1950 and revised in 1964 to align with newer national standards of soil classification. The first scientific soil survey of Prince Edward Island, Whiteside's study identified significant areas of erodibility.[107] Later, Department of Agriculture scientists examined the soil types of abandoned parcels and found a direct correlation between farm abandonment and PEI's erosion problems.[108] Despite these reports and the recently well-established scientific literature on soil erosion, the provincial Department of Agriculture did not take measures to educate farmers or protect island soils from erosion caused by intensive row cropping (see Arsenault, this volume).

Other federal Department of Agriculture initiatives in the early postwar period included a major potato study by P.J. Gilhooly and A. Gosselin. The paper found that most Island potato growers produced mainly seed potatoes, using long (five to six year) rotations, heavy commercial fertilizers (up to one ton per acre), and varieties such as Irish Cobblers, Green Mountains, Katahdins, and Sebagoes.[109] The report was openly biased toward large producers by eliminating farms with small (less than four acres) crops of potatoes. Interestingly, even the Island's largest potato producers, growing eleven acres each on average, complemented their root crop with fifty-three acres of grain and hay and twenty-four acres of pasture for their livestock. The largest capital expense on these mixed farms was not machinery but labour. The Island's most specialized potato growers were still mixed farmers.[110]

The federal Department of Agriculture was firmly convinced of the need to research and classify land use in the postwar period, and it used mapping and aerial photography to identify potential arable land and what it considered "inadequately utilized fields."[111] PEI was not in a position to expand its acreage, but it presented a useful laboratory for the government. In 1958, the Royal Canadian Air Force conducted an aerial photographic survey of the province through the contractors Kenting Aviation Ltd. of Charlottetown.[112] Larry Philpotts, a wartime fighter pilot and instructor who was expert in aerial photo interpretation, led the data analysis for the department. He examined the Island's agricultural, forest, and fisheries infrastructure in fourteen case-study townships, and he compared the 1958 survey with images from a 1935 survey to reveal change over time. Philpotts's team identified over 21,000 acres of abandoned land in these townships and 321 abandoned or rented farms. Similar to the general trend in the interwar period, abandoned farms were overrepresented in Kings County. Philpotts's case studies east of Lot 37 each lost between 17 and 24 per cent of their farms. Lot 45 to the north of Souris was the most dramatic site, with thirty-two farms abandoned, almost a quarter of the farms present two decades earlier (figure 7.11).[113]

In some townships, abandoned farms dotted the coast. Eleven farms along Northside Road near Big Pond in Lot 45 were a more realistic indication of one politician's apocalyptic vision of "hundreds of vacant farms" and "thousands of acres going back to spruce bush" along this shore in 1927.[114] Most abandoned homes were less visible, clustered along back roads like Gairloch and Selkirk roads in Lot 60.[115] The forest closed in quickly in these areas. Seven farmhouses along the Brothers Road near Peakes in Lot 38 were fully abandoned and returning to the earth, and the frames must have been haunting reminders to the two small farms that remained on that road. Only one farmhouse stands there now, flanked by grains, row crops, and two large potato warehouses. Anything that remained of the abandoned farms is lost in the poplar and white spruce.

In addition to the 21,000 acres abandoned on these farms, another 10,000 were evidently sold or rented to nearby farmers. Quite distinct from farm abandonment, this form of land consolidation was evidence of the growing size of farms in the postwar period. Identifying the phenomenon from the air was spotty at best, including observation of new paths between fields and the "predominant turn pattern" of tire tracks at the end of the lane, but it appears that the interpreters found a relatively consistent proportion of each township's agricultural land (between 4 and 9 per cent) being farmed in this way.

The department also examined the farms that remained. Using the aerial photos, Philpotts loosely classified these 1,857 farms by value and type of production. Fully half of the farms were "medium" producers, in

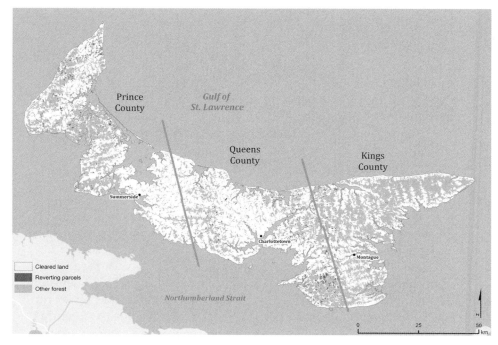

Figure 7.11 Land use and forest reversion, 1958.

terms of economic output.[116] In terms of land use, fewer than two dozen farms appeared predominantly focused on cash crops such as potatoes; specialization in livestock was far more common, with 729 such farms spread evenly across the study sites but particularly important in Lots 24, 31, and 40 (the areas around Rustico, New Haven, and Morell).[117] The third and most important category was farms with similar outputs from both livestock and crops. Even from the air it was evident that postwar PEI was still a mixed farm, and most operators were continuing to decide between going big or "going spruce."

An important 1961 federal-provincial study of land use and farm income attributed the decline in cultivated land to the farm labour problem. There were not enough young Islanders left in the countryside to justify increased production. The average age of farmers who took land out of cultivation was 64.4 years, while the age of operators adding to their holdings was just under 50 years. These ambitious farmers were also the younger ones; the mean age of the sample was 53.[118]

Federal researchers noticed that rural PEI's quality of life was different from the rest of the country's. Determining whether it was better or worse was more difficult. The 1961 federal-provincial report showed that only 53 per cent of Island farmers had electricity and 33 per cent had telephones; a similar survey in Ontario found power and telephones on 99 and 94 per cent of farms, respectively.[119] When asked about the disadvantages of living on Island farms, the most frequently identified problems (50 per cent of respondents) were economic. These included factors such as low and unpredictable income due to the fluctuation of price and yields, the difficulty of finding labour, and the difficulty of getting established as a new farmer. Forty-six per cent also identified poor infrastructure such as the roads, electricity, telephones, and schools in their community. The survey had more difficulty classifying the positive responses to farming, but most of them involved the "non-material aspects of rural life." Half of the respondents maintained that they felt close to nature, enjoying "the beauty of nature," the "open spaces," and the "fresh air," and over three-quarters simply called farm life personally satisfying. These farmers were deeply connected to their farms, claiming they enjoyed living independently and working on their own schedule. As some people phrased it, "the country is my home."[120]

Yet half of these homes were without the amenities enjoyed by most Canadians, and this life was not for the weak of heart. In 1965 Walter Shaw's government signed a federal agreement to conduct even more studies of the Island's economy. The province commissioned Acres International, which produced an eleven-volume report but made no specific recommendations.[121] In the 1967 session of the legislature, Premier Alex Campbell commissioned a white paper on economic planning and development by the economist Del Gallagher. The proposed development plan would enable PEI to "enjoy the benefits of economic growth which prevail generally in the Canadian society."[122] This was Gallagher's way of saying that PEI was a backward society but it could still be pulled into the twentieth century. In 1969, Raymond presented the findings of years of federal research to the Legislative Assembly. Campbell was both shocked and awed at the data. As historian and former Campbell staffer Wayne MacKinnon argues, Campbell was torn "between two cultures," and he was tasked with deciding how to approach development programs. Like his federal counterparts, the premier was committed to research, and he maintained that if Islanders only had the right information, they would make the right choices.[123]

At the federal level, the right information meant taking a scientific approach to determining the "best use" for farmland. The Land Development Corporation (LDC) was formed in 1969 to provide a financial and managerial vehicle for "land consolidation and more extensive land use." The LDC was charged with determining the "best use for agriculture, forestry or recreational purposes,"[124] and in this way the Comprehensive Development Plan helped push the long-established trend of consolidation and farm growth. This process occurred in a context of federal research programs that were designed to assess land and land use and create inventories that would help planners manage the land and determine the most productive ways to use it. The Canada Land Inventory was the culmination of this line of thinking. As a national system of land use classification and assessment, it represented the pinnacle of planning and incidentally produced the world's first Geographic Information System. In PEI, the poet Milton Acorn poignantly wrote that "nowhere is there a spot not measured by hands," and the Canada Land Inventory was the latest in a twenty-year attempt to measure the island, systematize local knowledge, and assess the land for its "best use."

In 1977, Campbell (by then the longest-serving premier in Island history) admitted that his government had pursued "growth and development after the central Canadian model" at the cost of the Island's traditional way of life. He began to realize that what they were searching for was self-sufficiency, and that elements of it had been there all along. Campbell felt that things local, regional, and small might still be beautiful, and he chastised other Liberals in the region for believing that "everything from away is better" and for "[selling] out to the centralist and the subsidy."[125]

In conclusion, federal and academic social scientists attempted to research and manage the Island's road to prosperity in the early postwar period, but by the 1970s, some of the same parties began to regret the changes they saw in the countryside. Efforts to keep young adults and their families at home took many forms, and it was evidently one of the reasons Alex Campbell modelled, or at least imagined, policies with the concepts behind E.F. Schumacher's *Small Is Beautiful* in mind.[126] As Graeme Wynn identifies (in this volume), a romantic belief in the superiority of farming and rural life, called Catonism by sociologists, grew popular in the twentieth century and was especially strong among external commentators and Island expatriates.[127] In the 1970s, demographers studying geographic mobility considered the effects of modernization sudden and irreversible. Large-scale urbanization caused "social breakdown" and what Schumacher called politically unstable "dual societies." Conversely, counter-urbanization and the growth of suburbs was considered by others "a clean break with the past."[128] It was tempting for historians and other social scientists to apply this language to Prince Edward Island, and indeed this period has been called "the break" and viewed as the threshold between "two cultures." However, the changes occurring in postwar P E I were already familiar to farmers. Rural outmigration is an important Island story, but it is not unique to P E I or even to the struggling economies of the Maritimes. Quebec and Ontario had each experienced large rural outmigration in the nineteenth century, and like the "rural beautification" movement sparked by this problem, "small is beautiful" was one effort to stem the tide.[129]

This chapter is not a lamentation for small-scale mixed farming on P E I, because it finds that small and large elements of agriculture existed cheek by jowl and fluctuated over time. Certainly, the postwar period witnessed great changes; however, it could be heralded as a time of growth in a long desolate landscape rather than the end of some sort of simpler time. It was not the first rise, or fall, of a significant sector. It was just as popular to lament the disappearance of new land in the 1890s, of sheep in the interwar period, or of hogs and beef herds in the early 2000s.[130] Even the development of a livestock economy and a thriving dairy industry was the peak of one phase that occurred in similar times and ways elsewhere. Thus, the postwar high-farming areas operated in many ways like other industrial farm landscapes, and when the critics of the Comprehensive Development Plan called it a model built for southern Ontario, Alex Campbell could rightly have stressed some of this Island's similarities and interconnections with that region rather than its uniqueness.[131] But in the 1960s, as Wynn argues (in this volume), that was not the "Island" way.

Islands are full of variation, and P E I is not a uniform laboratory.[132] By re-examining some of the wealth of historical census, survey, and cartographic data for P E I, we see the dynamic ebb and flow of land-use patterns. There was never a simpler time or a timeless place; at certain points southeast Prince County resembled industrial southern Ontario, and residents of eastern Kings might have felt more at home in the agroecosystems of Cape Breton than in other parts of their own Island. Further examination of these data and a detailed consideration of bovine metabolism and mussel mud show that terms like "traditional," "sustainable," and "self-sufficient" would have meant different things in different times and on different parts of the Island. Some Island farmers were large and specialized, and others were small-scale and pluri-occupational; some threatened habitat with extensive clearing, mussel mud digging, and repetitive row-cropping, but in the interwar period most were too small to have much impact.

Farms cannot be divided so easily into pre- and post-"break" categories. Prior to the 1860s, all but a few gentleman farmers concentrated around Charlottetown and Summerside were small, mixed, and vulnerable to crises like the hay shortage. In the late nineteenth century, farms expanded rapidly, but not equally, disturbing forest and estuarine ecosystems at wholly unsustainable rates. In the early twentieth century, some downscaled, others specialized and consolidated, and most took on other work. Early twentieth-century farms were not self-sufficient, pre-industrial, or ecologically responsible units of production. They responded to incentives, as their descendants did in the 1970s and do today. After the Second World War, many rural Islanders dropped the illusionary title of "farmer," and the kind of large-scale specialized farms covered by recent historians (see Arsenault, this volume) developed gradually in the 1960s and 1970s.

Rural depopulation has been a hallmark of the modern world; as nations develop advanced economies, their families move to cities, get better educated, and have fewer children. The difference on PEI and in the Maritimes was the absence of a metropolitan centre to absorb job-seeking families. Thus, the relatively normal process of rural depopulation here meant outmigration.[133] As with the growth of cities in the developing world today, the outmigration numbers speak plainly. The poor leave the country to get out of poverty.[134] No doubt they will care deeply about and possibly romanticize the places they leave behind, and like rural PEI, those places will always be complex and meaningful.

8

Agriculture and the Environment on Prince Edward Island, 1969–2014: An Uneasy Relationship

Jean-Paul Arsenault

The contemporary food economy does not reward farmers for doing things right, just for producing food as cheaply as possible. This explains, in part, why the relationship between agriculture and the environment has become an uneasy and conflicting one. It is also an example of market failure, since, in reality, the province of Prince Edward Island is mining its natural capital in return for short-term economic gain. Expanding world population and increasing demand for animal protein in developing countries will place even more pressure on food production systems. What impact will these trends have on agriculture and on its uneasy relationship with the environment that Islanders depend upon for their long-term well-being? Here, where the food is produced, how many farm families are already drinking bottled water or have installed nitrate filters? If industrial-scale agriculture were now being proposed for Prince Edward Island for the first time, would it pass an Environmental Impact Assessment?

This chapter attempts to make sense of a complex topic through analysis of available evidence, using simple language to present the facts. It describes the negative impacts of agriculture on the environment of this fragile Island under three main headings: erosion from water and wind; ground and surface water contamination; and wildlife habitat destruction. These categories have been chosen because the evidence is available and is supported by sound scientific research, because it can be weighed by an objective observer, and because it is possible to lay out the facts in clear language so that people can draw their own conclusions.

The problems framing this chapter – the threats to soil, water, and wildlife – are not limited to the late twentieth century. Environmental historians have identified these issues as some of the defining agricultural crises of the Anthropocene, and each of the land-use problems and policies discussed here has a long and complex history.[1] Some of that story, the longer agricultural history of Prince Edward Island, has been told by scholars such as A.H. Clark, David Weale, Georges Arsenault, William Janssen, Matthew Hatvany, and Wayne MacKinnon and Elinor Vass.[2] Still, there are many gaps to fill and revisions to make; this chapter focuses on the recent practices and policies that have created the situation we are in today.

In 2010, the Prince Edward Island government issued the most recent State of the Environment report, a comprehensive reckoning of how our natural environment has changed since the Round Table on Resource Land Use and Stewardship first proposed the use of key indicators.[3] The meaning of the word "indicator," as it applies to empirical environmental measures, may be found in the *2011 State of the Environment Report*, and I use selected indicators here to gauge the influence of the agriculture industry on the province's environment.

FRAMING AGRICULTURE

It has become a truism that environmental issues press harder on small islands with their finite land mass and resources. In the case of agriculture and Prince Edward Island, the environmental implications are even more sensitive. Agriculture has long been the largest single contributor to the Island economy and one of two dominant land uses on Prince Edward Island, accounting for 39 per cent of the land base in 2000, compared to 48 per cent in forest cover. Over the past ten years, food shipments averaged 60 per cent of the province's total manufacturing shipments and exports.[4] Only in Saskatchewan is agriculture a more significant contributor to provincial gross domestic product (GDP). But scale can be deceptive. As any wise farmer will tell you, "It's not what you bring in that counts, it's what you get to keep."

In 1928, net income on PEI farms was over 60 cents per dollar of gross revenue; by 2007, farms were reporting a net loss of 10 cents per dollar (figure 8.1). Realized net farm income has been in steady decline, crossing into negative territory for the first time in 2001. This is a staggering – not to mention disheartening – trend, given how much time, effort, and financial risk farmers invest in their operations. Statistics

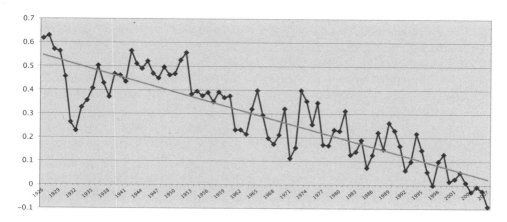

Figure 8.1 Net farm income per dollar of gross farm revenue.

demonstrate that most of the volatility in farm cash receipts and net farm income can be traced to fluctuations in yield and price of the province's main crop, potatoes. Supply-managed sectors, dairy primarily, benefit from stable cash flow and a net return based on cost of production. The beef and pork sectors have tended to be cyclical in nature, and their total contribution to overall farm incomes has changed little over time.

Measured against total provincial GDP, the value of agricultural production declined from 8.8 per cent in 2002 to 6.7 per cent in 2007. Comparatively, from 1986 to 2006, the number of farms dropped from more than 3,000 to 1,700, while the size of the average farm increased by 53 per cent, and the average capital value of a farm grew to over $1 million.[5] Put another way, it took 124 acres of land in crops to sustain a farm family in 1981; in 2006, that figure had grown to 250 acres, a twofold increase in just twenty-five years.[6]

Table 8.1 shows cash receipts from the sale of farm products. A number of facts are noteworthy. First, potatoes are the dominant crop, accounting for approximately 85 per cent of total value in 2009. Second, crops have contributed an increasing share of total farm cash receipts, now accounting for 65 per cent. Third, cattle, calves, and hogs have declined considerably, particularly hogs. Fourth, supply-managed sectors, dairy and eggs, have shown steady growth.

According to the report of the 2009 Commission on the Future of Agriculture and Agri-Food, the agrarian model of the nineteenth and early twentieth centuries was overtaken as farms grew in size to

Table 8.1
Farm Cash Receipts ($ thousands)

	1991	1994	1997	2000	2003	2006	2009
Grains	6,254	8,025	7,685	8,859	10,222	9,356	13,083
Potatoes	96,574	163,704	128,843	154,499	185,266	202,905	208,610
Fruits	2,255	2,453	2,080	4,856	4,521	7,644	5,800
Other crops	17,171	17,953	10,612	18,176	18,906	15,069	14,339
TOTAL CROPS	122,254	192,135	149,220	186,390	218,915	234,794	241,832
Cattle and calves	30,438	27,505	29,905	27,284	18,280	19,410	18,379
Hogs	21,931	22,326	29,181	29,526	26,510	23,630	10,748
Sheep and lambs	132	263	265	250	184	356	317
Dairy products	38,368	41,014	47,146	50,987	55,023	63,087	71,243
Eggs	2,955	2,618	2,948	3,172	4,276	3,689	4,071
Other livestock and products	4,969	5,631	7,471	8,533	9,395	10,496	12,966
TOTAL LIVE-STOCK	98,793	99,357	116,916	119,752	113,668	120,668	117,724
TOTAL CASH RECEIPTS	221,047	292,492	266,136	306,142	332,583	355,462	359,556

industrial scale. This transformation was characterized by fewer and more specialized farms, a concentration of processing and retail, declining economic viability, and environmental degradation. In other words, trends on Prince Edward Island mirrored general trends across the continent. The commission's report demonstrates how the intensification of agricultural practices resulted in increased environmental impact, loss of community respect and self-respect among farmers, a loss of new entrants, and, finally, a lack of innovation and investment in new technology. It calls this the industry's "vicious circle of decline," as illustrated in figure 8.2. The commission concludes that the trend is unsustainable, and it advocates a new approach, based on innovation and reforged

Figure 8.2 The circle of decline: farming in PEI.

relationships among farmers and suppliers, researchers, processors, consumers, and governments.

As the statistics show, while the value of exports is increasing, from the standpoint of profitability the agriculture industry is in decline. Moreover, the demonstrated negative impact of agriculture on the environment is a clear indication that the province is mining its natural capital and sacrificing long-term economic stability in return for short-term economic gain.

FRAMING THE ISSUES

The long-term impact of agriculture on the environment is difficult to assess, but signs show that the evolution of farming practices over the past forty years in particular has had a major impact, most of it demonstrably negative. Much of this can be traced to the evolution of the potato industry, potatoes and potato products now being the Island's number-one cash crop. Any discussion of the impact of agriculture on the environment must therefore focus on potato production.

In 2011 dollars, a grower of four hundred acres of potatoes must risk $1.12 million before receiving any return from the harvested product.[7] There is a tendency to focus on the decisions of individual potato farmers when assessing the impact of their practices on the environment.

However, evidence shows they are not the key drivers. Although they may own the land and drive the tractors, they have been responding to economic incentives that at best are perverse.

The 1987 report of the Royal Commission on the Future of the Prince Edward Island Potato Industry described an industry plagued historically by fluctuating returns and a lack of organization among producers.[8] At the time, the commission deemed the advent of the processing sector as a positive development, because it was seen as a means of stabilizing prices to the grower. In retrospect, the commission's view regarding the strategic importance of processing is understandable, and it may have remained so until the processing sector surpassed the seed and table sectors, beginning in 2001. Thereafter, as producers became more removed from the eventual customer, they became price-takers in a commodity-driven market.

In order to increase profit margins or, in down cycles, to simply survive, producers focused on increasing production and efficiency, falling in line with the industrial strategy of economies of scale. They expanded production, took out hedgerows, and ploughed closer to waterways – anything to make it easier to till larger fields with larger equipment and to optimize the use of their land base.[9] Flawed agricultural science is partly to blame as well. Agriculture scientists further refined the structural formulas of pesticide and fertilizer regimes and believed that modern chemistry could and should help squeeze every last kilogram of yield out of every last square metre. They focused mostly on soil chemistry and physics, and largely ignored soil biology. Similarly, government policy did nothing to discourage the expansion of individual production units and everything to encourage the development of the processing sector because of its economic spinoffs and the belief that it would promote stability in the potato industry.[10]

Figure 8.3 illustrates to what extent producer and consumer choices are influenced by a few so-called middle men. While, ultimately, many producers end up selling to many consumers, it is those who own the buying desks and the supermarkets who determine how much the producer receives and how much the consumer pays.

Over the past forty years, Prince Edward Island largely abandoned a seed potato industry that was based on high-value, small-quantity production in favour of commodity processing. While high-quality seed potatoes had been a key feature of the industry since the 1920s, the sector was susceptible to climate, disease, and market vagaries and by the 1990s had been eclipsed by potatoes for processing.[11] Today, when

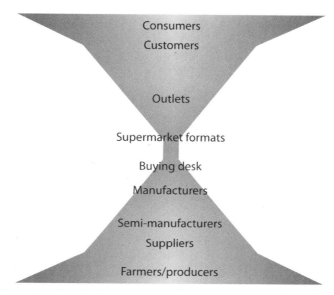

Figure 8.3 Funnel diagram: PEI producers, consumers, and "middle men."

representatives of the agriculture industry address the issue of economic return, it is most often in the context of what is happening to the potato processing sector and the drivers that influence French fry consumption. While the advent of the processing sector has reduced the producer's risk, it has not come without environmental consequences.

In addition, the balance between crops and livestock has been altered significantly by the concurrent expansion of the potato processing sector and the decline of the cattle and hog sectors. Given the importance of incorporating forages into a row-crop rotation and of using manure as a soil supplement, this trend is not seen by agriculture industry representatives and government policy-makers as a healthy one. Too often potato farmers feel they cannot afford to plant unprofitable crops or dabble in livestock as part of a program to replenish their soil, opting instead for shorter rotations that emphasize potato production and chemical use.

WASTING AWAY:
EROSION FROM WIND AND WATER

Being generally light and sandy, most soils on Prince Edward Island are prone to water and wind erosion when their covering vegetation is removed. Erosion causes infilling (siltation) of deeper water areas such as ponds and pools, degrades wetlands, covers gravel in streams and shell in estuaries, changes in-stream channel configuration, and enables the accelerated movement of chemicals carried in soil. The principal sources of siltation are water-borne erosion from agriculture, road construction, urban development, forestry operations, and other activities where soil is disturbed.

It is generally accepted that the maintenance of healthy soil in a row-crop production system on Prince Edward Island requires that the row crop be planted no more frequently than one year in three. Traditionally, potatoes were followed by a cereal crop and a forage crop in a three-year rotation, and this was indeed the practice in the era of the mixed farm. Manure was used as a fertilizer and soil supplement, and the forage crop ploughed under prior to potato seeding added much-needed organic matter to the soil medium. When applied to soils here, the Universal Soil Loss Equation indicates that the upper limit of sustainable soil loss is three tons per acre per year, a goal that can be achieved using a three-year rotation.[12]

Concerns about the impact of farming practices on soil quality began to emerge in the 1970s, when the agriculture industry was transformed from one characterized by smaller mixed farms to one dominated by larger, more specialized operations.[13] Unfortunately, threats to soil conservation and the need to maintain soil quality did not become a major and widespread issue until the major expansion of potato production in the 1970s and '80s was well underway (see table 8.1).

Prior to 1987, no research had been done into the application of soil conservation measures to Prince Edward Island conditions. Early research by the federal and provincial governments had demonstrated the devastating effects of soil erosion on land in row crops, but nothing was done to encourage soil conservation through incentives, technical assistance, or regulatory measures. The first modest efforts to construct erosion control structures, called terraces, began in the late 1980s.[14] Government incentives were put in place to encourage potato producers to adopt these, and technical assistance was provided free of charge. Other approaches were introduced, such as strip cropping and straw mulching and the use of cover crops and grassed waterways, again with government assistance, including cost-sharing with the landowner.

The Round Table on Resource Land Use and Stewardship devoted a chapter of its 1997 report to soil quality, labelling it the "number one land use issue on Prince Edward Island."[15] It reported that, while 81 per cent of cultivated land was at high-to-severe risk of erosion from water, only 10 per cent was under an acceptable form of soil conservation practice. The round table, in its consultations with farm groups, raised the possibility of mandatory three-year crop rotation but stopped short of making this one of its recommendations. Legislation was later enacted in the form of the Agricultural Crop Rotation Act (1998),[16] which calls for potatoes to be produced no more frequently than one year in three unless the producer has registered an alternative approved soil management plan with the Department of Agriculture. In 2008, the Commission on Nitrates in Groundwater repeated the call for mandatory three-year crop rotation, with no exceptions.

Two areas addressed by the round table did result in effective changes to legislation, making it illegal to plant row crops like potatoes on land with a slope greater than 9 per cent, and establishing mandatory grassed headlands and riparian buffer zones along watercourses and around wetlands. These are referred to as the Watercourse and Wetland Protection Regulations[17] and, while their primary focus is on the protection of surface water and aquatic habitat, they have had a definite impact on producers' soil management practices.

The chapter on soil quality in the 2010 *State of the Environment Report* begins by stating that soil is a fundamental but very fragile resource that is very susceptible to human mismanagement. The most important environmental issue related to agricultural practices is listed as soil erosion. The report goes on to identify four indicators of soil quality: frequency of row crops, area under soil conservation management structures, soil organic matter, and organic agriculture.[18]

For the first indicator, the Island government's stated objective is to ensure that row crops such as potatoes and corn are grown on the same field no more frequently than one year in three, unless an approved soil conservation plan is in place and being implemented. Results show that, from 1997 to 1999, 82 per cent of land in row crops met this standard and, from 2006 to 2008, the figure had improved to 89.6 per cent. The report notes that a decline in potato production is the key reason for the improvement in rotation length. Anecdotal information from the period when potato production was at its peak indicates that the average rotation at its worst fell to 2.4 years.

For the second indicator, soil conservation structures include terraces, grassed waterways, and farmable berms. When these are combined with soil management practices like strip cropping, erosion can be reduced to acceptable levels on excessively long or steep slopes. It is estimated that approximately 60,000 hectares of row-cropped land in the province require erosion control structures, strip cropping, or both. In 2009, approximately 21,600 hectares were under an acceptable form of soil conservation management system, although the term "acceptable" is not defined in the State of the Environment report. The figure represented an increase from 7,500 hectares in 1995. Government's stated objective is to add another 7,000 hectares by 2014.

Organic matter is a key indicator of the soil's capacity to support plant growth. It is important for maintaining soil structure, helps with water infiltration, and aids in resisting erosion. A level of 3 per cent organic matter content in the soil is considered the minimum acceptable. According to the *2010 State of the Environment Report*, "In 1999–2001, 68 per cent of samples had an organic matter content of three per cent or greater. In the 2006–2008 sampling period (on the same sites) this figure decreased to 48 per cent. Where potatoes were grown more frequently than once every three years in the crop rotation, soil organic matter levels dropped to below three per cent. When potatoes were grown once in every three years, and forages or cereals were incorporated into that rotation cycle, soil organic matter levels remained above three per cent. Soil organic matter levels are decreasing province-wide."[19] Government's stated objective is to see a positive trend in soil organic matter levels, but the report does not include a plan on how this will be done.

It is generally accepted that organic production techniques promote the maintenance of healthy soil. The State of the Environment report includes statistics on the area under organic agriculture and the number of Island farmers who are either certified producers or are in transition from traditional to organic production. Both trends are positive: hectares under organic production have increased from 600 in 2001 to 2,000 in 2009, and the number of certified producers has grown from 30 to 59 over the same period.[20]

In 2011, the evidence shows clearly that the quality of Island agricultural soils depends primarily on the decisions of individual potato producers and, more particularly, on trends in the potato processing sector. Forty years ago, the notion of having to modify farmers' soil management practices through incentives and regulations would have been considered absurd. Looking after the soil was part of a creed transmitted father to son and mother to daughter; the mixed farm made it possible, and the returns from the marketplace made it a rational decision from an economic standpoint. Much has changed, and if Prince Edward Island is to maintain its place as a producer of quality crops and livestock in the long term, it will have to continue to reduce soil erosion and show improvement in the key indicators of soil quality. The question becomes not whether to do this but how.

GROUND AND SURFACE WATER CONTAMINATION

As with the twin issues of erosion from wind and water, contamination of ground and surface water did not become a concern of Islanders until a number of signs – rain-gouged gullies across fields, a series of fish kills traced to pesticide poisoning, and nutrient-driven anoxic events – demonstrated that something fundamental had changed in farming practices. People began to notice that the rivers and streams ran red after every rainfall, that ponds were filling in at an increasing rate, and that the eutrophication of estuaries was happening more frequently.[21] Concerns about farming practices and their impact on water had been raised by the 1990 Royal Commission on the Land and were soon on the agenda of every environmental and watershed management organization in the province.[22]

However, government attempts to control watercourse contamination from agricultural sources prior to the mid-1990s were limited and ineffective. Farmers were free to use their best judgment in applying pesticides and fertilizers, and they were free to make their own decisions on how to manage land adjacent to watercourses. In fact, until very recently, the portion of a watercourse that flowed across a property was considered to be part and parcel of that property. "It goes with the land" was a strongly held principle handed down through the generations.

The hydrologic cycle on Prince Edward Island is illustrated with a set of simple numbers, as outlined in a 1996 report *Water on Prince Edward Island – Understanding the Resource, Knowing the Issues*:

- 1,100 millimetres (43 inches) of precipitation fall on the Island in an average year
- 40 per cent of this rises back into the air through evaporation and transpiration
- 27 per cent runs overland into watercourses
- 33 per cent soaks into the earth and becomes groundwater[23]

Nitrates are only one of many contaminants linked to agriculture that have had significant environmental consequences. They occur naturally in the environment and are an essential nutrient for plant growth. However, if there are more nitrates than plants can use, the excess can contaminate groundwater and affect surface water quality in rivers and streams. Over time, as agricultural practices have become more intensive, excessive fertilizer application has caused nitrates to become the most common chemical contaminant in ground and surface water. The key sources of nitrate pollution on Prince Edward Island are agricultural fertilizer, manure storage and spreading operations, septic systems, and fertilizers applied to lawns, golf courses, and other recreational facilities.

Phosphorus, in the form of phosphate, is also an ingredient in chemical fertilizers. When nitrates and phosphates are present in excessive amounts, they cause two problems in streams and ponds. The first, called eutrophication, results from a flush of plant growth. When these plants die, they are broken down by other organisms, and the process of decay uses up a great deal of oxygen. If too much oxygen is removed from the water, fish, invertebrates, and shellfish suffocate. The second problem is the changes in the composition and distribution of different species of plant and animal life that occur when excessive levels of nutrients are introduced into surface water. Significantly, there is a direct relationship between the magnitude of both problems and the proportion of cleared land in a given watershed.

In its 1997 report *Cultivating Island Solutions*, the Round Table on Resource Land Use and Stewardship identified two dimensions to the issue of Island groundwater quality: (1) human health and consumption, and (2) aquatic habitat and organisms living in Island watercourses. The round table pointed to the introduction of silt or sediment into watercourses as the single most important threat to surface water and aquatic habitat quality. Based on information available at the time, the round table reported that long-term average peak concentrations of suspended sediment in a representative sample of Island rivers were four times higher than would occur naturally. As an example, concentrations of suspended sediment in the Wilmot River, which runs through a high-farming district, were found to have exceeded the Canadian Guidelines for the Protection of Aquatic Life by a factor of eight.[24] Further concerns were registered two years later in the *Water Quality Interpretive Report* prepared for Environment Canada and the Government of Prince Edward Island's Department of Technology and Environment.[25]

In 2007, some ten years after *Cultivating Island Solutions* was published, the Environmental Advisory Council in its report *We Are All*

Downstream, We Are All Upstream, We Are All Part of a Watershed
stated that many presenters had identified water quality as the "first
issue": "It is inconceivable that the problem has been allowed to reach
this state and further delays in implementing sound farming practices
may be catastrophic."[26]

In July 2007, the provincial government appointed the Commission
on Nitrates in Groundwater to explore and recommend solutions to the
problem of nitrate contamination. The commission began its report:
"Over the past three decades, Prince Edward Island has experienced a
steady increase in the level of nitrates – both in the groundwater we rely
on for drinking water, and in rivers, streams and estuaries that are home
to a wide variety of wildlife and a source of livelihood and enjoyment for
many people. Islanders are concerned about this trend and the effects on
their health and the environment; and they are frustrated that nitrate
concentrations have been allowed to reach current levels without something being done to address the problem."[27] The report was the product
of an extensive research and consultation exercise focused exclusively on
nitrates, combining a human health issue and a very reliable indicator of
environmental health. The commission presented to government a series
of sweeping recommendations that, if implemented, would have a significant impact on agricultural operations. The three most controversial
recommendations call for amending land-holding legislation, matching
nutrients with crop needs to reduce nitrogen leaching, and identifying
high nitrate areas.[28]

The first recommendation was based on the commission's conclusion
that environmentally sensitive land devoted to processing potatoes must
be taken out of production. Recent amendments, generally seen as positive, were made to the Lands Protection Act to enable landowners to
exceed the normal land ownership limits when they set aside land that is
defined as sensitive.

The commission advocated a series of key management practices in
support of the second set of recommendations: reducing the amount of
fertilizer applied to potatoes; increasing the length of potato rotations;
managing soil organic matter through better conservation practices like
fall ploughing; and increasing forest cover. The commission also recommended mandatory three-year crop rotation with no exceptions, and the
development of a nutrient-management and accounting program for all
crop and livestock producers.

Regarding high nitrate areas, the commission called on government to
work with farmers and other landowners in watersheds "where national

standards for safe drinking water and healthy aquatic systems have been compromised." Remedial actions were identified, which included reducing fertilizer inputs, managing soil organic matter, increasing forest cover, reducing land in potato production, and encouraging wetland restoration. The commission also recommended that government enact legislated controls on nutrient management and mandatory accounting of nutrients in the identified high nitrate areas

The "Guidelines for Canadian Drinking Water Quality"[29] set the maximum acceptable concentration for nitrate at 10 milligrams per litre (mg/L). It is important to note, however, that this standard is currently under review by Health Canada and the United States Environmental Protection Agency, and it may be revised downward to further limit concentrations. Water tests done at a series of nitrate clinics in 2007 showed 6 per cent of private wells above the 10 mg/L guideline and another 11 per cent at the high end of the guideline, testing between 8 and 10 mg/L. A total of 2,511 water samples were tested for nitrates at the province-wide clinics in 2007.[30]

The 2010 State of the Environment report included updates on four key indicators of ground and surface water quality: nitrate in private well water, anoxic events in estuaries, nitrate concentration in surface water, and shellfish closures.[31] The level of nitrate in private well water is particularly important here, because 55 per cent of residents, the highest proportion in Canada, have their own well. Government's stated objective is to achieve an average nitrate concentration of 3 mg/L or less – province-wide – and no wells exceeding the maximum 10 mg/L guideline recommended by the "Guidelines for Canadian Drinking Water Quality." (Nitrate concentrations indicating "pristine" water conditions are typically in the range of 0.5 to 1.0 mg/L.) The average nitrate concentrations for private wells peaked at 4.1 mg/L in 2007, then declined to 3.2 mg/L in 2009. In 2009, 3.8 per cent of wells exceeded the 10 mg/L recommended by the guidelines.

While well testing focuses on groundwater, the frequency of anoxic events is an indicator of surface water quality and is linked to excess nutrient loading caused by land management practices, most commonly excess use of nitrogen fertilizer on agricultural crops. The susceptibility of an estuary depends on the strength of tidal flow, physical properties like depth, width, and length, and stratification of the water column. According to the State of the Environment report, the number of recorded anoxic events over the past nine years has ranged from a low of twelve in 2004 and 2005 to a high of twenty-one in 2010. In the report, government admits that, in certain watersheds, nutrient loads are so high that it is not clear that nutrient management alone will solve the problem.

Nitrate has been measured in the Mill, Dunk, and Morell rivers for more than thirty years, and for the Wilmot River since 1991. Long-term trends show nitrate levels increasing in all four of these test sites. Averages in the Mill, Dunk, and Wilmot rivers are routinely above the recommendations of the "Canadian Water Quality Guidelines for the Protection of Aquatic Life"[32] of 2.9 ml/L. Average nitrate values for the Wilmot River in 2008–09 exceeded 7.1 mg/L, while the values for the Dunk River exceeded 4.5 mg/L and those for Mill River approached 3.0 mg/L. Significantly, the Morell River is protected by a set of strong watershed management regulations and shows markedly lower levels of nitrate.[33]

Another more informal measure of water quality involves aquaculture. Closures in shellfish growing areas have affected the province economically by reducing the area available for harvesting shellfish. An increasing trend in the percentage of total area closed may indicate worsening water quality, while a decreasing trend may indicate improving water quality. Since the 2003 State of the Environment report was published, the relative percentage of approved area has changed little, showing an increase of 0.4 per cent overall since 2000. According to the 2010 report, this figure did not meet the stated objective of a 1 per cent increase in approved area compared to 2003.

The interconnectedness of systems influenced by human activity becomes obvious when one examines the influence of agricultural practices on key indicators of soil quality, and of ground and surface water quality. Organic matter content is directly affected by soil management practices, and it determines how efficiently plants can process nutrients in a soil medium. This same measure of soil quality has a major impact on the soil's ability to retain moisture and slow down erosion by water and wind. Shrinking forest cover and expanding field sizes have drastically reduced the environment's buffering capacity to the point where even normal weather patterns can cause erosion, eutrophication, and shellfish closures. In other words, there is only one "system," and it is very vulnerable to change.

What was suspected in 1997 by the round table is now known to be true. Ground and surface water contamination by chemical fertilizers and bacteria has emerged as a significant environmental and human health issue for Canadian agriculture. Nitrate tells a story because of its importance in potato production, the danger it poses to human and environmental health, and its value as an indicator. Unfortunately, as witnessed by the many farm families who have had to turn to bottled water because they contaminated their own wells, it is not a particularly happy one.

WILDLIFE HABITAT DESTRUCTION

One of the most superficially obvious environmental impacts of agriculture is its radical transformation of wildlife habitat. Even by the mid-nineteenth century, as European farmers spread out from the coastline into the interior, those impacts were readily apparent, and by the end of the century 70 per cent of Prince Edward Island was cleared for agriculture and in some form of food production. Much of the remaining 30 per cent has since been disturbed through the harvesting of timber products, so that very little, if any, area of land can truly be classified as undisturbed wildlife habitat.[34]

In the 1990s, the potato industry expanded rapidly just as demand for softwood timber grew. The number of hectares in potato production rose from 30,000 in 1990 to 45,000 in 2000, an increase of 50 per cent (see table 1). The round table referred to this period as "the mad dash for two-by-fours and for French fries that hang out over the box!" Farmers looking to expand their cleared land holdings sold standing softwood timber, mostly on ploughed forest, for as much as $5,000 per hectare, which more than paid for the cost of clearing the field, and ended up with good potato land valued at $7,500 per hectare.[35] Potato production has since declined by 25 per cent and the softwood timber sector has all but collapsed – industrial wood production stood at 666,000 cubic metres in 1999 versus 53,000 cubic metres in 2009 – both of them felled by the combination of global economic downturn and a high Canadian dollar.[36]

The forest cover itself is subject to important distinctions. The 2004 Forest Policy discussion paper presents an excellent description of the distinction between "ploughed" and "unploughed" forest, which is significant to any understanding of the impact of agriculture, past and future, on wildlife habitat:

Although the remaining forest has been extensively disturbed, forests growing on land that has never been cleared and ploughed are different from those regenerating on abandoned agricultural land. They are important reservoirs of native soils, species and genetic diversity, complex ecological interactions and carbon. They account for many of our remnant Acadian forest species such as American Beech, Yellow Birch, Sugar Maple, Eastern Hemlock, Eastern White Cedar and Black Ash, among others. Forests on unploughed lands cannot be created; at best, the current area could be maintained. However, pressures from other sectors continue to result in conversion of these areas to other uses such as agriculture and housing. Between 1900 and 2000, more than 23,000 hectares of this forest type was converted to non-forest uses, mostly since 1980. The trend is one of increasingly rapid decline.[37]

Government's new forest policy, released in 2006, calls for program changes meant to increase forest restoration efforts, particularly on unploughed forest, to manage for a diversity of forest species, to protect wildlife, and to enhance wetlands and watercourses.[38] All of these favour wildlife habitat protection and improvement, considerable challenges on a small island characterized by high population density and widespread farming.

The chapter in the 2010 *State of the Environment* report on biodiversity begins with a recognition of the complexity of the issue and its relevance for the Island's environmental health:

Biodiversity (natural variability) is more than just a count of species. It encompasses the genetic diversity within species, their relative abundance, as well as the diversity of habitats in the landscape. "Healthy" habitats can have many species (like older forests) or few species (like sand dunes). The health of a habitat is defined by its ability to resist and recover from natural threats such as fire or disease, and not the number of species present. Biodiversity serves as the base of our Island's natural capital. The province's long history of settlement and land clearing has resulted in the loss of natural biodiversity at all levels. Habitat loss and invasive species are the two greatest threats to biodiversity. As our impact on the Island's landscape grows, the stress on local habitats and the native species they support will increase. Land management practices which better maintain natural biodiversity and focus on habitat restoration are essential if we are to maintain the natural checks and balances that ensure our ecosystems are healthy, resilient and abundant with life.[39]

In the report, the provincial government provides an update on four indicators: forest communities, forest cover types, protected land area, and species number.

Forest communities growing on land that has never been cleared and farmed are classified in the provincial forest inventory as upland forest, wet rich forest, and black spruce forest.[40] These communities contain the only remaining reserves of natural forest soil biodiversity – insects, bacteria, and fungi. They are home to hundreds of native plant species, including many that are important for ecological or economic reasons and that are not found in other Island forest communities. Moreover, areas of unploughed forest are better able to resist disturbances such as disease, fire, and insects because they are comprised of a diversity of species and ages of trees and shrubs. As noted above, these areas came under increasing pressure between 1990 and 2000 as the result of a combination of factors, including land clearing for agriculture. That pressure, in turn, fed the appetite for creating protected areas.

The Government of Canada recognizes the International Union for Conservation of Nature (IUCN)'s definition of a protected area as "a clearly defined geographical space, recognised, dedicated and managed, through legal or other effective means, to achieve the long-term conservation of nature with associated ecosystem services and cultural values."[41] Natural area, as defined in the provincial Natural Areas Protection Act, means a parcel of designated land that contains natural ecosystems or constitutes the habitat of rare, endangered, or uncommon plant or animal species; contains unusual botanical, zoological, geological, morphological, or palaeontological features; exhibits exceptional and diversified scenery; provides haven for seasonal concentrations of birds and animals; or provides opportunities for scientific and educational programs in aspects of the natural environment.

The 2010 International Year of Biodiversity provided an opportunity to take stock of Canada's assembly of protected areas.[42] The Government of Canada reported that it had set aside 9.9 per cent of its lands as protected areas. Prince Edward Island set a target of 7 per cent, or 12,479 hectares. As of 2010, the State of the Environment report showed that the province had achieved 57 per cent of its target, representing 7,141 hectares protected under the Natural Areas Protection Act.[43]

The 2010 *State of the Environment Report* includes the measure of species number but cautions that, since it is such a simple measure of biodiversity, as an indicator it must be used carefully. For example, the province's salt marshes have low plant diversity but rank among the most important and productive habitats. A cutover forest can have high plant diversity, but many plants found there will be exotic species or common generalists that can survive anywhere. Additionally, the number of species known to be present on Prince Edward Island is influenced by how much effort has gone into looking for them.[44]

That agriculture has had a significant impact on wildlife habitat and species biodiversity is not in question. The evidence shows that 70 per cent of the Island's land base is or has been devoted to this form of land use, and there is no indication that the pattern will change. However, recent attempts by government, non-profit organizations, and private landowners – which have not been properly measured and evaluated – are indicators of positive change. These markers include an amendment to the Lands Protection Act that allows farmers to increase their land holdings in return for setting aside environmentally sensitive areas; successful efforts by the Government of Prince Edward Island, the Nature Conservancy of Canada, and the Island Nature Trust to protect lands under the Natural Areas Protection Act; legislative changes requiring farmers to set aside buffer areas along watercourses (which have the added effect of creating wildlife corridors); and relief from provincial property tax for private land designated under the Natural Areas Protection Act and the Wildlife Conservation Act.

PESTICIDES, LANDSCAPE, AND LAND USE CHANGE

That this chapter has highlighted only three topics should not be taken to mean that others – pesticide use, landscape, and land use management, for example – are less important. In fact, many people believe that pesticide use is just as important, if not more so, than any of the three listed above. The problem is that while there is evidence concerning the impact of pesticides, it is often conflicting, anecdotal, or pertains to some other geographic area. For this reason, it is difficult to arrive at a finding of fact that is of much use to anyone. As for landscape and land use management, I will briefly discuss them here.

In its 2010 State of the Environment report, the provincial government reported on three indicators of pesticide impact: occurrence of residue in groundwater, occurrence of fish kills, and sales as measured in kilograms of active ingredient.[45] Based on limited data from 2004 to 2008, changes in the occurrence of pesticide residues in drinking water samples showed a variable pattern in terms of number of wells affected, but all samples remained well below health-based recommendations for maximum concentration in drinking water. The number of fish kills from 1993 to 2010 varied from highs of eight in 1999 and 2002 to several years when none were registered. The report notes that enforcement efforts have increased considerably and that certain pesticides have been removed entirely from use in agricultural operations. From the available evidence, it is possible to conclude that pesticides, if properly applied and regulated, can be tolerated by our environment until a more natural system is found to produce food in sufficient quantities to feed the world's growing population.

Regarding landscape, changing agricultural practices have had a drastic impact on the appearance of farmed areas. Not surprisingly, when it comes to defining beauty in a landscape, not everyone sees things the same way. The Council of Europe came up with the following definition of landscape in 2004: "A zone or area as perceived by local people or visitors, whose visual features and character are the result of the action of natural and/or cultural (that is, human) factors."[46] On Prince Edward Island, the issue of landscape was addressed in several reports including the 1973 and 1990 Royal Commissions, the 1997 Round Table Report, and the 2010 Report of the Commission on Land and Local Governance.[47] Although the Planning Act and the Heritage Places Protection Act provide the legislative authority to regulate development and preserve landscapes, government's efforts to date have been very limited, and the recommendations of previous reports have been ignored. A not-for-profit organization, the L.M. Montgomery Land Trust, has focused its efforts on an area along the Gulf of St Lawrence seacoast between French River and Park Corner, which it has named the L.M. Montgomery Seashore. Its objective is to preserve what remains of a remarkably beautiful working rural landscape in an attempt to stifle a runaway real-estate market.

The most reliable empirical data regarding the attractiveness of our landscape come from visitors' surveys conducted by or on behalf of the provincial government. The 2009 Travel Intentions Survey conducted by the Tourism Research Centre at UPEI compared the expectations and experiences of visitors to Prince Edward Island with those of visitors to nearby destinations.[48] Among the highest rated features were the uniqueness and unspoiled nature of the environment. Visitors like what they see in the Island landscape; historically, landscape has been consistently rated as one of the Island's main attractions.[49] Similarly, despite the many changes to the scenic environment resulting from the adoption of modern, industrial-scale farming practices, there has been no consistent cry of alarm from Islanders.

Finally, a related example of the impact of agriculture on the environment is the loss of resource land – farmland and land in transition to forest – to other uses such as transportation, housing, or commercial or industrial development. In this case, the change in use may be better or worse from an environmental standpoint, but the overall impact is assumed to be neutral since the change is really only from one human system to another. A recent study, the report of the Commission on Land and Local Governance, concluded that one of the greatest threats to the future of the agriculture industry is the conversion of farmland, especially to housing and cottage developments, as farmers facing financial uncertainty increasingly consider their land as a liquid asset rather than the foundation of their livelihood. Unfortunately, there has been little research into the impact of non-agricultural land uses on key indicators of environmental well-being.

CONCLUSION

Looking back over the past forty years, the facts show clearly – other factors notwithstanding – that the degree of pressure to which the environment has been subjected is directly related to processing potato production. The ebb and flow of key environmental indicators has overwhelmingly depended on how many hectares were grown for French fries. It is that simple. It is generally believed by potato industry representatives and government policy-makers that the current level of production is sustainable from an environmental standpoint, assuming legislated standards are applied aggressively and programs to encourage producers to farm more responsibly are maintained. However, in the event of further expansion of the processing potato sector, current mechanisms may not be adequate, and key environmental indicators will continue to decline.

There are those who believe the contract between the producer and the processor is the most powerful tool available, and that potato processors are in the best position to fix problems by requiring that producers meet standards or lose the opportunity to sell their potatoes. For example, the processing potato contract could include mandatory adherence to crop rotation legislation and to a nutrient management program, or both. Market signals are encouraging in this regard, but it is too early to tell if this will happen.

Without question, agricultural diversification is key to ensuring healthier relationships between industry, environment, and the public.

Watersheds identified in the report of the Commission on Nitrates in Groundwater as being under greatest pressure from nitrates and other contaminants simply cannot sustain the area currently under crop production. Even by implementing all measures recommended in various reports, it will be impossible to maintain soil and water quality and to protect wildlife habitat unless the area devoted to agriculture is reduced in threatened watersheds. Strategically the best approach to managing the environment – and the complex relationships between users – may be to provide farmers with financial incentives to convert land to other uses and to encourage the formation of more active watershed management groups.

If one thing is clear from the retrospective view, it is that government and the agriculture industry have failed in their joint responsibility to be good stewards. Islanders have shown great patience with farmers, largely because so many Islanders are only one or two generations removed from the farm. But how long will this level of tolerance last? The disastrous fish kills in western Prince County in the summers of 2011 and 2012 proved that some potato growers – although they knew better – would not take adequate measures to protect watercourses adjacent to their fields from pesticide contamination. That serious charges were laid and convictions obtained is a clear indication that the period of grace is over.

Agriculture and the environment can achieve a healthy coexistence, but it is all about balance and understanding that a systems approach is needed. Modern farming aims to control nature instead of working with nature. Organic farming practices feed and build the soil, which in turn feeds the plant, whereas modern hydroponic agriculture views the soil as an inert medium to hold the roots while the plant is fed directly. In the past, on-farm food production was diversified and based on an integrated crop and livestock system. It was balanced, and the system worked. The livestock side provided organic fertilizer in the form of manure and at the same time created a demand for feed and forage crops that rotate well with potatoes. Over the past forty years in particular, the agriculture industry has moved away from animal husbandry and mixed farming in favour of potato production, and the system is under strain – environmentally, socially, and economically.[50]

As consumers increasingly demand answers to questions about where and how their food is produced, the impetus for change is likely to come not from innovations in production technology but from the market for food products. This shift should put farmers back in the driver's seat and provide them with more choices. The one great strength of Island farmers is their ability to adapt. Although this attribute has not always been evident over the past forty years, there is a fount of knowledge here, and a deep-set desire to keep abreast of market trends and to do things right. More importantly, there seems to be a growing realization by farmers and governments that environmental degradation is no longer acceptable and that emerging market forces will lead to more responsible farming practices. If that happens, Island agriculture may find its balance after all.

9

Lines in the Water:
Time and Place in a Fishery

Edward MacDonald and Boyde Beck

In essence, all fisheries rely on three factors: desirability, attainability, and sustainability. Is the species something that you want? Is it something that you can catch? And, if you want it and can catch it, can it withstand the pressure that you put on it? How those questions have been answered over time frames the environmental history of Prince Edward Island's marine fisheries.[1]

It is tempting, though dangerous, to view the backstory of the Island's fisheries in teleological terms, as a morality tale trending relentlessly towards today's sense of impending crisis. But the long sweep of history also teaches how difficult it is to pierce the mystery of what goes on beneath the sea's surface or what happens when fishers – or historians – drop their lines into the water.

FISH ...

For the first ten thousand years of human habitation on Prince Edward Island, sustainability posed no problem to any fishery. Archaeological evidence makes it clear that successive native cultures relied heavily on marine resources (species such as seals, shellfish, lobster, salmon, eels, herring, and smelts), but they lacked the numbers, the technology, or, perhaps, the necessary cosmology to seriously overtax them.[2] They also lacked any economic motive. That was something Europeans would supply.

When sustained European contact with the Gulf of St Lawrence began in the early 1500s, the main attraction was the fishery. For the next two hundred years, Prince Edward Island played sporadic host to Europeans fishing off its northern coastline. Basque whalers may occasionally have hunted its waters, though by the early seventeenth century they had driven the whale stocks in the Gulf to the point of commercial extinction. In any case, the major resource exploited off Island shores was that most lucrative of New France commodities – more lucrative even than beaver fur – cod. After explorer John Cabot famously stumbled upon the world's richest cod-fishing ground on his 1497 voyage of discovery, the fishing fleets of Western Europe had crowded sail behind him. By the 1520s the fishery was spreading steadily along the inshore waters of what is now Atlantic Canada. Jacques Cartier may not have encountered any fishermen when he coasted the North Shore of Prince Edward Island in the summer of June 1534, but in the 1620s Samuel Champlain found Basque fishermen already making themselves at home there.[3]

Whether the Basques (or the Portuguese, as Farley Mowat once maintained[4]) occupied a semi-permanent fishing station anywhere along the North Shore is mere conjecture – loose sand and persistent wind are a poor combination when drying cod – clearly the Island had become a familiar location for fishermen. "Île Saint-Jean" tends to be little more than a vague notion on seventeenth-century maps of the region, but the transient place names on those maps are almost always along the northern coast, the most convenient location for an inshore cod fishery.[5]

Over the course of the seventeenth century, the French Crown included Île Saint-Jean in charters to a succession of individuals with real or pretended plans to use the Island to exploit the cod, seal, and walrus fishery in the Gulf of St Lawrence.[6] But most of the fishing (most of it unrecorded) was done by French or Basque fishing crews with no formal title to the shoreline. Only when the Treaty of Utrecht stripped France of mainland Nova Scotia and its fishing base in Newfoundland in 1713 did Île Saint-Jean figure more prominently in French plans for the region. Even then the emphasis was agricultural rather than aquatic. In the grand post-1713 strategy for the region, the new fortress of Louisbourg on Île Royale (Cape Breton) would anchor the French cod fishery while Île Saint-Jean, with its conjectured fertility, would be developed as the "granary" of Louisbourg.

Yet when the Comte de Saint-Pierre and his Compagnie de l'Île Saint-Jean sent out some three hundred *engagés* to the Island in the spring of 1720, their express intent was to fish, not farm.[7] Saint-Pierre's royal charter may have required settlement, but his motives were purely economic, and that meant exploiting an industry that did not require clearing and planting, only putting lines in the water. On arrival, about two-thirds of the settlers went directly to the north shore of the island to begin fishing cod from bases at Havre Saint-Pierre (in honour of le Comte) and Tranche Montagne (North Lake). They would have found at least one fisherman already in residence, Francois Douville of Normandy, who had arrived in 1719.[8]

By October 1724, the Compagnie de l'Île Saint-Jean was bankrupt. Its fate foreshadowed many of the problems that would bedevil the Island's fisheries for the next 150 years. Misfortune at sea, competition from other fishers, the high start-up costs for a sedentary fishery (the Compagnie spent over a million livres in five years), distance from markets and supplies, and erratic returns on investment would repeatedly turn bold beginnings into financial shipwrecks.[9] The only thing not lacking was fish.

Although Saint-Pierre's venture failed, Havre Saint-Pierre quickly became the major fishing port during the French regime on Île Saint-Jean, and remained its largest community. By 1752, there were nearly three hundred permanent settlers there, almost all of them tied to the cod fishery. From Saint-Pierre and other harbours along the North Shore, small *chaloupes* (shallops) slipped out to hand-line just offshore, while schooner-like *goelettes* fished the deeper waters of the Gulf. In the beginning most of the resident fishers came, like Francois Douville, straight from the fishing ports of Normandy and Brittany, but gradually intermarriage merged the fishing community with the trickle of Acadian farmers who were slowly making their way into Île Saint-Jean.

After 1749, distant officials, determined that the Island fulfill its agricultural destiny, restricted fishing to two designated ports, Tracadie and Havre Saint-Pierre, in order to force Acadians to focus on farming.[10] Given the succession of quasi-biblical plagues that afflicted French-era farmers, many of the colony's settlers would probably have starved had the fishing regulations been strictly enforced. Like the Mi'kmaq before them, they fished to survive, and local officials generally turned a blind eye to the practice. Already many Acadians were practising the occupational pluralism, divided between land and sea, that would eventually become the hallmark of the Island's fishing culture. Subsistence fishing supplemented subsistence farming, a pattern of living that would survive the cataclysm of the British conquest in 1758 and the wholesale deportation that followed. It would also survive the best – or worst – efforts of fisheries promoters in the century that followed.

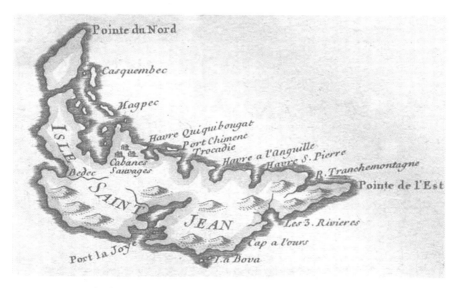

Figure 9.1 Detail of French map of Acadie, 1744.

... OR CUT BAIT

The Island's fishing potential was not lost on British authorities. By the time the Treaty of Paris permanently delivered Île Saint-Jean into British hands in 1763, British fishing entrepreneurs were already active there, and it was the potential of the fishery that helped make the Island valuable in the eyes of imperial officials, early promoters, and would-be proprietors.[11] That perception coloured Samuel Holland's famous survey of 1764–65, which divided the island into sixty-seven townships. Potential for the fishery helped determine Holland's estimation of each township, and when they were finally lotteried off to various claimants on the Crown's largesse in July 1767, a Fisheries Reserve, a five-hundred-foot wide strip of shorefront running along all coastal lots, was set aside for the use of fishermen. Although the Reserve provision was in practice ignored, it reflected the Board of Trade's faith in the Island's fishing potential.[12] So did the decision to grant two townships directly to merchant companies that had already set up fishing operations there. Township 40, which encompassed much of St Peter's Bay, went to George Spence, John Mill, and Lt George Burns, while Township 59, fronting on the superb harbour formed by Cardigan Bay, was given to Hutcheson Mure, Robert Cathcart, and fishing captain David Higgins.[13]

The fisheries' potential was also reflected in local legislation once Prince Edward Island became a separate colony in 1769. The first bill ever enacted by an Island government, in September 1770, was An Act for the Better Regulating the Carrying [on of] the Sea Cow Fishery on the Island of St. John, which established a licensing system and a closed season for hunting walrus. It was badly needed. Valued for its hides, ivory tusks, and, especially, the train oil that could be rendered from its blubber, walrus had once been common in the Gulf of St Lawrence, especially on the shelving beaches of the Magdalen Islands and Prince Edward Island, but they had been hunted ruthlessly in the eighteenth century. The act was entirely self-interested – it meant to preserve walrus from interfering Americans so that Islanders could kill them – and, in environmental terms, salutary. By 1810 the walrus was essentially extinct in Island waters.[14]

While Island legislators were struggling to conserve walrus stocks, the Island's early fishing entrepreneurs were themselves becoming an endangered species. Among the original proprietors *cum* fish merchants in Lots 40 and 59, George Burns and David Higgins, respectively, were the managing partners. Like that of the Comte de Saint-Pierre, their fates offered inauspicious auguries for the fishing industry. After three decades on the Island, Burns returned to the British Isles, crushed by debt. Higgins's fishing enterprise miscarried, despite substantial financial backing from proprietor James Montgomery and Boston merchant Job Prince. Bankrupt and cuckolded, he drank himself to death in 1783.[15] Other ventures that combined fishing and trade would follow, notably John Hill at Cascumpec near present-day Alberton, and John Cambridge at Murray Harbour.[16] Their struggles seemed to confirm what the first fishing companies' fates had suggested: the Island fishery was unfeasibly risky.[17]

The specific factors that conspired against early British fishing entrepreneurs – for example, the disruption of trade caused by the American Revolution that financially unhinged David Higgins – masked more systemic problems. One of them may well have been the Island's pervasive system of leasehold land tenure, which saddled tenants with the necessity of paying rents to proprietors. Fishing might provide a subsistence and allow a little trade with one's neighbours, but most observers insisted that farming was the best way for tenants to make their rent. According to the prevailing wisdom, fishing was something you did if you were an incompetent farmer. And to do both was to do neither well. Condescension drips from Lord Selkirk's account of the Acadian fishermen at Rustico:

"They are not however regular fishermen, but follow it at intervals of their agricultural business – a combination which never succeeds."[18]

Over and over again, British officials and local observers would decry the tendency among Acadians and other settlers to mix fishing and agriculture. "Fishing is so enticing an employment," wrote the Island's first British governor, Walter Patterson, "that the Common people can scarcely refrain from it a sufficient time in the year to raise themselves a little Bread."[19] Only when the colony's farmers could cheaply feed the colony's fishermen, argued Patterson, would the fishery consistently turn a profit. Patterson's contemporary John Stewart echoed those arguments three decades later in his *Account of Prince Edward Island*. "In the first seven years after the commencement of the settlement," he scoffed, "ten times as much money was thrown away on fishing projects as on the cultivation and improvement of the lands."[20]

By the time Stewart published his book in 1806, Islanders seemed to have learned their lesson. Few others followed their example, and by the early nineteenth century the Island's fishing industry had dwindled into insignificance. In 1829 the *P.E.I. Register* would count only eleven vessels and thirty-eight men engaged in commercial fishing.[21]

But just because there was no Island fishery did not mean that no one was fishing in Island waters. Settlers continued to harvest different fish for their own use, especially pelagic species such as herring, gaspereaux, mackerel, and smelts. Having made his case for "farming before fishing" in the colony's development, Stewart had rolled out a long list of potential Island fisheries, chief among them cod. At the moment, he pointed out, the Island's cod were being caught mostly by New Englanders. As many as six hundred Yankee vessels, he claimed, fished the north side of the Island each year.[22] The War of 1812 temporarily barred those opportunistic Yankees from the Gulf fishery. When they returned, under the provisions of the Anglo-American Convention of 1818, they soon turned their hand to another of the fisheries that Stewart's account had extolled: mackerel.

Cod had always dominated the North Atlantic fishery. It was large and plentiful, provided good return on the effort spent catching it, and was easily preserved. Mackerel had never enjoyed such popularity. Small and oily, it did not cure well, and while it schooled in immense shoals on the surface of the water, it was expensive to fish using a hook and line for the simple reason that eighteenth century hooks were expensive to make. If one hook catches one fish, then the bigger the fish the better, giving cod the advantage. Besides, to jig mackerel in commercial quantities required fishers to rapidly "slat" each fish into barrels with a snap of the wrist that tore the hook out of the mackerel's jaw. Too often, instead the hook bent or the line broke. Then, during the 1810s, New Englanders perfected the mackerel jig, which weighted the shank of hooks with a plummet of lead. The simple innovation solved the problem of rapidly landing mackerel by jigging.[23] Pickled in brine, mackerel could now be sold to rising urban populations and plantation owners in need of cheap food for their field hands.

The conjunction of numbers, need, and technology soon engendered a major new fishery. In 1830, declining stocks in New England waters drove the first Gloucester mackerel schooners into the Gulf of St Lawrence. They found arguably the best mackerel fishing grounds in the world. The following year, 1831, New England fishers salted a record 450,000 barrels of mackerel, much of it from the "Bay" of St Lawrence, and for the next half-century the annual catch would average 225,000 barrels.[24] Each June the Yankee mackerel fleet, 650 vessels strong, would follow the mackerel north into the Gulf, converging where the fish schooled thickest: New Brunswick's Chaleur Bay, the Magdalen Islands, and, from August through October, the North Shore of Prince Edward Island.[25]

The sudden rise of a valuable new fishery on Islanders' doorsteps helped signal a shift in government attitude towards its marine resources. With settlement advancing and agriculture securely established, the Island's legislature had begun modestly to promote a colonial fishery in the 1820s through regulation (1825) and then reward (1829), paying bounties to vessels exclusively engaged in fishing for cod.[26] The encouragement fell on deaf ears, and fisheries historian Kennedy Wells was only exaggerating about Island attitudes towards the fisheries when he wrote, "Like the weather, it was a subject about which everyone talked, but almost no one did anything."[27] In the 1770s Governor Patterson had worried that fishing would lure farmers away from the land; now the tables were turned. In 1839, John Hill's son, S.S. Hill, complained about the temptations of farming: "The life of a fisherman ... is not so luxurious as that of a farmer; and as fishermen in Prince Edward Island will spend much of their time among the farmers during the winter, there is danger of their changing their proper pursuit to follow the cultivation of the land."[28] A Yankee sea captain put it more bluntly: "Men possessed of such farms hadn't oughter take to fishing for a livelihood."[29]

Of course, there was more to it than that. Besides a shortage of fisher-men, the Island fishery wanted capital. Almost anyone might catch quan-tities of cod, herring, or mackerel with a couple of lines and a leaky shallop, but a fishing *industry* needed boats, bait, salt, stages, ships, gear, flakes, barrels. That required money, and Islanders with scarce capital to invest in the 1830s and '40s evidently found less risk and more profit in the colony's burgeoning shipbuilding industry. As a result the Island mackerel fishery developed almost in slow motion. In 1831, fish contrib-uted only £1,600 to Island exports of £42,000. Twenty years later, in 1851, the ratio remained low: £6,700 of £61,000, with still only five fishing companies operating on Prince Edward Island.[30]

When a significant Island mackerel fishery did finally emerge in the mid-1850s, it was primed with American capital that flowed north dur-ing the Reciprocity era of 1854–66, when American fishermen had free access to the Island's inshore waters, the right to trans-ship their catch from Island ports, and (through local statute) the right to own property in the colony.[31] As a result, American merchants such as J.H. Myrick, I.C. Hall, and C.C. Carleton began fishing operations on Prince Edward Island.[32] By 1861, there were eighty-nine fishing companies on the Island, and mackerel had become the king of a modest Island fishery that employed more than 2,300 men and 1,200 boats.[33]

Over time, mackerel schooners got bigger and faster, allowing them to spend more time fishing and less time sailing to and from port. At the same time, fishing technology grew more efficient. Jigging with hand-lines (two to four lines per crewman) slowly gave way after 1850 to purse seines that could literally bag shoals of mackerel at a time.[34] By the 1870s the conversion from hook and line to seine nets on New England vessels was largely accomplished. The short-term results were spec-tacular. In 1884, the New England mackerel catch set a new record, 478,076 barrels. But the subsequent decline was as swift as the rise had been slow. Two years later, in 1886, the catch plummeted by 75 per cent. Indeed, the mackerel catch for 1883 to 1885 exceeded the total catch for the next twenty-three years, which averaged only 43,000 barrels per year. Over-fishing, made possible by increased effort and enhanced tech-nology, had essentially ruined the mackerel fishery, which never recov-ered its former importance.[35] The collapse of mackerel stocks might have been devastating for the Island's fishing industry, but even before mackerel's collapse, another new fishery had risen that would prove much more lucrative and, within certain limits, far more durable.

Figure 9.2 Fishing out of North Rustico Harbour in 1877.

"COLOSSAL PROPORTIONS": THE RISE OF LOBSTER

Lobster had always been abundant on Prince Edward Island, washing up on the shore in windrows after heavy storms like so much seaweed. They were easily caught, in some cases right on the shore at low tide or with a cleft stick or a scoop net in shallow water.[36] But they had little value. "As to lobsters," wrote S.S. Hill in 1839, probably exaggerating for effect, "the best description of their abundance that can be given, is to say that they are on that, and that account only, despised by the older settlers ... When they are brought to the wharf at Charlotte Town ... the boys who usually catch them, sell for [a] halfpenny or a penny a piece."[37]

The handicap facing lobster as a potential fishery was frustratingly simple: there was no effective way to preserve the meat long enough to get it from where it was caught to the large urban markets where it would be eaten. But then canning technology – invented by the French, improved by the English, and adopted by the Americans – solved the logistical dilemma that faced would-be lobster fishers. By the 1830s,[38] canning had spread to the New England lobster fishery, and the technology quickly spread northwards, as dwindling lobster stocks in New England waters pushed American money and interest into the Maritimes.[39] By the late 1840s, the earliest lobster factories were operating in New Brunswick. The first record of lobster canning on Prince Edward Island dates from March 1858, yet in 1873 there were still only two lobster "factories" in the new Canadian province.[40] That year the Island fishery was valued at $288,863, of which only $10,592 derived from lobster canning.[41] In 1874, the lobster "pack" was a paltry 1,443 pounds, but the following year, the number had climbed to over 151,000 pounds, and two years later, in 1877, the pack was 664,000 pounds.

The mushrooming growth did not come at the expense of other fisheries. Instead, the catalyst was probably the collapse of another major industry, shipbuilding, which sent Island entrepreneurs in search of new investment opportunities.[42] After a mid-decade rally, the struggling shipbuilding industry suddenly imploded. In 1877–78, production fell by two-thirds and did not recover. Over the same period, the amount of lobsters canned on the Island more than doubled, from 640,000 to 1.6 million pounds. Looking back three decades later, Georgetown merchant Archibald John Macdonald would remark on this seesaw effect: "About this time also passed away the building of ships & it looked as if there was nothing else left for labor & commerce. But a few years of hard times was followed by the rise of the Lobster fishing."[43] For a brief time it did seem as if the lobster industry might take shipbuilding's place as the engine that drove the Island's export economy.

In 1879, thirty-five lobster factories canned nearly 2.3 million pounds of lobster around Island shores, the bulk of it shipped in one-pound cans to markets in Great Britain. The location of these early factories is revealing. Twenty-five of them operated on the Northumberland Strait shore, many in areas where there was no strong tradition of commercial fishing for cod or mackerel.[44] Although the North Shore would eventually yield the highest catches, lobster fishing there first had to overcome the inertia of an entrenched mackerel and codfish industry. The south coast of Kings County, where the earliest factories clustered, had no such impediment.[45]

Over the second half of the 1870s, the lobster pack had roughly doubled each year. In 1881, the industry took another giant leap when 6.5 million pounds of lobster were canned in 118 factories, greater than the combined pack of Nova Scotia and New Brunswick. Prince Edward Island had suddenly become Canada's leading lobster packer.[46] That year the value of the Island fishery soared to $1.95 million, nearly seven times the 1873 figure. Lobster accounted for 60 per cent of that total, $1.2 million. Marvelled the inspector of fisheries, John Hunter Duvar, "Lobster fishing has suddenly increased to colossal proportions."[47] No one could have predicted it at the time, but it would be over sixty years before the Island fishery surpassed those dollar totals.

Figure 9.3 Beach Point lobster factory, 1880.

The great lobster boom was full throttle, wide open, and almost completely unregulated – that is to say, unsustainable. Over the next five years, ever greater effort yielded ever smaller packs fetching ever lower prices. Even the lobsters were smaller. Where the factories of the late 1870s had needed to shell only two or three lobsters to fill a one-pound can, by 1888 seven were required.[48] Inspector Duvar, who had trumpeted the rise of the lobster fishery, was the first to sound the alarm, and the most alarmist: "The lobster fishery has taken another year's step towards its early extinction," he wrote in his 1884 report.[49] In 1887, the lobster pack was less than one-third of the 1881 total, and catches fell off so badly as the season wore on that over half of the 132 canneries closed in mid-July "for lack of lobsters."[50] After less than fifteen years, just at the same time as the mackerel fishery was collapsing, the lobster industry had reached the brink of disaster.

And then a curious thing happened. Those responsible for the industry backed away from the edge. Unlike the migratory mackerel and cod, which ignored international boundaries, the lobster fishery on Prince Edward Island was prosecuted exclusively in Canadian waters and so fell entirely under Canadian jurisdiction. A special commission, the first of many, was appointed in 1887 to address the lobster crisis. Of twenty-six written submissions from Island lobster packers, fifteen supported a moratorium on lobster fishing of one to three years to allow stocks to recover. (The actual fishermen were not consulted.) The commissioners themselves split on the issue. In the end, Ottawa opted for a less draconian remedy, choosing regulation over closure. After some tinkering, two-month closed seasons were established, one for the North Shore and one for the South. A licensing system was imposed, first on fishermen and then on canneries. Minimum size limits for lobsters were set, and it became illegal to take moulting or "berried" (that is, spawning) lobsters.[51]

Enforcement would be a persistent problem; there were always too few inspectors and too many fishermen willing to ignore the regulations.[52] For a time, the number of lobsters needed to pack a one-pound can with meat continued to rise.[53] Yet the measures seemed to work. Although they would fluctuate unpredictably from year to year, lobster catches stabilized, and, if there was no return to the halcyon days of 1880–81, the lobster fishery had reached a sustainable equilibrium by the mid-1890s.[54] It would continue to be the reliable backbone – or, maybe, exoskeleton – of the Island fishery, accounting annually for 60–65 per cent of its total value. After falling to only $877,000 in 1888, the estimated value of the Island's fisheries bounced back. For the next half century it generally averaged about $1 million per year, sometimes dipping below, rarely going much above. Chronic doubts were expressed about the resource's carrying capacity, yet stocks proved remarkably resilient.

Islanders had finally found a fishery that agreed with their agricultural lifestyle. While a handful of fishermen in a few localities fished from spring breakup to fall freeze, catching whatever fish was in season, the bulk of the Island's roughly 4,500 fishermen were part-timers, who practised a sort of occupational pluralism, using the short lobster season to generate cash income to supplement the production from their subsistence farms.[55] A generation earlier, they might well have hired out to one of the Island's many shipyards. Now they fished, either providing their own gear – traps, boats, lines – or using gear provided by the factory owners. Another factor that made the part-time fishery possible was that it did not demand the infrastructure of a deep sea fishery. The essentials were cheap to acquire: a homemade boat you hauled up on the beach, an anchor made from stones,[56] and traps made with wood otherwise classed with the weeds. Lobsters did not even demand fresh bait, and the fisherman could supply it himself by setting nets for herring in the early spring.

Besides entrenching the part-time nature of Island fishermen, the rise of the lobster fishery fundamentally changed the fishing landscape. Since the lobsters were fished from small, oar-powered, sail-assisted boats that could not travel far or fast, they must be canned close to where they were caught. As a result, lobster factories sprang up all along the shore like beads on a necklace, usually two or three kilometres apart but sometimes separated by only a few hundred metres. The little clusters of stages, bunkhouses, cookhouses, and cannery buildings provided the lobster industry with a distinctive architecture.

The demographic landscape changed as well. In Newfoundland, women had for centuries played an important onshore role in the cod fishery, especially in tending the flakes on which the fish were spread to dry.[57] Now women entered the Island fishery through the open door of the lobster factories, where unmarried or widowed women found work in the cookhouse or packed cans with freshly boiled lobster meat. Not only did fishermen and factory staff (men, women, and boys) work at the shore, they generally lived there as well, given the vicissitudes of Island land travel each spring and fall. For two months or so each year, temporary communities coalesced around the lobster factories, creating a whole new layer in Island society.[58]

The number of those lobster factories climbed steadily in the 1890s, peaking at 246 in 1900. As the 1887 commission had discovered, there were essentially two types of lobster factory, high end or low end: "Excepting a comparatively few first-class establishments, worth $3,000 and $5,000 apiece with all modern appliances, lobster factories are inexpensive buildings, roughly erected on the beach with boards, furnished with no other appliances than a table or two and brick fireplace and flue and a metal boiler, and suitable for no other purpose excepting, perhaps, as fish curing houses. When factory buildings are done with the boards, they are hauled away to build barns, so that the materials are not wholly wasted."[59] In the smallest operations, the fishermen were often also the canners, packing a few cases (each holding forty-eight, one-pound cans) a week and selling them to wholesalers.[60]

With their colourful labels and grandiose brand names, Island-packed lobster tins looked impressive from the outside, but the contents often told a different story. As early as 1887, London buyers were complaining about blackened and spoiled lobster meat.[61] "I am sorry to say your lobsters opened so poor that I would not care to buy them," one wholesaler wrote to W.P. Irving of Cape Traverse on 12 August 1899. "One can in 3 which I opened here was black. I am afraid you will have trouble with them. Better have them labeled with a nice label and shipped to the United States."[62] As pathologist Dr Andrew Macphail discovered, when the federal government hired him to investigate in 1896, sanitary standards at canneries were only part of the problem. Conventional canning wisdom was also at fault. After the cans were packed and sealed, packers "bathed" them in boiling water to sterilize the contents – but then punctured the lids to release any trapped air before resealing the cans and re-boiling. The practice opened the door for pathogens, then sealed them in with the lobster meat.[63] Of course, solving the spoilage problem was arguably less difficult than persuading cost-conscious Island packers to change their ways. Part of the federal response was to

Figure 9.4 Fishing boats at Malpeque Harbour heading out into Malpeque Bay, 1960.

address quality issues by curtailing the availability of packing licenses, and after 1900, the number of lobster factories began slowly to decline.

By 1910 the rituals and practices of the lobster fishery seemed largely set. Gaffs and hoop nets had long since given way to semi-cylindrical lobster traps built of lathe and twine, at first the big "double-enders," then, beginning in the 1890s, the smaller "parlour" traps familiar to today's fishers.[64] Fastened to snood ropes, they were ferried out to the fishing grounds at the start of the season and tied to long back lines, typically 75 to 150 per line, in a process called "setting" or "running" the lines.[65] For the rest of the season, weather permitting, they were hauled daily (Sundays excepted), by hand, producing generations of lean Island fishermen with preternaturally muscular forearms.

In an Island society often criticized for its stubborn aversion to change, Island fishermen are usually condemned as conservative and short-sighted.[66] And yet, by 1910, they were embracing an innovation that would have far-reaching consequences for the Island lobster fishery. Even as the Prince Edward Island legislature was legislating a ban on automobiles in 1908, convinced of their faddish impracticality, Island fishermen were converting from muscle to motor power at sea. The transition was astonishingly rapid. The first marine gas engines appeared around 1905.[67] In 1910, 166 Island fishing boats boasted marine engines, while 1,993 relied on a combination of sails and oars. By 1917, the figure was almost exactly reversed: 1,688 boats with engines and only 445 without.[68]

The early marine engines, mostly "Imperials" manufactured by Bruce Stewart & Co. of Charlottetown ("The Motor That Never Fails")[69] or Acadia engines made in Nova Scotia, were easy to operate but underpowered, generally only 4 to 10 hp. Affectionately dubbed "make-and-break" engines or "putt-putts," they were barely stronger than the tide, but they made travel to and from the fishing grounds far easier. Over time, powerful car engines replaced the early marine models.[70] Clive Bruce's experience is probably typical. Beginning in the 1920s with a 4 hp Acadia engine, the Kingsboro fisherman graduated to a 235 (i.e., displacing 235 cubic inches) Chevrolet, then, successively, a 292 Chev, a 354 Perkins diesel, and, in his last boat, another 292 Chevrolet.[71] Once the more powerful engines were fitted with power take-off shafts, they could help with the work of hauling the lines. By the 1950s, trap haulers, with their churn-shaped – and politically incorrect – "nigger heads" had become a staple feature of Island lobster boats. The enhanced hauling ability encouraged fishermen to fish more traps, even as their boats' increased mobility allowed fishermen to break up the long backlines into small, ten to twelve trap trawls (called "dumps" or "sets," depending on the locality) that could target more precisely the patches of rocky bottom where the lobster lurked.

Bigger engines also made possible bigger, more capacious vessels, and the ubiquitous dories and small shore boats of the nineteenth century gradually gave way to multiple variations on the high-prowed Cape Island design familiar today. Bigger boats in turn needed better berths. Where fishermen had once simply anchored their dories in the shallow water of sheltered bays or winched them ashore above the high-water mark with capstans and rollers, they would now increasingly congregate in wharf-lined "runs" leading back into small rivers or saltwater lagoons.[72]

Marine engines also indirectly accelerated the decline in the number of lobster factories in the first half of the twentieth century. Motorization seldom propelled the fishermen onto new fishing grounds, but it did make it faster to get to and from those familiar grounds. Lobster packers had once needed to go where the lobster were caught; now, marine engines brought the lobsters to them. Instead of lining the coastline, factories slowly began to cluster around the new fishing runs.

While such changes were far from cosmetic, they did little in the beginning to alter the fundamental nature of the lobster fishery. Lobsters crawled into traps, the traps were emptied into crates, the crates were dumped into boilers, and the boiled meat was packed into cans while the shells were dumped or salvaged for fertilizer by local farmers.[73] The size or speed of boats and even the design of traps had little measurable impact on the number of lobsters caught. Occasional tinkering with the idea of exporting fresh or live lobster, made difficult by the Island's comparative distance from American and Canadian markets, did little to lift lobster prices. Though stable, the lobster fishery in the early 1900s had essentially flat-lined in terms of growth.

COAXING NATURE

If greater effort and more efficiency could not elevate lobster catches, federal officials reasoned, then perhaps it was possible to increase (or, at least, preserve) the supply by giving nature a hand. In an early attempt at aquaculture, the Department of Marine and Fisheries began establishing lobster hatcheries across Maritime Canada. The science was simple. Spawn were scrubbed off female lobsters, incubated artificially, and then released into the safety of contained, saltwater lagoons to mature before being released into nature. The first Canadian hatchery was established in Nova Scotia in 1891, and between 1903 and 1912, fifteen more were opened, two of them on Prince Edward Island.[74] Each year annual reports published eye-popping statistics as billions of lobster fry were released into the wild. And for a time, optimism reigned. "A hatchery has been erected in 1903 at the Block House [at the western entrance to Charlottetown Harbour]," Lt-Gov. D.A. MacKinnon reported in a 1906 fisheries article, "with capacity for an output of one hundred million fry each year. In a year or two more the result of this distribution of young lobsters around our coasts must greatly aid in the future production."[75] MacKinnon was a better politician than prognosticator. In 1917 federally commissioned research concluded that female lobsters were better incubators than scientists; the artificially propagated lobster fry were having no provable impact on lobster stocks. The hatcheries were closed.[76]

The author of the damning report, Professor A.P. Knight, was employed by the Fisheries Research Board, which periodically brought its portable Biological Research Station to Malpeque Bay. While he was researching lobsters in 1917, Knight's colleagues had been focusing on another shellfish with an even longer fisheries pedigree and even bigger problems: oysters.

Since at least the 1840s, Island oysters had enjoyed an enviable reputation as a fashionable delicacy, and it was to protect them from wholesale destruction that the Assembly in 1825 banned their export (and
their burning to produce lime as fertilizer) for a period of seven years.[77]
Bedeque Bay oysters commanded early attention,[78] but by the Confederation era, it was "Malpeque oysters" that defined the oyster export
industry to cities such as Montreal. In 1882, in the midst of the great
fisheries boom, the value of the oyster industry had climbed to $171,000.
Afterwards, the industry declined, apparently because of overfishing
and wasteful methods, but also because of the damage to oyster beds
from another Island custom, dredging "mussel mud" from the bottoms
of bays and estuaries to use as fertilizer.[79] Yet its promise continued to
tantalize. Malpeque Bay, argued fisheries inspector J.A. Matheson, "is
in the nature of a little Klondike to all those employed in the business
who with no capital except a dory and a rake, can earn one to four dollars per day."[80] Klondike or no, the oyster fishery continued to struggle.
In 1882, 57,000 barrels of oysters were harvested; in 1910, the figure
was 11,300.[81]

It was the problems and potential of the oyster industry that first
brought Fisheries Research Board scientists to Malpeque Bay in 1903.
As far back as 1887, a special oyster commission had advocated both
research and better regulation, and the federal Department of Marine
and Fisheries ultimately retained its own expert, Ernest Kemp, to find
ways to strengthen the industry.[82] Both government and experts were
concerned with the health of existing oyster stocks, but they also were
prodded by the possibility of seeding new beds. In 1912, after a tedious
squabble with Ottawa over jurisdiction, the Island government began
leasing to private entrepreneurs tracts of seabed in river mouths and
bays that were deemed suitable for oyster culture. Dozens of oyster companies were formed, and by 1913 five thousand acres had been leased to
them. The provincial government boasted in its 1914 Throne Speech
that the oyster fisheries "now promise to become a great source of provincial wealth."[83]

Therein lies an environmental fable. To stock the new oyster leases in
Malpeque Bay, eight Island companies began to import oyster spat from
Chesapeake Bay in the United States in 1913–14. But along with the
spat, the companies also imported a deadly and highly infectious patho-
gen – mortality rates from it were over 90 per cent – that quickly spread
from bay to bay. Over the next few years "Malpeque disease" virtually
destroyed the Island's oyster stocks. It would take decades to restock

Island waters with spat from the disease-resistant survivors, and even longer for aquaculture to regain its allure.[84]

TREADING WATER

The twentieth century's two world wars were bookends for the Island's fisheries. After initially staggering the industry, they fed demand-driven boom periods.[85] In between, the Island's various fisheries drifted along, becalmed by low prices. Lobster continued to provide an income, if not a living, to several thousand Islanders, while a much smaller number dabbled in groundfish, mostly cod and hake, or, at various times and to varying degrees, netted herring and mackerel (mostly as lobster bait) or fished for smelt. The collapse of fish prices following the First World War drove down the value of the Island fishery to a post–lobster boom low of $468,791 in 1921, less than half the total in 1920, but that was an aberration. The fishery rebounded to something approaching "normal" by the mid-1920s, only to pitch into the black trough of the Great Depression after 1929, bottoming out again in 1933 at a value of $519,165. Between 1930 and 1933, the price of cod fell by 50 per cent to 20–75 cents per hundredweight (depending on fish size), split, gutted, and ready for salting;[86] herring prices fell by about 66 per cent; mackerel by more than 70 per cent; oysters and smelt by more than 60 per cent. According to economist H. Scott Gordon, Island fishermen's incomes fell by at least 50 per cent between 1929 and 1937.[87]

Paradoxically, instead of driving fishermen out of the fishery, desperation pushed many Islanders back into it. The number of fishermen actually climbed by 50 per cent during the 1930s to 3,310, from 2,202 in 1929. The number of lobster traps soared too, from 278,000 in 1929 to 426,000 eight years later. Although more Islanders were fishing, fewer were canning. The number of factories, already in steep decline after the First World War, continued to slide as profit margins shrank. "All through at lobster," Tignish-based factory owner C.F. Morrissey told his diary on 30 June 1930. "Worst year in 15. Damn near broke. Hard times." In Morell, factory owner "Big Jim" MacIntyre was reduced to peddling cases of lobster from the back of his car at $6 per forty-eight pound case.[88] Many factories simply closed up shop. In 1930 there were eighty-five of them; by 1945 there would be sixty-eight, nearly half in Prince County.

The spike in demand for foodstuffs produced by World War II and its immediate aftermath restored a measure of buoyancy to the fishing industry. In 1946, as Island lobster factories retooled to can finfish to meet the urgent needs of the United Nations Relief and Rehabilitation Agency, the value of Island fisheries smashed all previous records, topping $3 million.

Island canneries' postwar moment in the sun was fleeting. The transportation revolution that had begun on the water before the First World War shifted to the land after the Second. A spreading web of paved roads made it even less necessary to locate canneries near landing places. Meanwhile, cold storage facilities, refrigerated trucks, and improved sea and air links with the mainland made shipping live or fresh lobster increasingly feasible. As it became easier and faster to ship "market" lobsters in their shell, they increasingly supplanted the small "canners" in North American consumer markets and fetched much higher prices. Federal economist H. Scott Gordon might have been premature in 1952 when he asked "whether the canning of lobster is worthwhile at all,"[89] yet the number of lobster factories continued to fall. In 1900, there had been 246; by 1960, there were 28.[90] Twenty years later, the number was closer to a dozen. Nor did fishermen and factory hands need to live at the shore anymore. Like other commuters, they now drove to work, and the ad hoc communities that had once shaped the Island shoreline quickly vanished. The one thing that did not change was the Island fishery's reliance on lobster, which continued to account for two-thirds of fishing revenue. Rising prices pushed values steadily higher during the 1950s and '60s, though not fast enough to keep pace with the expectations of governments and their economic planners.

GROWING PAINS

H. Scott Gordon's 1952 report for the federal Department of Fisheries was itself something of a watershed. In the nineteenth century, the federal Department of Marine and Fisheries had taken its advice from "knowledgeable" persons such as lobster canners. In the early twentieth century, it had turned to scientists for answers to specific questions about fish stocks. In their postwar romance with regional development planning, both the federal and provincial governments (the province founded its own Department of Fisheries in 1956) increasingly delivered the future of the fisheries into the calculating hands of economists bent on expansion and efficiency.[91]

The rise of a fisheries bureaucracy in the second half of the twentieth century created a familiar dialectic of outsider versus local, theoretical versus practical, broad objectives versus individual needs. In his report, Gordon primly observed that "adherence to conservation regulations is poor" and enforcement "unpopular, ineffective, and even dangerous" – particularly in western Prince Edward Island, "where the law has had such little popular support for so many years that undersized lobsters are sold openly to reputable packers."[92] For much of the next half-century, behind a veneer of collaboration, the "experts" would often treat fishermen with paternalistic condescension, while fishermen would regard "science" with undisguised scorn. Both shared the goal of a more prosperous, more sustainable fishing sector, but it often seemed as though they were pushing on opposite sides of the same door.

Convinced that the lobster fishery had been operating more or less at capacity for many years, Gordon advocated fewer lobstermen in a better regulated fishery – a constant refrain in subsequent studies. At the same time, he urged greater exploitation of other fisheries, some old and some new. The oldest of all, of course, was the ground fishery.

Because the Island fishing industry was not keyed to cod, it largely missed the wrenching dislocations of the 1920s that affected the rest of Atlantic Canada, as offshore dragger fleets displaced the old Banks schooners, and fresh or frozen products eroded the traditional markets for salt fish. Island fishermen had continued to fish the way they had always fished, handlining or hauling their multi-hook cod trawls. By his own calculation, Clive Bruce of Kingsboro had, over the course of his sixty-seven-year fishing career, hauled himself 2.75 times around the world on his backline, baiting a hook every six or seven feet. He vividly remembered his best catch of cod: 5,219 pounds from four days of fishing twenty-nine lines.[93]

Given the small number of Island fishers, Bruce's hook-and-line fishery posed little threat to groundfish stocks. On the other hand, it gave little prospect of economic expansion. In 1950, the provincial government launched a Fisheries Development Program to help finance the creation of an offshore dragger fleet. The first Island-owned dragger, paradoxically named the *Souris II*, was launched in September 1950.[94] By 1961, twenty-four wooden draggers had been constructed. Four years later, Bathurst Marine in Georgetown launched a new wave of vessels with its first steel-hulled dragger. The dragger fleet's greater catches also catalyzed the development of modern fish processing plants. By 1970 there would be three plants geared directly to the offshore fishery, two in Souris and one in Georgetown.[95]

But as the Comte de Saint-Pierre had discovered in the 1720s, catching lots of fish was no guarantee of prosperity. Of the two dozen draggers

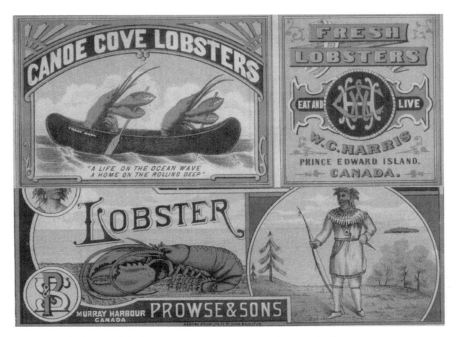

Figure 9.5 Lobster labels from various PEI canning plants in the late 1800s.

launched in the 1950s, only ten were still afloat by 1967, and if depreciation was factored in, none of them had made any money.[96] The processing industry itself faced cutthroat competition, and the "forced development" fiasco represented by Bathurst Marine and Gulf Garden Foods in Georgetown, which in four years swallowed up $9.3 million in provincial funds to generate a debt in excess of $6.2 million, should have shaken the confidence of planners.[97] It did not.

The impact of the dragger fleet on fish stocks was even harder to measure than its effect on the Island economy. Blessed with hindsight, veteran fishermen would have few doubts on this issue. All agree that the dragger fleet destroyed the ground fishery in Island waters. Not only were the draggers guilty of overfishing (and of defining "offshore" in very loose terms); not only was there appalling waste, as unwanted or unprofitable fish were simply dumped overside; but the heavy drags on the seine nets also destroyed the fragile sea-bottom habitat. Gus Gregory of Souris, who had both handlined from a dory and crewed on the draggers, was haunted by the memory of one particular scene off Cape George in the Northumberland Strait. A wolf pack of some fifty boats

Figure 9.6 Wooden dragger fleet in Murray Harbour, PEI.

was dragging: "The nets were small little nets that a herring couldn't get through. And they dragged everything up and picked the best out of it, and shoved the rest out through the scupper hatches ... flushed everything out through."[98] Only the small size and competitive disadvantage of the Island dragger fleet would prevent the province from playing a larger role in the ecological collapse that led to a federal moratorium on the East Coast's northern cod fishery in the early 1990s.

FISHING FOR DOLLARS

Even as the romance with modern industrial fishing followed its dollar-driven course, the search for alternative fisheries continued, increasingly stoked by government intervention. As early as the 1930s, scallops had been identified as a potential new fishery, but it would be another four decades before scallop dragging found a precarious anchorage in the stormy waters of early spring and late fall. The scallop catches in the Northumberland Strait peaked in value in 1998 but were not sustainable. A seaweed fishery targeting Irish moss followed a different trajectory but ended in a similar state of collapse related to overexploitation and use of destructive gear (see Novaczek, this volume). The bottom-dragging technologies used to capture both scallops and Irish moss removed rocks, flattened the three-dimensional structure of mixed bottom habitats, and smashed juvenile lobsters, spurring lobster fishers to lobby to have both scallop and Irish moss dragging banned from the productive lobstering grounds along the Island's North Shore. Scallop dragging was also restricted on certain rocky habitats in the Northumberland Strait. But need is a fierce driver. Although scallop fishing destroyed lobster habitat, many fishers pursued both fisheries, even as poor catches threatened to make neither one commercially viable. Recent attempts to revitalize scallop grounds in the Strait by seeding out cultivated juvenile scallops has been hampered by shifting sediments on the sea bottom that smother the vulnerable juveniles in their "grow-out" cages. The increasing sediment loads, in turn, have been traced to shoreline erosion.

While ecology and methodology bedevilled moss and scallops, more traditional issues overtook yet another new fishery. In 1965, government officials began testing a bluefin tuna fishery. Island fishermen had never found a use for the huge "horse mackerel" that often wreaked havoc by tangling in their nets. Now it was rebranded as a premiere game fish. Quickly, another seasonal fishery developed. The tuna fishery eventually developed two main branches: a commercial fishery centred in West Prince and a high-end sport fishery headquartered in North Lake – the "Tuna Capital of the World" – in eastern Kings County. Both found lucrative markets in Japan. But tuna fishery profits proved highly variable, being entirely dependent on market forces, the changeable migration patterns of a large game fish, and tuna's vulnerability to over-fishing. As with other species, fisheries officials resorted to quotas to regulate human pressure on tuna stocks while they migrated through Canadian waters. How successful this effort has been is an open question. The intense international debate in the twenty-first century about whether or not to designate bluefin tuna as an endangered species is a reminder of the political nature of conservation, the power exerted by market demands, the challenge of managing migratory fish species that cross international boundaries, and the inherent difficulty in counting something that lives underwater.[99]

The emergent mussel industry of the 1970s and '80s posed no such difficulties. Mussels were the poster child of the state's ambitious efforts to create new fisheries during the 1970s.[100] Though ubiquitous, wild mussels had been largely ignored by European settlers,[101] but in 1974 the provincial Department of Fisheries Aquaculture Division began experimenting with cultured mussels, adapting to North American

Figure 9.7 The early days of mussel harvesting, 1970s.

winters the European technique of growing mussels on lines suspended in tidal currents above the sea bottom. Private growers were enlisted as partners, and in 1978 the first cultured mussels were harvested from the Cardigan River in central Kings County. At the start of the century, the province had leased sea bottom; now it leased thousands of acres of water in bays and river estuaries to would-be mussel growers. By 1988, after a decade of state-assisted marketing and financial growing pains, and despite a deadly shellfish poisoning outbreak,[102] the value of the industry topped $2.4 million, and "Island Blues" had carved out a market niche in North American kitchens.[103]

Production would continue to rise dramatically into the new millennium even as profit margins shrank. By 2000, mussel lines crowded virtually every farmable expanse of inshore water, competing with each other for food. Meanwhile, invasive species such as tunicates (which smother mussel socks), oyster drill whelks, and green crab (predators of juvenile mussels) posed new challenges for growers.[104] Despite such obstacles, mussels continued to rank second only to lobsters among Island fisheries. In 2009, the mussel harvest fetched almost $24 million, accounting for 20 per cent of the total value of the Island fishery.[105] No other aquaculture venture has yielded comparable results.[106]

FISHERS OF MEN ... AND WOMEN

The government investment in mussel farming during the 1970s was just one part of a much grander design. In March 1969, Ottawa and the province had launched the Comprehensive Development Plan, an unprecedented fifteen-year, $725 million federal-provincial program aimed at transforming the province's economy and society. Its architects had the fishing sector squarely in their sights. Since the 1950s, economists had complained that the Island had too many fishermen (roughly three thousand by 1969) chasing too few dollars, and the Development Planners felt the same way. In his 1970 analysis of the industry, Cecil M. Birch was especially blunt: "Fishermen have got to get out, inefficient producers have to change or die, facilities have to be concentrated and 'rationalized,' fewer, larger scale operations in fishing and processing have to be accepted, market regulation is essential, and so are planning and cooperation."[107]

Besides spreading out the fishing effort among more species, the Development Plan's fisheries strategy planned to reduce the number of fishers to a thousand, concentrated in fourteen to twenty designated ports with Georgetown and Souris the locus for an offshore fishery.[108] But even as Birch was delivering his economic ultimatum, politicians were backing away from the planners' Stalinesque approach to rationalizing the fishing sector.[109] By 1974 the relocation program had been abandoned.[110] Instead, as lobster landings declined, fisheries officials changed tack. Already in the late 1960s the federal Department of Fisheries and Oceans (DFO) had adopted a limited entry licensing system to control the number of fishers and had imposed limits on the number of traps.[111] In 1977 the DFO piloted a three-year, voluntary licence buy-back scheme designed to achieve an overall reduction in the number of fishing licences, especially for the main resource fishery, lobster.

Then, just as the buy-back system was beginning to show results, a curious thing happened. After hitting a twenty-seven-year low in 1974, lobster landings began climbing rapidly in the late 1970s, soon reaching 2.5 to 3 times the average landings for the first seventy-five years of the century. Prices rose even faster during the inflationary cycles of the period. Between 1969 and 1988, the average price for lobster nearly quadrupled.[112] The rise in landings combined with the steady increase in prices produced a sustained lobster boom between 1980 and the early twenty-first century. In 1969, Islanders landed 8.2 million pounds of lobster valued at $5.4 million. The comparable figures for 2008 were 21.9 million pounds and $107 million.

By the turn of the millennium, the fishing landscape, physical and human, had changed dramatically. Federal fisheries policies had pushed many small-scale operators out of Atlantic fisheries while allocating quota to industrial fleets. The inshore fishing enterprises that remained were "encouraged" to professionalize and focus on single species rather than follow the traditional, multi-species harvesting strategies that allowed them to switch targets according to market signals and local stock fluctuations.[113] More and more women now went fishing, partly to maximize Employment Insurance benefits and keep profits in the family in the face of rising costs and partly in a reflection of crumbling gender barriers.[114] Despite fierce resistance in parts of the region, federal policy had bankrolled Native peoples' treaty right to fish commercially.[115] Meanwhile, the farmer-fisherman, once the mainstay of the Island fishing population, had all but vanished – in part because so few Islanders now farmed and many of these had adopted single commodity models of industrial agriculture.[116] Rural fish plants, with few exceptions, did not survive. Waves of consolidation, abetted by improved transportation infrastructure and government policy, centralized fish buying and processing almost entirely out of the province. The dragger fleets were long gone, and by 2007 low prices hobbled a lobster fishery where the costs of doing business had risen steadily.

But still there were lobster to fish. The continued resilience of lobster stocks defies easy explanation, although it clearly involves both fish and fishers. The lobster fishery is often held up as one of the few fisheries where fishers themselves have, through their unions and associations, developed and imposed local rules and limits to fishing that maintain it as a relatively labour-intensive small boat fishery. Fishers' grudging acceptance of ever more layers of regulation may also have helped: limits to the number and size of traps, rules against the harvesting of very small and very large lobsters, and new escape mechanisms that allow small lobsters to get out of traps – all, admittedly, offset by the ever-increasing efficiency of fishing technology. In the end, changes in the structure of marine ecosystems, rather than good management, may well be the true cause of the lobster's persistence.[117] The large cod, now gone, had been predators capable of keeping numbers of lobster, shrimp, and other crustaceans in check. And while pundits warn of an inevitable collapse in lobster stocks should fishing pressure remain high, the current crisis in the lobster fishery is not so much a function of declining stocks (with the exception of the Northumberland Strait fishery) as low market prices.[118] Yet as other fisheries rose and fell like the tide, lobster remained in 2012, as it had been since the early 1880s, the one constant in the Island fishing sector, accounting annually for roughly two-thirds of the landed value of the Island catch.

MURKY WATERS

It is difficult to know which of the Island's two principal fisheries, lobster or mussels, offers the best guide to the future. Conventional scientific wisdom maintains that relentless overfishing and habitat degradation will surely kill the world's fisheries within decades. Already, one recent study suggests, human impacts have decreased formerly important fish species in areas such as the southern Gulf of St Lawrence by more than 90 per cent.[119] A 2009 study of women's actual and potential roles in the Island's fishery documents fishing families' sense that the province's fisheries are "on the brink."[120] But if the future trajectory of a sustainable fishery arcs from capture to culture, what are we to make of lobster's stubborn abundance? And if fish aquaculture is the future, what moral can be drawn from Advanced Lobster Technology's much publicized, but ultimately bankrupt lobster-farming venture in Victoria, PEI, during the early 1980s? Can the path to the future be found by leaping from buoy to buoy along the Island's mussel leases? Or does it lie in the controversial experimental production of genetically modified salmon in land-based tanks at Aqua Bounty Farms in Fortune Bay?

History explains, but it seldom predicts. A survey of the chequered history of Prince Edward Island's marine fisheries does offer several lessons. It teaches us that, given the "right" technology and sufficient economic motive, we are more than capable of destroying our fisheries. It cautions us about our limited ability to achieve sustainable fisheries through top-down regulation or management. Finally, it tells us that, in many cases, we do not know what we know. We do not really know what happens beneath the surface of Island waters. We do not fully understand the workings of the marine environment nor our effect on it. The seemingly inevitable shift from a "capture" to a "culture" fishery is not just a defence against the spectre of depleted species and the gaping maw of human need: it is an attempt to provide a measure of certainty and predictability to an uncertain sea. In the waters surrounding Prince Edward Island, where overfishing has profoundly altered ecosystems, climate change is now exacerbating conditions. Water temperatures are rising, acidity is rising, oxygen levels are dropping.[121] Over the centuries hope has always been the fishers' best bait. That may no longer be enough.

The Landscapes of Tourism:
Scenic Images in Prince Edward Island
Tourism Literature

Alan MacEachern

Since the late nineteenth century, Prince Edward Island has been actively promoted as a tourism destination.[1] The image being sold to tourists has in one sense not changed all that much along the way. Then as now, the province has been portrayed as a place of pastoral beauty, a relaxing retreat from the modern world. But a glance through old and new guidebooks would show that different landscapes have been chosen to epitomize Prince Edward Island over time, and they have been presented in different ways. Rivers and streams once attracted more attention than beaches did. Tree species trended, if not as quickly as activities and attractions. Even the Island's colours – even its air – have been subject to redefinition.[2]

It is difficult to determine exactly what any such changes in the tourism literature signify. They may in part reflect shifts in tourism and Islanders' attempts to adapt to them. They may reflect what Islanders believed their home to be or what they believed visitors wanted it to be. Or they may be a mix of all these. A humanities-style Heisenberg Principle comes into play: the representations of landscape cannot logically claim to accurately reflect the authors', Islanders', and tourists' desires for it, as well as the Island as it truly was, all at the same time. And yet it is still worth trying to pull apart meaning.[3] Tourist guidebooks have over time become the dominant synthetic expression of Prince Edward Island to the world. That the provincial government has since the 1950s produced annual visitors guides – renaming them "visitor's" guides in 2010 so as to shift the focus from the Island's luring of the masses to the traveller's own individual experience – has even meant this image has official sanction. The annual guides have in turn become a key means by which Islanders have both constructed and absorbed a sense of self. When the Department of Tourism and Culture recently considered doing away with the guides altogether, questioning their necessity in the Internet age, it was Island tourism operators rather than tourists who strongly objected.[4]

In the chapter that follows, I explore how representations of Prince Edward Island's landscapes have evolved in the photographs and, to a lesser extent, texts of tourism guidebooks.[5] As Island scholars routinely note, the province makes for a good case study: as both an island and a full Canadian province, it is coherent, manageable, and significant. For my purposes, it also benefits from having had a healthy tourism industry for well over a century and government-administered, regularly produced tourism promotion for almost that long. And because Prince Edward Island has never relied on a single natural landmark such as Niagara Falls, tourism promoters have had considerable latitude to choose any landscape – indeed, any location on the small island – as one worth praising. Utilizing what I believe to be significant and yet representative images from successive eras, my fundamental goal here is not to craft an overarching thesis as to how nature has been used for tourism. Rather, it is to trap those moments that best exemplify the classification and reclassification of what elements of nature are deemed worthy of people's attention – the constant, incremental redefining of beauty.

I think of Jacques Cartier as Prince Edward Island's first tourism promoter and the first one to draw attention to the beauty of the Island landscape. Upon reaching the Island in 1534, the French explorer in his journal described the land around Cape Kildare as "*la plus belle qu'i soict possible de voir*."[6] This declaration has been passed down in the Island's tourism literature for more than a century now, usually translated as "the fairest land 'tis possible to see" (although on what basis "'tis" is thought to be characteristic of sixteenth-century French usage is not clear). It is never mentioned, though, that Cartier offered such testimonials wherever he went. A harbour in Labrador was "one of the best in the world," an island off Newfoundland "the best land we have seen," and the land around Chaleur Bay – visited shortly after Prince Edward Island – "as fine and as good land ... as any we have ever seen" and "the

finest it is possible to see." Like any good tourism booster, Cartier knew
better than to be stingy with his praise.

But it was really in the late nineteenth century that Prince Edward
Island tourism promotion began in earnest, when the steamship and railway companies that brought visitors to the province began publishing
guidebooks with sections devoted to it. We might expect hucksterism in
such literature, and there was certainly much of that. But there was also
more honest appraisal than anticipated, perhaps because the companies
were not affiliated with a single locale and perhaps because they wished
their guidebooks to impersonate the independent travel writing genre.
The Intercolonial and PEI railways' 1905 *Forest, Stream and Seashore*
began its Island section with British writer William Cobbett's line about
"a rascally heap of sand, rock, and swamp, called Prince Edward Island,
in the horrible Gulf of St. Lawrence."⁷ Of course, the guidebook then
worked diligently to counter this judgment.

But perhaps it was such editorial decisions that spurred the Island
toward tourism self-promotion by the early twentieth century. If transportation companies could attract tourists by promoting the province
for a few pages as just one of their destinations, how much more could
be accomplished if those who knew the Island best wrote about it alone?
The *Charlottetown Examiner* published *Prince Edward Island Illustrated* in 1897, and two years later the provincial government followed
with the first officially sanctioned guide, *Prince Edward Island Garden
Province of Canada*. Since tourism and publicity were conflated in this
period, these guidebooks promoted the Island simultaneously as a destination for tourism, immigration, and business investment. Early in the
new century, municipal and private tourism information agencies began
popping up, as did a short-lived Development and Tourism Association.
From 1899 to 1912, stenographer and Legislative Assembly librarian
W.H. Crosskill was the provincial government's one-man tourism promotion branch; his successor, seventy-four-year-old J.E.B. McCready,
held the job into his nineties, often borrowing liberally from Crosskill's
prose. The homegrown tourism literature was not noticeably different in
style or substance from other work promoting PEI; the only real difference was that it focused solely on the Island.

The photographs in the visitors guides of these first decades tended to
be of either prominent Charlottetown buildings or the bucolic Island
countryside – pastoral scenes along rivers or streams, with forests as
backdrop. These two foci are unsurprising in purely logistical terms,
since steamship passengers tended to land in the capital, and both steam

and rail passengers spent much of their time there when not travelling the province's interior by rail. But the images also represented the Island as these companies, and then Islanders themselves, thought it should and could be reasonably portrayed. The urban photos assured readers that Prince Edward Island was modern, prosperous, and civilized, the rural photos that it was old-fashioned, charming, and picturesque. A montage from the 1917 *Summer Provinces by the Sea* (figure 10.1) is indicative of how the Island and its people were depicted together (as well as of how small many guidebook images were). A fallen tree resting over a secluded brook, a private fishing spot, a farm as seen from a forest, and five generations posed together like a string of pearls spoke of a place where people and nature existed in tandem, the calm constancy of one reinforcing the calm constancy of the other.

What is largely missing from images of the Island in early guidebooks such as *Summer Provinces by the Sea* is the "by the sea" part, beaches in particular. Whereas the 1917 guide has approximately twenty pictures of Island harbours, bays, rivers, and streams, only two reference any sort of beach. Other travel guides of the era were somewhat more generous to the seashore – *A Summer Paradise*, published in 1913 by the provincial government, contains a few photos of swimmers frolicking – but none gave the beach pride of place. "On the North Shore" in *Forest, Stream and Seashore* (figure 10.2) is quite unusual in showing a beach devoid of people, yet even this image suggests the picturesque appeal of wind-worn trees and stones rather than the beach itself.[8] Prince Edward Island tourism today is so closely associated with the beach that this indifference to the seashore in early promotional images is certainly surprising. It is even more so given that beaches of the North Shore in particular were being touted in the texts – and were appearing in visual form in other media, including postcards and the 1880 Meacham's *Atlas*. A century ago, the Island's islandness may well have been as important to tourism in terms of healthy sea air as in terms of the seashore itself. In the days before air conditioning, the chance to escape hot and overcrowded, unsanitary cities for the cool, bracing air of a small island had clear medicinal value. Air did not photograph well, but on the other hand it spread over the Island equally, bringing the possibility of tourism well beyond the coast – a windfall for inland landscapes, if you will.

What with a number of parties creating these first guidebooks, and the image that Prince Edward Island would project for tourists still in its infancy and thus very much in flux, it can be difficult to spot trends in how the province was promoted. Still, there are indications the

Figure 10.1 *Summer Provinces by the Sea* (1917).

guidebook was slowly evolving. The small jumbled collages of snapshots slowly gave way to larger, more dominant photographs. When .the Intercolonial published *Prince Edward Island: The Garden of the Gulf*

Figure 10.2 *Forest, Stream and Seashore* (1905).

in 1913, it largely copied the Prince Edward Island section of its 1905 *Forest, Stream and Seashore* but added almost twice as many photographs and removed a paragraph on the Island's colours. Even black-and-white images apparently did a better job than text of conveying colour. The 1913 edition also dropped the section on farming. Moving further into the twentieth century, there are fewer and fewer descriptions of Prince Edward Island's day-to-day existence as a living community. In the same vein, discussion of Island history and showcasing of prominent churches and public buildings – staples of earlier accounts – began to disappear. Travel guides no longer bothered describing the province as a bustling place with a promising outlook and focused instead on it being a destination of unchanging serenity. W.H. Crosskill's 1906 claim that most tourists went to the North Shore "to revel in the surf and strong air of that famous region" was touched up by J.E.B. McCready seven years later as "to revel in the surf and clear air of that famous region."9 "Strong" was fine for some places, but the Island's image was becoming fixed as one of clarity and calm.

Tourism and its promotion slowly started to snowball during the 1920s. A new Tourist and Publicity Association established in 1923 devoted itself almost exclusively to advertising, ignoring the need for better accommodations and more attractions. In its first year the association printed 15,000 copies of a new guide – notably entitled *Restful Summer* – and by the end of the decade it was distributing 40,000 brochures per year. Much of this rising interest was thanks to the automobile. Cars revolutionized North American tourism, allowing families to explore the countryside without being confined to the routes of ships and trains; everywhere was a potential destination. Prince Edward Island had been slow to accept the automobile, banning it outright from 1908 to 1913 and allowing it only limited access until 1919, but tourism promoters embraced it wholeheartedly. A photo in *Prince Edward Island: Its Resources and Opportunities* showed a car travelling along a tree-lined road, the caption promising "The highways are in good condition and there is no traffic problem."[10] Camping alongside the road – "gypsy camping" – was popular, and the guidebooks assured readers that Islanders would be ever-ready, ever-subservient hosts, a characterization that must surely have rankled. The 1926 edition of *Its Resources and Opportunities* claimed, "At most of the farm houses throughout the island meals or lodging can be secured when necessary at reasonable rates." Every single word in the 1927 edition of the book was the same but for one: "most" farmhouses had become "many."[11]

The car opened up all Island landscapes to tourism, but it did not immediately transform how these landscapes were perceived. To some degree, the image of the Island as offering a pastoral retreat from modernity became more solidly entrenched. The 1928 *Official Motor Guide* claimed that the province was "emphatically a Land of Rest, appealing to the jaded in spirit – the wearied in body. There is no rush or bustle here, no jarring sounds, no traffic noises."[12] But in the longer term, the car could not help but reshape how places were viewed and used by tourists, because it broadened both who could travel and what they could choose to see and do. Even as the back cover of *Vacationland of Heart's Content* told 1939 readers to "Come to 'the Island' – *and rest,*" its centrefold cartoon map (figure 10.3) promised a beehive of activity (also, Vikings).

The Island's tourism literature of the late 1930s through wartime suddenly seems much more like the tourism we know today. There were far more images than before of the North Shore beaches and of happy families at play on them – a response in part to the 1937 creation of the national park, the province's first specific tourist attraction. And the beaches were pictured as teeming with people in a way that no previous

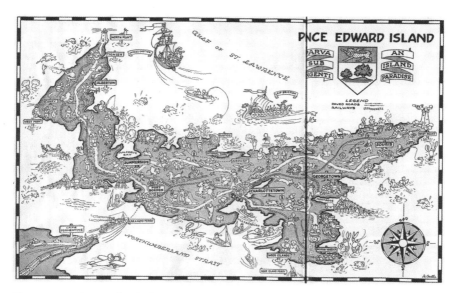

Figure 10.3 *Vacationland of Heart's Content* (1939).

landscape had been. Much more than a field, a brook, or a forest, the beach was interpreted in this era as a social landscape that required the presence of other people to give it meaning. One of those meanings concerned sex; the promotional literature exploited the fact that societal convention permitted more flesh to be bared at the beach than anywhere else. Six bathing beauties gambolled through the pages of the patriotically themed 1941 brochure *Prince Edward Island: The England of Canada*, in one shot peeking coyly out from behind the rocks. The caption read, "Modern mermaids on the shores of the age-old sea beckon you and your family to join them in a happy, carefree holiday in Prince Edward Island's beautiful National Park. 'Breathes there a man with soul so dead' as to refuse?"[13] It would seem that the family man with a wandering eye had been targeted as a key demographic. In the following year's *Prince Edward Island: The Birthplace of Canada*, women were *literally* typecast, the pinups used (and reused) to spell out the province's initials (figure 10.4).

The cover of *The Birthplace of Canada* illustrates another landscape feature that rose to promotional prominence alongside the beach: the birch. Beginning around the late 1930s and continuing through at least the early 1960s, guidebooks extolled the beauty of the Island's white birches in text and photos.[14] It is unclear what drove this campaign:

Figure 10.4 The cover of *Prince Edward Island: The Birthplace of Canada* (1942).

while the trees are attractive and distinctive, they are also widespread throughout North America. Perhaps it is worth considering that the white birch is a pioneer species, colonizing open spaces following disturbances such as forest fires or forestry – or declining agricultural land use such as Prince Edward Island experienced at the beginning of the century.[15] It may well be that the birches that came to maturity in mid-century and that drew the attention of tourist promoters were, unobserved, the perfect symbol of the Island economy's gradual transition from agriculture to tourism.

With the end of the Second World War, North American travel boomed, assisted by a rising standard of living and a related growing belief that recreation, including a yearly vacation, should be the right of all. While the Prince Edward Island government was coming to respect tourism's great economic potential,[16] few Islanders – least of all "the Farmer Premier," J. Walter Jones – could yet imagine it challenging agriculture as the basis of the Island's existence. Tourism promotion languished through the early 1950s, with the publicly sponsored but privately run Prince Edward Island Travel Bureau doing what it could with quite limited funds. Yet despite relative government inattention, the Island began to develop what historian Matthew McRae memorably calls an "accidental tourism industry."[17] More by push factors than pull, tourism to the Island bloomed postwar: between 1946 and 1950, the number of vehicles arriving on the Cape Tormentine ferry quadrupled, and the number of visitors to the national park doubled.[18]

The photographs from the 1952 Travel Bureau guidebook *Prince Edward Island* reflect this era of tourism promotion in at least three ways. First, there are simply more people. A family of campers relax within five metres of the family at the adjacent site. In the clichéd pose of a woman looking out over the dunes, she is not contemplating solitary nature but rather a beach full of people. Second, photographs are becoming dominant, claiming a larger share of the brochures. Taking pictures is itself becoming recognized as an important vacationing activity; one section of the guidebook is presented as a series of snapshots. Third, and presumably most specific to the Island's circumstances, tourists are pictured enjoying a wide range of activities – fishing, golfing, horseback riding, sunbathing, and so on – while locals are shown going about their business – loading hay, picking potatoes and strawberries, hauling lobster traps, tonging oysters, and so on – in distinctly separate sections. Tourists play the province while Islanders work it, but there is little sense of this being shared space.

With tourism's growing significance to the economy, the province committed more to what was becoming accepted as a real industry. One result was that the Travel Board (soon, Bureau) had sufficient funds to produce annual visitors guides. The literature it produced in the 1950s and 1960s was in one sense exceptionally generic; presumably because the government did not want to be seen as favouring individual businesses over others, it was unusual for specific accommodations, restaurants, or even attractions to be mentioned by name. (The 1960s was the "typical" decade, in which seemingly every picture of a beach, sailboat, golf course, and even bikini-clad woman was labelled "typical" of the kind the tourist would see.) Yet this very lack of specificity, coupled with the need to produce a new edition of the guidebook every year, means that it is easier than ever to see how images of Island landscapes were being produced for tourism and how those images evolved incrementally in response to tourist trends or simply to marketing experimentation.

A series of *Come to Prince Edward Island Canada* guides from the 1960s demonstrates this evolution.[19] At first the guides appear all but identical – opening, for example, with sections about the beaches and countryside. But the text is constantly shifting. The description of the beaches starts out matter-of-factly in 1960 – "If it's swimming you're after, come to Prince Edward Island where the warmest salt water north of Florida awaits you. Your bathing suit will be a cherished possession during the summer holiday here." But by 1962 the language is florid – "Beaches of dazzling pink and white sand, sloping gently to the sea, stretch for more than a thousand miles around the shoreline of beautiful Prince Edward Island, a red and green fairyland set like a gem in the blue waters of the Gulf of Saint Lawrence on Canada's Atlantic Coast." (Island beaches turn pink for a few years, until red again prevails.) By 1968, the prose has been toned down once more, but waterskiing is now mentioned even before swimming. As often as the text changes, the images change faster, rearranged for every edition and quite often replaced. Occasionally, the image changes so fast that the accompanying caption does not change to keep pace.[20] This suggests that photographs have become the key discourse in tourism promotion. Their size and quantity increase, and the content of the images changes, too. As the opening pages of the beaches sections from 1960 versus 1968 demonstrate (figures 10.5 and 10.6), compositions are growing more formal, more geometric – and soon, even psychedelic. But more noticeable is that the landscapes are emptying out. The tourism industry was discovering that after the frenzy of the baby boom, people wanted to get away from it all, including other people, when on vacation.

The 1970s saw a continuation of this trend, with would-be visitors seduced by the promise of quiet contemplation rather than intense activity. The guidebooks also suddenly seemed self-aware, their authors realizing that neither tourism nor its promotion was a novelty any longer and that all parties understood exactly what was going on. "Let's be frank," states Premier Alex Campbell to introduce the 1974 edition. "This book is intended to lure you to Prince Edward Island. We want you to spend your entire vacation here if you can. And we want you to come back, again and again."[21] This self-awareness undoubtedly contributed to the reduction of text, including captions: it seemed gratuitous over-selling to explain in words what could more easily and more coolly be communicated in pictures.

A two-page spread from 1975 encapsulates the sense of serenity and seclusion. There is no text, just a landscape of dunes and gulf and, in the foreground, a near-naked woman partially obscured by dune grass – and by the staple, since this is the guide's centrefold (figure 10.7). This is certainly the most voyeuristic photo in the history of Prince Edward Island tourism promotion, with the camera playing the part of the tourist who stumbles upon the scene. The following year's centrefold is by contrast much more direct, the bikini-clad girl front and centre, the scenery less scenic and less central. But arguably the most interesting thing about the turn to sexuality was that it was so short lived. Although these photographs constitute an alluring and even plausible representation of the interplay between Island landscape, climate, and tourism, they do not conform to the brand that the province had been building over the century, one that tourists and Islanders alike had come to expect: that is, the Island as a pastoral retreat from modern existence. Getting away from it all may not actually have meant getting away from sex, but it at least meant that sexuality would be too discreet to be hinted at in the visitors guide.

As inconsistent as those cheesecake photos were with the Island's longstanding image, they at least offered a vision of how the province might be portrayed. But the late 1970s saw Prince Edward Island tourism promotion enter its least visually interesting decade by far. With tourism's economic significance intensifying, there were more calls to develop the industry beyond its Queen's County core and more pressure on the government to be seen as treating all locales and all attractions equally. The result was that almost overnight the visitors guides went from not advertising many specific sites to advertising all of them. Whether Green Gables house or Burlington Go-Karts, every attraction qualified for one small picture and about one hundred words. Never before or since was the guidebook so overtly a catalogue of experiences to be purchased.

By the late 1980s the Department of Tourism had come to terms with the fact that even where all attractions are equal, some attractions are more

Figure 10.5 *Come to Prince Edward Island Canada* (1960).

equal than others. And critically, it also recognized that the province's overall image was more than the sum of these attractions, and that this image could best, or only, be displayed through archetypes: a hayfield, a lobster dinner, a sunset, a smiling child. Photographs of seashores and rolling countryside once again grew common. This era also saw the increased fragmentation of tourism and its promotion. In 1988 the province chose, significantly, as its inaugural year-long tourism theme "Touch Nature," a celebration of the Island's "quiet but spectacular beauty, unspoiled environment and traditional way of life."[22] Campaigns such as "We're Akin to Ireland" followed (although in the case of that 1990 promotion, distinctly less so in the French version), with the guidebooks targeting specific kinds of visitors even as they emphasized the Island's core image. This move to distinct annual themes was brief, however, because each theme excluded some subset of tourism operators, did not yield the expected jump in tourist numbers, and was presumably a great deal of work.

It is more difficult to map the changing portrayal of landscapes for tourism promotion in recent decades. Unlike at mid-century, when text

Figure 10.6 *Come to Prince Edward Island Canada* (1968).

and photos changed incrementally each edition, now virtually all text and many photos are fresh each year.[23] We are also conditioned to see more contemporary portrayals as more accurate, self-evident, even "natural" representations of the world. And perhaps we tacitly assume that, with a century of experience, tourism promotion must surely by now be getting it right, presenting the Island simultaneously as it is and in its best light. Yet the Island's nature has continued to be relentlessly reinterpreted. The case of Elephant Rock captures this nicely. Sometime around 1990, a pachyderm was spotted just off the northwest coast of the Island; since it was made of easily-eroded sandstone, it may not have existed in that shape for long. Western Prince County was a corner of the Island that did not see many tourists, and the provincial government was always on the lookout for new ways to draw visitors there. Elephant Rock first appeared in the visitors guide in 1993 as a highlight of the Island's "North by Northwest" region (figure 10.8). Notably, this was also the first year that the guide contained expanded sections devoted to the six regions; introducing Elephant Rock may have resulted in some measure simply from the need to find more attractions to fill each section. By 1996, Elephant Rock had made its way onto the Prince Edward Island map (figures 10.9 and 10.10). But a 1998 winter storm sheared

Figure 10.7 *Visitors Guide* (1975).

the head and trunk off the rock, consigning the attraction to an elephant graveyard. It sank from the visitors guide and map by 2000 (figure 10.11).

As long as there is tourism, Prince Edward Island's landscape will by necessity be constantly reimagined for it, thanks to changing aesthetic trends, metaphors and associations, and tourism and consumer demands – not to mention the land use (local and global) that will physically reshape the nature that is being subject to interpretation. And occasionally, as in the Elephant Rock case, nature will change entirely on its own.

Historian Edward MacDonald argues convincingly that Prince Edward Island's pastoral landscape – and, by extension, the promotion of it for tourism – faces an unprecedented demographic threat.[24] While the Island's population is greater today than ever before, the number of farms and people living on farms is only one-tenth of what it was a century ago. Rural, much less agricultural, hegemony is no more. As working mixed farms have gone to seed, been split into lots, or consolidated into large corporate farms, the traditional pastoral landscape of hedgerows, livestock, and rotating crops has been disappearing. With it disappears the strata of the Island population that worked that land or, increasingly, even experienced it as such. The 2014 *Visitor's Guide*, the current one at my time of writing, offers some indication of how the Island is responding to such changes – as always in the case of tourism

Figure 10.8 *Visitors Guide* (1993).

promotion, probably somewhat with deliberation and somewhat because the contemporary reality makes certain paths seem self-evident. There is by the 2014 guide greater emphasis on Islanders themselves than ever before. The first sections are dedicated to "Culture," "Craft," and "Culinary" before turning to the landscape-centred "Golf" and "Beaches." But the Island way of life presented in these early pages is one of ceilidh and pow-wows, hooked rugs and pottery, lobsters and new potatoes – that is, what might diplomatically be called the tourist season way of life. A later section on "Experiences" appears to promise connection to more traditional year-round occupations, but its images are of clam-digging, folk art, and charter fishing. There is no attention paid to those who tend the pastoral landscape, which surely suggests either the declining significance or the taking for granted of the pastoral landscape itself. Will that landscape, the long-time heart of Prince

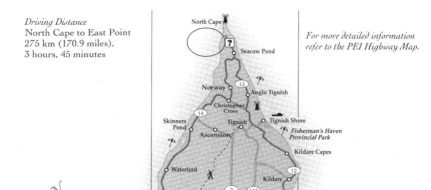

Figure 10.9 *1995 Visitors Guide* map.

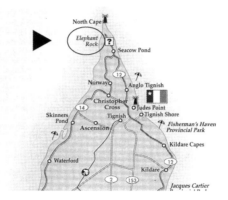

Figure 10.10 *1996 Visitors Guide* map.

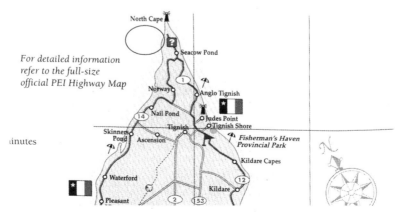

Figure 10.11 *2000 Visitors Guide* map.

Edward Island tourism promotion and of the Island itself, turn out to have had its day, differing from birch trees, pink sand, or Elephant Rock only in the amount of time it takes to go out of fashion? It would seem a bad omen that of the perhaps one thousand photographs in the 2014 guidebook, there are several of Cows Ice Cream but none showing actual cows.

At left: Elephant Rock first appeared as a tourist attraction in 1996, but by 2000 its trunk had slipped into the ocean, and it disappeared from the *Visitors Guide* map.

Two Centuries of Energy
on Prince Edward Island

Kathleen Stuart

Energy has driven development, both literally and figuratively, through-out the history of Prince Edward Island, from the first Amerindians seeking sources of heat and light to the modern state's forlorn attempts to jump-start manufacturing industries in a province with the highest energy costs in Canada. On a superficial level, a small island without coal, oil, natural gas, or any significant hydroelectric potential may seem to tell a simple story of learning to live with built-in limitations. The reality is much more complex, and it poses instructive questions about the capacity for innovation, flexibility, and sustainability on small islands with limited energy resources.

Lewis Mumford's proposed development continuum for the evolution of the machine in human society[1] posits an Ecotechnic energy regime of wood, wind, and water power, which has given way to the Paleotechnic (coal, steel, and steam) and Neotechnic (hydroelectric power and nuclear power from metal alloy) energy regimes. Mumford's thesis has endured since the interwar period, although recent historians often speak of the changes between organic and mineral energy regimes.[2] As we will see, Prince Edward Island had only indirect access to the mineral and hydro-electric sources of energy. This situation was both limitation and impetus for innovation.

Fundamentally, earth receives its energy from nuclear fusion in the sun. Some solar energy is captured by plants and then provides food fuel for humans and other animals. Some plant energy is ultimately stored in the form of fossil fuels. Solar energy also drives winds, waves, and cur-rents, and the hydrological cycle that moves water across the face of the planet. Since ancient times and in pre-industrial civilizations, domestic animals and humans (at times labouring under political control or slavery) have provided the muscle (somatic energy) for mobility, tool making, construction, food gathering, and agriculture to meet basic human needs. Somatic energy was also used to process biomass (such as wood or peat) to provide thermal energy for comfort and cooking.

As exemplified by the Dutch Golden Age of the seventeenth century,[3] various water- and wind-driven technologies (waterwheels, windmills, sailing vessels) were developed to meet the growing energy needs of expanding human populations and expanding European empires. In the eighteenth century the invention of practical and efficient steam engines ushered in the Industrial Revolution (1760–1850) and the ability to convert non-renewable fossil fuels (coal, oil, gas) into usable mechanical power for manufacturing and transportation. Electricity was developed as a carrier for power. Throughout the turbulent twentieth century, energy use grew and technological innovations, including nuclear energy, diversified, while human populations continued their burgeoning growth.[4]

In the developed world, the idea of "progress" in society has been linked to the shift from dependence on somatic energy through wind and water, biomass, coal, and steam, culminating in hydroelectricity, high-energy fossil fuels, and nuclear power. During much of the twentieth century, unprecedented development of coal mines, oil fields, large-scale power generation, and high levels of energy consumption helped persuade generations of North American historians to embrace the ideology of technological determinism and link cultural and social progress directly to technological triumph.[5] This model of cultural progress has been challenged by the environmental movement, which arose following detonation of the hydrogen bomb in 1952 and was further galvanized by Rachel Carson's *Silent Spring*.[6] Seeing the planet from space for the first time in 1961, ordinary citizens became increasingly aware of and concerned about Earth's limits to growth. More recently, concerns centre on the various ethical and environmental issues attached to nuclear power development, and on atmospheric and toxic pollutants and climate changes inherent in continued combustion of fossil fuels.

Although progress in a society is still often measured by the quantity of energy it consumes, a more nuanced and contextualist approach has developed since the 1970s, focusing on how social conditions, prices, traditions, popular attitudes, interest groups, class differences, and government policies shape new technologies.[7] But despite this shift in thinking, and the growing need to reduce carbon emissions, fossil fuels continue to dominate our energy supply, illustrating that community commitment to any particular energy technology may be difficult to change. However, this does not imply that the community lacks agency or ability to innovate.

For a small island that is more or less distant from mainland energy infrastructure, providing cost-effective energy to its residents presents particular challenges. This is true for Prince Edward Island (PEI) even though it is close to mainland Canada. This chapter examines the historical pattern of changing energy use and technologies on PEI, an island place in time that has clearly evident limits in terms of available human, economic, and energy resources, and where the environmental and socio-economic impacts of adoption of successive energy technologies have been quickly apparent. The Island's pastoral landscape, Victorian architecture, and nostalgic culture, viewed from offshore, might imply a general reluctance to adopt new ideas; however, the view through a contextual lens challenges such an assumption.

Like many small islands worldwide, PEI is overwhelmingly reliant upon the importation of fossil fuels and electricity because, as noted above, it has no coal, petroleum, natural gas, or large-scale hydropower of its own. But since earliest settlement, Island entrepreneurs have derived mobility, heat, and light from whatever was available locally, including domestic animals, wind, water, sunshine, local forests, and rivers. Islanders' adoptions of a broad range of energy technologies (with some outcomes proving more successful than others) illustrate independent thinking, sustained resourcefulness, and acceptance of considerable risk in pursuing development goals. Examining this "Island microcosm" reveals a complex trajectory of technological innovation over time. The story of energy provides a unifying thread to the other narratives in this volume, which speak to particular historical phases and economic sectors of Prince Edward Island. The history of energy illuminates some of the available choices and motive forces behind successive economic and industrial activities that have affected the Island's environment over time. It also reveals that some preconditions considered necessary for creation of alternative energy technologies have been evolving in PEI since the early nineteenth century. This historical, contextual approach can assist us in understanding current conditions and developing energy policy for the future.

Adopting new technology is not merely a matter of transporting hardware into a different environment; it is a slow and difficult process influenced by many factors, including the labour market situation, local natural resources, social and institutional frameworks, education and skills of the labour force, attitudes and social objectives of the community, as well as the willingness to take on financial and political risks.[8] The experience of the small northern country of Finland, consisting of islands and a sparsely populated mainland peripheral to a vast continent, resonates with that of PEI in many of these ways. Eminent environmental historian Timo Myllyntaus has examined electrification in the late-industrializing Finnish agrarian economy.[9] He identifies five strategies for creating technological capability: (a) imitating foreign technology, (b) learning by doing, (c) adapting foreign technology to domestic circumstances, (d) improving foreign technology, and (e) making original inventions and innovations.[10] This chapter examines how, on PEI over the past two hundred years, entrepreneurs and governments have pursued developments in energy services for transportation, heating, lighting, and electrical power. My discussion uses Myllyntaus's typology as a framework for examining the Island's trajectory over the past two centuries. I begin with a broad overview of energy technologies on PEI, followed by in-depth examinations of several historical technologies, leading to a discussion of overall trends and options for the future.

HISTORICAL OVERVIEW OF ENERGY TECHNOLOGIES ON PRINCE EDWARD ISLAND

The timeline of energy technology on PEI begins around 8000 BCE, following the retreat of glaciers, when non-agricultural Aboriginal peoples relied on somatic and solar energy as they hunted and fished on the island (see Kristmanson and Keenlyside; Curley, this volume). Somatic energy continued its dominance in the 1700s. During the French regime (ca. 1720 to 1758), relatively small numbers of French fishers and Acadian settlers, both making space for agriculture, employed hand tools and beasts of burden (oxen and horses, which foraged for themselves in patches of cleared woods[11]) to clear forests and ingeniously dyke wetlands.

British colonists arrived after 1763, and the rate of settlement increased in the 1800s. Wind, water (i.e., Ecotechnic) and later, steam-powered (Paleotechnic) technologies were adopted alongside traditional somatic energy practices. To borrow Graeme Wynn's phrase, they were "settlers in a wooden world."[12] Under British rule, unrelenting exploitation of the forested land for shipbuilding, settlement, and conversion to agriculture

accelerated throughout the nineteenth century. Some ecological consequences of this early industry are detailed elsewhere in this volume (see
Sobey's discussion of forests; MacFadyen's history of agriculture;
Curley's exposition of impacts of dams on wildlife). As Sobey's chapter
reflects, the cultural ethic of the period paid scarce attention to values
inherent in environmental resources beyond the utilitarian. Early legislative efforts to curb or mitigate ecological damages were limited in scope
and effectiveness (see appendix).

Wood was a critical resource for home heating (see Sobey, this volume). Fireplaces typically heated colonial homes, and food was cooked
using fuel wood. As deforestation increased in the late nineteenth century, developing networks of railroads and steamships enabled better
access to ports and coalmines in Nova Scotia.[13] Eventually, fossil fuels
largely displaced renewable fuels for home heating but it was a long
process. Biomass, wind, and solar energies have each played important
roles in the twentieth century, and as will be seen below, increased
application of renewable energy technologies are under discussion as
energy sources for the twenty-first century. New transportation technologies of the nineteenth century, fuelled by coal, oil, and gas, helped
to transform the landscape and provided incentives for increased industrial development.

The first electric plant went into operation on Prince Edward Island
as early as 1884, but electricity spread slowly across the province.[14]
Modernization followed trends elsewhere in rural Canada, but the cost
of electricity remained one of the highest in the country, owing to
the lack of access to hydroelectricity and large-scale transmission grids.
The relatively small scale and remoteness of Island industries, as well
as regional and federal political influences, combined to constrain economic development.[15]

In the 1970s the spiralling cost of oil prompted both a movement for
development and adoption of renewable energies and an energy conservation movement on PEI, bolstered by the creation of PEI's Institute
of Man and Resources (IMR).[16] This constellation brought experts in
alternative energy technology to PEI and gave the Island a brief, global
reputation as an energy innovator.[17] In a telling development, a change
of government provincially, access to cheaper electricity, and a fading
sense of crisis as oil prices dropped contributed to the rapid decline
and then demise of the IMR. However, its legacy was a foundation
of energy consciousness that, connected with the rural culture of self-
sufficiency, informed the knowledge economy[18] and set the stage for a

wave of wind-energy development in the early twenty-first century when large wind farms erected at each end of the Island created surplus "clean, green" power. Nonetheless, mobility and space heating still depend largely on fossil fuels, causing concern whenever fuel costs soar to new heights. The following section examines a number of these developments of energy capacity in PEI in more detail, to expose the technological incentives that have motivated socio-economic development on the Island and mediated the relationship between Island people and their ecological environment.

EARLY MOTIVE FORCES: WOOD, WIND, WATER AND SOMATIC ENERGY

The somatic energy regime (for travel, hunting, gathering, and fishing) of Aboriginal people on PEI is thought by some scholars to have been seasonal from about 8000 BCE until well after European colonization.[19] In 1534, when Jacques Cartier sighted Île Saint-Jean on behalf of France, he found it completely covered in mixed forest. The island, 1.4 million acres in area, remained under the control of France until 1758 without much utilization of the timber except for house building and firewood for cooking and warmth.[20] Fires often escaped into the forest, becoming extensive in 1724, 1736, and 1742.[21] European colonists supplemented human muscle power with that of domestic animals and running water. The De la Roque census of 1752 counted 2,223 people possessing 100 horses, 800 oxen, 1,300 other cattle, 1,200 sheep, 1,300 pigs, 2,300 fowl, 300 geese, 100 turkeys, and 12 ducks; the inhabitants grew wheat, peas, turnips, and cabbages, and had four gristmills and two sawmills.[22] Roads were required and a few were built,[23] but because settlers lived close to rivers and estuaries, many moved by canoe in summer and along the same (now frozen) routes on foot or with snowshoes in winter.[24]

The French population peaked at about 4,700 settlers in 1758, but over half of these were little more than refugees from the mainland deportations of 1755; another third had been less than a decade on the land. Following mass deportation of the Acadians in 1758, Île Saint-Jean became a British colony and was renamed Prince Edward Island in 1799. British settlement pushed the human population to 71,000 by 1855; it had reached 108,000 by 1880.[25] By 1833 there were roughly 30,000 cattle, 50,000 sheep, 20,000 pigs, and 6,000 horses; much of the farming was handwork with spade, hoe, sickle, scythe, and axe. Traction animals hauled two-wheeled carts or, after winter freeze-up, more efficient sleds.

During the first third of the century, numbers of oxen had scarcely doubled while horses increased six times owing to the development of more roads and the open fields required for pasturage and feed crops.[26]

When Britain's traditional sources of Baltic timber were threatened by Napoleon in the early 1800s, PEI entrepreneurs found opportunity to exploit the Island's timber to build wind-powered ships that carried lumber, selling both the ship and its cargo upon arrival in Britain. As is discussed in more detail by Sobey (this volume), the Island became the point of origin of wooden sailing vessels over a 130-year period, beginning in the 1780s. There were also regional markets for Island-built schooners and brigantines in Newfoundland and for the local coasting trade.[27] External trade was small but vigorous by the mid-nineteenth century as forest products, oats, potatoes, oatmeal, live animals, and various kinds of fish were exported from ten shipping ports on the island to Britain, the United States, Nova Scotia, and Newfoundland. The "Golden Age" that PEI enjoyed in the 1850s and '60s was surely enhanced by wealth created by shipwrights and the tenant farmers who largely cut the trees. For example, the Three Rivers area in Kings County produced 396 vessels between 1787 and 1920; fifty sailing ships were built in the port of Montague alone between 1847 and 1907.[28] Overharvesting for timber and firewood, along with frequent forest fires, gradually changed the age structure of the forest and its species makeup so that by 1860 wood suitable for shipbuilding was becoming scarce (see Sobey, this volume, for a more detailed account).[29]

Shipbuilding and other domestic industries required energy inputs. By 1860, there were 176 sawmills and 141 gristmills powered by or located near streams, nine kilns for making clay bricks, and 48 lime-burning establishments, along with 55 tanneries and 46 wool-carding mills. Although there was enough stored energy in Island millponds to power the hundreds of small mills scattered around the province, there was limited room for expansion. After 1880, small-scale artisanal agricultural and fishery products such as canned lobster, laundry starch, butter, and cheese were widely produced.[30] On the water where the lobsters were caught, fishermen were quick to mechanize: more than half of the Island lobster fleet was powered by imported gasoline by 1915.[31]

As in milling and lobster fishing, scale was an important factor in agricultural development. As demographic pressure mounted after the 1850s (the end of immigration being offset by high birth rates) and competition from within Canada burgeoned, Island agriculture struggled to find and hold markets. Only by increasing yields, finding new products, putting more acres into cultivation, or increasing efficiency could agriculture provide an adequate living to the rising population. After 1880 Islanders tried all of these strategies, but the very pattern of small farms that gave Island society its great stability also placed social constraints on agricultural expansion (see MacFadyen, this volume). When the population grew faster than the available economic – and energy – resources, Islanders left. Out-migration, a trickle in the 1870s, became a steady river of humanity in the decades that followed.[32]

As those who were left struggled to adapt to the changing circumstances of the new century, ways of harnessing energy to produce food changed dramatically, even though today's land-use still traces early settlement patterns. The iconic family farm had evolved over decades of backbreaking manual labour and animal power as settlers fertilized and stabilized the acidic red clay soil as it became stripped of forest. Locally available soil additives containing stored solar energy (including mussel mud, lobster shells, seaweed, manure, and ashes) were hauled by animals to the fields. After World War II, demand grew for imported fossil fuels and their by-products, including herbicides, pesticides, and chemical fertilizer.[33] The result was growth without prosperity. By 1960, the provincial government carried the highest per capita debt in Canada; the unemployment rate was the second highest in Canada; per capita incomes and output were only half the national average or just slightly over.[34] Thus, in the 1970s, in a radical social engineering experiment that attracted attention abroad, the PEI "way of life" was again fundamentally altered, this time with introduction of the $725 million Comprehensive Development Plan, a cost-shared development agreement between Ottawa and Prince Edward Island to diversify and "rationalize" the economy.[35]

ENERGY FOR MOBILITY

The importance of the wooden shipbuilding industry flags the ubiquity of sail-powered wooden vessels as the prime means of marine transportation on Prince Edward Island during the 150 years of European colonization. By 1865, however, improvements to the compound steam engine and development of the screw propeller had signified the impending eclipse of the wooden sailing vessel market in Britain as more economical steam-powered ships fuelled by coal began to appear in the international trade.[36] On Prince Edward Island, the collapse was sudden and catastrophic, telescoped into a period of about three years, 1878 to

1880. In the century to follow, the emerging fossil fuel economy and its technologies depended on coal, oil, and other fuels from elsewhere to ship PEI agricultural, forestry, and fisheries products to distant markets by roads, rails, and ferries, for better or worse. (See Sobey; MacFadyen; Novaczek; Arsenault; and MacDonald and Beck, this volume, for discussions of the environmental impacts.)

Even as shipbuilding first began to falter, the local colonial government of the early 1870s was investing in steam power – on land, not water. Following trends elsewhere in the region, construction began on the Prince Edward Island Railway in 1871, and by 1875 steam-powered locomotives travelled on 286 miles of rail across the province.[37] Routing the shiny new technology provided a significant social and cultural boon that would deliver coal, lumber, and produce to local markets and ports, link settlements, create jobs, and distribute patronage to many of the Island's inhabitants.[38] The customized railroad meandering down the 286-mile, narrow-gauge track from one small station to another also allowed Island culture to flourish. Besides moving heavy goods and passengers, the train supported theatrical productions, funeral processions, and inter-community sporting events, and even enabled a wider pool of marriage partners. In retrospect, the technology enabled cultural and economic development. At the time, the application of the technology was heavily influenced by local communities, demonstrating both "learning by doing" and "adapting foreign technology to domestic circumstance" as per Myllyntaus's typology of ways to create technological capacity. But the railroad illustrated another point as well, concerning development on a small island with limited resources. Despite its economic and cultural importance, the PEI Railway was a perennial money loser. Its construction and operation came at a great price to the British colony in economic (capital cost, \$3.8 million) and political terms. The threat of state bankruptcy drove the Island into Confederation in 1873 (with Ottawa agreeing to take over completion and operation of the railway and promising continuous steam communication with the mainland). Construction of the railway also furthered the destruction of the forest (approximately 3,000 wooden railway ties were required per mile).[39] The railway continued to provide passenger and freight service for much of the twentieth century, but without achieving economies of scale or efficiency. By 1989, the railway service had been discontinued, and over the following years the last remaining railway cars and ties were sold off.

Modes of individual transportation and the power behind agricultural activities changed more slowly. In 1891, 37,000 horses (driving and draught) were providing land transportation. Sixty years later (1951), nine out of ten farms still had horses, and less than 40 per cent of farm families owned automobiles.[40] The widespread adoption of the automobile was inextricably linked to the availability of all-weather roads. The first rural asphalt (1.8 miles) was laid on the Malpeque Road in 1930.[41] The spread of pavement during the 1950s and '60s was a key development and the enabler for a great deal of social and demographic change. In 1943, there were 206 miles of pavement in the province, representing 6 per cent of Island roads. By the end of the 1950s, taking advantage of federal cost-shared programs, 656 miles of pavement existed, and a decade later, the Island had a higher percentage of paved roads than any province in Canada.[42] The effects of this transportation revolution were far reaching. For example, the number of horses plummeted by two-thirds from 21,349 to 7,867.[43] With the demise of the railway, the trucking sector expanded to carry heavy, perishable agricultural products as rapidly as possible (initially via ferry and later by bridge) to urban markets in Central Canada and New England. As the five hundred or so one-room school districts where students used to walk to school became consolidated into fewer, much larger units, a need for fleets of gasoline- or diesel-powered school buses was created. The need or desire for more mobility only continued to grow, as women gained more freedom from farm chores and increasingly commuted to jobs off the farm. Although the number of Island farms shrank, non-farm residents did not necessarily move to the city: in 2006, the 77,000 people living in rural areas (often commuting to town for work) continued to outnumber the Island's urban population of 61,700.

The rural population still (in 2014) relies largely on private vehicles for mobility, as regular public transit does not exist outside of urban areas. Ironically, the use of automobiles was initially outlawed on Island roads (from 1908 to 1913) by the province for the sake of safety and because the vehicles were deemed impractical.[44] Some restrictions remained until 1919,[45] but today there are almost two vehicles for every household. The 2006 census counted 53,135 households in the province. In 2011, vehicle registrations numbered 113,301, of which 71,193 were private passenger vehicles and 23,987 were trucks; total gasoline sales in that year reached 207.3 million litres.[46] An infrastructure of paved and gravelled roads extends to all areas of the province. PEI's paved roads require intensive maintenance due to the structure of the soil, the spring freeze-thaw cycle that damages roads, and winter snow-removal activities. Gravel can be quarried at a few sites on the Island, but granite and most other heavy road-building materials must be imported from the mainland by ferry or barge and trucked to construction sites. In total, 742,765 metric tonnes of sand, stone, and gravel were unloaded at the four Island ports in 2010, along with 87,711 tonnes of fertilizer and 360,167 tonnes of petroleum products.[47] Moving all of these heavy loads damages roadbeds and burns imported fuel, while storage and handling require infrastructure. Demand for energy is therefore greatly exacerbated whenever economic expansion involves heavy construction.

In the late nineteenth and early twentieth centuries, prior to the advent of the "fixed link" (Confederation Bridge), subsidized steamship service provided the province's major link to the rest of the world. After 1917, the federal government established a regular, all-season ferry service that could carry railcars between Cape Tormentine, New Brunswick, and Port Borden, PEI; in 1941 a federally subsidized private ferry link to Pictou, Nova Scotia, opened at Wood Islands. Three diesel-powered car ferries continue to cross the fourteen-kilometre waterway separating PEI and NS, running from May to December when the strait is free of ice. Another car ferry links PEI's eastern town of Souris to Quebec's Magdalen Islands (Îles de la Madeleine) that lie 134 kilometres to the north in the Gulf of St Lawrence. Four commercial ports handle small ocean-going vessels; smaller harbours around the coast service inshore fishing boats and pleasure craft during ice-free months.[48]

LIGHTING AND ELECTRICAL POWER

With regard to artificial lighting and electricity, which are technologically intensive, Prince Edward Islanders have been inventive and innovative but ill situated to compete with other jurisdictions in obtaining cheap electrical power. The Charlottetown Gas Light Company first supplied gas to some sixty houses in the capital city in 1854, and there were 125 street lamps by 1879. However, it was expensive, and the quality of the gas was poor. The company had wound up operations by 1896, eclipsed by the electric lighting that had arrived in the previous decade.[49]

The first electric street lighting in North America went online in New York City in 1882, and it was not long after – 1884 – that the City of Charlottetown adopted the new technology. The Royal Electric Engineering & Construction Company of Montreal was contracted to light city streets with electricity produced from high-pressure steam, using coal for fuel.[50] The Full Electric Company plant, which used incandescent technology, appeared in 1885. An electrical generating plant operated by the Prince Edward Island Electric Company was completed on 14 May 1886 to supply arc lighting. By 1901 all competing firms had amalgamated to form Charlottetown Light and Power, a monopoly with three plants for generating electrical power in the city.[51] Maritime Electric Ltd from Fredericton, NB, purchased the local firm in 1918. Between 1909 and 1919, a two-cent rate hike went into effect, raising the price to fifteen cents per kilowatt, "owing to the increased cost of coal, which is now double that of two years ago."[52]

In rural areas, electricity became available to wealthier subscribers near small, privately owned hydroelectric generators built on eight Island rivers, which were dammed for this purpose. By 1928, eleven power plants used a combination of mill-fed water wheels and engine-powered turbines for a total production of 2.3 million kWh of electricity.[53] Compared to the rest of Canada during the first half of the twentieth century, central electric service on PEI remained expensive and localized (see table 11.1). Capacity for small hydro was limited by the maximum elevation (152 m or 466 ft) and by the fact that streams, although numerous, were short and seasonally variable. Due to limited demand and low capacity, rural subscribers typically received power only a few hours at night and, after the gradual introduction of electrical appliances, on washing day. The result was a checkerboard pattern of electrification, both spatially and temporally.

By 1931 Maritime Electric Ltd had expanded into outlying areas of PEI through the purchase of the Montague Electric Company (incorporated in 1899). By 1950, it had absorbed seven more rural electric companies and served 4,441 rural customers consuming 3.97 million kWh, as well as 4,861 city customers consuming 14.28 million kWh.[54] After rural electrification became an official government program in 1953, the remaining small hydro facilities were absorbed by Maritime Electric, which was installing ever-larger steam generators and expanding distribution lines into rural areas.[55] By 1960, Island power companies had strung over six hundred miles of wire to 22,000 customers, and 5,700 farms had been electrified.[56] Shortly afterwards, Maritime Electric acquired Scales Hydro, the last of PEI's small, rural, independent producers of electricity, and became a widely held corporation listed on the Montreal and Toronto Stock Exchanges. By 1970, Maritime Electric was generating over 20 million kWh per month, using 45,000 gallons of

Table 11.1
Customers with central electric service, PEI and Canada, 1921–1951

	PEI		Maritime Provinces		Canada	
	Number of homes with service	*Percent of all homes with service*	*Number of homes with service*	*Percent of all homes with service*	*Number of homes with service*	*Percent of all homes with service*
1921	2,801	15	46,169	23	830,062	47
1931	3,980	21	83,196	40	1,336,721	59
1941	5,531	27	128,379	53	1,755,917	63
1951	10,624	47	240,097	84	2,951,988	88

Source: Canada Dominion Bureau of Statistics, Census of Industry, Central Electric Stations in Canada, 1922 (Ottawa, 1923[?]); Census of Industry 1931, Central Electric Stations in Canada (Ottawa 1933); Government of Canada, Census of Industry, 1948 (Ottawa, 1949); and Central Electric Stations in Canada, 1951 (Ottawa 1953)

cooling water per minute and consuming 20,000 gallons of Bunker "C" oil per week.[57]

By then, the Comprehensive Development Plan's ambitious vision of an expanded manufacturing base on Prince Edward Island was already butting against the reality that industrial expansion requires cheap energy – and the Island's electrical rates were the highest in Canada. Not for the first time, access to energy – and its cost – was frustrating dreams of economic development.

Maritime Electric clearly needed access to more cost-effective electricity, but with its small customer base the private utility was hard-pressed to justify passing on the full cost of establishing a cable connection to the mainland – a technically challenging feat at least ten times the cost of a landline. A solution came in 1977 when government stepped in. As part of the Comprehensive Development Plan, the provincial government became the owner of two 138 kV three-phase submarine cables between NB and PEI, leasing them to Maritime Electric. Financing partners included the federal Departments of Regional Economic Expansion and Energy, Mines and Resources, and the Government of PEI. Electrical capacity rose significantly in 1979 with installation of high-voltage undersea transmission cables to transfer bulk electricity from New Brunswick.

Today Maritime Electric distributes the conventional electricity supply, generated mainly from nuclear, hydroelectric, and coal-fired sources in New Brunswick, to approximately 66,000 Island customers over a

5,000 km network of power lines.[58] In 2011, the total electricity supply was 1,259,126 megawatt hours (MWh), of which only 22.7 per cent was generated within PEI. The net peak load within the province was 221 MW, yet the net generation capability within the province reached a whopping 414 MW, of which 163 MW (39.4 per cent) was wind generated.[59] Maritime Electric has diesel electrical generating stations in Charlottetown and Borden-Carleton which are kept in standby mode, being put into operation only when the energy supply from off-Island sources is interrupted. The company also purchases up to 52 MW of wind generation from the provincially owned PEI Energy Corporation.[60] Also worth noting is the municipally owned Summerside Electric Company. An independent power generator and distributor, it was originally incorporated in 1896. It has been granted exemptions to sections of the Electric Power Act, and since the Renewable Energy Act was enacted, it has installed four wind turbines. It now generates 10 MW electricity from fossil fuel and wind for its city residents and provides backup power to Maritime Electric.

The electrical utility does not operate entirely without public scrutiny. The Island Regulatory and Appeals Commission (IRAC), which has a narrow mandate and limited resources, hears and resolves disputes over land use on PEI and administers the Electric Power Act and, since 2005, the Renewable Energy Act. IRAC regulates energy prices, including the timing and degree of all energy price increases proposed by Maritime Electric. The quasi-judicial body conducts public hearings on rate applications, making their reports available to the public on the commission's website (www.irac.pe.ca). In 2005, after a rigorous public hearing process, Maritime Electric was allowed to install and commission a new generator worth $35 million in Charlottetown.[61] The 50 MW combustion turbine, fired on diesel fuel, provides backup capacity for energy purchases from off-Island sources and contingency backup for the submarine cables. In hindsight, it seemed a straightforward purchase of foreign technology: service personnel from General Electric in California were flown to PEI to install the unit, essentially one 747 aircraft engine. The installer reported that running this turbine for one day requires six tanker-trucks of fuel.[62] The unit is capable of providing enough power to supply almost one-quarter of the peak electrical demand on PEI and can be adapted for a variety of fuels, including natural gas and biofuels, should local sources be developed. By 2014, however, Maritime Electric was yet again advertising an imminent need to increase its electricity supply in order to meet spiralling energy demands.

The high cost of electricity remains a preoccupation for many consumers on PEI, but only about 13 per cent of the province's total energy requirement is supplied by electricity from all sources, including bulk purchases from neighbouring provinces and the abundant but intermittent electricity generated on PEI from wind. Of greater concern is the overwhelming percentage of the energy supply required for mobility and space heating. Energy for mobility is mainly derived from burning fossil fuels; most thermal energy for heating homes, commercial buildings, and powering industrial operations is supplied by burning light and heavy oil or propane, plus a small percentage from biomass and municipal waste.[63] Therefore, improving energy efficiency is a highly significant component of any strategy that seeks to manage energy costs and encourage more energy self-reliance.

ENERGY FOR SPACE HEATING AND HOUSEHOLD CONVENIENCES

In the balmy days of summer, visitors easily forget that winter conditions on PEI dictate climate-controlled housing for people, livestock, and their food supplies. Situated at 46° north latitude, the crescent-shaped island in the southern Gulf of St Lawrence experiences a wide range of weather conditions during the year, making it a good climate laboratory. Islanders love to talk about the weather in a place where mean temperatures range between 23.2°C and 13.8°C in July, and between minus 3.3°C and minus 12.6°C in January. Precipitation averages 84 mm in July and 102.4 mm in January, with wide fluctuations.[64] Air conditioning is not normally required in the summers, but the cold winters and windy conditions justify considerable home insulation, extra window glazing, and space heating from fall to spring, as well as climate-controlled barns and warehouses for agricultural livestock and stored produce.

Modern amenities seem far removed from the early settlers' drafty log houses with gaping fireplaces and chimneys that were wood-framed and clay-lined due to the scarcity of stone on the Island. The transition to electricity and fossil fuel heat was generally a gradual process throughout many parts of rural Canada, and PEI was no exception.[65] Only 11 per cent of dwellings on the Island were using oil for domestic heating in 1951, relying instead on burning wood or coal, as shown in table 11.2. The percentage of dwellings with electric and fuel-consuming

Table 11.2
Fuel use for domestic heating in Prince Edward Island dwellings, 1951

Tenure	Number of Homes	Coal		Coke		Wood		Oil	
		Number	Percent	Number	Percent	Number	Percent	Number	Percent
All	22,455	9,165	41%	320	1%	10,340	46%	2,545	11%
Owned	18,305	6,710	37%	215	1%	9,745	53%	1,575	9%
Rented	4,150	2,455	59%	105	3%	595	14%	970	23%

Source: Census of Canada, 1951, volume 3 Housing and Families, Table 25: "Occupied Dwellings by Tenure Showing Principal Heating Fuel, for Counties and Census Districts 1951," 25-1–25-13.

conveniences in 1941 is outlined in table 11.3, highlighting major differences between farm and non-farm areas. By 1959, although Charlottetown, Summerside, and some smaller areas of PEI had access to locally generated hydroelectricity earlier in the century, 53 per cent of farms had electricity and 33 per cent had a telephone.[66] As soon as households could afford it, they retrofitted their kitchen wood stoves with Kemac oil burners and installed electric pumps and indoor plumbing with hot water; they bought refrigerators, washers, dryers, and a host of other labour-saving appliances. Heated air, which had previously wafted from a labour-intensive wood furnace in the basement through open grates in floors and ceilings to rooms above, could now emerge on demand from hot water registers in every room of the house, produced by an oil-fired boiler that circulated hot water through copper pipes.

When alternative energy research at the Institute of Man and Resources was sparked by the oil crisis in 1973, wood energy became its most extensive program: 40 per cent of the Island was wooded, and many households already recognized the value and economy of heating with wood.[67] IMR's research had determined that by 2005, as much as 60 per cent of homes and 100 per cent of commercial, retail, and public buildings could be supplied by wood energy upon the improvement of forest management. IMR, promoting energy efficiency and state-of-the art ecological goals of the day, encouraged the use and manufacture of wood furnaces and stoves that were more efficient and adaptable. The institute was also attuned to cultural goals whereby some simply preferred the radiant heat and romantic image of self-sufficiency that a wood fire represents, using it either as a primary heat source or as a supplement to other sources of warmth. Today the IMR legacy has ensured that

Table 11.3
Percentage of dwellings with electric and fuel consuming conveniences, 1941

	Estimated number of occupied dwellings	Electric lights	Gas or electric cooking	Refrigeration (ice or mechanical)	Radio	Automobile	Telephone	Electric vacuum cleaner	All four preceding conveniences
Farm									
Prince	5,013	6.7		11.8	57.2	33.1	20.1	2.5	1
Queens	5,177	8.8		18.2	55.2	36.6	21.1	2.7	1.8
Kings	3,417	2.6		7.1	48.7	17.5	11.4	0.3	0.3
Non-farm									
Prince	2,100	45.8	1	1.4	62.1	24.4	20.3	10.3	6.4
Queens	3,505	78.3	4.3	48	75.8	26.4	34.2	14	8
Kings	800	33.6	1	21.8	61.4	18.9	11.8	7.9	3.1
Summerside	998	85.6	1	65.9	83.5	35.1	41.2	22.7	15.5
Charlottetown	2,910	95.7	5.6	55.6	83.2	24.5	39.5	18.5	10.5

Source: Census of Canada, 1941, volume 9 Housing Table 30, "Summary of housing and related data for electoral districts, farm and non-farm, and cities of 30,000 and over, 1941," 140–55; Census of Canada 1941, Volume 9 (housing), Table 31, "Summary of Housing and Related Data for Urban Centres of 4,000 to 30,000," 156–67.

firewood logs, pellets, and wood chips compete with oil and electricity as alternative forms of energy for space heating despite the risk of known hazards to health from air pollution.

Spreading knowledge about energy issues and convincing Islanders to embrace healthy new attitudes and opportunities remain key elements in energy policy. Education has been a priority in PEI since the early nineteenth century, an outcome of receiving a settler society from the British Isles that sought to equip youth for industrial manufacturing and agricultural services. The traditional classical curriculum of the nineteenth century along with practical manual training and a movement during the early years of the twentieth century encouraged domestic science (home economics) for women and a parallel stream of informal education through Mechanics' Institutes, agricultural societies, Farmers' Institutes, and university extension departments.[68] Emphasis on practical knowledge and appreciation of high standards of craftsmanship spread beyond the regular classroom.

Recent developments have taken education about energy issues to a new level. On the same site as land set aside for a college in 1804, federal and provincial politicians opened a new building at Holland College in 2011 to provide advanced educational opportunities in energy technology. This new program represents the mainstreaming of "alternate" thinking about energy on PEI. The new building itself demonstrates advanced energy technologies in its construction while its trainees learn to apply practical skills and knowledge in solar and wind power technologies and heritage building restoration. Across town, the University of Prince Edward Island announced later in the same week that it had become the only university in Atlantic Canada to receive Building Environmental Standards Certification from the Building Owners and Managers Association of Canada (BOMA) for twenty-two of its main campus buildings.[69] While new state-of-the-art structures may resemble valued heritage buildings on the outside, their interior components incorporate significant improvements in energy efficiency, drawing upon ancient ideas such as rooftop gardens and sunshine capture for heating and cooling. Meanwhile, older structures valued for their architectural style are being retrofitted, revealing how thinking about thermal energy has dramatically changed since they were built. These PEI educational institutions disseminate knowledge about energy applications while modelling energy efficiency and alternatives to create technological capability for future generations, resonating with the Myllyntaus typology.

RENEWABLE ENERGY AND "GREEN POWER"

Energy innovation is often driven by need, but it also exploits opportunity. The story of the PEI Railway did not end when the rails were removed in 1989. The old rail bed was transformed into a 235-kilometre linear park of international recreational significance, and became the first-completed province-wide section of the Trans-Canada Trail for twenty-first century cyclists, hikers, and birdwatchers. Growing environmental and health-conscious sensibilities, vestiges of social capital in Island rural communities, and local individual leadership championed the conversion of the structure into an element in the province's alternative energy infrastructure. This innovative conversion encouraging the use of somatic energy can be compared to the fifth step in Myllyntaus's model.

Another traditional source of energy, wind, has enjoyed a significant renaissance on Prince Edward Island. Despite the reliable presence of prevailing wind, early settlers made only limited use of wind as an energy source (other than to power water craft). Whether for cultural reasons or convenience, most Island mills were water-powered.[70] But by the 1970s, scientists and planners had begun to remark on PEI's excellent wind regime, and the province showed increasing interest in wind energy. During the 1970s and '80s, the Institute of Man and Resources seeded a number of experiments in the efficient use of wind energy; a line can be drawn between its activities and the creation of the Atlantic Wind Test Site at North Cape, and its successor, the Wind Energy Institute of Canada (WEICan). In 2008 the new Institute was slated to receive over $3.5 million from the federal government and over $0.9 million in land and assets from the province. Additional funding for annual maintenance was to come from both partners in the years following.[71] As Canada's national wind laboratory, WEICan focuses on testing and certification, research and innovation, industry training and public education, and technical consultation and assistance. Gaining support for energy R&D within PEI suggests another instance of the fifth strategy in the Finnish model: making original inventions and innovations.

Of course, wind power is a political hot button in a province where politics is a favourite sport. To address the growing need for new economic and environmental measures to combat over-dependence on imported fossil fuels, in December 2005 the province proclaimed the Renewable Energy Act. This forward-thinking legislation addressed renewable energy, demand-side management, and net metering, which allowed small-capacity wind generators on approved sites such as large industries, farms, and municipalities to sell their excess electricity back to the public utility. The act included a Renewable Portfolio Standard of 15 per cent by 2010 to encourage and develop wind resources for electricity; that goal has since been exceeded by a wide margin.

The PEI Energy Corporation, a provincial Crown corporation established in 1978 as an incubator for alternative energy technology, had installed eight large wind-powered generators at North Cape in November 2003, with a total capacity of 10.56 MW. Aeolus PEI also installed what was claimed to be North America's largest wind turbine there, the V-90, for an additional 3 MW of capacity.[72] Given the increased instability in the system from the high level of wind power being generated, collaboration began with Maritime Electric to adapt wind technology to domestic circumstances. In an endorsement of the province's initiatives, further turbines were brought online in 2007 by another commercial generator using European technology, with 9 MW installed that year and a further 99 MW in 2009.[73] Ten even bigger turbines became operational in early 2014.[74]

As wind technology advanced, one way to provide for the extra cost was for electricity users to pay a premium for green power. The wind farm at North Cape was made possible because the governments of Canada and PEI agreed to pay a premium for most of the electricity it would generate and designate it for use in government buildings in PEI.[75] Up to 20 per cent of the output from the wind farm was made available for sale to the public through Maritime Electric's distribution system. The public utility was already purchasing this electricity from the wind farm at a price equal to the cost it would have incurred to purchase or generate this electricity from fossil fuels. Despite its premium price, the public fully supported green power, and all of the electricity available under this program very quickly became fully subscribed.[76] Maritime Electric passed these green power premiums on to the PEI Energy Corporation which owns and operates the original wind farms. Since the energy produced was not actually cheaper, it is difficult to say what lay behind Islander consumers' ready subscription to these green power initiatives, though one suspects it was a blend of eco-awareness and economic nationalism. Although outside observers occasionally scoffed at the claim, the provincial government touted its green energy in

2008 by introducing a line of license plates featuring a windmill on a red Island cliff with the slogan "Canada's Green Province."[77]

The vagaries and shifting fortunes of politics are of critical importance as a risk factor in outcomes for a small jurisdiction, in local as well as inter-jurisdictional spheres, especially in a federation as complex as Canada. On 18 November 2005, prior to an election, it was announced that the federal government and Maritime Electric would cost-share equally a $60-million project to run a new 200 MW capacity cable inside the Confederation Bridge between PEI and New Brunswick.[78] This project was expected to double the current cable capacity to 400 MW, allowing the Island to export its wind power and to act as a backup for the two existing cables. As envisioned under its Energy Framework of 2004, the government of the day in PEI had hoped to attract a range of new private-enterprise wind generation facilities. It reasoned that besides reversing the outflow of capital, an additional 200 MW of wind power could cut greenhouse gas emissions by an estimated 500,000 tonnes and sulphur dioxide levels by 5,700 tonnes. The provincial environment minister of the day was quoted as saying "That's equal to removing 75,000 cars from PEI roads."[79] In January 2006, an opposition party became the minority federal government in Ottawa. Meanwhile the PEI government also changed stripes in 2007. The administration in Ottawa was not prepared to honour the pre-election promise of its predecessor to participate in the cable project despite reasonable economic and environmental arguments in its favour.[80]

The commercial and environmental promise of wind, a "clean" energy source that may lessen our dependence on external energy sources, has not gone uncontested. The concerns are similar to those in other jurisdictions, but again compounded by the close confines of a small, densely settled island. Opposition to wind turbines runs the gamut from conflicts over most appropriate land use and the visual aesthetics of wind farms in a pastoral landscape through health concerns over emissions from transmission lines and human sensitivities to turbine noise, to the risk posed by whirring blades to birds and bats. Often, too, criticism crosses over into the realm of economics (expensive mechanical problems with the technology and the ethics of "polluting" the Island landscape with wind farms owned off-Island that create energy for export rather than Islanders' own use). Such issues have been addressed without being resolved, but they have failed to dampen the state's current amour with wind energy.

LESSONS FROM THE PAST TO GUIDE THE ENERGY FUTURE OF PEI

Today as a Canadian province, although small in absolute terms, PEI shares with the nation one of the highest ecological footprints on the planet.[81] Energy-poor by Canadian standards, the Island lacks its own sources of large-scale hydroelectricity, coal, petroleum, natural, gas, or uranium. It imports all of its petroleum products at world price and almost 80 per cent of its bulk electricity from neighbouring provinces. The consistently high cost of electricity proved to be beyond its control throughout the twentieth century. It was a price taker subject to marketing strategies and energy production capacities at the source: at first it was from the early unregulated entrepreneurial electricity generators using limited hydro and thermal capacity; later, with the advent of undersea cable, it was from neighbouring jurisdictions at the gateway to the continental electricity grid. But as a province, PEI has ample jurisdictional capacity and access to political power at national, provincial, and community levels. PEI governments have been successful in varying degrees at leveraging public policy and federally funded programs to offset the disadvantages of scale and distance. Thus there are many reasons why PEI, first as an independent British colony, and later as a province of Canada, has experimented with a broad range of energy technologies in its continuing quest to solve the energy problem.

Each conversion from one form of energy into another (kinetic, chemical, thermal, or radiant) involves loss or diffusion (usually as heat) into the environment. For example, humans are only about 18 per cent efficient (horses about 10 per cent) in converting the calories in their food to mechanical energy.[82] Modern, large-scale, technology-intensive power systems are particularly complex, requiring significant capital and long-term planning. While the cachet of new technology grabs headlines and our imaginations as we look towards the future, we are still surrounded by vestiges of past energy use in our homes, watersheds, fields, and forests, as well as in our mindsets. The environmental impacts of individual and collective actions are often invisible or overlooked in the short term. Thus, in-depth investigation of the history of energy technologies over the *longue durée* helps us identify how past Islanders have adapted to the challenge of finding the energy they needed on Prince Edward Island. In a world where the voracious appetite for energy is now blamed for unprecedented climate change, knowledge of past practice may help mitigate the negative environmental effects of certain practices and make more efficient use of others.

Just as PEI used its small scale to its advantage and became the first province in Canada to implement a province-wide household waste management program in 2002, it has also been singular and sometimes quirky in creating legislation or regulations to reject ideas "from away." An early example was the initial banning of motorcars. More recently, the Campbell government in 1975 chose not to purchase a portion of the nuclear power generated in Point Lepreau, NB, on moral and political grounds, even though the deal might have included a new undersea transmission cable and cheaper electricity rates.[83] Islanders were not simply saying no to new ideas: they were rejecting those that seemed irrelevant, inappropriate, or downright dangerous. On the other hand, they were also capable of embracing new technologies in advance of mainland jurisdictions. Also in 1975, to carry out practical and applied research on alternative energy, and to showcase PEI to the rest of the world, the Campbell government created the internationally recognized Institute of Man and Resources.[84] The province had quickly established a program to subsidize home insulation when the price of fuel oil sky-rocketed in 1973–74.[85] That campaign soon had homeowners focused on energy efficiency, perhaps aided by Islanders' tradition of conserving warmth in the colder months by "banking" their homes with locally available straw bales or seaweed.[86] Enabled by a government subsidy, panels for passive solar water heating appeared on the roofs of homes throughout the Island, providing significant energy savings on domestic water heaters connected to oil-fired furnaces. Some of those panels are still at work on roofs today.

In 1986, the city of Charlottetown garnered international attention by being the first in Canada to supply district heating from woodchips and municipal solid waste plus some fuel oil.[87] Today, this model system still provides trouble-free hot water heating to about 125 downtown public and private buildings and generates 1,200 kW of electricity, most of it used internally, with the balance sold to the power grid.

Wind has gained value as a natural resource, such that an unprecedented 40 per cent of the province's electrical capacity is now available from large wind farms using adopted European technology. Solar power also has potential in PEI, which has 288 days of measurable sunshine per year.[88] Solar arrays for lighting and smart controls for efficiency have recently been incorporated into new public buildings in

Charlottetown. Individual farmers experiment with growing energy crops and oils for biodiesel as part of less intensive crop rotations. The Island's history of advancing alternative energy technologies and the knowledge economy has created a pool of local expertise that will surely be mobilized as the complex environmental challenges of climate change emerge.

Lessons of Time, Place, and an Island

Claire Campbell

PROLOGUE: A LIFE IN FOUR ISLANDS

Camp Hurontario, Thirty Thousand Islands, Georgian Bay, June 1973. My parents, married the autumn before, are working at the island summer camp for boys. They are given the Hamelin cabin, a quiet acknowledgment of their status as still-newlywed staff. My father has lived nearly all his summers on the granite islands and crystal waters of the Georgian Bay; my mother, though, is entirely out of her element. A prophetic beginning.

Sanibel Island, December 1984. We have driven through Pennsylvania snow and Georgia pines to Florida, at the start of a decade of family trips in a Volkswagen Westfalia camper. My father, a teacher, takes care that we visit the colonial fort at St Augustine and walk the boardwalks in the Everglades with their interpretative plaques. But for a ten-year-old, it is the wide white beach of Sanibel Island that is the real attraction. Palm trees exist, not just on television, however odd they seem wrapped in Christmas lights. Warm, sunny, far from winter, school, reality.

Dingle Peninsula, June 1999. I am driving, alone, around two islands: first Britain, now Ireland. On a bare rocky hillside sloping to the sea, I look west, as my ancestors must have done. But I am looking west with longing. For weeks now I have missed trees – real forest, not low-lying gorse scrub, or neat estate rows, or pines seeded after the wartime deforestation of the Highlands. This land looks as though it has been grazed, worn to the bone. I feel exposed, self-conscious, trapped at the water's edge. I am Canadian. I want to be lost in a woods, on a mainland with no end.

Slotsholmen, Copenhagen, August 2009. Beneath Christianborg Palace, in its nineteenth-century imperial grandeur, we descend to the twelfth-century ruins of Absalon's Castle, once a medieval fortress in a Baltic *havn.* The canals and footbridges outside are the only reminder of the older waterscape. The jumbled stones are cold, shadowed, and hushed, a hidden foundation for the palace and city above it. Two years later I will take a ferry to Samsø to see how an island can determine a different, independent future in energy. A millennium apart, islands of time.

TIME AND PLACE: LEARNING ABOUT ISLANDS

The French word for coastline, *littoral,* has become in English a word that suggests a space between – between land and sea, between two kinds of nature. It's a fitting term for this book, itself born of a week of movement between city, woods, farmland, and shoreline, and between fields of study. The 2010 conference Time and a Place: Environmental Histories, Environmental Futures, and Prince Edward Island began with three principles: that environmental histories and futures are fundamentally entwined; that the discussion of sustainability needs humanists, scientists, and policy-makers sharing their knowledge; and that islands are excellent places to begin this conversation. These essays are the result of that conversation. How do we know what a forest used to look like? We gain glimpses from material artifacts, surveyors' field books, conservation legislation, and tourism photos. Despite our usual thinking that the environment is a matter for scientists and lawmakers, sustainability is a democratic project: one that requires, and invites, everyone to share what we know and how we respond to environmental change.

It also is constantly revealing how much we still have to learn. As several essays here remind us, the New World was judged by those with a specific frame of reference – a particular demand for fish, a long-standing lack of trees – while Indigenous knowledge was until recently marginalized and ignored. But the transience of coastal encounters and the changeability of the coastline disrupt the surety of knowing especially an island's history. We cannot know where and how many and for how long French and Basque fishing crews stayed on the north shore (just as Parks Canada has never been able to count the number of visitors to Georgian Bay Islands National Park). Ever-changing shorelines long made it difficult to map Prince Edward Island's estuaries and bays; it hasn't got much easier with climate change and storm surges now rearranging the coast. After three centuries of forests clearing, biologists are still discovering new species (another argument against constructing highways through the Island's scarce remaining woods). And while some artifacts have been washed away with the tides, archaeologists at work offshore in places like Denmark and Newfoundland are discovering sites of occupation on what was once dry land. Our knowledge of global history and geography is sand that is constantly shifting, just like the Greenwich dunes.

Much simpler and therefore much more durable, perhaps especially among those of us from away, are our *ideas* of islands. Or more precisely, the abstraction of *island*: a place of escape, a gaze of white beach framed by a leaning palm, unoccupied, awaiting only us. From Kauai to Avonlea, we cultivate islands as playgrounds, remnants of paradise where we can "touch nature" or the past in a purer, simpler form. The rose (aqua) haze of tourism ads is, of course, a product of our desires and our imagination more than nature, but those images have had an indelible effect on how we have – or have not – understood and managed island environments. What lies behind and beyond that beach? What can we, mainlanders and islanders both, learn from the environment and the history of Prince Edward Island *as* an island?

LESSON I: A BLUE-BROWN-GREEN-WHITE PLANET

Looking at a satellite image of Prince Edward Island, I am struck by how fragile it seems. Beaches on the north break into the gulf in sandbars; red soils dissolve into the Northumberland Strait; the whole province is nearly cleaved into several islands by the Hillsborough River, West River, Malpeque Bay, and St Peter's Bay. Here is a place where "the ceaseless voice of many waters"[1] is never far away – a much-needed reminder for land-dwelling souls that our planet is more marine than terrestrial. Eastern First Nations tell of earth as an island borne on Turtle's back, or of the god Kitchikewana throwing handfuls of earth into a lake. Forty years ago, astronauts on the Apollo 8 mission read aloud how the firmament was created in the midst of the waters, showing us for the first time what is truly a blue planet.[2] But as John Gillis writes in this volume, "Reformulating and revitalizing environmental history means not only going offshore but also following the waters inland." Protected dunes and buffer zones along riverbanks recognize the presence of water inland on PEI. And while tourist photographs cannot show sea breezes or aquifers but only the sandy beaches beneath our feet, water and wind surround us in three-dimensional ways. While gales and hurricanes, the ultimate combination of wind and water, are the stuff coastal myths are made of, only recently have we been willing to recognize our part in their creation and our vulnerability to their effects.[3]

Just as islands connect us with water, they also connect us with history: archipelagos of time as well as space. In the past, scholars from Charles Darwin to Andrew Hill Clark tended to treat islands as convenient laboratories, isolated yet indicative, and as Alan MacEachern writes in this volume, "coherent, manageable, significant." But many of the essays in this book take the long view, believing that global events in the distant past – the creation of the North Atlantic oceanic basin, or the advance and retreat of glaciers – may bear quietly but daily and forcefully on the island environment. Islands reveal one of the fundamental tenets of environmental history, that geography is not a fixed and permanent thing. The Atlantic shoreline asks us to imagine a seabed in motion: as the glaciers retreat, the Grand Banks subside from islands into underwater hummocks, and an ancient Northumbria is flooded to divide PEI from the mainland; millennia later, the Great Northern Peninsula still rises out of the sea, released from glacial weight in isostatic rebound. As Arctic ice shrinks further, rising sea levels lap at the already narrow Chignecto isthmus, making it easy to picture a future island of Nova Scotia. If the continental great plains symbolized the iconic frontier of the nineteenth century, Greenland regaining its green shores from melting icecaps represents the new frontier of the twenty-first.

Islands are constant reminders of humanity's transoceanic pasts and how we have connected them by our movements. Most of Canada's history has been a story of "migratory and sojourning" ventures along coasts and waterways. While some sojourning marked out sites for our largest cities, other routes are now forgotten. Less than a century ago, fishing stations like Battle Harbour were crammed with fleets sailing the highways of the day; only now and only from land do these outposts seem remote and isolated. Part of what feels so unnatural about driving onto PEI is the straight, direct, and confined view from the bridge – neck craned over the concrete barriers for glimpses of shoreline – so unlike that from a rocking ship or a gliding canoe. Islands invoke a sensual echo of memory, an older perspective.

People, plants, and animals alike migrate to favourable habitats or cultivate new ones. The Norse sailed from one northern island to the next in search of greener pastures, finding in the Gulf of the St Lawrence the mythical Vinland. (In 1939 the PEI government included Vikings under sail on its map of the island, promising a new generation of visitors a land of "Heart's Content.") Archaeologists along Canada's Atlantic coasts have found evidence of long-standing trade between Baffin Island and Greenland centuries before colonies in the Caribbean and the north Atlantic began exchanging sugar for cod. We also carry islands with us, taking from them what we need or desire. How much of PEI's forest was sailing the world in ships in the nineteenth century? The seashell pocketed on a summer vacation, multiplied by the hundreds of thousands, recalls the billions of tons of shell mud dug and spread by farmers. Countless fish, lobster, and other marine species have been shipped from one side of the Atlantic Ocean to the other, and now to both sides of the Pacific.

Islands have been bound for centuries by webs of human exchange, for better and for worse. They are themselves easily traded, neat geographical currency, whether as a lease for Hong Kong or the purchase of the US Virgin Islands. In Atlantic Canada, coastal riches have always seemed compromised by mainland entanglements. It is surely no coincidence that it was the two islands, PEI and Newfoundland, that resisted confederation with Canada until the financing and politics of land-based projects like railways proved too much. For the second half of the twentieth century, farmers and fishermen alike on PEI struggled with consolidation, off-island ownership, and international competition, their harvests and catches determined by factors a world away from those who actually "own the land and drive the tractors." We should be cautious about overestimating the possibilities of island self-sufficiency. But today's industrial dependencies are products of particular decisions we have made in the past. There have always been other paths not taken, other paths that we might explore.

LESSON 2: A WORLD IN MINIATURE, A CACHE OF RICHES

Prince Edward Island is a small place. You can walk across it at its narrowest in an hour – and at its widest, run the annual marathon. Yet the essays that make up this book show that even a small island contains an enormous amount of life. Mi'kmaq, French, and British knew and harvested fish and fowl, sea mammals and sea plants. Even with two-thirds of the Island now devoted to agriculture, its biodiversity is astonishing, an indication of the special richness of a terraqueous ecology. At the same time, by their boundedness, islands encouraged settlers to fully exploit as many and as much of nature's abundances as possible, so that biodiversity became a driver of incautious innovation. Nearly all these

essays itemize not only the range of species on or near PEI but our ingenuity in finding a use and profit for nearly everything we could find here
(although to the modern palate, the idea of plovers with sauces is somewhat off-putting). Different peoples used the same resources in different
ways but in escalating intensity: the rivers, for example, travelled and
fished, then harnessed for mills for half a dozen industries; the trees, for
building and heat, then for timber and ships, progressing systematically
and relentlessly through hardwoods to softwoods as each species was
depleted. An ironic and perverse turn on the old axiom "waste not, want
not" – using everything to exhaustion – has become a metaphor for
much of human history.

PEI's rich but contained and accessible biodiversity nurtured a kind of
economic diversity, one that knitted together resources and revenues. If
not quite "halfe on land and halfe in sea," by fishing and farming, clearing fields and keeping woodlots, gathering seaweed and fuel, Islanders
developed a truly mixed economy. This versatility often perplexed colonial authorities, unaware of the natural fertility of the marshlands that
enabled Acadian agriculture, or the suitability of what scholars later
called occupational pluralism. Even in 1937, L.M. Montgomery could
picture on the north shore "a rather neglected rapscallion family who
lived in a ramshackle house where the spruce barrens ran down to a
curve of the harbour shore known as Hungry Cove. Nobody knew how
Solomon Snowbeam contrived to feed his family … he fished a little and
'worked out' a little and shot a little … [The children] were impudent,
friendly little creatures who certainly did not looked starved."[4]

Another member of Montgomery's community of Lantern Hill is
Step-a-Yard, a hired man who, as part of his duties, goes mudding, like
other farmers harvesting nutrients and energy from the mussel beds (a
reminder for Maritime energy utilities today promoting biomass, which
our predecessors knew meant much more than scrap wood). As Edward
MacDonald and Boyde Beck show here, the lobster fishery boomed
because it complemented an agricultural lifestyle, requiring time and
equipment that farmers could supply.

A way of life once judged as neither industrious nor virtuous has in
recent decades become part of our image of a rural golden age. The modest but well-provisioned family farm found along the road to Avonlea
has understandable appeal to those who have sought more sustainable
ways of living: back to the (is)land, slower foods, hundred-mile living
(PEI, after all, is not much more than one hundred miles long). This
vision suggests a knowledge and familiarity with the land that many lack

today, a more responsible system of production and consumption answerable to local circumstance, an appreciation of different resources rather than a singular reliance on one, whether lobsters, potatoes, or Anne of Green Gables. For if islands embody nature's wealth, they also are powerful reminders of its limits. It is when we have diverged from what the Island can provide to what we want it to provide that we have sought to breach those limits, not without cost. Mono-crop farming required intensive chemical fertilizers; more intense industrialization required imported fossil fuels. This is not to endorse subsistence or pre-industrial agriculture, but as with all history, to identify the limits and the lessons of past practice: what to leave and what to learn from. The diverse but limited riches of an island are perhaps the best reminder of moderation in all things.

LESSON 3: THE RESOURCES OF MEMORY AND MEANING

One of the lessons of environmental history is that while the twentieth century had no monopoly on avarice, advances in technology and demand did enable it to an unprecedented degree. And while we should not romanticize a simpler, pre-industrial account of using nature, whether by natives or newcomers, we *can* find in Island culture a body of knowledge comprised of myriad forms of what Kathleen Stuart here calls social capital: traditions of practice, memories of past adaptations, deeply rooted social connections, and cultural attachments to place. Several of this book's chapters note the limited utility of ideas of management or conservation imported from the mainland, relative to local – but not parochial – information, as when the PEI census counted a key energy source (i.e., mussel mud) in a way that Canada's would not, or when fishers persisted with older techniques like handlining simply because they worked. Memories of more sustainable practices may be close at hand, for many of these practices have only recently been overshadowed: we are in many ways only two generations removed from traditional mixed small-scale farming. Recognizing the different ways in which communities are invested in their industries and in the environments that support those industries, as sites of skill and identity as well as revenue, is essential to mobilizing public support for environmental protection. Watershed groups, land trusts, local energy companies, and other citizen groups demonstrate how Island will is itself a resource. As we are confronted with and occasionally overwhelmed by the scale of environmental degradation, the island may represent the best way to "think globally, act locally."

At the same time, social capital may be, and may need to be, found elsewhere. Around the world, coastal environments have generally been shared but divided spaces: places for fishing weirs and canneries for some, beaches and golf courses for others. Such diametrically opposed aesthetics of scenery and use are bound to cultivate resentment. But rather than presuming difference, it may be that the past forty years (the same period in which we have departed most consistently from sustainable industry on PEI) have seen environmental protection become common enough in the political arena to provide a common vocabulary, a shared concern, for those who live near coasts and those who are drawn to them. The growing popularity of *terroir*, with its respect for human-scale production and the dignity of tradition as well as environmental character, demonstrates that even those seeking a vacation and not an environmental critique wish to support sustainable industry. Speaking of "Islanders by choice" rather than those "from away" recognizes the concern of those born off-Island for their adopted place, sentiments to be respected and made use of. We might take inspiration from what Helen Kristmanson and David Keenlyside refer to as "forms of alignment" between the Mi'kmaq and Acadians, when the north shore was more a space of alliance and exchange than of exclusive possession. To make such "alignments" happen, we need to have a greater sense of environmental history in our everyday experiences of places, so that people new to the Island learn that even its idylls are the work of human hands, scenic *because* they are lived and worked.

LESSON 4: HISTORY FOR SUSTAINABILITY

Environmental debate is infused with an air of perpetual crisis, of catastrophes happening *right now*, with an imperilled future. And islands, with their ever-present intersectionality of land and water, remind us constantly of the problems of both. The essays here reference almost too many such problems to count: water contamination and soil exhaustion; some species invasive, others endangered; oceanic deoxygenation and acidification; climate change bringing sea-level rise, volatile weather, and shoreline erosion. Little wonder that it is the most vulnerable islands, like Tuvalu, that plead the loudest for more global attention to climate change.

Yet sustainability is about addressing and redressing situations that originate in both the industrial and the deep past. Historical ecologists and bioarchaeologists show that issues of the moment, such as climate change and the exhaustion of fish stocks, in fact date back over centuries. The role of the historian is to recognize the moment of human intervention, the effect of human action, the range of human responses, and the layers of human imprint. Though neither insular nor insulated, the boundedness of an island telescopes our attention, inviting us to delve deeply into the past in one place. It makes understandable the palimpsest of the environmental past, of competing and successive uses of the same land and the cumulative impact of human history on it. On Prince Edward Island the marks of these older decisions are everywhere, in the lines of settlement, transportation, and woodlands. Most of the trees we see on the Island are pioneer species colonizing sites of human disturbance; fields "gone spruce" or pretty stands of birch show a forest actively recovering from two centuries of forest fires, timber harvests, farm clearance and abandonment. Place names too are ever-present reminders of past occupation and dispossessions, from Havre Saint-Pierre to St Peter's Bay. Sometimes a map is the best history book.

Why does this matter? For one, environmental history makes a silent and at times ostensibly remote past more present. It broadens the public and political discussions about sustainability to consider historical context and long-term change, which can only produce more considered and more far-sighted policy. As an archive of environmental/human interaction, it allows us to speculate on (if not precisely anticipate) the possible effects of new and untried managerial decisions. This collection is full of "environmental fables" that are all too disturbingly prescient. The fate of the oyster industry a century ago – touted as "a little Klondike" where anyone could strike it rich, quickly ruined when the rush to seed new beds introduced a devastating infection – is surely a lesson for today's aquaculture advocates. The lobster fishery seemed to weather the collapse of other fisheries at the end of the twentieth century, but history and prudence suggest that such pressure on a single species is unwise, and fishing down the food chain as far as invertebrates shows how completely we have emptied the sea.[5] Even with the full weight of tourist promotion marketing lobster as both luxurious and regionally distinct – in comparison to the mid-twentieth century when it was disdained as food for the poor – lobster prices have sunk so low that the market has been flooded with too-small lobsters as fishers try desperately to claim some income. Historians are reluctant advisors, but we should not be.

While we cannot fairly judge or condemn our ancestors for making unsustainable choices, we can hold ourselves to a higher standard. We can distill from past experience more extensive and more rigorous criteria for our own actions (as per Jean-Paul Arsenault's wry query, "If industrial scale agriculture were now being proposed for Prince Edward Island for the first time, would it pass an Environmental Impact Assessment?"). PEI is groaning under the weight of reports and recommendations that in many ways say much the same thing, whether about an eighteenth-century fishery reserve or last year's state of the environment review. However atomized and eclectic past legislation has been, it nonetheless exists, a body of knowledge and a set of prior experiments showing the emphases and limits of generations of environmental management. We have, quite literally, been here before.

Scarcity is hardly ideal, but the truth is that it prompts economy, and exhaustion drives innovation. What land there is must be reused, so farm abandonment allows for forest and habitat restoration; the smallest province produces the first provincial conservation strategy. Island cities like Manhattan or Stockholm have developed some of the world's best systems for green energy and public transit. To put it another way, human history demonstrates that we have little incentive to change until forced to do so. Prince Edward Islanders are not and have never been inevitably environmentalists, but they have confronted nature's limits and, as Graeme Wynn says, "came to understand that the consequences of squandering nature's bounty could rarely be avoided in situ." So the other fable of note is that islandness actually opens new avenues for creativity. Some Island actions (like the banning of cars in 1908) may seem quirky, but the autonomy to respond to local concerns or to depart from conventional practice can be extraordinarily valuable. While the rest of Atlantic Canada since the 1960s has chased fossil fuels ever further afield and negotiated more pipelines and transmission lines between them, PEI has ventured to "go it alone" in renewable energy, from the Institute of Man and Resources to the wind farms at North Cape, seeking allies in other island nation-states like Denmark rather than on the mainland. Like the other small islands of the world, it has good reason to do so.

In closing, I find myself thinking of Prince Edward Island National Park – the Russian doll of islandness, itself a series of islands, an island of federal jurisdiction and protected status within a province, and a collection (an archipelago?) of ideas about our relationship with nature developed over time. The park's ecological integrity is weak because of its popularity,[6] and, in an inescapably circular logic, it is popular precisely because of its coastal setting. Concerns about dune erosion and plover habitat, are, as we know, recent things: the park was designed to be PEI's "first specific tourist attraction" and for decades was pictured as teeming with people. Today the cracked and overgrown highway leading onto Robinson's Island reminds us that the park was deliberately landscaped to invite people into nature, and that these decisions brought unanticipated and uninvited changes to that very setting. A subsequent generation of Islanders derailed a proposed second park by opposing the kind of expropriation of land that had created the first. Acknowledging that people lived and worked along the shoreline long before the arrival of bikinis, Parks Canada introduced interpretative sites like Stanhope to demonstrate the park's cultural heritage. The subsequent addition of Greenwich, with its focus on dune ecology, represented another evolution in park thinking. And Greenwich and Basin Head point to where we need to go next, in establishing offshore, alongshore, and marine protected areas. Within a single park we can see the lessons of history.

PEI National Park reminds us that a protected area, like an island, is an imperfect sanctuary. Both can guard ecological integrity and experiment with improving it, but they are never sealed off from outside influence; these are not life rafts of sustainability. Yet we persist in thinking of both as such, as fragments of "calm constancy" somehow safe from degradation, the ideal that forgives us our more destructive daily practices elsewhere. In 2010, Ottawa announced that Sable Island – a curved sandbar on the edge of the Scotian Shelf, three hundred kilometres from the mainland, home to wild horses and centuries of shipwrecks – was to become a national park. Two years later, however, the province of Nova Scotia issued the largest call for offshore bids in its history, granting billions of dollars of exploration rights to the north, south, east, and west of Sable. Meanwhile, after six years of construction, the first natural gas production began in 2013, forty kilometres from the island.[7] Drilling platforms and sandbars: so different, yet both islands in their way, marking our twin desires of finding resources and redemption in the ocean.

A WORLD OF ISLANDS

Two things happen when the water level drops in the Thirty Thousands Islands of the Georgian Bay, as it has been doing quite dramatically in recent years. As the water retreats, it exposes the lakebed of Canadian

Shield. Former islands become simply heights of the same rock, extensions of each other and the mainland, joined by great bands of curving pink and black granite. And a way of movement and life on water is suddenly hobbled. Boating routes become impassable; docks and cribs sit exposed, ungainly and unusable. Those on the islands lose not only their sense of orientation but also their reason for being there, not only how to live there but why they do. As this collection demonstrates time and again, the island is a multi-layered metaphor for humanity's place on this earth. Alluring in their individuality, symbols of undiscovered riches and new beginnings, islands are interconnected by historical pathways and contemporary vulnerabilities. Intertwined with the rise and fall of civilizations, they are also the most sensitive barometers of environmental degradation. The history of Prince Edward Island, as that of all islands, reveals what we have sought in nature and at what cost. A world in miniature, an island frames the weight of centuries and the scope of global change in a scale of time and place that we can understand. Most importantly, it tells us what we have done and what we need to do now. Historians do not predict the future, but perhaps islands can.

APPENDIX

Laying Down the Laws:
A Table of Environment-Related Legislation
on Prince Edward Island, 1770–1970

Colin MacIntyre

It is hardly surprising that Islanders' attitudes toward the environment have evolved over time.[1] What follows is a table of the major pieces of legislation related to Prince Edward Island's environment prior to the 1970s. Before a conscious "environmental movement" began in the 1970s, Islanders had concerns over the environment, but as the legislative chart (along with many of the essays in this collection) shows, those concerns generally revolved around conserving natural resources so that Islanders could use them. If governments have sporadically acted as stewards of the land, the driving force has been economic, even when the focus is recreational, and while there has sometimes been a groping instinct towards sustainability, in many cases such legislation (such as An Act to Regulate the Carrying on of the Sea Cow Fishery in 1770) has been less concerned with the resource than who should have access to it.

As the power of the state grew, so did its willingness to intervene in the environment. More or less on par with other jurisdictions, Island legislation has been used as a blunt tool variously to encourage exploitation (for example, through bounties), manage use, protect desired species, eradicate undesirable ones, or introduce new ones. Each act, in its own way, is about consumption: nature is cut, killed, coaxed, fed, sprayed, weeded, and watched over. But in the pre–*Silent Spring* era, there is little sense of consumption at any aesthetic level. Only by the end of the 1960s did legislation begin to reflect the emergence of a more self-conscious environmental awareness. And only now, perhaps, are policy-makers becoming more sensitive to the finite nature of resources on a small island

In all of this, the environmental history of Prince Edward Island was affected by its "islandness." The limited geographical area and amount of natural resources likely made the need for protective legislation evident well before any detrimental changes would have become noticeable in large continental areas. Arguably, the bounded area of the Island may also have given the impression that the environmental problems could be more easily fixed – perhaps the reason why federal economic planners gravitated toward the Island to experiment with development plans in the postwar period.

How can future government policies and environmental histories benefit from compilations such as this book? As A.H. Clark maintained, they can bring us a little closer to "understanding what we are" by offering "a clearer view of what we have been."

Table A.1
Summary of PEI environment-related legislation and policy trends, 1770–1970

Year	Reference	Title	Details
1770	Ratified by first Assembly in 1773 in 14 Geo.III, cap. 1	An Act to Regulate the Carrying On of the Sea Cow Fishery	Hunting regulation
1773	14 Geo. III, cap. VII	An Act for Indemnifying Persons Who Shall Burn Small Bushes, Rotten Wind-Falls, Decayed Leaves, and All Other Brush and Rubbish upon the Lands and in the Woods on This Island	Forest regulation
1780	20 Geo. III, cap. IV	An Act to Prevent the Cutting of Pine or other Trees without Permission of the Proprietor, and to Prevent the Cutting Down and Destroying of Fences	Forest regulation
1780	20 Geo. III, cap. V	An Act for Preventing the Running at Large of Stone-Horses or Stallions, and for the Killing of Partridges at Improper Seasons	Hunting regulation
1780	20 Geo. III, cap. V (second session)	An Act to Regulate the Salmon, Salmon-Trout, and Eel Fishery.	Fishing regulation
1781	21 Geo. III, cap. VI	An Act for a Reward for Killing Bears.	Hunting regulation
1798	39 Geo. III, cap. VI	An Act to Repeal an Act Entitled, "An Act for Indemnifying Persons Who Shall Burn Small Bushes, Rotten Wind-Falls, Decayed Leaves, and All Other Brush and Rubbish upon the Lands and in the Woods on This Island"	Forest regulation
1801	41 Geo. III, cap. I	An Act for Granting a Bounty for the Growing and Cultivation of Hemp	Farming regulation
1808	48 Geo. III, cap. III	An Act for Repealing an Act Entitled "An Act to Prevent the Throwing of Ballast into Rivers and Creeks on this Island, and for empowering the Governor, Lieutenant Governor, or Commander in Chief for the time being, to appoint Ballast Masters, and to Regulate Their Duty"	Watershed regulation
1825	5 Geo. IV, cap. XII	An Act to regulate the Fisheries of this Island	Fishing regulation
1831	1 Wm IV, cap. III	An Act to establish a reward for the Destruction of Bears and Loupcervier	Hunting regulation
1832	2 Wm. IV, cap. II	An Act to prevent the Destruction of Oysters by Burning the same, for the purpose of converting the Shells Thereof into Lime	Fishing regulation
1832	2 Wm. IV, cap. VII	An Act Regarding the Better Preservation of Forests	Forest regulation

Year	Reference	Title	Details
1832	11 Geo. IV, cap. VI	An Act to alter and amend an Act … entitled "An Act to prevent the throwing of Ballast into Rivers and Creeks on this Island, and for empowering the Governor, Lieutenant Governor, or Commander in Chief for the time being, to appoint Ballast Masters, and to Regulate Their Duty"	Watershed regulation
1833	3 Wm. IV, cap. XVIII	An Act for the Preservation and Improvement of the Herring and Alewives Fisheries of This Island	Fishing regulation
1840	3 Vic., cap. XII	An Act to regulate the floating of logs, scantling, deals, and other kinds of Wood, down the Rivers and Lesser Streams in This Island	Watershed regulation
1843	6 Vic., cap. IX	An Act to amend the Act regulating the floating of logs, scantling, deals and other Kinds of wood, down the Rivers and Lesser Streams in this Island, and for Other Purposes Therein Mentioned	Watershed regulation.
1844	7 Vic., cap. XXV	An Act for the Encouragement of the Seal and Cod Fisheries.	Fishing regulation
1844	7 Vic., cap. X	An Act to Alter and Amend an Act … for the appointment of Harbour and Ballast Masters, and for more effectually preventing the throwing of Ballast into Harbours and Navigable Rivers	Watershed regulation
1844	7 Vic., cap. XVII	An act for raising a Fund for the encouragement of Agriculture, to be expended in the erection of Lime Kilns, and the burning of Lime	Farming regulation
1844	7 Vic., cap.	An Act to establish a reward for the destruction of Bears and Loupcerviers	Hunting regulation
1845	8 Vic., cap. XX	An act for the regulation of the mackerel fishery	Fishing regulation
1852	15 Vic., cap. XLII	An act relating to … appointment of Protectors and Overseers of the Fisheries, and to prohibit the taking of Salmon after a certain period of the year.	Fishing regulation
1852	15 Vic., cap. II	An Act to Continue … Acts therein mentioned relating to the floating of logs, scantlings, deals, and other kinds of wood down the rivers and lesser streams in this Island.	Watershed regulation
1852	15 Vic., cap. XXIV	An Act to regulate the sale of arsenic and other poisons therein mentioned.	Regulation of poisons
1862	25 Vic., cap. XXXIII	An Act to prohibit the exportation of Juniper, Hackmatack timber, or knees	Forest regulation
1864	27 Vic., cap. XI	An Act relating to Partridges or Tree Grouse, and to repeal certain portions of the several Acts Therein Mentioned	Hunting regulation

Year	Reference	Title	Details
1869	32 Vic., cap. XXVII.	An Act for the better protection of the Salmon Fisheries, and to Repeal a Certain Act Therein Mentioned	Fishing regulation
1872	35 & 36 Vic., cap. XVI	An Act to define the law with regard to Seaweed and Kelp on the seacoast or outside the shores of this Island.	Watershed regulation
1873	36 Vic., cap. VI.	An Act for preventing the killing of Wild Ducks, Snipe, Woodcock, and Bittern, at Improper Seasons	Hunting regulation
1878	41 Vic., cap. II	An Act relating to the destruction of the Canadian Thistle	Farming regulation
1879	42 Vic., cap. VII	An Act for the Protection of Game and Fur-Bearing Animals.	Hunting regulation
1883	46 Vic., cap. III.	An Act to prevent the spread of the Potato Bug in Prince Edward Island.	Farming regulation
1884	47 Vic., cap. VIII	An Act to Protect Wild-Fowl.	Hunting regulation
1895	58 Vic., cap. X.	An Act for the Reclamation of Marsh Lands in Prince Edward Island.	Farming regulation
1895	58 Vic., cap. XI	An Act to Prevent the Spread of Black-knot on Plum and Cherry Trees	Farming regulation
1898	61 Vic., cap. VIII.	An Act for the Preservation of Partridge.	Hunting regulation
1901	1 Edw. VII, cap. XXXIII	An Act to Prevent the Destruction of Woods, Forests, and Other Properties by Fires	Forest regulation
1903	3 Edw. VII, cap. VI.	An Act Respecting a Forestry Commission	Forest regulation
1906	6 Edw., cap. IX.	The Prince Edward Island Fish and Game Protection Act, 1906.	Hunting and Fishing regulation
1906	6 Edw. VII, cap. VII	An Act to Incorporate the Prince Edward Island Fish and Game Protection Association	Hunting regulation
1906	6 Edw. VII, cap. 23	An Act respecting the oyster fisheries of Prince Edward Island	Fishing regulation
1906	6 Edw. VII, cap. XVI	An Act to prevent the spread of Noxious Weeds	Farming regulation
1907	7 Edw. VII, cap. VII.	An Act to amend "The Prince Edward Island Fish and Game Protection Act, 1906"	Hunting and Fishing regulation
1917	7 Geo. V., cap. XI.	The Beaver Protection Act.	Hunting regulation
1919	9 Geo. V., cap. XXXVI	An Act for the prevention and suppression of fires.	Forest regulation

Year	Reference	Title	Details
1920	10 Geo. V., cap. XIX.	An Act for the Suppression of Infection and Contagious Disease Among Bees, and For Instruction in Beekeeping.	Farming regulation
1921	11 Geo. V, cap. VI.	An Act to amend an Act for the prevention and suppression of fires.	Forest regulation
1925	15 Geo. V., cap. XI.	An Act to Amend the Statute Law ... Protection for partridge ...	Hunting regulation
1928	18 Geo. V., cap. XVI.	The Prince Edward Island Fish and Game Protection Act, 1928	Hunting and Fishing regulation
1934	24 Geo. V., cap. XIX.	An Act to Amend an "Act to Prevent the Destruction of Woods, Forests and Other Property by Fires"	Forest regulation
1937	1 Geo. VI., cap. XIII.	The Prince Edward Island Fish and Game Protection Act, 1937	Hunting and Fishing regulation
1938	2 Geo. VI., cap. IX	An Act to Amend "The Game Act, 1937"	Hunting and Fishing regulation
1939	15 Geo. VI., cap. XVIII.	The Forest Fires Act	Forest regulation
1939	3 Geo. V., cap. LI.	An Act to Prevent the Spread of Noxious Weeds	Farming regulation
1940	4 Geo. VI., cap. IV.	Animals' Protection Act	Farming regulation
1940	4 Geo. VI., cap. IX.	An Act Respecting Bacterial Ring Rot	Farming regulation
1940	4 Geo. VI., cap. XXXI.	An Act to Amend "The Game Act, 1937"	Hunting and Fishing regulation
1941	5 Geo. VI., cap. XI.	An Act to Amend "The Game Act, 1937"	Hunting and Fishing regulation
1943	7 Geo. VI., cap. IV	An Act to Amend "The Game Act, 1937"	Hunting and Fishing regulation
1944	8 Geo. VI., cap. XI.	An Act to Amend "The Game Act, 1937"	Hunting and Fishing regulation
1945	9 Geo. VI., cap. 4.	An Act Respecting Bacterial Ring Rot	Farming regulation
1945	9 Geo. VI., cap. XIV.	An Act to Amend "The Game Act, 1937"	Hunting and Fishing regulation

Year	Reference	Title	Details
1947	11 Geo. VI., cap. XVI	An Act to Amend "The Game Act, 1937"	Hunting and Fishing regulation
1948	12 Geo. VI., cap. II	An Act to Amend an Act Respecting Bacterial Ring Rot and Other Plant Diseases and Pests	Farming regulation
1948	12 Geo. VI., cap. XV	An Act to Amend "The Game Act, 1937"	Hunting and Fishing regulation
1949	13 Geo. VI., cap XVI	An Act to Amend "The Prince Edward Island Fish And Game Protection Act"	Hunting and Fishing regulation
1951	15 Geo. VI., cap. XII	The Forestry Act	Forest regulation
1951	15 Geo. VI., cap. XIII	The Prince Edward Island Fish and Game Protection Act	Hunting and fishing regulation
1951	15 Geo. VI., cap. CXIV	The Potato Production Act	Farming regulation
1956	5 Eliz. II., cap. XXVI	An Act to Amend the Plant Disease Eradication Act	Farming regulation
1962	11 Eliz. II., cap. I	An Act Respecting Agricultural Rehabilitation and Development.	Farming regulation
1964	13 Eliz. II., cap. XXIV	An Act to Control and Regulate the Distribution and use of Pesticides and Poisonous Top Killing Sprays.	Farming Regulation

Notes

INTRODUCTION

1 The Milton Acorn selections quoted in this essay may be found in the collection *The Edge of Home*, edited by Anne Compton.

2 Indeed, this entire paragraph borrows shamelessly from MacEachern's "What Can This Place Teach Us?"

3 Cobbett, *Rural Rides*, 535.

4 MacNeil, "The Acadian Legacy," 1–16.

5 Devor, "Explanatory Power," 70–1.

6 Piper, "Colloquial Meteorology," 102–23.

7 Devor, "Explanatory Power," 64; Havatny, "Tenant, Landlord, and the New Middle Class," PhD diss., University of Maine, 1996.

8 Jørgensen, "Not by Human Hands," 479.

9 Way, "Cosmopolitan Weed," 357.

10 For the province's place in Canadian electrification, see R.W. Sandwell, "Mapping Fuel Use in Canada," 239–68.

11 Albert C. Saunders, "Rapid Progress," 56–9.

12 Of two recent environmental histories of Canada, MacDowell's *Environmental History of Canada* contains a single index reference to Prince Edward Island (and that appears as a subheading under "regions"), while Wynn's groundbreaking *Canada and Arctic North America*, xvii, makes elegant apology for its scant reference to Canada's smallest province.

13 The term is coined in their *Lessons from the Political Economy of Small Islands*.

14 "I, Milton Acorn," in Compton, *Edge of Home*.

15 The most sustained criticism is made in Bumsted, "'The Only Island There Is.'"

16 Forbes, "In Search of a Post-Confederation Maritime Historiography," 5.

17 Sager and Panting, *Maritime Capital*, 14, 177.

18 Acheson, "National Policy," 3–8, 28; Wynn, *Canada and Arctic North America*, 182–4; MacDonald, *If You're Stronghearted*, 30, 119–21.

19 To cite just two examples: Weale and Baglole's defiant *Prince Edward Island and Confederation* and A.H. Clark's classic *Three Centuries and the Island*, discussed at some length by Wynn in this volume.

20 Abel, *Changing Places*, xxii–xxiii, 13; Anderson, "Reindeer, Caribou," 2–3.

21 See, particularly, Baldacchino, *A World of Islands*; Depraetre, "Challenge of Nissology," 17–36.

22 As explained in DeGrace, "Bathygnathus Comes Home," 12–13.

23 As briefly summarized in Campbell and Summerby-Murray's cogent introduction to *Land and Sea*. On the importance of the bio-regional approach, see Flores, "Place: An Argument for Bioregional History," 31–50.

24 A short list would include Clark's *Three Centuries and the Island* and its less auspicious predecessor, Stilgenbauer's "The Geography of Prince Edward Island"; also MacEachern's *Natural Selections*; Martin's *Watershed Red*; MacQuarrie's *Bonshaw Hills*; and several Island-based essays in Campbell and Summerby-Murray's *Land and Sea*.

25 MacEachern, *Natural Selections*; *The Institute of Man and Resources*.

26 To cite some of the more prominent examples, Bolger, *Canada's Smallest Province*; Bumsted, *Land, Settlement, and Politics*; Robertson, *Tenant League Movement*; Bittermann, *Rural Protest on Prince Edward Island*; *Sailor's Hope*. Hatvany's "Tenant, Landlord, and the New Middle Class" takes a much more overtly environmental history approach, assessing tenants' exploitation of land and ability to pay their rents, but even he uses the Land Question as the point of departure for his examination.

27 MacEachern and Turkel, *Method and Meaning*, xii. MacEachern, in turn, is referencing Worster's *The Ends of the Earth*.

28 Robin, "No Island Is an Island."

29 Cronon, *Nature's Metropolis*.

30 See Gillis, this volume; also Gillis, *The Human Shore*.

31 McNeill, "Of Rats and Men," 299–349; Diamond, *Collapse*, chapter 3.

32 "I, Milton Acorn," in Compton, *The Edge of Home*.

CHAPTER ONE

1 Beer, "The Island and the Aeroplane," 271.

2 Carson, *The Edge of the Sea*, 1.

3 Nunn, "Island Origins and Environments," 132.

4 Grove, *Green Imperialism*, 9; Crosby, *Ecological Imperialism*, iv.

5 Crosby, *Ecological Imperialism*, 13; on the Galapagos, see Larson, *Evolution's Workshop*.

6 Rainbird, "Islands out of Time," 216–32.

7 Gillis, *Islands of the Mind*, chapter 6; Broodbeck, *An Island Archaeology of the Early Cyclades*, chapter 1.

8 Quammen, *Song of the Dodo*, 19.

9 Gillis, *Islands of the Mind*, chapter 4.

10 Rainbird, "Islands out of Time," 232.

11 Rozwadowski, *Fathoming of the Ocean*, chapter 1.

12 Raban, *Coasting*, 300.

13 Epeli Ha'uofa first coined this term in reference to the South Pacific.

14 Broodbeck, "Insularity of Island Archaeologists," 234.

15 Erikson, "In Which Sense Do Cultural Islands Exist?" 133–47.

16 Berry, *The Unsettling of America*, chapter 9.

17 Mandelbrot, "How Long Is the Coast of Britain?," 636–8.

18 Nunn, *Vanished Islands and Hidden Continents of the Pacific*; Strommel, *Lost Islands*.

19 Gillis, *Islands of the Mind*, 143.

20 Ibid., chapter 2.

21 Weale, *Chasing the Shore*, 10.

22 Nunn, "Island Origins and Environments," 132.

23 Sauer, "Seashore," 309.

24 Crawford, "A Role for LIPS," 7–32.

25 Marean et al., "Early Human Use of Marine Resources," 905–8.

26 Berry, *Unsettling of America*, 174.

27 Nunn, *Vanished Islands*, 59.

28 Ibid., chapter 5.

29 Nunn, "The A.D. 1300 Event," 1–23; "Environmental Catastrophe in the Pacific Islands," 715–40; "Origins and Environments," 124–5.

30 Nunn, "Environmental Catastrophe," 732–3.

31 Kennett, *The Island Chumash*, chapters 5–8.

32 Cunliffe, *Europe between the Oceans*, 89–139.

33 Clarke and Maquire, *Skara Brae*.

34 Childe, *Skara Brae: A Pictish Village*, 2.

35 *A Dictionary of Creation Myths*, viii.

36 Jacobsen, *The Living Store*, 128.

37 Mancke, "Spaces of Power in the Early Modern Northeast," 35.

38 Mack, introduction to *The Sea*.

39 Loefgren, "From Peasant Fishing to Industrial Trawling," 154. See also Schei and Moberg, *The Orkney Story*, 147.

40 Lewes Roberts, *Merchants Mappe of Commerce* (London, 1638), quoted in Pope, *Fish into Wine*, 234.

41 Stilgoe, *Alongshore*, chapter 13. Also see McKenzie, *Clearing the Coastline*.

42 Cronon, *Changes in the Land*, 39, 53.

43 Jacobsen, *The Living Shore*, 103–28; Cronon, *Changes in the Land*, 51.

44 On the changing nature of the Maine coast, see Conkling, *Islands in Time*.

45 Stratford et al., "Envisioning the Archipelago," 120.

46 Grove, *Green Imperialism*, introduction and chapter 1.

47 Wilson and MacArthur, *Theory of Island Biogeography*.

48 Putz, "A Singular Community," 122.

49 Ian Jared Miller, "Bitter Legacy, Injured Coast," *New York Times*, 20 March 2011, 12.

50 The realization that the natural environment is more man-made than we think stems back to the 1950s, but it has been recently reinforced by McNeill in *Something New under the Sun*. See also Glacken, "Changing Ideas of the Habitable World," 73.

51 Bolster, "Opportunities in Marine Environmental History," 567–97; "Putting the Ocean in Atlantic History," 19–47. See also Richards, *The Unending Frontier*, chapter 15.

52 Roberts, *Unnatural History of the Sea*. See also Edward MacDonald and Boyde Beck's account of the serial collapses of PEI fisheries, this volume.

53 Gastner, *Rachel Carson*, 64.

54 D'Arcy, *People of the Sea*, 30–9.

55 D'Arcy, "Maritime History in the Age of Sail."

56 D'Arcy, *People of the Sea*, 16, 98–9.

57 Ibid., 168.

58 Stilgoe, *Alongshore*, 407.

59 Jay, "Scopic Regimes of Modernity," 3–28.

60 Norimitsu Onishi, "Japanese Town's 'Great Wall' Provided a False Sense of Security," *New York Times*, 2 April 2011, A4.

61 Mack, *The Sea*, 105. Navigators sit naked on the deck, their testicles sensitive to every movement of the waters.

62 Theroux, "The True Size of Cape Cod," 148.

63 Gastner, *Rachel Carson*, 125.

64 See Pilkey and Young, *The Rising Sea*.

65 Lewis and Wigen, *The Myth of Continents*.

66 See, for example, *Encylopedia of Islands* (2009), which still treats islands as bounded entities.

CHAPTER TWO

1 The island-novel comparison is made by Emma Marris in "Reconstituted Edens," 414, a review of T.C Boyle's *When the Killing's Done* (New York: Viking 2011). The quotations are taken from this review.

2 Carson, *The Sea around Us*, 110.

3 Sullivan, foreword to *Anne of Green Gables*.

4 Parks Canada, Green Gables Area Plan Concept, 27. For a fuller treatment of these developments see Squire, "Literary Tourism and Sustainable Tourism," 119–34.

5 Montgomery, *Anne of Green Gables*.

6 Epperly, *Fragrance of Sweet-Grass*, 18.

7 Gammel, "Embodied Landscape Aesthetics," 228–47.

8 For example, botanist Quentin Cronk has written: "In conserving palaeo-endemics we are conserving ancient patterns of diversity: islands as museums. In conserving neo-endemics we are conserving the result of special processes of evolution: islands as laboratories" ("Islands," 488).

9 Prichard, *Researches into the Physical History of Man*, 248–9.

10 Morgan, *Systems of Consanguinity*, 448–9. There is a useful discussion of this history in Spriggs, "Are Islands Islands?," 211–26.

11 Grove, "The Culture of Islands."

12 Losos and Ricklefs, "Adaptation and Diversification on Islands," *Nature*, 830–6: "Because many islands are young and have relatively few species, evolutionary adaptation and species proliferation are obvious and easy to study. In addition, the geographical isolation of many islands has allowed evolution to take its own course, free of influence from other areas, resulting in unusual faunas and floras, often unlike those found anywhere else."

13 Quammen, *Song of the Dodo*.

14 Grove, *Green Imperialism*.

15 Diary of Joseph Banks, quoted in Grove, "The Culture of Islands," and in Grove, "The Island and the History of Environmentalism," 158

16 Marsh, *Man and Nature*. This much-celebrated book has been described as "the beginning of land wisdom" in the United States and the starting point of the conservation movement; see Lowenthal, *George Perkins Marsh*, for a detailed assessment.

17 This was Haddon's second visit to Torres Strait. His team included C.S. Myers, W.H.R. Rivers, S.H. Ray, William McDougall, and C.G. Seligman. The results were published between 1901 and 1931 as *Reports of the Cambridge Anthropological Expedition to Torres Strait*. See Moore, *The*

Torres Strait Collections of A.C. Haddon; Haddon, "Cambridge Anthropological Expedition to the Torres Straits and Sarawak"; Radcliffe Brown, *The Andaman Islanders*; Malinowski, *Argonauts of the Western Pacific*. For a general account, see Harris, *Rise of Anthropological Theory*. There is a brief review in Boomert and Bright, "Island Archaeology," 3–26, and an assessment in Kuklick, "Islands in the Pacific," 611–38.

18 Boomert and Bright, "Island Archeology," 5.

19 Farbotko, "Wishful Sinking," 54.

20 Mead, *Growing Up in New Guinea*; *Coming of Age in Samoa*. See also Baldacchino, "The Coming of Age of Island Studies," 272–83.

21 Spate, "Islands and Men," 253–64.

22 Vayda and Rappoport, "Island Cultures," 133–42.

23 Clark, *Three Centuries and the Island*.

24 Wynn, "Geographical Writing on the Canadian Past," 108–11, in Conzen, Rumney, and Wynn, *A Scholar's Guide*.

25 Hartshorne, *The Nature of Geography*. For further assessment of the implications, see Wynn, "A 'Deep History,'" 153–6.

26 Clark, *Three Centuries*, 222–3.

27 Hartshorne, *Perspective on the* Nature of Geography, 49

28 For more on Sauer and his influence see Conzen, Rumney, and Wynn, *A Scholar's Guide*, 25–33, 173–6.

29 Spriggs, "Are Islands Islands?," 216.

30 Goodenough, "Oceania and the Problem of Controls," 146–55, quote on 146; the other papers were Sahlins, "Differentiation by Adaptation," 291–300; and Goldman, "Variations in Polynesian Social Organization" 374–90. Mead's introduction appeared in *Journal of the Polynesian Society*, 145.

31 Clark, "South Island, New Zealand and Prince Edward Island, Canada," 150.

32 Roger Duff, a New Zealander, had used the idea of islands as laboratories in a book written in 1947–48, viz., *The Moa-Hunter Period of Maori Culture* (Wellington: R.E. Owen, Government Printer 1950). Noting this occurrence, Spriggs observes: "The statement is unreferenced, suggesting it was a commonly used idea at the time." Clark lived in and worked on New Zealand in the mid-1940s, and he was generally cognizant of work in the social sciences in this period

33 See Fosberg, *Man's Place in the Island Ecosystem*, and Evans, "Islands as Laboratories," 517–20.

34 Moore Jr., *Social Origins of Dictatorship and Democracy*, 490–3.

35 Robertson, *Sir Andrew Macphail*, 279.

36 This notion of the end of the nineteenth century as an intellectual precipice below which seethed social and moral chaos is taken from Haultain and used by Shortt, *The Search for an Ideal*.

37 See, for instance, Reich, *The Greening of America*; Roszak, *The Making of a Counter Culture*.

38 For the *Whole Earth Catalogue*, see Kirk, *Counterculture Green*; for *Mother Earth News*, see Armstrong, *A Trumpet to Arms*, 194–8. Note that "British Columbia: Paradise on the Pacific," "Coastal British Columbia," "Alberta's Homestead Sales and Land Leases," "Wild Foods of British Columbia" "Back-to-the-Land in Southern Ontario," and "Homesteading in the Kootenays," appeared in *Mother Earth News*, issues 3–5, 1970 (as noted by Weaver, "First Encounters," 4.)

39 Macphail quote from 1912 in Robertson, "Sir Andrew Macphail," 8. For a more general overview see also Shi, *The Simple Life*. These ideas have long and complicated genealogies and manifest in all sorts of forms and places. For a recent much-noticed version see HRH The Prince of Wales, Juniper, and Skelly, *Harmony*; and the brief but probing review by Stott, "A Magical Process," 764.

40 Berry, *The Unsettling of America*.

41 "Wendell Berry's *The Unsettling of America*: A Look Back at His Seminal Work," http://resident-theology.blogspot.com/2010/04/wendell-berrys-unsettling-of-america.html.

42 Berry, *The Gift of Good Land*.

43 Gower, "The Impact of Alternative Ideology on Landscape"; Simmons, "But We Must Cultivate Our Garden"; Vonnegut, *The Eden Express*; Gloin, "Living Green before Their Time"; McDaniel, "Homesteading in Maine"; Sue, Nelly, Dian, Carol, Billie, *Country Lesbians*.

44 Weaver, "First Encounters," 1–30.

45 MacEachern, "Narrative"; Ryan O'Connor and Alan MacEachern, "Back to the Island," http://niche-canada.org/member-projects/backtotheisland/home.html.

46 O'Connor and MacEachern, "Back to the Island."

47 Interview with Steve Knechtel at O'Connor and MacEachern, "Back to the Island," and MacEachern, "Narrative."

48 Interview with Laurel Smyth, at O'Connor and MacEachern, "Back to the Island."

49 MacEachern, "Narrative."

50 Ibid.

51 Jacob, *New Pioneers*, xii. See also Gould, *At Home in Nature*.

52 Schumacher, *Small Is Beautiful*, 28, 18.

53 These developments are well treated in (and my discussion of much that follows derives from) MacEachern, *The Institute of Man and Resources*, quote from pg. 17. See also Doern and Toner, *The Politics of Energy*; Canada, *Development Plan for Prince Edward Island*.

54 MacEachern, *Institute*, 21.

55 *Charlottetown Evening Patriot*, 15 April 1975, quoted by MacEachern, *Institute*, 25.

56 MacEachern, *Institute*, 30.

57 Quotes from ibid., 35.

58 Ibid., 49, referencing articles in *Chatelaine* and *Saturday Night* magazines.

59 MacEachern, *Institute*, 48.

60 Ibid., 82.

61 Evans, "Islands as Laboratories."

62 Clifford, *The Predicament of Culture*, 1988; Clifford and Marcus, *Writing Culture*; Taussig, *Shamanism*. See also Rainbird, "Islands out of Time," 216–34; Comments, 234–58; Reply, 259–60.

63 Spriggs, "Are Islands Islands?"; Barrowclough, "Expanding the Horizons," 27–46.

64 Patton, *Islands in Time*, 181.

65 Boomert and Bright, "Island Archeology"; Patton, *Islands in Time*.

66 J.E. Robb, cited in Lape, "The Isolation Metaphor," 226.

67 Lape, "The Isolation Metaphor," 224–9; Gosden and Pavlides, "Are Islands Insular?" 162–71.

68 See Weaver, "First Encounters."

69 McRobie, *Small Is Possible*, 174.

70 Norman Hall, director of the PEI Enersave program, as quoted by MacEachern, *Institute*, 85.

71 As noted by MacEachern, *Institute*, 116; see also Hall, "The Commission of Conservation," 236–63; and Girard, *L'écologisme retrouvé*.

72 Smith and Mackinnon, *The 100-Mile Diet*; Rees and Wackernagel, *Our Ecological Footprint*.

73 Here I consciously echo the thoughtful New Zealand sheep farmer, ornithologist, and nature writer W.H. Guthrie Smith, as discussed in Wynn, "Remapping Tutira," 418–46.

74 Speth, "Environmental Failure"; Robinson, "Squaring the Circle?," 369–84.

75 Hough, *Forestry of the Future*, 74–6; and in Grove, "Culture of Islands."

CHAPTER THREE

1 Archaeologists, geologists, and other scientists use "years BP" or "years before present" to denote a past period of time. Within this convention,

"present" means AD 1950 when radiocarbon dating was first applied to archaeological and other scientific research.

2 Unique environmental conditions at or near glaciers.

3 Dyke, Dale, and McNeely, "Marine Molluscs," 125–84.

4 Stea, "Geology and Palaeoenvironmental Reconstruction."

5 Mott, "Palaeoecology and Chronology of Nova Scotia," 39–54.

6 Ibid., 49, 50.

7 Keenlyside, "Ulus and Spearpoints," 25–7.

8 Miller, "Late Glacial and Post-Glacial Fauna," 77–90.

9 Anderson, "Holocene Vegetation," 1152–65.

10 Ibid.

11 Keenlyside, "Palaeo-Indian Occupations," 163–73.

12 Shaw, "Geomorphic Evidence of Postglacial Terrestrial Environments," 149.

13 Shaw and Forbes, "Short- and Long-Term Relative Sea-Level Trends," 291–305.

14 Miller, "Late Glacial and Post-Glacial Fauna," 77.

15 Ibid., 85.

16 Ibid., 53.

17 Gramly, "The Vail Site."

18 MacDonald, *Debert*, 141. Carbon-14 or radiocarbon dating is a technique for determining the age of carbon-bearing minerals, including wood and plant remains, charcoal, bone, peat, and calcium carbonate shell. A valuable tool for archaeologists, geologists, and other scientists, it is used to date organic material up to 75,000 years old. A raw carbon date cannot be used directly as a calendar date because the level of atmospheric C14 has not been constant over time. Thus, lab C14 dates are adjusted or recalibrated to provide consistent calendar ages.

19 See, for example, Keenlyside, "Ulus and Spearpoints"; MacDonald, *Debert*; Turnbull and Allen, *More Palaeo-Indian Points*.

20 See Greer, Strand, and Sias, "People, Caribou and Ice."

21 See McCaffery, "Aboriginal Occupations," 99–101; Pintal, "Aux Frontières de la Mer."

22 Keenlyside, "La periode Paleoindienne," 119–26.

23 Archaeologists generally divide stone tools into two classes: ground and flaked. Ground stone tools are further divided into two sub-categories: those tools that are ground and polished through grinding, pounding, or crushing of plants, animals, and mineral resources (milling stones, mortars, pestles) and those tools where grinding or polishing was key to their manufacture (axes, adzes, net sinkers, or plummets). Flaked stone tools, such as projectile points, cutting, and scraping tools, are produced by the

removal of flakes or "chips" from vitreous stone through percussion or pressure flaking processes known as "flint-knapping." Some ground stone tools are flaked at an early stage of their manufacture, and some flaked tools are ground as a means of sharpening.

24 See Kristmanson, "The Ceramic Sequence."

25 Kristmanson, "Archaeological Investigations."

26 See Sanger, *The Carson Site*, and Keenlyside, "Progress Report Sutherland Site."

27 Denys, *Histoire Naturelle des Peuples*.

28 See Kristmanson, "Archaeological Investigations"; Keenlyside, "Prehistory of the Gulf of St Lawrence 'Southern Basin,'" 124–31.

29 See Hoffman, "Historical Ethnography of the Micmac," 230; Snow, *Archaeology of New England*, 32–3.

30 Miller, "Aboriginal Micmac Population," 122.

31 In the seventeenth century, French chroniclers in what is present-day Nova Scotia referred to some Aboriginal people as Souriquois; today we understand that this term referred to ancestral Mi'kmaq people living in part of the Maritime Provinces (Hoffman, "Historical Ethnography," 88). Souriquois is not what the Aboriginal people called themselves, and its meaning is not fully understood, though various explanations have been put forth. Champlain, for example, encountered a group of Aboriginal people camped near a river they called Souricoua, south of the Miramichi in New Brunswick (see Miles, "Introduction," 14). Others interpret the term as a French spelling of *zurikoa*, a Basque word meaning "that of the whites," which had become the name of the pidgin language used for trade in the North Atlantic area from about AD 1500–1650 (Holm, "Pidgins and Creoles," 628). In addition to their mother tongue, the Souriquois also spoke this pidginized form of Basque. Similarly, the term Mi'kmaq, also not an Aboriginal self-referent, is thought to derive from *nikmaq*, a pidgin greeting comprised of elements from local Aboriginal and Portuguese languages from the late sixteenth and early seventeenth centuries (Whitehead, "Proto-Historic Period," 240). The Aboriginal people today known as Mi'kmaq historically referred to themselves as Inu'k or L'nu'k, "the people" (Whitehead, "Nova Scotia," 5).

32 Hoffman, "Historical Ethnography," 231.

33 Miller and Hamell, "A New Perspective," 311–28.

34 Hamell, "Strawberries, Floating Islands," 72–94.

35 Deal, *Prehistory of the Maritime Provinces*; Leonard, *Mi'kmaq Culture*.

36 Whitehead, *Stories from the Six Worlds*.

37 Martin, "Four Lives of a Micmac Copper Pot," 11–133.

38 Our use of the expression 'Middle Ground' derives from White, *The Middle Ground.*

39 Kristmanson, "Archaeology at Pointe-Aux-Vieux, Part 1."

40 As narrated in Upton, *Micmacs and Colonists.*

41 Allen, "Final Report," 33.

42 Ibid., 33.

43 Ibid., ii.

44 Cronon, *Changes in the Land,* 41.

45 Ibid., 183n32.

46 Biard, "Missio Canadensis," 73.

47 When adapted for the Prince Edward Island Mi'kmaq population, other estimates include 3,288 (Dobyns, "Estimating Aboriginal American Population, 395–416); 281–1124 (Kroeber, "Native American Population," 1–25); and 723 (Steward, *Theory of Culture Change*).

48 Mooney, "Aboriginal Population of America North of Mexico," 1–40.

49 Wallis and Wallace, *Micmac Indians of Eastern Canada,* 17; Hoffman, "The Historical Ethnography," 96.

50 Miller, "Aboriginal Micmac Population."

51 Bock, "Micmac," 117; also Snow, *Archaeology of New England,* 36.

52 Snow, *Archaeology of New England,* 34.

53 Ibid., 31–42. Using Snow's formula, the historic Aboriginal population of New Brunswick (total area of 72,908 square kilometres, or 21,300 square miles) was 8,733, and the historic Aboriginal population of Nova Scotia including Cape Breton and some 3,800 coastal islands (total area of 55,284 square kilometres, or 21,300 square miles) was 11,541. Taking into account the larger land masses in New Brunswick and Nova Scotia, these calculations are compatible with Cronon's estimate.

54 Hoffman, "Historical Ethnography," 229.

55 Ibid., 231–3.

CHAPTER FOUR

1 To give a precise figure: by 1935 only 32 per cent of the Island's land area was still under forest (Glen, "Prince Edward Island 1935/1936 Forest Cover Type Mapping"), though by 1990 this had increased to 49 per cent (Prince Edward Island Forest Inventory 1990/1992).

2 Scott, *Canada's Vegetation.*

3 See Sobey, *Early Descriptions,* part 3, for an assemblage and analysis of extracts from twentieth-century studies that have touched on the forests of the Island. All serve to place the Island's forests in the context of

continental or regional forest types (Halliday, *Forest Classification*; Rowe, *Forest Regions*; Loucks, *Forest Classification*), or, with forest description being peripheral to other aims, have been entirely qualitative and descriptive (Stilgenbauer, *Geography*; Erskine, *Plants*; MacDougall, Veer, and Wilson, *Soils*). The best previous attempt at an understanding of the pre-settlement forest is to be found in Erskine, *Plants*, 15–22.

4 Sobey and Glen, "Forests of Prince Edward Island," 585–602.

5 MacDougall Veer, and Wilson, *Soils*, 2–15.

6 These have been assembled in Sobey, *Early Descriptions*, 1 and 2 (extracts).

7 For the maps, see Sobey and Glen, "Mapping the Pre-Settlement Forests." The surveyors' field-books are still in the process of being analyzed.

8 Russell, *How Agriculture Made Canada*, 200. See Sobey, *Early Descriptions*, part 2, Analyses, 24–30 for an assemblage in tabular form of all of the early comments on the use of the forest trees as an indicator of soil quality.

9 As a substitute for the lack of any quantitative records on the relative abundance of the different trees in the historical accounts, I have resorted to tallying the number of different references to each tree found in all of the forest-related historical accounts taken together (excluding their mentions in tree *lists*, where the aim was to list all of the trees of the Island) (see Sobey, *Early Descriptions*, part 2, Analyses, 221–6). There will be biases favouring the mention of particular trees for reasons other than their abundance in the forest, but even so, the tally has produced a useful quantitative indicator of the relative abundance of the different trees that makes ecological sense.

10 Especially informative is John Stewart's statement in 1806 that beech "grows in great abundance, probably better than half of the Island is covered with it, in some districts forming nine-tenths of the forest" (Stewart, *Account*, 36). See also Sobey, *Early Descriptions*, part 2, Analyses, 188, for other early comments indicating the importance of beech in the forest.

11 For examples of the occurrence of areas of softwood in the "hollows" within hardwood areas, see Sobey, *Early Descriptions*, part 2, Analyses, 11. There are also comments to that effect on the manuscript maps in the provincial Archives: the best example is to be found on a map of Lot 28 dating from 1773 (Map 0,539): "From Tryon River to the North Boundary Line soil very good chiefly hard Wood/Except in the Valleys Hemlock, Spruce & Pine." The area to which this description applies covers some sixteen hundred hectares (see Sobey and Glen, "Mapping the Pre-Settlement Forests," 107).

12 Such as in evidence to the Land Commission of 1875 (*Report of Proceedings*). See Sobey, *Early Descriptions*, part 2, Extracts: 185–95.

13 The earlier immigrants' handbooks had usually characterized land under conifers as unsuitable for farmland, but by the 1870s some witnesses to the Land Commission of 1875 were describing it as "second class land" (see Sobey, *Early Descriptions*, part 2, Analyses, 25–9).

14 Sobey, *Early Descriptions*, part 2, Analyses, 12–15.

15 Ibid., 71.

16 This distinction in drainage was also evident in the classification of the present-day Black Spruce Forest, the plots of which were subdivided into a wetter bog-type forest and a drier lichen-heath-type forest (see Sobey, "Analysis of the Ground Flora," 92–5).

17 Sobey, *Early Descriptions*, part 2, Analyses, 15–16.

18 Ibid., 10.

19 Ibid., 20.

20 Ibid., 21.

21 Ibid., 21.

22 Ibid., 18–20.

23 Ibid., 24–31.

24 Ibid., 31–3.

25 Ibid., 22–3.

26 Sobey, *Early Descriptions*, part 1, 151–4; part 2, Analyses, 252–3.

27 The only recorder to provide any geographical information is Bain in 1890 (*Natural History*), who stated that the boreal component of the Island's forests, as well as the swamps and the barrens, were largely confined to the eastern and western counties, which is in broad agreement with the distribution of their present-day descendants (see Sobey, *Early Descriptions*, part 2, Analyses, 16–17).

28 See Sobey and Glen, "Analysis of the Ground Flora," 30–5; and Sobey and Glen, "Mapping of the Present and Past Forest-types," 504–20.

29 Pastor and Mladenoff, "Southern Boreal," 216–40; Scott, *Canada's Vegetation*.

30 Anderson, "Holocene Vegetation," 1152–65.

31 Sobey, "Analysis of Historical Records for the Native Fauna," 384, 392. The absence of the moose and the beaver from the Island (two of the Mi'kmaq's principal winter foods) made their subsistence on the Island in the winter difficult, if not impossible.

32 Lower, in *Settlement and the Forest Frontier*, 28–31, was the first to distinguish between these two types of motivations among immigrants to Canada.

33 There were also settlers who came from elsewhere in North America, namely, the Acadians and the Loyalists.

34 Sobey, *Early Descriptions*, part 2, 24–5; part 2, Analyses, 110–13.

35 As did Robert Clark at New London and James Montgomery at Stanhope and Three Rivers (see Bumsted, *Land, Settlement and Politics*, 51–5, 62–4).

36 Men such as Joseph Pope and James Peake (see De Jong and Moore, *Shipbuilding*).

37 They are represented in the early records by the artisans Thomas Curtis and Benjamin Chappell (see Sobey, *Early Descriptions*, part 2, Extracts, 34–43).

38 In the written records for the Island are found examples of virtually all of the various attitudes to the forest that were recorded elsewhere in North America (see Nash, *Wilderness*).

39 Sobey, *Early Descriptions*, part 2, Analyses, 114–23.

40 See Sobey, "Analysis of Historical Records," for the conclusion, based on an analysis of the evidence, that the species was the red-backed vole (*Clethrionomys gapperi*) rather than the meadow vole (*Microtus pennsylvanicus*).

41 See Sobey, *Early Descriptions*, part 2, Analyses, 131–7, for examples of the conflict over the ownership of the timber, and the occurrence of theft.

42 The man was William Dawson, principal of McGill University, who carried out a study of the Island's peat resources which was published in 1871 (Sobey, *Early Descriptions*, part 2, Analyses, 141). Noting the "rapid disappearance of the forests," he expressed concern about the sustainability of the firewood supply of the Island, and added cautiously that it was "worthy of consideration whether measures should be taken by the Government for the protection of the remainder of the forests." It is somewhat surprising that the most extended statement on the need for forest conservation (albeit also from a utilitarian viewpoint) is that of the French minister of the Marine, the count of Maurepas, in 1732 (Sobey, *Early Descriptions*, part 1, 27).

43 Johnstone, *Series of Letters*, 115. See also Sobey, *Early Descriptions*, part 2, Analyses, 16.

44 By "aesthetic" I mean the impact the forest made on the *senses* of the observer, in terms, for example, of its visual beauty or pleasantness. In fact, the first European to describe the Island's trees, Jacques Cartier, in 1534, used aesthetic criteria, rather than utilitarian, in his assessment of the forest (see Sobey, *Early Descriptions*, part 1, 26).

45 Robert Gray in 1793, and Isabella Bird in 1851 (see Sobey, *Early Descriptions*, part 2, Analyses, 127–8).

46 Samuel Hill in 1839, and Francis Bain in the 1880s (see Sobey, *Early Descriptions*, part 2, Analyses, 129).

47 MacGregor, *Historical and Descriptive Sketches*, 259–60.

48 Such an attitude, the roots of which can be traced to the Bible (see Nash, *Wilderness*, 13–20), was recorded by L.M. Montgomery (*Selected Journals*, vol. 1, 302, 359–61) and Sir Andrew Macphail (*Master's Wife*, 157–8) in the rural post-pioneer Island communities in which they grew up in the late nineteenth century.

49 See Sobey, *Early Descriptions*, part 2, Analyses, 44–8 for a compilation of the many descriptions of the methods of forest clearance, the best of which are those of Douglas ("Settlement Formed in Prince Edward's Island," 182–3) and Johnstone (*Series of Letters*, 107–11). The prior killing of the trees by girdling (the stripping of a ring of bark) was not often used on the Island, despite the statement of Clark (*Three Centuries*, 78).

50 As Johnstone (*Series of Letters*, 126) and Lawson (*Letters*, 30–1) point out, many farms on the Island took the form of a long narrow strip with 10 chains (660 feet) of frontage along a river or coastline, or later along a road, and 100 chains of depth (a legacy that has remained ever since, as can be seen in the cadastral maps of the Island published by the Meacham Company in 1880 (*Illustrated Historical Atlas*).

51 I have not come across any references in the Island literature to the size of the area that should have been retained as a farm woodlot in order to supply firewood and fencing materials (see Sobey, *Early Descriptions*, part 2, 77).

52 Several recorders stress that this was a common occurrence: Douglas, *Diary*, 19; Stewart, *Account*, 138; Johnstone, *Series of Letters*, 104.

53 Douglas (*Diary*, 19), Stewart (*Account*, 138), and MacGregor (*Historical and Descriptive Sketches*, 57) state that forest fires were more common in the spring or the beginning of summer because this was the time when most of the settlers burnt the wood left over from their clearance operations.

54 Stewart, *Account*, 138.

55 See Sobey, *Early Descriptions*, part 2, Analyses, 57–8.

56 MacGregor, *Historical and Descriptive Sketches*, 20.

57 Johnstone (*Series of Letters*, 106) stressed the loss of firewood: "when the hard wood is burnt upon a farm, the people have no convenient way of supplying themselves with fuel for their fires at home."

58 Aptly described by Stewart (*Account*, 138–40) and MacGregor (*Historical and Descriptive Sketches*, 173).

59 Stewart (*Account*, 139), Johnstone (*Series of Letters*, 106), and MacGregor (*Historical and Descriptive Sketches*, 58) describe how after a forest fire,

"fire-weed" and other successional species "sprang up," "entirely impoverishing the land."

60 This is most vividly described by Johnstone (*Series of Letters*, 106–7), and is also mentioned by Lawson (*Letters*, 31).

61 Johnstone (*Series of Letters*, 104) especially notes this effect.

62 Johnstone, ibid., alludes to this.

63 I have found two acts of the Legislature (1773, 1825), the draft of one undated bill to be put before the Assembly, and one proclamation by a governor (1815), that are all concerned with the control of forest fires, though there may have been other acts as well as regulations that I have not come across (see Sobey, *Early Descriptions*, part 2, Extracts, 28–31).

64 See Sobey, *Early Descriptions*, part 1, 22–4, for an analysis of the French period records for the two fires, and part 2, Analyses, 54–6, for retrospective British period comments on the extent and effect of the fires. See also Sobey and Glen, "Mapping the Pre-Settlement Forests," 177–95.

65 This value was obtained by estimating by eye the proportion of each township that was burned, as shown in figure 4.5, taking the area of each township to be the number of acres as "measured" by Clark (*Three Centuries*, 261). The total area of the burn came to 171,000 acres or 69,300 ha, which is 12.1 per cent of the total land area of the Island (574,000 ha) as given by MacDougall, Veer, and Wilson (*Soils*, 22). Of course, not all of the forest within the area would have been burned, as was commented on shortly after the fires (see Sobey, *Early Descriptions*, part 1, 24).

66 Stewart, *Account*, 33.

67 Holland, *Letter to Lord Hillsborough*. This statement led me to the realization that on the large-scale map (4000 feet to one inch) that Holland constructed at the end of his survey in 1765, his cartographers had marked parts of the burned area with special symbols (short vertical strokes) representing such columnar burnt trees. The map is now in the British National Archives at Kew and is catalogued as CO700/Prince Edward Island 3. See Sobey and Glen "Mapping the Pre-Settlement Forests," 177–95.

68 We have evidence of such from Johnstone (*Series of Letters*, 105–6), Douglas (*Diary*, 19), Stewart (*Account*, 33), and in testimony recorded by the Land Commission of 1875 (*Report of Proceedings*, 190, 224, 468). (See Sobey, *Early Descriptions*, part 2, Analyses, 61–2, for further comment and analysis.) I note that Tubbs and Houston (*Fagus grandifolia*, 325–32) state that on account of their thin bark beech trees are "highly vulnerable to injury by fire."

69 A statement recorded by the Land Commission of 1875 indicates that such did occur (*Report of Proceedings*, 468).

70 Gesner (*Report*, 8) stated that the barrens at St. Peters had been "overrun by fires from time to time." See Sobey, *Early Descriptions*, part 2, Analyses, 12–15.

71 This process drew the attention of Johnstone (*Series of Letters*, 106–7), and MacGregor, (*Historical and Descriptive Sketches*, 58–9). See Sobey, *Early Descriptions*, part 2, Analyses, 23, for other references.

72 The number of "occupiers of land" recorded in the census of 1861 was 11,241. See Sobey, *Early Descriptions*, part 2, Analyses, 66, for how these estimates were arrived at.

73 See Sobey, *Early Descriptions*, part 2, Analyses, 72–3, for the basis of these fencing estimates.

74 See ibid., 105–7, for a brief assessment of the domestic and local industrial uses of wood products, and 107–10, for the non-wood materials that were harvested from the forest. See also Sobey, "Analysis of Historical Records," 393, for an assessment of the records of the hunting of forest mammals for game and furs.

75 "Wood pasture" is the term used for this very ancient practice in the British Isles (see Rackham, *Ancient Woodland*, 11–20). For an extended analysis of the records for this practice on the Island, see Sobey, *Early Descriptions*, part 2, Analyses, 52–4.

76 MacGregor (*Historical and Descriptive Sketches*, 261) states that one of the first tasks of the pioneer farmer was to make "a fence of logs to keep off the cattle and sheep."

77 See Sobey, *Early Descriptions*, part 2, Analyses, 387, 388, 394.

78 The first attempt was made by the Company of Île Saint-Jean sometime between 1720 and 1723, and the second was in 1727 and 1728 by the Department of the Marine, the government department responsible for the colonies. For a detailed study of these ventures, see Sobey, "Department of the Marine," *The Island Magazine*, 10–18, and Sobey, "Department of the Marine," *The Northern Mariner*, 1–18.

79 See Glen and Sobey, "The Fall – and Rise? – of White Pine," 6. Since that paper was published, new information has emerged revealing that eighty-eight masts were "laded" and that the person responsible was David Higgins, who continued as an entrepreneur associated with the Island. (This information was brought to my attention by Earle Lockerby; its reference is Library and Archives Canada, MG55/23-N.44, vol. 1, p. 1.)

80 See Glen and Sobey, "The Fall – and Rise? – of White Pine," 7, for discussion of the short length of the period (February 1763 to July 1767) during which the "broad-arrow" laws, under which large pine trees were reserved for masts for the Royal Navy, would have been applicable to the Island's pine resource.

81 Wynn, "Administration in Adversity," 49–65.

82 The Island's House of Assembly stipulated [1 George IV, C. III] in 1820 "That no *Pine, Spruce,* or *Hemlock Ton Timber* shall be less than *twelve feet* in length nor any Birch or other Hard Wood, less than *ten feet* in length, nor shall any *Ton Timber,* be considered Merchantable, unless the same shall square *eleven inches* at least" (italics as in original). See Sobey, *Early Descriptions,* part 2, Analyses, 81; Extracts, 30.

83 Lower, *Great Britain's Woodyard,* 30–1; Wynn, *Timber Colony,* 35, 41–3.

84 See Sobey, *Early Descriptions,* part 2, Analyses, 89–90.

85 These values are from the PEI Customs records as cited by De Jong and Moore, *Shipbuilding,* 26.

86 See Wynn, *Timber Colony,* 30–1, for details on the imposition of the timber tariffs.

87 From the P.E.I. Customs records as cited by De Jong and Moore, *Shipbuilding,* 26.

88 Lower, *Great Britain's Woodyard;* Wynn, *Timber Colony.*

89 Johnstone, *Series of Letters,* 103; MacGregor, *Historical and Descriptive Sketches,* 20; Hill, *Short Account,* 30.

90 See Sobey, *Early Descriptions,* part 2, Analyses, 95–7.

91 The data in figure 4.6 have not yet been published and I thank William Glen for allowing me to use it. His summation of the ton-timber exports from the Island for all of the years from 1803 to 1847 (excluding the four years between 1828 and 1831, for which the records appear to be missing) comes to 246,728 tons of softwoods (mostly pine) and 51,220 tons of hardwoods (mostly yellow birch). I have added estimates for the missing four years based on the graphical trends on either side of these years (21,336 SW, and 4,476 HW), which gives a total of 268,064 tons of SW and 55,696 tons of HW, or a grand total of 323,760 tons of wood.

92 See Sager and Fischer, *Shipping and Shipbuilding,* for a review of the factors that led to the establishment of a ship-building industry in Atlantic Canada.

93 These figures are based on compilation of data in De Jong and Moore, *Shipbuilding.*

94 The only numerical statement that I have come across on the relationship between a ship's tonnage and the amount of wood needed to build it is in Greenhill, *Evolution,* 112: "Before the introduction of iron knees in the 1820s, it was reckoned that a load-and-a-half of timber was required for every ton of merchant shipping. After the use of iron knees became almost universal, a 200-ton vessel could be built of some two-thirds of a load of timber per ton; a vessel of between 100 and 200 tons ... of three-eighths of

a load per ton, and smaller vessels of up to half-a-load per ton." For problems with this statement, and the estimates based on it, see Sobey, "Shipbuilding," 82–9.

95 This was calculated by dividing the vessels into Greenhill's three size-classes, and by assuming that iron knees were used in all of them.

96 The following is based on Sobey, "Shipbuilding."

97 Lloyd's Register of Shipping was the main British society responsible for the classification of vessels. It provided its trained surveyors with detailed "Rules" which included the rating (expressed in years) to be assigned to each of the structural components of a vessel, based on the wood-types used in that component. The overall rating assigned to a vessel was determined by the *lowest* rating given to any of its structures.

98 The "Mixed Material Rule," first evidenced in a Lloyd's circular letter of 26 June 1869, stated: "if in vessels built of Spruce … the stem, apron, and inner and outer sternposts were made of Pitch Pine or Hackmatack" [and provided other stated conditions hold] "such vessels might be allowed … one year additional classification." See Sobey, "Shipbuilding," 64.

99 See Sobey, "Shipbuilding," 79n192, for a compilation of the evidence submitted to the Land Commission of 1875 (*Abstract of the Proceedings*) which suggests that by that time, even in the later settled areas of western Prince County, only a few stands of suitable timber remained. The witnesses talk mostly of spruce and cedar (the pine was long gone), and most of this seems to have been harvested within the memory of many of those giving testimony to the commission.

100 Smethurst, *Narrative of an Extraordinary Escape*, 41.

101 The percentage contribution in figure 4.1 of white spruce, balsam fir, red maple, white birch, trembling aspen and pin cherry (*Prunus pensylvanica*) comes to 74.7 per cent. In the pre-settlement forest some of these species, and especially the red maple, would have been a component of the climax forest, with some of the trees very large, though most of the red maple today is early successional, never achieving the sizes it did then.

102 De Jong and Moore (*Shipbuilding*) tabulate quantitative evidence indicating the importance of ship "transfers" (i.e., the sale of ships outside the Island, usually in the United Kingdom) in the Island's balance of trade: for the thirty-four years for which they give data between 1822 and 1876 (see their tables, pp. 39, 100, 128, 166), the value of the ships exported averaged 40 per cent of total exports. If we were to add the monetary value of the timber exported for the same years the percentage would rise considerably.

103 Burke proposed that the government set up a commission to oversee the growth of trees on the 16,000 acres of provincial lands (either through natural growth or planting), as well as encouraging "private individuals in the preservation and extension of their present wood plots and in the reafforestation of the denuded places on their holdings, ... [and in] the placing of windbreaks and shade trees generally about the steadings" ("Forestry," 84).

104 The fact that the wording of the act of 1903 that created the commission (III Edward VII, C. VI) largely reflects the proposals that Burke ("Forestry," 84) made in his speech to the Canadian Forestry Association is presumably a reflection of his influence. See Gaudet, *Forestry*, 46, and McAskill, "The People's Forest," 27–8, for a review of some of the developments in Island forestry in the twentieth century.

105 That is, apart from one significant change that began to occur from the 1930s, when, for the first time since the beginning of European settlement, woodland began to make a comeback on the Island as farms on the more marginal land (mostly in the east and west) began to be abandoned.

CHAPTER FIVE

1 MacEachern and Turkel, *Method and Meaning in Canadian Environmental History*.

2 As famously articulated in Margaret Atwood's *Survival*.

3 Marsh, *Man and Nature*. See also the insightful reflections in Brian Drake's review of Marsh's *Man and Nature* in *H-Environment, H-Net Reviews*, January 2004, http://www.h-net.org/reviews/showrev.php?id=8754.

4 While environmentalists (naturalists, wildlife users, legislators and scientists) make a clear distinction between "preservation" and "conservation," there has always been a blurring of lines between the terms on Prince Edward Island. Even though legislation historically has used the term "preservation," conservation (i.e., wise use) was the intent. Moreover, in this densely settled island province, there has been no true "wilderness" worthy of preservation for nearly two centuries, so that "preservation" in practice generally resembles "conservation."

5 Wildlife Policy for Canada, 1990.

6 This is the mantra of Wildlife Habitat Canada. See their website, accessed 3 March 2013 at http://www.whc.org/.

7 Miller, "Environmental History," 13–33.

8 Belland, "Mosses," 179–96; Scudder and Vickery, "Grasshoppers," 371–9.

9 Keenlyside, "Ulus and Spearpoints," 25–7.

10 Keenlyside, "New Finds," 10–12.

11 Keenlyside, "In Search of the Island's First People," 3–7.

12 O'Grady, "In the Footsteps of Jesse Walter Fewkes," 10–16.

13 Wallace Ferguson, "Selective Exploitation."

14 Keenlyside, "In Search of the Island's First People."

15 Keenlyside, "Ulu and Spearpoints."

16 Cronon, *Changes in the Land*; Pyne, "Indian Fires," 6–11; Lewis, "Reconstructing Patterns of Indian Burning," 80–4; Williams, *Clam Gardens*.

17 Stewart, *Account of Prince Edward Island*, 80, 82.

18 Harold F. McGee Jr. summarized Nicholas Denys's 1672 account of the Mi'kmaq taking beavers in winter, only as needed, by scaring them from their lodges and harpooning them. See McGee, "Use of Furbearers," 17. Calvin Martin describes a similar relationship in the pre-Contact period between the Mi'kmaq and the species they hunted. See Martin, *Keepers of the Game*.

19 Bailey, *Conflict of European and Eastern Algonkian Cultures*, quoted in McGee, "Use of Furbearers," 18.

20 Ray, "Fur Trade in North America, 21–30.

21 Ibid.

22 Sobey, "An Analysis of the Historical Records," 384–96. Sobey discounts the archeological evidence of a beaver tooth and a beaver-chewed stick found in peat, as well as several other less-convincing written references to beaver.

23 Keenlyside, "In Search of the Island's First People," 3–7. See also Wallace Ferguson, "Selective Exploitation of Shellfish."

24 Harvey, *French Regime in Prince Edward Island*, 21.

25 Ibid., 28.

26 Sobey, "Analysis of Mammalian Fauna," 393.

27 Ibid.

28 Stewart, *Account of Prince Edward Island*, 63–5.

29 Harvey provides this information in his introduction to Walter Johnstone's *Travels in Prince Edward Island*, but for some reason did not include the actual passages that reference fur-buying. The contents of *Journeys to the Island of St. John or Prince Edward Island, 1775–1832*, edited by Harvey, shows "Walter Johnstone: 'Letters' and 'Travels,'" and the introduction precedes both texts.

30 MacGregor, *Historical and Descriptive Sketches*, 24–7.

31 Sobey, "An Analysis of the Historical Records," 389. Holland reported "some, but very few carriboux."

32 Glen, *Prince Edward Island Wildlife Legislation*, 47–9. Doug Sobey believes that the marten and otter might have easily adapted to greatly altered

landscapes (see "An Analysis of the Historical Records," 394) as they have in the British Isles, but there was a limited amount of time for them to adjust on the Island, decades, rather than centuries. Examples closer to home also bear examination. There are no North American marten populations that live in agricultural landscapes.

33 Sobey, "Shipbuilding," i–ii.

34 Glen, "Prince Edward Island 1935/1936 Forest Cover Type Mapping."

35 Marten are small, relatively long-lived animals that require large blocks of mature coniferous or mixed wood forest for hunting, though they are capable of using regenerating forest. But there are no North American marten populations that live in agricultural landscapes. See COSEWIC, Assessment and Update Status Report on the American Marten, 9–10, http://publications.gc.ca/collections/collection_2007/ec/CW69-14-46-2007E.pdf.

36 Glen, *Prince Edward Island Wildlife Legislation*, 125–32.

37 Melquist and Dronkert, "River Otter," 629.

38 Gallant et al., "Habitat Selection," 422–32. Otter are distributed in protected areas (e.g., Kouchibouguac National Park) at much higher densities than in surrounding disturbed areas. This distribution is attributed to better environmental quality in the river systems of the protected areas.

39 Melquist and Dronkert, "River Otter."

40 Sobey, *Early Descriptions of Forests*, 388.

41 Sightings of otter or otter signs are occasionally reported; for example, one drowned in a fishing net in Seal River near Cardigan in 1969. It is noteworthy that otters are capable of swimming to Prince Edward Island but have not re-established a population there, perhaps because immigrant otters are mainly males. Reintroduction of the otter is currently being discussed, but success is not assured.

42 Hornby, "Bear Facts," part 1, 9.

43 Sobey, *Early Descriptions of Forests*, 392.

44 Hornby, "Bear Facts," part 1, 3.

45 Vass, "The Black Bear on Prince Edward Island: A Natural History," 8–9.

46 Hornby, "Bear Facts," part 2, 27.

47 Vass, "Black Bear," 9.

48 In Upper Canada, the practice of shooting game declined soon after settlement, but its persistence on Prince Edward Island has not really been traced. See McCalla, "Upper Canadians and Their Guns," 121–37.

49 Stewart, *Account of Prince Edward Island*, 73.

50 Ibid., 77.

51 Bell, "Mr. Mann's Island," 12.

52 Stewart, *Account of Prince Edward Island,* 76.

53 MacGregor, *Historical and Descriptive Sketches,* 30.

54 Glen, *Prince Edward Island Wildlife Legislation,* 121–3.

55 MacQuarrie and Guignon, "Hunting for Money," 13.

56 Smith-Alley Collection, Public Archives and Records Office of Prince Edward Island (hereafter, PARO), Acc. 2702, Series 20, vol. 304 (1876).

57 Hogan, "Infinite Number of Wood Pigeons," 24.

58 For more information on Robie Tufts, see Acadia University Archives, Esther Clark Wright Collection (2009). Robie W. Tufts fonds, http://library. acadiau.ca/archives/research/acadia_archives/Tufts_Robie.pdf.

59 Tufts, *Birds of Nova Scotia,* 176.

60 It is today listed federally as endangered rather than extinct because occasionally someone thinks they have seen one.

61 Tufts, *Birds of Nova Scotia,* 163–6.

62 Ibid., 186. Hunting was especially a problem in the United States during spring migration when knots stopped to fuel up on horseshoe crab eggs. Today the eastern subspecies is considered endangered due to overharvesting of horseshoe crabs in Delaware Bay. See also COSEWIC, http://www. sararegistry.gc.ca/species/speciesDetails_e.cfm?sid=980.

63 Erskine, *Atlas of Breeding Birds,* 75.

64 Erskine, "Great Cormorants of Eastern Canada," 9.

65 Taverner, *Birds of Eastern Canada,* 62.

66 Hogan, "Breeding Parameters of Great Cormorants."

67 Mineau, "Birds and Pesticides," 12–18.

68 The key lobbying role played by recreational anglers is not well documented on Prince Edward Island, but very important elsewhere. See, for example, Parenteau, "A 'Very Determined Opposition,'" 436–63.

69 All cormorant data were supplied by Forests, Fish and Wildlife Division, Prince Edward Island Department of Agriculture and Forestry.

70 Erskine, *Atlas of Breeding Birds,* 28.

71 Taverner, *Birds of Eastern Canada,* 123 and 164, lists the stomach contents of one of Prince Edwards Island's common raptors, the marsh hawk or harrier, and sums up, "The balance is evidently in favour of this species which is incapable of taking any fowl but small ones and then only when they wander into its habitat." Of the great blue heron, he writes, "Occasionally Herons may visit trout streams ... but such cases are rare and insufficient for the condemnation of the species. Herons often frequent the pound nets of the fishermen, but the limited size of their gullets precludes their taking anything of economic importance." On the American crow, he pronounces, "Insects form a large part of the Crow's food and

balancing the useful with the harmful species, the result is obviously in the bird's favour."

72 Federal-Provincial-Territorial Task Force on the Importance of Nature to Canadians, "The Importance of Nature to Canadians: The Economic Significance of Nature-related Activities," http://publications.gc.ca/collections/Collection/En47-312-2000E.pdf.

73 Hill and Blaney, "Exotic and Invasive Vascular Plants," 216.

74 MacArthur and Wilson, *Theory of Island Biogeography*.

75 Arsenault, "The Malpeque Bay Acadians," 9.

76 Clark, *Three Centuries and the Island*, 33, 37.

77 Sobey, "An Analysis of the Historical Records," 83–8.

78 Dupuis, "The Early History of Atlantic Salmon on Prince Edward Island," 22.

79 Meacham, *Illustrated Historical Atlas of Prince Edward Island*.

80 Ibid., 44.

81 Dupuis, "Early History of Atlantic Salmon," 22.

82 In contrast to other parts of Eastern Canada, where sport fishing was an important lobby that found itself in opposition to Native fishers and local settlers. See Parenteau, "Very Determined Opposition," 436–63; and "Care, Control and Supervision," 35.

83 Sobey, *Early Descriptions of Forests*, part 2, 85.

84 Dupuis, "Early History of Atlantic Salmon," 23.

85 Yet we know of no species that was extirpated because of dams. This is a possible research topic.

86 Canada, *Annual Report of the Department of Marine and Fisheries, 1889*, 130. Angling remained so a century later. In 1973, adults and those under 16 years of age comprised 11,195 anglers participating in fresh water angling, from a population of 115,000; another 18,440 anglers fished only in salt water. See Thompson, *Sportfishing in Prince Edward Island*, 41–2.

87 Canada, *Annual Report of the Department of Marine and Fisheries, 1882*, 176.

88 Sobey, "Shipbuilding," i–ii.

89 Dupuis, "Early History of Atlantic Salmon," 21–25.

90 Canada, *Annual Report of the Department of Marine and Fisheries, 1896*, 140.

91 MacIntyre, "Environmental Pre-History of Prince Edward Island," 89.

92 White, "Some Observations on the Eastern Brook Trout," 101–8. White was possibly unaware that the phosphorus component of fertilizer is the most important factor in determining freshwater productivity, entering streams bound to soil particles eroded from the land.

93 J. Armand DesRoches, *Report of the Commission on Nitrates in Ground-water. Province of Prince Edward Island* (2008), http://www.gov.pe.ca/photos/original/cofNitrates.pdf.

94 Heyland, "Decline of Gray Partridge," 20.

95 See, for instance, Henny et al., "North American Osprey Populations," 579–603.

96 "Osprey Helped," 18–19; see also MacDougall, "Return of the Bald Eagle," 5.

97 DDT use in Canada was banned in 1973. See Erskine, *Atlas of Breeding Birds*, 51.

98 Mineau, "Birds and Pesticides," 14. The author is senior research scientist in pesticide ecotoxicology at Environment Canada.

99 Garron, Davis, and Ernst, "Near-Field Air Concentrations," 688.

100 Health Canada Pest Management Regulatory Agency, "Re-evaluation Decision," 1.

101 Smith, "Prince Edward Island Trout Fishery," 9–11.

102 "Fish and Wildlife Director Is Critical of Most Dams," *Charlottetown Guardian*, 31 May 1969. For more information see Johnston and Cheverie, "Repopulation of a Coastal Stream," 107–10; Gormley, Teather and Guignion, "Changes in Salmonid Communities," 671–8; Mutch et al., "Pesticide Monitoring," 94–115.

103 Botkin, *Discordant Harmonies*, 12.

104 McGee summarized Nicholas Denys's 1672 account of the Mi'kmaq taking beavers in winter, only as needed, by scaring them from their lodges and harpooning them. See McGee, "Use of Furbearers by Native North Americans after 1500, 17.

105 Hornby, "Bear Facts," part 2, 27–31.

106 Sobey, *Early Descriptions of the Forests*, part 1, 145–50.

107 Ibid., part 2, 235–58.

108 Dupuis, 24.

109 Stewart, *Account of Prince Edward Island*, 36–94; MacGregor, *Historical and Descriptive Sketches*, 31.

110 See Vass, "Mrs. Haviland's Plants," 23–6, and the accompanying sidebar by Ian MacQuarrie.

111 Martin, "Francis Bain," 3–8.

112 Wake, "Prince Edward Island's Early Natural History Society," 33.

113 Its members are heavily involved with birding and related "citizen science" projects such as Christmas bird counts, the Maritimes Breeding Bird Atlas project, and more recently, the Maritimes Butterfly Atlas.

114 Glen, *Prince Edward Island Wildlife Legislation*. For more on the role of anglers' associations in regulating fishing habitats, see Parenteau, "Very Determined Opposition to the Law."

115 Cameron, *Mammals of the Islands*, 42.

116 Erskine, *Plants of Prince Edward Island*, 6–10.

117 Leonard, "Archaeological Remains."

118 Godfrey, "Birds of Prince Edward Island," 155–213.

119 Cameron, "Mammals of the Islands," 1–165.

120 Erskine, *Plants of Prince Edward Island*.

121 Bleakney, "Zoogeographical Study," 1–119. See also Cook, "Analysis of the Herpetofauna."

122 Brown, McAlpine and Curley, "Northern Long-Eared Bat," 208–9.

123 McAlpine, Harding, and Curley, "Occurrence and Biogeographic Significance of the Pickerel Frog," 95–8.

124 Gormley, Teather and Guignion, "Distribution and Abundance of Slimy Sculpin," 192–4.

125 Majka, "Sugar Shack Bugs," 20–1.

126 *Public Consultations on the PEI Museum System*.

127 Cameron, "Mammals of the Islands," 53.

128 Heyland, "Decline of Gray Partridge," 43.

129 Ibid., 83.

130 Forester and Forester, *Silver Fox Odyssey*, 1.

131 Curley, "Population Dynamics," 7. At the same time, Prince Edward Island was for many decades an exporter of fox breeding stock and the two-way trade homogenized the gene pool of the various subspecies elsewhere, as on the Island.

132 The main goal of the Biodiversity Convention signed in Rio de Janeiro in 1992 is to promote human well-being by maintaining biodiversity at the ecological, species, and genetic levels. The fundamental code of life is revealed at the genetic level. See Secretariat of the Convention on Biological Diversity, Sustaining Life on Earth, United Nations Environment Programme and Government of United Kingdom (2002), http://www.cbd.int/convention/guide/.

133 Forester and Forester, "Silver Fox Odyssey," 12.

134 Ibid., 14.

135 Jones, *Fur-Farming*.

136 Croken, "Early Experiences of a Ranch Veterinary," 72.

137 MacIntyre, "Environmental Pre-History," 77.

138 Curley, "Population Dynamics." Changing fashions and a decline in quality control were also factors in the decline.

139 The same question might be raised with respect to aquaculture initiatives for Arctic char and Atlantic salmon.

140 Curley, "Introducing the Striped Skunk," 20–23.

141 Dibblee, "Beaver on Prince Edward Island," 18–22.

142 Ibid.

143 Ray, "Fur Trade in North America," 27.

144 Clark, *Three Centuries and the Island*, 252n59. In the twenty-first century, mink are a mainstay of fur ranching, housing many of the genetic mutants with varying coat colours that have been developed since ranching began. A possible consequence of mink ranching (which can never be totally proven at this late date) is the introduction of Aleutian mink disease virus to Prince Edward Island within the past sixty years.

145 Heyland, "Decline of Gray Partridge," 63–5.

146 Glen, *Prince Edward Island Wildlife Legislation*, 109–35.

147 Although known locally as "bypass ponds," these are online ponds that do not divert water away from the watercourse. They cause ponding by slowing the flow with an earthen dam, and the water continues downstream around one side of the dam through a "run-around," returning to the natural watercourse.

148 MacIntyre, "Environmental Pre-History," 153.

149 Prince Edward Island Dam Inventory.

150 Data were supplied by biologist Alan McLennan, Prince Edward Island Forests, Fish and Wildlife Division.

151 Dibblee, "The Beaver," 18–22.

152 Randy Dibblee, personal communication to author, 12 May 2011.

153 That politics and science can make an uncomfortable marriage is made glaringly apparent in Bavington, *Managed Annihilation*.

154 McClellan, "Changing Patterns of Land Use," 101–14.

155 Martin, *Watershed Red*.

156 See *Prince Edward Island Environeer* 3, no. 4 (1975).

157 "Prince Edward Island Conservation Strategy," 27–8, 28 for reference to wildlife.

158 Wildlife Policy for Prince Edward Island, 1995, http://www.gov.pe.ca/photos/original/95wildlfpolicy.pdf.

159 Wetland Conservation Policy for Prince Edward Island 2007, http://www.gov.pe.ca/photos/original/fae_wetland_con.pdf.

160 A recent evaluation of the legislated ten-metre buffer zone between streams and farm fields concluded that pesticides lethal to aquatic organisms are still passing into rivers surrounded by "shallow sloped fields." This conclusion also applies to the newer fifteen-metre buffer

zone. See Dunn et al., "Evaluation of Buffer Zone Effectiveness," 868–82.

161 The *Charlottetown Guardian*, 31 May 1969, ran a page-two headline: "Fish and Wildlife Director Is Critical of Most Dams." The story included information on continuing misuse of pesticides resulting in "stream kills regularly each year," meaning loss of all life in the streams. There have been sixty recorded fish kills on the Island since the 1960s. For more information, see Gormley, Teather and Guignion, "Changes in Salmonid Communities," 671–8; Mutch et al., "Pesticide Monitoring and Fish Kill Investigations," 94–115.

162 See Arthur Smith, "Stream Improvement – Valleyfield Watershed," PEI *Environeer* 3, no. 4 (1975), 10–11.

163 Daryl Guignion, a UPEI biology professor, was a prominent figure in the steering committee while local conservationist Frances Cobb contacted the landowners for assent. Gilbert Clements was the provincial minister of municipal affairs who defied dissenting landowners and supported the dream of a natural river brimming with fish, particularly Atlantic salmon. The stated purpose of the Morell River Conservation Zone in regulation is (a) to maintain the recreational value of the Morell River; (b) to retain its unspoiled state for the use and enjoyment of present and future generations; and (c) to protect it from encroachment of undesirable and incompatible land uses. The zone extends for three chains on either side for much of the length of the river.

164 Reports of the Montague Watershed Project to Wildlife Habitat Canada, including "Summary Report Number 3," "Integrated Land Management," 31 March 1988, and "Interim Report No. 6, Cooperative Watershed Management Project," September 1989 are all sources of information, along with personal knowledge of the author.

165 IUCN's definition of a protected area (2008) is available at http://www. iucn.org/about/work/programmes/gpap_home/.

166 See the map of Victoria Park in the *Illustrated Historical Atlas of the Province of Prince Edward Island*.

167 See MacEachern, *Natural Selections*, 7.

168 Ibid., 14.

169 Ibid., 244.

170 Personal communication from Colin MacKinnon, Canadian Wildlife Service, Environment Canada, Sackville, New Brunswick.

171 Order-in-Council P.C. 1956–1060, as detailed in a letter from Brian G. Carter, Dominion Wildlife Officer to Harvey Moore, 16 August 1956.

172 Breeding populations of Canada geese were a novelty item in the 1950s. Most southern jurisdictions now recognize their nuisance value.

173 Smith and Fyfe, "A Proposal for the Acquisition of Land in the Vicinity of Deroche Point," 3–4. Richard Fyfe led the charge for peregrine falcon recovery in North America at the famous (but now closed) peregrine captive breeding facility in Wainwright, Alberta. Allan Smith's work led to the establishment of several National Wildlife Areas in Nova Scotia and New Brunswick.

174 Ralph Cameron, "Land Going for a Wildlife Area," *Charlottetown Evening Patriot*, 27 May 1969, 1.

175 "1800 Acres Involved: Land Expropriation Being Looked Into," *Charlottetown Guardian*, 28 May 1969.

176 Canadian Committee for the International Biological Programme, "Ecological Reserves in the Maritimes," xi.

177 Ibid., 192.

178 "Prince Edward Island Natural Areas Survey."

179 "Endangered Spaces Report," 33.

180 Begley, "The Wave-Lined Edge of Home," 25.

181 Prince Edward Island Land Use Commission, Written Decision, Boughton Island Appeal Hearing, 1989.

182 Weeks, *Minding the House*, 37.

183 Letter from G. Douglas Murray, director, Provincial Parks, to Monte Hummel, president, World Wildlife Fund dated 3 May 1990, and attached "Update on Protected Areas."

184 Hummel, *Protecting Canada's Endangered Spaces*, 14.

185 Griffin, "Prince Edward Island," 128–33.

186 North American Waterfowl Management Plan, "Strategy for Cooperation."

187 "Eight New Wildlife Management Areas Proposed," accessed 5 November 2015, http://www.gov.pe.ca/newsroom/index.php?number=news&dept=&newsnumber=1093&lang=E.

188 "More Natural Areas Designated," accessed 5 November 2015, http://www.gov.pe.ca/newsroom/index.php?number=news&dept=&newsnumber=7718&lang=E.

189 Parks Canada Agency, "*Unimpaired for Future Generations?*" I-9–10.

190 Wilson, *Future of Life*.

191 See Rockström, Steffen, Noone et al., "A Safe Operating Space for Humanity," 472–5.

192 Thomas and Dibblee, "Coyote, *Canis latrans*," 565–7. It is now considered to be a native mammal.

193 Most Prince Edward Island residents refer to the bank swallow as "cliff swallow," but the cliff swallow is a separate species which also nested in the province; its last known colony (in 1986) was located in Peakes. The

bank swallow was listed as Threatened by COSEWIC at its April 2013 meeting. The decline of avian aerial insectivorous appears to be more pronounced in the east. See, for example, Nebel et al., "Declines of Aerial Insectivores."

194 COSEWIC assessment and update status report on the Gulf of St. Lawrence aster *Symphyotrichum laurentianum* in Canada, 2004. http://www.sararegistry.gc.ca/species/speciesDetails_e.cfm?sid=252.

195 Chouinard and Swain, "Predicted Extirpation of the Dominant Demersal Fish," 2315–19.

196 "Big One Didn't Get Away: Ronald Gormley Receives Premier's Cup for Landing Largest Tuna," *Charlottetown Guardian*, 8 March 2012, A6.

CHAPTER SIX

1 The oldest known "modern" seaweed fossils were found in China in 2011; see http://reefbuilders.com/2011/02/16/seaweed-fossils/.

2 For an early account of the emerging understanding of plate tectonics and global climate change, see Nance, Worsley, and Moody, "The Supercontinent Cycle," 44–51.

3 Van den Hoek, "Phytogeographic Distribution Groups," 153–214, and "World-Wide Latitudinal and Longitudinal," 227–57; Van den Hoek, Breeman, and Stam, "Geographic Distribution of Seaweed Species," 55–67.

4 For some examples of research into these phenomena see Novaczek, "Response of Gametophytes," 241–5, and "Response of *Ecklonia radiata* (Laminariales) to Light," 263–72; Breeman, "Relative Importance of Temperature," 199–241.

5 For an early exposition, see Setchell, "Law of Temperature," 287, and "Temperature Interval," 187–90. For a modern hypothesis, see Breeman, "Expected Effects," 69–76.

6 Novaczek and McLachlan, "Investigations of the Marine Algae," 91–143.

7 Hardin, "Tragedy of the Commons," 1243–8.

8 Named by National Research Council scientist Dr Jack McLachlan after a Nova Scotian phycologist of the twentieth century, Tikvah Edelstein.

9 Gurgel, Fredericq, and Norris, "Phylogeography of *Gracilaria tikvahiae*," 748–58.

10 Murchison and Murchison, "Quantity Survey of *Gracilaria*," 151.

11 Atlantic Geoscience Society, *The Last Billion Years*, 134–43.

12 Wilson, "Did the Atlantic Close?" 676–81.

13 Luning, *Seaweeds*, 102.

14 Laboratory experiments and cladistic studies to elucidate the possible transpolar migration of seaweeds from the Pacific to the Atlantic Ocean

have been conducted by marine biogeographers including Van den Hoek, "Phytogeographic Distribution Groups," 153–214; Lindstrom, "Possible Sister Groups," 245–60; Luning, Guiry, and Masuda, "Upper Temperature Tolerance," 297–306; Brodie, Guiry, and Masuda, "Life History and Morphology," 183–96.

15 Van den Hoek, "World-Wide Latitudinal and Longitudinal," 251; Luning, *Seaweeds*, 22; Van den Hoek and Breeman, "Seaweed Biogeography of the North Atlantic," 59, 80.

16 An early attempt to explain algal distributions can be found in Van den Hoek, "World-Wide Latitudinal," 247, 251; for a more comprehensive treatment, see Van den Hoek and Breeman, "Seaweed Biogeography," 59, 80.

17 Rhatigan, *Prannie Rhatigan's Irish Seaweed Kitchen.*

18 See Keenlyside and Kristmanson, this volume.

19 Baye, "Dynamics of Barrier Beach and Dune Systems."

20 Bousfield and Thomas, "Postglacial Changes," 47–60.

21 Wallis and Wallace in *The Micmac Indians*, 13, recount how Mi'kmaq used dulse as a worming agent. Seaweed also figures in a Glooscap legend about the creation of Spencer's Island, Nova Scotia (see hrsbstaff.ednet. ns.ca/hughson/LegendNameConnection.htm).

22 Dillehay and Rosen, "Plant Food"; Dillehay et al., "Monte Verde."

23 Information gathered from elders of Mi'kmaq and Williche communities is documented in Levangie and Soto Quenti, *Medicinal Seaplants of the Mi'kmaq and Williche.*

24 See De la Pylaie, *Flore de l'Ile de Terre-Neuve*; Farlow, *Marine Algae of New England*; Hay and MacKay, "Marine Algae of New Brunswick"; and the overview by South, *Guide to the Common Seaweeds.*

25 Hugh Bell and Constance MacFarlane made significant contributions to the knowledge of marine plants in Atlantic Canada in the early and mid twentieth century. Their seminal works include the first attempt at a comprehensive list of marine plant species: "The Marine Algae of the Maritime Provinces of Canada I," 265–79; and an overview of marine plant ecology in "The Marine Algae of the Maritime Provinces of Canada II," 280–93. In 1957 Taylor followed up with a comprehensive flora for Eastern North America, *Marine Algae of the Northeast Coast of North America.*

26 Hoarau et al., "Glacial Refugia and Recolonization Pathways," 3606–16.

27 The introduction and migrations of *Fucus serratus* can be traced through the series of reports by Hay and MacKay, "Marine Algae"; Robinson, "Distribution of *Fucus serratus*," 132–4; Bell and Macfarlane, "Marine Algae of the Maritime Provinces," I and II; Edelstein et al., "Investigations," 2703–13; Dale, "Phytosociological Structure," 2652–8;

and Novaczek and MacLachlan, "Investigations of the Marine Algae of Nova Scotia XVII."

28 *Ascophyllum nodosum* is from the same family as *Fucus* and has similar chemical and medicinal properties. For a recent account of its commercial importance and ecology, see Raul Ugarte's presentation in *Constance MacFarlane Seaplant Symposium*, DVD 5.2.

29 De la Pylaie, *Flore de l'Ile de Terre-Neuve.*

30 The movements of *Furcellaria* after its introduction were traced by Bell and MacFarlane, *Marine Algae of the Maritime Provinces*; MacFarlane, "Ecological Observations," 151–4; Holmsgaard, Greenwell, and McLachlan, "Biomass and Vertical Distribution," 309–13; Novaczek and MacLachlan, "Investigations of the Marine Algae of Nova Scotia XVII"; Bird, Greenwell, and McLachlan, "Biology of *Furcellaria lumbricalis*," 61–82.

31 Brodie, Guiry, and Masuda, "Life History and Morphology of *Chondrus nipponicus*," 183–96.

32 Bouck and Morgan, "The Occurrence of *Codium* in Long Island Waters," 384–7.

33 Garbary, Vandermeulen, and Kim. "*Codium fragile ssp. tomentosoides*," 537–40.

34 Fralick and Mathieson, "Ecological Studies of *Codium fragile*," 127–32.

35 See Ed MacDonald and Boyde Beck's account of the oyster fishery, this volume.

36 J. Jenkins, Fisheries and Oceans Canada, personal communication recorded in Novaczek, "Macroalgal Invasions."

37 PEI Aquaculture Alliance, n.d.

38 The Pacific origins of Irish moss have been discussed by, *inter alia*, van den Hoek, "Phytogeographic Distribution Groups," and explored experimentally by Luning, Guiry, and Masuda, "Upper Temperature Tolerance."

39 The Community Museum Association of PEI has placed blancmange recipes online. See "The Harvests of Prince Edward Island: Irish moss," http//:www.museevirtuel-virtualmuseum.ca.

40 Properties of carrageenan are outlined in Chopin, "The Red Alga *Chondrus crispus*," 1514; Neushul, *Method for the Treatment of AIDS Virus*; Vaugelade et al., "Non-Starch Polysaccharides," 33–47; Pearce-Pratt and Phillips, "Sulfated Polysaccharides," 173–82; Smit, "Medicinal and Pharmaceutical Uses," 245–62, among others. New information on medicinal properties commonly appears in the online medical database www. pubmed.nl.

41 Needler, "Irish Moss Industry."

42 Chopin and Ugarte, "Seaweed Resource of Eastern Canada."

43 See MacFarlane, "Seaweed Industry"; and Jim Craigie's account of Dr MacFarlane's work on DVD 1.2, *Constance MacFarlane Seaplant Symposium*.

44 Larkin, "Our Way of Living."

45 Owens, "Effects of Ice," 95–104.

46 *C.F.'s Diary, 1913–1952*; entry for 21 October 1941 concerns Irish moss harvesting.

47 "Marine Plant Harvesting Requires Special Licence," *Charlottetown Guardian*, 27 May 1977. This was also the year that certain destructive dragging technologies were banned; see Fisheries and Oceans Canada 1981.

48 MacFarlane, *Irish Moss*, 12.

49 Keough, *Slender Thread*.

50 Local stories and photos of Irish moss harvesters are archived on the online "Island Narratives Program" of Robertson Library, UPEI, at http://vre2.upei.ca/cap/node/278 (concerning North Shore), and http://vre2.upei.ca/cap/node/456 (concerning western PEI). A history of the industry including names of local and multinational moss buyers can be found in Chopin and Ugarte, "Seaweed Resource."

51 Larkin, "Our Way of Living," 99–103, 107–8.

52 Chopin and Ugarte, "Seaweed Resource."

53 See ibid. for a discussion of the evolution of moss harvesting technology. Primary data on impacts of drag raking can be found in Pringle and Sharp, "Multispecies Resource Management," 711–20; Pringle and Semple, "Dragrake Harvesting Intensity," 342–5; Chopin, Pringle, and Semple, "Impact of Drag Raking" and "Impact of Harvesting"; Sharp et al., "Recent Changes." In his presentation to the Constance MacFarlane Seaplant Symposium, Maxime D'Eon recounted early attempts to promote less damaging gear, 2008 (*Constance MacFarlane Seaplant Symposium*, DVD 1.3). This history is also recounted in Hanic, "Testing and Evaluation."

54 Pringle, "Structure of Certain North American Fishery Agencies," 11–20.

55 "Find Irish Moss Raking Leads to Lobster Injuries," *Charlottetown Guardian*, 27 March 1971.

56 Bird, Saunders, and McLachlan, in "Biology of *Furcellaria lumbricalis*," provide a comprehensive account of the history and attributes of *Furcellaria*.

57 A brief history of the moss fishery, including a discussion of the impact of *Furcellaria* on commercial viability of moss beds, can be found on the DFO website, http://www.glf.dfo-mpo.gc.ca/e0006845.

58 For Dave MacEwen's review of the history of the Irish moss fishery; see *Constance MacFarlane Seaplant Symposium*, DVD 4.1.

59 Porter, "Women in Fishing Households."

60 The National Film Board's documentary film *Room for a Co-op* chronicles the rise and fall of the Marine Plants Co-op. See also Anderson, Frenette, and Webster's unpublished report, "Global Village?"

61 Needler, "Irish Moss Industry," 1–5.

62 Ibid., 4.

63 "Forget Report Bad News for Fishermen."

64 Mossing was the first Island fishery industry where women played leading roles as spokespersons as well as harvesters and processors, providing an active, sometimes militant leadership. Boyd, "Of Price and Prices," deals with the strike, while Novaczek et al. in *At the Table*, 17–24, also provide a brief account of the role of women in the moss fishery, as part of a larger study of women in PEI fisheries.

65 Ellsworth, "Irish Moss Strike," 8.

66 Allan Critchley presented a history of Irish moss from the point of view of processors at the Constance MacFarlane Seaplant Symposium, 2008 (*Constance MacFarlane Seaplant Symposium*, DVD 4.2).

67 Glyn Sharp related the story of *Furcellaria* in PEI at the Constance MacFarlane Seaplant Symposium 2008 (*Constance MacFarlane Seaplant Symposium*, DVD 4.3).

68 See PEI's virtual museum site, http://www.museevirtuel-virtualmuseum.ca/edu/ViewLoitCollection.do;jsessionid=11BF8EEA7AF08305E196350E107 7C7E9?method=preview&lang=EN&id=17003.

69 http://www.tasteofnovascotia.com/members/acadian-seaplants-limited/.

70 Jim Craigie related the story of Constance MacFarlane at the Constance MacFarlane Seaplant Symposium 2008 (*Constance MacFarlane Seaplant Symposium*, DVD 1.2).

71 Glyn Sharp told the history of Basin Head and the giant moss at the Constance MacFarlane Seaplant Symposium 2008 (*Constance MacFarlane Seaplant Symposium*, DVD 5.3).

72 Prince Edward Island, *2010 State of the Environment*, 22.

73 Andrew Lush, personal communication, December 2011. The formal report on these trials was viewed in its draft form in January 2012.

74 ACOA, the Atlantic Canada Opportunities Agency, is a regional economic development agency.

75 Novaczek, "Exercising Community Control," 28–9.

76 Anne of Green Gables is a fictional character of the PEI writer L.M. Montgomery, whose stories are the basis for many touristic products and experiences on the Island.

77 A set of DVDs available from www.islandstudies.com documents the presentations from the three-day symposium.

78 See www.tignishtreasures.ca and the article by Wayne Roberts, "Fish Sticks These Ain't," in *This Magazine*, November–December 2007, at http://www. thismagazine.ca/issues/2007/11/fishsticks.php.

79 In public meetings conducted in communities along the Northumberland Strait in 2006, the Institute of Island Studies and PEI Fishermen's Association documented testimonies from fishermen concerned about increasing siltation and disappearing rocky bottom habitats. These concerns are reflected in Gilles Theriault & Associates, *Report on Consultations on Ecosystem Overview Report for the Northumberland Strait* (Fisheries and Oceans Canada 2006).

80 Temperature limits of Irish moss were explored experimentally by Luning, Guiry, and Masuda, "Upper Temperature Tolerance."

81 In 2012 the DFO issued a report on the state of the Gulf of St Lawrence ecosystem that explained how the gulf has been changing in recent decades, with rising water temperatures, increasing acidity and dropping oxygen concentrations. See Benoit et al., "State of the Ocean Report."

CHAPTER SEVEN

1   MacDonald, "A Landscape … with Figures," 61–79.

2   "Variety of Crops Grown in Maritime Provinces."

3   McNeill, "Report of the Superintendent of the Census Returns," 6; MacDonald, *If You're Stronghearted*, 135.

4   For a recent summary of the many agricultural crises explored by Canadian historians see Russell, *How Agriculture Made Canada*.

5   Whiteside, *Soil Survey of Prince Edward Island*; Dyck, "Land Use and Farm Income," 101; DeGrace, "In the Story of the Earth," 2–6.

6   Cronon, *Nature's Metropolis*, 226.

7   Judd, *Second Nature*, 72; Donahue, *The Great Meadow*, 166.

8   Olmstead and Rhode, *Creating Abundance*, 263.

9   For a historiographical discussion of the Land Question, see Hatvany, "Tenant, Landlord and Historian."

10 Prince Edward Island. Land Commissioners' Court – 1862, *Abstract*; Sobey, *Early Descriptions*, part 2, 162.

11 Wilson, *Tenants in Time*, 54, 162.

12 Olmstead and Rhode, *Creating Abundance*, 271.

13 The number of milch cows, 1855–71, is estimated using the number reported in Nova Scotia in 1871 (2.6). Note that the number of horned cattle was also 2.6 in Nova Scotia, and in New Brunswick 2.4, so the estimate seems reasonable.

14 MacKinnon and Wynn, "Nova Scotian Agriculture in the 'Golden Age.'"
15 Sharpe, *A People's History*, 147.
16 Callbeck, "Economic and Social Developments," 334.
17 Bruce and Cran, *Working Together*, 37.
18 Social differentiation in nineteenth-century Prince Edward Island resembles other parts of the Maritime region. See, for example, Bittermann, "Hierarchy of the Soil"; McNabb, "The Role of the Land."
19 Hatvany, "'Wedded to the Marshes'"; Curley, "The Essential Salt Marsh," 21; Judd, *Second Nature*, 72, 74–5.
20 Prince Edward Island, *Abstract of the Census ... 1861*.
21 Hatvany, "Wedded to the Marshes."
22 The estimates used for these caloric ratios were extremely conservative (less than a third of what horses and cattle consume today and half of the recommended sheep feed).
23 MacKinnon and Vass, *Best of the Past*, 13.
24 MacKinnon and Walder, "Agriculture in Atlantic Canada, 1851," plate 12.
25 "Blue Books," in *Journal of the House of Assembly of Prince Edward Island* (Charlottetown: George T. Haszard, 1830, 1851, 1856, 1861, 1866).
26 Livestock experts recommended 80–100 pounds of turnips per day for fattening a beef cow in this period (Morton, *Cyclopedia of Agriculture*, 532, 535). Henry Stephens and John Stuart Skinner recommended much higher rations for English dairy cattle of 1 bushel of turnips or carrots per day (half in morning and half in afternoon). This was presumably only during milking season, which could not have been more than 300 days per year (*Book of the Farm*, 22).
27 Sobey, *Early Descriptions*, part 2, section A, 52–3.
28 Quoted in D.C. Harvey, *Journeys to the Island*, 129.
29 Hudson and Meggison, *Preserving the Past*, 84–5; Sobey, *Early Descriptions*, part 2, section A, 53.
30 Vass, "Agricultural Societies of Prince Edward Island," 32, 35.
31 Prince Edward Island, *Abstract of the Census ... 1871*, Appendix: "Abstract of General Remarks."
32 Banner and Urban oats were the most popular varieties of white oats; other varieties included Victory, Abegweit, Gary, and Peace River oats. Black oat varieties included American Beauty and Black Norway. See MacKinnon and Vass, *Best of the Past*, 4–5.
33 Bruce and Cran, *Working Together*, 36–8; Clark, *Three Centuries and the Island: Historical Geography of Settlement and Agriculture in Prince Edward Island, Canada*, 158, 160, and figure 100.

34 *Census of Prince Edward Island*, 1861; Clark, *Three Centuries and the Island*, 134, table 9.

35 On 24 January 1866, his son Doug went "to town with the first load of wood 8/6" (PARO, John MacEachern Diary, acc. 3192, item 1).

36 Glen, "Prince Edward Island 1935/1936."

37 At this point, the colony had 80,900 residents; it had been growing by more than 30 per cent per decade since 1841.

38 Clark, *Three Centuries and the Island*, 122–5.

39 Most Island soils have an average pH below 5.

40 The "land fertilized with lime" variable is problematic, because although it was an attempt to get at the degree to which land had been "improved," it was not specified if the question was regarding land that had ever been treated with lime, land that had been recently treated, or land that had been treated in the previous twelve months only. Because the question was also asked of mussel mud, which was widely known to last for a decade or more on the land, I have taken the figure to mean land that was ever treated with these calcareous fertilizers.

41 MacFadyen, "Drawing Lines in the Ice"; Weale, "Mud Diggers"; Hudson and Meggison, *Preserving the Past*, 92–4; Shutt and Wright, *Peat, Muck, and Mud Deposits*.

42 Hoffmann and Winiwarter, "Making Land and Water Meet"; MacGregor, *British America*, 331; Sherman, "Daniel Webster," 480.

43 Similar restrictions were enacted in Virginia. See Holmes, "Aboriginal Shell-Heaps"; MacIntyre, "Environmental Pre-History of Prince Edward Island"; O'Grady, "In the Footsteps."

44 Griffin, "Canada," 354; Bain, "Every Lowly Tribe."

45 MacGregor, *British America*, 331.

46 Prince Edward Island, "Land Commissioners' Court – 1862, Abstract, 121."

47 Weale, "Shell-Mud Diggers."

48 In the early 1870s it was assumed that "If a man hauls more than two miles it does not pay." Prince Edward Island, Commission under Land Purchase Act (1875), 375.

49 David Weale noted that one of the first mud diggers in Bedeque Bay was a commercial operator. Basil MacNeill's diary for 1912 shows that he purchased his mud from a variety of operators at the shore. Quoted in *Goin' to the Corner*, vol. 1, 105.

50 Reg Thompson's interview of Vernon McCarvill, *Island Voices*, 17 December 2003, http://www.islandvoices.ca/interviews/detailview/ivoices:i voices20100601acass009; other farmers modified their sleighs for mud

hauling, such as Basil MacNeill who in early February recorded that he "rigged up a sleigh box for to go at the mud" (Basil MacNeill diary entries, 6 February, 1912, and 8 February, 1912, quoted in *Goin' to the Corner*).

51 Allan Graham, *Photo History*, 53–4; "Summerside News," *Island Guardian*, 7 March 1892, 4.

52 Basil MacNeill diary entries, quoted in *Goin' to the Corner*.

53 PARO, John MacEachern Diary.

54 The Anderson daughters' diary (transcription courtesy of Winifred Wake, Friends of the Lower Bedeque School), noted that "Father took a load of hay to Summerside," in April 1879. MacEachern managed to keep oats through the winter in a "stack from across the brook." This was the point on his farm furthest from the house and the road, and it may have even been inaccessible for much of the winter. The stacks kept crops off the ground and relatively dry, and protected them from wandering livestock.

55 Prince Edward Island, Commission under Land Purchase Act (1875), 31, 465, 507.

56 Brian Donahue, *Great Meadow*, 172.

57 MacKinnon and Vass, *Best of the Past*, 5; Canada, *Third Census*, vol. 4, table 2.

58 Quoted in MacKinnon and Vass, *Best of the Past*, 12.

59 PARO, Ledger of Roderick Munn, Acc. 4325.

60 This does not take into account the size of Munn's hay fields, but as he was not clearing land and other crops remained steady, the hay acreage presumably did as well.

61 Munn specified the experimental use of sea manures such as lobster offal and mussel mud on his turnip crops, but these were very small areas, and presumably the bulk of the mud was directed toward hay fields. His farm was eventually featured in Premier Albert C. Saunders's "The Rapid Progress of Prince Edward Island."

62 For more on the Island dairy industry and the promotional work of J.W. Robertson in the 1890s, see Bruce and Cran, *Working Together*, 51–5; MacDonald, *If You're Stronghearted*, 28.

63 Clark, *Three Centuries and the Island*, 163.

64 The Bruntland report suggested that "as a system approaches ecological limits, inequalities sharpen" (UN World Commission on Environment and Development, *Our Common Future*, chapter 2, part 2).

65 Whiteside, *Soil Survey*, 6.

66 Clark, *Three Centuries and the Island*, 122–3, figure 72.

67 Raymond and Rayburn, "Land Abandonment"; Edward MacDonald notes "the Dominion census in 1901 revealed a net loss of six thousand people

in the Island's population" [about a 5.5 per cent loss] and the loss continued (*If You're Stronghearted*, 30, 119–21). For Maritimers' New England destinations, see Beattie, "The 'Boston States,'" 253–4.

68 Wynn, *Canada and Arctic North America*, 184.

69 Forbes, *Maritime Rights Movement*; Forbes, *Challenging the Regional Stereotype*; Inwood, *Farm Factory Fortune*; Henderson, "A Defensive Alliance."

70 Gwyn, "Golden Age or Bronze Moment?"; Inwood and Irwin, "Land, Income and Regional Inequality," 157–8.

71 Stoll, "Farm against Forest," 65–6.

72 Burke, "Forestry in Prince Edward Island," 82–3.

73 *Census of Canada*, 1931, cxliv.

74 MacFadyen and Glen, "Top-Down History."

75 Montgomery, *Jane of Lantern Hill*, chapter 34.

76 Raymond and Rayburn, "Land Abandonment"; Ramankutty, Heller, and Rhemtulla, "Prevailing Myths," 503.

77 Bittermann and McCallum, "'One of the Finest Grass Countries'"; Callbeck, *Cradle of Confederation*, 238.

78 MacDonald notes that even in the height of the seed potato expansion in 1928, the average Association member was only growing seven acres of potatoes. *If You're Stronghearted*, 134–8.

79 Clark, *Three Centuries and the Island*, table 8.

80 Ibid.

81 Ibid., 220.

82 MacDonald, *If You're Stronghearted*, 28.

83 Note "fertilizer" included manure. *Sixth Census of Canada, 1921*, vol. 5 – Agriculture, (Ottawa: F.A. Acland, 1925), ix; *1941 Census*, vol. 8, part 1, PEI, table 1, 56–7, xiv.

84 Hatvany, "Tenant, Landlord, and Historian."

85 MacFadyen, "Drawing Lines in the Ice."

86 Quoted in MacKinnon and Vass, *Best of the Past*, 14.

87 Cunfer, "Manure Matters"; Sheridan, "Chemical Fertilizers"; Shutt and Wright, *Peat, Muck, and Mud Deposits*, 24.

88 Cunningham, "Limestone Study for Prince Edward Island."

89 For the ages of farmers, see Janssen, "Agriculture in Transition," 120.

90 MacKinnon and Vass, *The Best of the Past*, 20; see also Prince Edward Island AgriAlliance, "Innovation Road Map for the Prince Edward Island Agriculture & Agri-Food Sector," figures 8 and 9.8, February 2013.

91 In the 1961 Census, a farm is defined as "an agricultural holding of one acre or more with sales of agricultural products during the past 12 months

of $50 or more." That was a change from 1951 and 1956, where a farm was either a) three acres or more in size, or b) one to three acres in size with production valued at $250 or more. Canada, Introduction, *1961 Census*, vii.

92 Clark, *Three Centuries and the Island*, 216.

93 McClellan, "Changing Patterns of Land Use," 101.

94 Raymond and Rayburn, "Land Abandonment," 80.

95 Ibid.

96 Clark, *Three Centuries and the Island*, 12, table 2, 220.

97 Janssen, "Agriculture in Transition," 123.

98 Clark, *Three Centuries and the Island*, 12, table 2.

99 Dyck, "Land Use and Farm Income, 108, table 4.

100 Ibid., 102, table 1.

101 MacDonald, *If You're Stronghearted*, 28, 138.

102 Dyck, "Land Use and Farm Income," 103, table 2.

103 Clark, *Three Centuries and the Island*, 12, table 2.

104 Ibid., 255n11.

105 For more on the development plan, see MacDonald, *If You're Stronghearted*; MacKinnon, *Between Two Cultures*; Holloway, "'Give Us This Day.'"

106 Lattimer had extensive experience in research on the Island. See Lattimer, *Taxation in Prince Edward Island*; *Economic Survey*, 4; MacKinnon and Vass, *Best of the Past*, introduction.

107 See Whiteside, *Soil Survey*, 35. Whiteside presented the results of the first survey in 1950 and was later commissioned to produce an update with new analyses in response to new crops.

108 Philpotts, *Aerial Photo Interpretation*, 13.

109 Gilhooly and Gosselin, "Farm Management Study," 38. In addition to Irish Cobbler and Green Mountain varieties, MacKinnon and Vass identified Dakota Reds, Early Rose, and MacIntyre Blues (*Best of the Past*, 5).

110 Gilhooly and Gosselin, "Farm Management Study," 39.

111 Thomson, *Skyview Canada*, 167.

112 McDonald and Glen, *1958 Forest Inventory*.

113 Philpotts, *Aerial Photo Interpretation*, 11, 18, tables 3 and 7.

114 Quoted in MacDonald, *If You're Stronghearted*, 136.

115 Philpotts, *Aerial Photo Interpretation*, figures 24, 26, and 28.

116 "Medium" was defined as gross product of between $1,200 and $5,000. Only 132 produced more than the medium farms, and 338 produced less than $250.

117 Strangely, most of the potato specialists were in the Egmont townships in West Prince.

118 Dyck, "Land Use and Farm Income."

119 Dyck, "Farmer's Views," 136–7.

120 Ibid., 134–5.

121 MacKinnon, *Between Two Cultures*, 102–3.

122 Ibid., 104.

123 Ibid.

124 *Journal of the House of Assembly of Prince Edward Island*, 1969, 13.

125 MacKinnon, *Between Two Cultures*, 244.

126 MacEachern, *Institute of Man and Resources*.

127 Catonism was particularly strong in Quebec where economists like Esdras Minville promoted a back-to-the-farm doctrine and argued that Quebec had become too urban. Robin Neill, *History of Canadian Economic Thought*, 40–2.

128 Schumacher, *Small Is Beautiful*, 51; Woods, *Rural Geography*, 75; Vining and Strauss, "Demonstration."

129 Harris and Mueller, "Making Science Beautiful," 109.

130 Burke, "Forestry in Prince Edward Island"; Clark, *Three Centuries and the Island*, 221.

131 See interview with Alex Campbell in the NFB film *The Prince Edward Island Development Plan: Part 1, Ten Days in September* (1969), http://onf-nfb.gc.ca/en/our-collection/?idfilm=12673.

132 As Hans Rosling and Zhang Zhongxing argue for Africa, a nuanced understanding of the data is necessary before universal policies can be made ("Health Advocacy," 11–14).

133 McCann, "Living a Double Life." For more on PEI's urbanization experience, see Clark, *Three Centuries and the Island*, 122–5, 259n13.

134 VanWey, Guedes, and D'Antona, "Out-Migration and Land-Use Change."

CHAPTER EIGHT

1 McNeill, *Something New under the Sun*, 22–6, 35–48, 212–16, 262–4; Pimental et al., "Soil Erosion and Agricultural Productivity," 277–92; Ramankutty and Foley, "Estimating Historical Changes in Land Cover," 381–96; Turner et al., *Earth as Transformed by Human Action*.

2 Geographer A.H. Clark's classic account of settlement and adaptation is *Three Centuries and the Island*. David Weale takes more of a folk history approach in his best-selling *Them Times*. Georges Arsenault concentrates on Acadian agriculture in several of his many publications. The best overview can be traced in Arsenault's *The Island Acadians;* see also Arsenault's *L'agriculture chez les Acadiens*. Elinor Vass and Wayne MacKinnon collected traditional farming lore and practice in *The Best of the Past;* see

also Vass's "Agricultural Societies of Prince Edward Island." Matthew Hatvany focuses on the early colonial period, most notably in his doctoral dissertation, "Tenant, Landlord, and the New Middle Class." Finally, William Janssen takes aim at the postwar era in "Agriculture in Transition."

3 Prince Edward Island, *2010 State of the Environment.*

4 PEI, *36th Annual Statistical Review.*

5 Ibid.

6 Figures derived from a comparison of Department of Finance and Municipal Affairs annual statistical reviews, Prince Edward Island.

7 *Charlottetown Guardian*, 25 April 2011. Excerpt from a speech given by Gary Linkletter, chairman of the PEI Potato Board, to the Hillsborough Rotary Club.

8 PEI, *Royal Commission on the Future of the Potato Industry.*

9 For more on the effects of hedgerow removal, see Peters and Lovejoy, "Terrestrial Fauna," 353–70. See also Terrasson and Tendron, "Case for Hedgerows," 210–21.

10 The generalizations offered here are based on the several reports cited in this essay and the confidential observations of experts obtained by the author.

11 As narrated in MacDonald, *If You're Stronghearted,* 134–8, 356–61.

12 Ontario, "Factsheet on Universal Soil Loss Equation," http://www.omafra. gov.on.ca/english/engineer/facts/12-051.htm.

13 Many publications on soil conservation appeared in the 1970s, including several experimental plot reports by Norbert Stewart of the PEI Department of Agriculture and Forestry. Other examples include de Belle, *Roadside Erosion and Resource Implications;* Harza of Canada Ltd, *Soil Conservation Program;* Howatt, "Farming Today," 12. See also MacQuarrie, *Soil Erosion;* Prince Edward Island, *And So Goes the Soil;* PEI, *Current and Proposed Programs in Soil Conservation;* Willis, *Report on the Comparative Study of Regimes.*

14 "Champion of the Soil," *Charlottetown Guardian*, 6 June 2011, is about Ron Dehaan's induction into the Canadian Conservation Hall of Fame.

15 PEI, *Cultivating Island Solutions.*

16 Agricultural Crop Rotation Act, RSPEI 1988.

17 Watercourse and Wetland Protection Regulations, http://www.gov.pe.ca/ law/regulations/pdf/E&09-16.pdf.

18 PEI, *2010 State of the Environment.*

19 Ibid., 69.

20 Ibid., 70.

21 Eutrophication is defined as "the enrichment of bodies of fresh water by inorganic plant nutrients (e.g., nitrate, phosphate)." It can occur naturally

but can also result from human activities such as fertilizer runoff or sewage discharge. See Lawrence, Jackson, and Jackson, *Longman Dictionary of Environmental Science*, 144–5.

22 PEI, *Everything before Us.*

23 PEI, *Water on Prince Edward Island.* The 1996 figures do not necessarily take into account climate change impacts, but they are the most recent available.

24 PEI, "Impact of Land Based Activities."

25 Somers, Raymond, and Uhlman, *Water Quality Interpretive Report.*

26 Prince Edward Island, *We Are All Downstream*, 34.

27 Idem., *Report of the Commission on Nitrates in Groundwater.*

28 Ibid.

29 http://www.hc-sc.gc.ca/ewh-semt/water-eau/drink-potab/guide/index-eng.php.

30 PEI, *2010 State of the Environment.* Aquatic life in our rivers, streams, and estuaries are more sensitive to nitrate pollution. Recent studies suggest that a maximum nitrate level of 2 mg/L would be appropriate to protect the most sensitive freshwater species.

31 Ibid.

32 http://ceqg-rcqe.ccme.ca/en/index.html#void.

33 Morell River Conservation Zone. See section 67 of the Subdivision and Development Regulations under the Prince Edward Island Planning Act.

34 PEI, "Creating a Vision for the Future." The complex topic of soil microbiology is beyond the scope of this chapter.

35 Personal communication with Brian Brown, PEI Department of Energy and Forestry.

36 PEI, *36th Annual Statistical Review.*

37 Ibid.

38 PEI, *Restoring a Balance in Island Forests.*

39 PEI, *2010 State of the Environment.*

40 Ibid., 47–8.

41 "Protected Areas: What Are They? Why Have Them?" *International Union for Conservation of Nature*, http://www.iucn.org/about/work/programmes/pa/pa_what/.

42 Canada's Terrestrial Protected Areas Status Report 2010.

43 PEI, *2010 State of the Environment.*

44 Ibid., 52.

45 Ibid., 20, 53–56.

46 Council of Europe, *European Landscape Convention.* See also Prince Edward Island, *Report of the Commission on Land and Local Governance*, 55–9.

47 PEI, *Report of the Royal Commission on Land Ownership and Land Use*; PEI, *Everything before Us*; PEI, *Cultivating Island Solutions*; PEI, *New Foundations*.

48 "Travel Intentions Survey," 19–20.

49 See, for example, MacDonald, "A Landscape ... with Figures," 70–85.

50 While quantitative evidence is currently lacking, it would appear that similar scenarios may have played out in miniature in the mid to late nineteenth century as poor farming practices overtaxed marginal farmlands and an overemphasis on the most valuable commercial crop, grain, exhausted soils in some districts.

CHAPTER NINE

1 This essay focuses on marine fisheries rather than freshwater species. While marine resources have attracted much scientific study, historical treatments of the fishery on Prince Edward Island are less common. The most comprehensive is Wells, *The Fishery of Prince Edward Island*, which is somewhat updated in MacDonald, *If You're Stronghearted*. Cecile Gallant focused on Island Acadians in *Histoire de la pêche chez les Acadiens de l'île-du-Prince-Edouard*. More specific topics, such as the lobster fishery, have attracted separate treatments, most of them in *The Island Magazine*, but see also Boyde Beck, *A Lobster Tale*. The province does not figure largely in broader studies of the North Atlantic fisheries.

2 Mi'kmaq cosmology, for example, made humans a part of nature rather than giving them dominion over it. The prehistoric fishery is covered in much more detail elsewhere in this volume by Keenlyside and Kristmanson.

3 Samuel de Champlain, *Voyages*, quoted in Clark, *Three Centuries and the Island*, 15. "The Basques go there frequently," Champlain reported, though his knowledge was hearsay.

4 Mowat makes the assertion in his book *Sea of Slaughter*, but when pressed by author Kennedy Wells in a telephone exchange, could not document the statement. Wells decided not to include Mowat's claim in his own history of the Island fishery (recollection of Edward MacDonald, who was Wells's researcher on the history of the Prince Edward Island fishery project).

5 A number of such maps, among them Visscher (1666), Coronelli (1695), and Moll (1720), can be viewed on UPEI's *Island Imagined* website, http://www.islandimagined.ca/.

6 This is concisely summarized in Wells, *Fishery*, 84–8.

7 The most complete accounts are Lockerby, "Comte de Saint-Pierre," 7–14, and Arsenault, "Settlement of Havre Saint-Pierre," 25–30. Saint-Pierre's

royal charter authorized Saint-Pierre to establish settlers and a shore-based fishery within a land grant that eventually encompassed Prince Edward Island, Miscou, and the Magdalens.

8 Arsenault, "Settlement of Havre Saint-Pierre," 26.

9 Jean-Pierre Roma and his Compagnie de l'Est du Île Saint-Jean fared little better at Three Rivers along the eastern coast in the 1730s and '40s. Roma's fishing settlement was destroyed in 1745 by New England militia. See Margaret Coleman, "Roma, Jean-Pierre," *Dictionary of Canadian Biography* online, http://www.biographi.ca/009004-119.01-e.php?&id_nbr'1630.

10 Arsenault, " Settlement of Havre Saint-Pierre," 28. In taking his census in 1752, Sieur de la Roque quarrelled with official policy: "There has been for a long time a mistaken belief, founded on a lack of experience of the conditions, that the settlers who follow the fisheries neglect the cultivation of the soil." Quoted in Harvey, *French Regime in Prince Edward Island*, 173.

11 Although Prince Edward Island would officially be known as St John's Island until 1799, for the sake of convenience we will freely use the term Prince Edward Island throughout, except when quoting from period documents.

12 The Fisheries Reserve became a long-running legal tangle that is best dissected in Bittermann and McCallum, "One That Got Away."

13 Canada, "Minutes of Meeting of Trade and Plantations, 8 July 1767," 7. The London merchants had requested land grants in exchange for launching a fishery in November 1763. See Bumsted, "British Colonial Policy," 5.

14 According to Governor Walter Patterson, an American named Gridley was having his employees prevent walrus from landing on Island shores in order to drive them into his waiting arms on the Magdalen Islands. The most complete of several modern accounts is Hogan, "White Gold and Train Oil," 19–22. For a contemporary account, see Stewart, *Account of Prince Edward Island*, 90–4.

15 See J.M. Bumsted, "Higgins, David," *Dictionary of Canadian Biography Online*, http://www.biographi.ca/009004-119.01-e.php?&id_nbr'1949. Technically, he died of a fever after a four-month drinking binge.

16 See J.M. Bumsted, "Hill, John," *Dictionary of Canadian Biography Online*, http://www.biographi.ca/009004-119.01-e.php?&id_nbr'3442. Hill linked his fishing activity on Prince Edward Island with his involvement with the Newfoundland cod trade. For more on Cambridge, see H.T. Holman, "Cambridge, John," *Dictionary of Canadian Biography Online*, http://www.biographi.ca/009004-119.01-e.php?&id_nbr'2786. Cambridge's

failed attempt to start a fishery is referenced in the diary kept by Thomas Douglas, 4th Earl of Selkirk, who spent time on the Island in 1803.

17 That was certainly the lesson derived by James Montgomery, one of the most active of the early proprietors on Prince Edward Island, from his experience in business with David Higgins on Lot 59. See Bumsted, "Sir James Montgomery," 76–102. Nor did it help when a Norman expatriate named LaSeur launched a major fishing enterprise at Rustico in 1813–14, employing "almost all the males in the area," only to sail off in the schooner he had bought but neglected to pay for. See Lt-Gov. C.D. Smith to Lord Bathurst, Colonial Secretary, 9 August 1814, CO 226/29, 93 and 122, Special Collections, Robertson Library, University of PEI, Charlottetown; MacGregor, *British America*, 295–6.

18 Lord Selkirk's Diary, 1803, cited in Wells, *The Fishery*.

19 Quoted in Wells, *The Fishery*, 100.

20 Stewart, *Account of Prince Edward Island*, 122–3.

21 *Prince Edward Island Register*, 1829.

22 Stewart, *Account*, 291–304. He also lists eels, oysters, herring, gaspereaux, and mackerel.

23 The introduction of the mackerel jig is discussed at length in Goode et al., *Materials for a History of the Mackerel Fishery*, 85–6, http://www.archive. org/stream/materialsforhistoounit/materialsforhistoounit_djvu.txt.

24 A barrel in mackerel fishing was commonly understood to hold three hundred pounds of salted fish.

25 See MacDonald, "Yankee Gale," 17–25.

26 See An Act to Regulate the Fisheries of this Island, 5 Geo. IV, Cap. XII, which dealt mostly with terms of employment; and An Act for Encouraging the Fisheries by Granting Bounties, 9 Geo. IV, Cap. VI, reprinted in *Prince Edward Island Register*, 28 April 1839. The bounty legislation was periodically renewed. See, for example, the *Royal Gazette*, 5 February and 12 March 1839; *Royal Gazette*, 19 May 1840. A bounty rewarding sealing vessels was added in the 1840s. See *Journal of the House of Assembly of Prince Edward Island* (hereafter Assembly Journal) 1844, 96; Assembly Journal, 1846, 74; and Assembly Journal, 1848, 40, http://eco.canadiana. ca/view/oocihm.9_00960. The sums paid out were modest.

27 Wells, *The Fishery*, 108. For one example among many, see the *Charlottetown Islander*'s report (23 April 1843, 3; 12 May 1843, 3) of a lecture to the local Mechanics' Institute on the development of an Island fishery by a Charlottetown cooper named James Kelly. Kelly felt the six hundred farms along the coast could support a fishing population of 240,000.

28 Hill, *Short Account of Prince Edward Island*, 74.

29 Quoted in Lawson, *Letters on Prince Edward Island*, 31.

30 Statistics here are culled from census reports and export statistics recorded annually in the appendices of the Assembly Journal.

31 See "The Alien Bill," *Charlottetown Islander*, 9 September 1859, 2–3. Given royal assent in May 1859, "An Act to Enable Aliens to Hold Real Estate" allowed aliens to "take, hold, convey, and transmit Real Estate in this Island."

32 Myrick's, especially, came to dominate the economy of West Prince County for the next century.

33 Census Abstract, Assembly Journal, 1862.

34 Seine boats dispatched from the schooner encircled the school of mackerel with seine nets up to 1,350 feet long and the "purse" was then closed by drawing together the bottom edges of the net. For detailed descriptions of both jigging and seining mackerel, see Goode et al., 55–62, 93–7.

35 The collapse was explicitly blamed on the purse-seining. See, for example, Canada, *Annual Report of the Department of Marine and Fisheries, 1892*, 35–7, 41–2. Ottawa banned the use of purse seines in Canadian waters, but it was too late.

36 Stewart, *Account*, 81, describes the cleft stick method. Gus Gregory of Souris could remember his neighbours catching lobster from the shore in the early twentieth century. See interview with Gregory by Reg "Dutch" Thompson, 28 March 1995, http://www.islandvoices.ca/islandora/solr/search/fish/-/dismax.

37 Hill, *Short Account*, 47. In the early twentieth century, when lobster prices remained low, lobster was supposedly associated with poverty, and a pervasive folk tradition insists that children were ashamed to take lobster sandwiches to school.

38 For a useful overview of the historical lobster fishery in Maine, see Martin and Lipfert, *Lobstering and the Maine Coast*.

39 Rutherford, Wilder, and Frick, *An Economic Appraisal of the Canadian Lobster Fishery*, 3. At this point, the issue for American canners was the amount of effort required to keep the New England factories supplied rather than an absolute shortage of lobsters. But by 1876, the Canadian Department of Marine and Fisheries would note, "It seems that excessive fishing has exhausted the lobster fishery along the northeast coast of the United States; and that enterprise which was embarked in the same has now been transferred to Canada." See Canada, *Annual Report of the Department of Marine and Fisheries*, 1876. The northward expansion of the lobster fishery reached the west coast of Newfoundland at about the

same time as it began booming on Prince Edward Island. See Korneski, "Development and Degradation," 21–48.

40 Summarized in Wells, *The Fishery*, 131–4.

41 Statistics cited for the 1873–1917 period are for the most part taken from the Prince Edward Island section of the annual reports of the federal Department of Marine and Fisheries, published in the Sessional Papers of the Canadian Parliament. As Statistics Canada warns, the statistics for catch and value during this period were guestimates and notoriously unreliable. (See Statistics Canada, Historical Statistics of Canada: Section N: Fisheries [by N. H. Morse], http://www.statcan.gc.ca/pub/11-516-x/sectionn/4057755-eng.htm.)

42 Only detailed cross-referencing of Island lobster canners and Island shipowners during this period will confirm this speculation, but preliminary research points to the migration of interest from one sector to the other.

43 Macdonald, "Father's Memoirs," 42. Macdonald also mentions the rise of cheese and butter factories in the 1890s.

44 The locations are recorded on the cadastral maps published in the *Illustrated Historical Atlas of the Province of Prince Edward Island*, published by Meacham in 1880 but based on surveys done in 1878 or '79.

45 See Canada, *Annual Report of the Department of Marine and Fisheries 1877*, Sessional Paper No. 5, Appendix 17, which breaks down canning statistics by district. Of the 362,676 pounds of lobster canned in the previous year, an estimated 200,000 pounds were produced between "South Point" (perhaps a typo for Beach Point) and Little Sands on the south shore of King's County. The *Daily Examiner*, 24 March 1885, 1, put the pre-1878 canneries at Canoe Cove, Murray Harbour, Cascumpec, Little Sands, and Darnley.

46 Unlike New Brunswick and Nova Scotia, which were closer to New England's urban markets, Prince Edward Island had no live lobster export trade of any significance in the nineteenth century.

47 Canada, *Annual Report of the Department of Marine and Fisheries, 1882*, Sessional Paper No. 5, 175.

48 Hunter Duvar provides these estimates in Canada, *Annual Report of the Department of Marine and Fisheries 1889*, Sessional Paper No. 8.

49 Canada, *Annual Report of the Department of Marine and Fisheries 1884*, Appendix No. 5, report of J.H. Duvar, inspector of Fisheries for Prince Edward Island, 175.

50 Canada, *Report of the Canadian Lobster Commission, 1898*, 5.

51 Self-evidently, the regulations fell very much within the paradigm of conservation to assure sustainable exploitation outlined in the appendix of this collection (MacIntyre).

52 When Commander William Wakeham, special commissioner and inspector of fisheries for the Gulf of St Lawrence, toured West Prince County in 1909–10, some fishermen claimed ignorance of any regulations regarding minimum size, moulting, or spawning lobsters. See "Lobster Fishing: Evidence ... ," especially 235–494.

53 Some packers claimed in 1898 that it took as many as ten. See "Report of the Canadian Lobster Commission, 1898."

54 The effect of the regulations was less clear in 1893, when Francis H. Herrick lamented the lobster fishery's "gradual but certain decay" because of over-fishing and castigated the "perverted logic" of past fisheries legislation. See Herrick, "Protection of the Lobster Industry."

55 See Canada, *Annual Report of the Department of Marine and Fisheries, 1888*, Appendix No. 5, 168.

56 Known as a "killick."

57 See Keough, *Slender Thread*.

58 For more on the subject of canneries and canning communities, see Gorveatt, "'Polluted with Factories,'" 10–21; Arsenault, "Packing Lobsters on the Beach," 13–21.

59 Canada, *Report of the Canadian Lobster Commission, 1898*, 7.

60 The practice was still common in the interwar period. See, for example, the interview with John Alex Murchison, Point Prim, who packed lobsters in one of his farm buildings and sold them to wholesaler J.W. Windsor Co., PARO 2924/22.

61 See Wells, *The Fishery*, 143–4; also, for example, *Charlottetown Presbyterian Witness*, 14 August 1880, which reported that a shipment of Island lobsters to London, "bearing well known Island labels – have proved to be trash."

62 [Illegible], Charlottetown, to W. Irving, 12 August 1899, PARO 2590/243.

63 Andrew Macphail, "Discoloration in Canned Lobsters." The problem was by no means confined to lobster or to Island canneries. See, for example, Petrick, "Ambivalent Diet," 35–8.

64 When George Leard interviewed elderly fishermen in the Souris area in the 1960s, they spoke of pre-trap methods, generally a hinged hoop and a gaff. See "Fishery – Lobster," George Leard Papers (microfilm copy), PEI Collection, Robertson Library, University of Prince Edward Island, Charlottetown. The earliest known reference to lobster traps describes their use at Davies and McFadyen's lobster factory at Poverty Beach ("On the Road," *Charlottetown Examiner*, 25 October 1875). The introduction of the "Wheeler" or parlour trap is referenced in Canada, *Report of the Canadian Lobster Commission, 1898*, Sessional Paper No. 11c. Its gradual adoption is traced in the evidence given before Commander Wakeham in 1909–10.

65 A reporter from the *Charlottetown Daily Examiner* described the event in dramatic terms for the 25 April 1903 edition. See MacDonald, "Running the Lines," 9–12.

66 For an iconic – and oft-quoted – characterization, see Croteau, *Cradled on the Waves*, 85: "Fishermen are just about the hardest people to organize ... As a class they tend to be irresponsible and improvident." Later, he adds, "Generally speaking, backwardness and a lack of push, characterize the fishing industry of the Maritimes" (89).

67 *Fisheries in the Atlantic Provinces*, 1. See also Daly, *Prince Edward Island*, 16, which puts the first marine engine in the Murray River area in 1904.

68 Again, these figures are culled from annual reports of the Department of Marine and Fisheries published yearly among the Sessional Papers of the Canadian Parliament.

69 Undated advertisement, from "Fisheries Files," Prince Edward Island Museum & Heritage Foundation, Charlottetown. See also PARO, 3019/1-19.

70 For example, Don Stewart, Stratford, interview by Edward MacDonald, 22 March 1984. Stewart stated that by the time its plant burned down in 1946, Bruce Stewart & Co. were no longer manufacturing marine engines because car engines had driven them out of the market.

71 Clive Bruce, Kingsboro, PEI, interview by Reg "Dutch" Thompson, 26 April 1996, http://www.islandvoices.ca/interviews/detailview/ivoices: ivoices20100504acass006.

72 A remnant shore fishery is chronicled in McKenna, "Marooned in the Past," 22–7.

73 In his annual report in 1886, John Hunter Duvar reported factories selling lobster waste for fertilizer at $1 per ton (Sessional Paper No. 11b, 1886, Appendix 3, No. 7, p. 250.) By the 1920s, according to Stilgenbauer, "The Geography of Prince Edward Island," 60, it was being sold for $1 a cart-load, but most oral interviewees remember it being given away. See, for example, John Alex Murchison, interview by Jeannie Macleod, Belfast Historical Society Fonds, PARO 2924/22; Johnny Chuck MacAdam, Morell, interview by Reg "Dutch" Thompson, 5 February 1999, http://www. islandvoices.ca/interviews/detailview/ivoices:ivoices20100816acass001.

74 Nicosia and Lavalli, "Homarid Lobster Hatcheries." The authors trace the first attempts to propagate lobsters artificially to Brittany in 1858. It would appear the two Island hatcheries were at Blockhouse Point at the entrance to Charlottetown Harbour in 1903 and Georgetown in 1909, although there is an early twentieth-century postcard of Tignish Run labelled "Lobster hatchery." A salmon hatchery had been tried on the Dunk River

in the nineteenth century, and both trout and salmon were spawned at a hatchery in Southport in the twentieth.

75 MacKinnon, "Fisheries," 171.

76 Knight, *Official Report on Lobster Investigations, 1917*.

77 An Act for the Preservation of Oysters, 5 Geo. IV, cap. 2, Acts of House of Assembly or Legislative Assembly.

78 See Abraham Gesner's approving appraisal of Bedeque oysters in his "Report of the Geological Survey of P.E.I.," Assembly Journal, 1847, Appendix D; also, Crosskill, *Handbook*, 89. The Bedeque beds were quickly fished out.

79 For more on the oysters and mussel mud digging, see Josh MacFadyen's essay in this volume.

80 Quoted in Wells, *The Fishery*, 148.

81 A table of oyster harvests since 1876 was published in Canada, *Annual Report of the Department of Marine and Fisheries*, 1911, Sessional Paper No. 22, lxxi.

82 Johnstone, *The Aquatic Explorers*, 38.

83 Quoted in MacDonald, *If You're Stronghearted*, 71. The jurisdictional dispute over the sea bottom in bays and estuaries can be tracked in the J.A. Mathieson Papers, PARO, RG 25.23. The enabling legislation is 6 Edw. VII, c.2 (amended in 1912), and 3 Geo V, Cap. 6, Acts of House of Assembly or Legislative Assembly. The areas involved included Malpeque Bay, Cascumpec Bay, North River, Bedeque Bay, New London Bay, Pownal Bay, St Peters Bay, Tryon River, St Mary's Bay, Orwell Bay, and the Hillsborough River.

84 Summarized in Wells, *The Fishery*, 159. The Fisheries Research Board was tasked with studying the disease in 1917, but could find no cure. See Johnstone, *Aquatic Explorers*, 84.

85 See, for example, "The Lobster Canneries, Shall They Be Closed for the 1915 Season," *The Busy East of Canada*, January 1915, 17–18; and "Lobsters and the War," *Charlottetown Guardian*, 28 October 1914, 4. The aggregate values are taken from N.H. Morse, "Historical Statistics of Canada, Section N: Fisheries," Statistics Canada, http://www.statcan.gc.ca/pub/11-516-x/sectionn/4057755-eng.htm.

86 The percentages are furnished here by Gordon, *The Fishing Industry of Prince Edward Island*, 11. The prices come from various oral interviews in the Reginald "Dutch" Thompson Collection, http://www.islandvoices.ca/.

87 Gordon, *Fishing Industry*, 12.

88 *C.F.'s Diary*; Johnny Chuck MacAdam, Morell, interview by Reg "Dutch" Thompson, 5 February 1999, http://www.islandvoices.ca/interviews/detailview/ivoices:ivoices20100816acass001.

89   Gordon, *Fishing Industry*, 38.

90   Weir, "Rural Reconstruction," 45.

91   The trend is traced in some detail in MacDonald, *If You're Stronghearted*, especially chapters 7 and 8. Fishermen themselves were often studied but seldom consulted and rarely listened to in this period.

92   Gordon, *Fishing Industry*, 30.

93   Clive Bruce, Kingsboro, interview by Reg "Dutch" Thompson, 26 April 1996, http://www.islandvoices.ca/interviews/detailview/ivoices:ivoices 20100504acass006.

94   "First P.E.I. Owned Dragger Now Ready for Launching," *Charlottetown Guardian*, 8 September 1950, 5.

95   *Agreement Covering Development Plan*, 44–5.

96   Proskie, "Costs and Earnings," 1–2.

97   Summarized in MacDonald, *If You're Stronghearted*, 268–70.

98   Gus Gregory, Souris, interview by Reg "Dutch" Thompson, 28 March 1995, http://www.islandvoices.ca/interviews/detailview/ivoices:ivoices 20100430acass001.
     See also Robbie Robertson, Kingsboro, PEI, interview by Reg "Dutch" Thompson, 10 February 1988 and 28 March 1995, http://www.island-voices.ca/interviews/detailview/ivoices:ivoices20100504acass003; Clive Bruce, Kingsboro, PEI, interview by Reg "Dutch" Thompson, 26 April 1996, http://www.islandvoices.ca/interviews/detailview/ivoices:ivoices 20100504acass006.

99   The debate rages online as well. See, for example, "Endangered Species Listing for Bluefin Tuna Not Warranted," *National Oceanic and Atmospheric Administration*, 27 May 2011, http://www.noaanews.noaa. gov/stories2011/20110527_bluefintuna.html; "Bluefin Tuna Is Endangered, Scientists Say," *CBC News Prince Edward Island*, 9 May 2011, http://www.cbc.ca/news/canada/prince-edward-island/story/2011/ 05/09/pe-bluefin-tuna-endangered.html (both accessed 7 February 2012).

100 For more on mussel growing technology, see Scarratt, *Handbook of Northern Mussel Culture*.

101 Or worse. In some communities, they were thought to be poisonous.

102 Gilgan, Burns, and Landry, "Distribution and Magnitude of Domoic Acid Contamination," 469–74.

103 Prince Edward Island, *37th Annual Statistical Review*, 86.

104 *Help Stop the Spread*.

105 Finfish aquaculture, for example, topped out at a value of only $3.2 million in 2004 and a maximum output of 99 tonnes in 1997.

106 Birch, "Fishing Industry."

107 *Agreement Covering Development Plan*, 42–3, does not specify the desired number of fishers, but economist Copes does in *The Development of the Fishing Industry in Prince Edward Island*. Theoretically, the displaced fishermen would be retrained for other occupations.

108 For example, see the election promise published in the *Charlottetown Guardian*, 5 May 1970, 3.

109 See APEC, "History of the Prince Edward Island Comprehensive Development Plan," PEI Collection, Robertson Library, University of Prince Edward Island, 73.

110 The limited entry system was adopted in 1967 and the trap limit (originally four hundred traps, but later reduced to three hundred) at about the same time. See Wells, *The Fishery*, 69.

111 The summary offered here is based on annual reports of the provincial department of fisheries for the period and Spierenburg, *Historical Statistics*.

112 The trend also reflects the increasing mechanization of the fishery, which placed less emphasis on the physical strength of the fishers. For more on women in the fishery and the dynamics of fishing households, see Maureen Larkin, "Our Way of Living"; Porter, "Women in Fishing Households."

113 See Hutchings and Myers, "Biological Collapse of Atlantic Cod," 37–94.

114 See, for example, Wells, "An Extinct Breed?" 15. A degree of occupational pluralism still thrives in rural communities especially among "non-core" fishing families who target minor species such as eels, smelts and clams, and supplement this by firewood cutting and other rural pursuits.

115 Novaczek, Angus, and Lewis, "Evolution of Post-Colonial Indigenous Peoples' Fisheries Management Systems," 188–207.

116 See Lotze, Lenihan, et al., "Depletion, Degradation, and Recovery Potential," 1806.

117 DFO 2012 State of Canada's Oceans (Gulf of St Lawrence section), http://www.dfo-mpo.gc.ca/Library/345310.pdf.

118 That lobster can be pushed to the brink of commercial extinction was demonstrated on the west coast of Newfoundland in the late nineteenth and early twentieth centuries. See Korneski, "Development and Degradation," 21–48.

119 Novaczek, Angus, and Lewis, "Evolution of Post-Colonial Indigenous Peoples' Fisheries Management Systems," 5.

120 The company's ill-fated attempt can be traced in a series of newspaper clippings from the local press in the Vertical File of the PEI Collection, Robertson Library, University of Prince Edward Island.

121   These trends are charted in CASC's "Canadian Marine Ecosystem Status and Trends Report," 22–7.

CHAPTER TEN

1   For the history of Prince Edward Island tourism, see MacDonald, "A Landscape ...with Figures," 70–85; McRae, "Manufacturing Paradise"; MacEachern, "No Island Is an Island"; Adler, "Tourism and Pastoral," 131–54.

2   In 2010, the artist group Dodolab showed visitors to the Confederation Centre Art Gallery photographs of different colours, skies, and other landscape features of the Island, and asked which images were the best representations of the province. The survey produced a composite "Prince Edward Island Postcard" and an "Un-Prince Edward Island Postcard."

3   Likewise, what are we to make of the fact that the first visible minority to appear in an Island visitors guide, with the exception of the very occasional Mi'kmaq, was apparently a wax Michael Jordan in an advertisement for "Wax World of the Stars" in 2004? This is extraordinary, if only because the Island had by that point been promoting itself to Japanese tourists for more than a generation.

4   Personal communication with David Mackenzie, deputy minister of tourism and culture, Prince Edward Island.

5   The guidebooks are such a voluminous and consistently produced source base that I have elected to explore them alone here. Admittedly, incorporating promotional films, the government's tourism website, or other media may well have yielded somewhat different findings.

6   Biggar, *Voyages of Jacques Cartier*, 40.

7   Intercolonial Railway and Prince Edward Island Railway, *Forest, Stream and Seashore*, 162.

8   It might be supposed that early photography demanded too long an exposure time to capture wave action, and so beach shots were avoided; in fact, cameras were able to photograph waves from at least the 1850s.

9   Crosskill, *Handbook*, 34; McCready, *Prince Edward Island*, 33.

10 *Prince Edward Island: Its Resources and Opportunities*, 22.

11 Ibid., 63.

12 MacDonald, *If You're Stronghearted*, 121.

13 *Prince Edward Island: The England of Canada*, 9. Devotion to England typically figured in wartime tourism material. The 1945 guide *Prince Edward Island* clumsily begins, "'There'll Always Be An England – in Canada' while there's a Prince Edward Island."

14 Birches also made the cover of *Prince Edward Island: Canada's Garden Province*. See http://www.ourroots.ca/e/toc.aspx?id=4902.

15 In similar fashion, the blueberry canning industry that developed in Maine in the 1860s was the indirect result of early nineteenth-century forest fires. See Pyne, *Fire in America*, 55.

16 "The tourist industry has developed into one of our major enterprises..." in *Submission by the Province of Prince Edward Island to the Royal Commission on Transportation*, 79–80. See also pp. 61, 66, and 67.

17 McRae, "Manufacturing Paradise," 84.

18 Ibid.; MacEachern, *Natural Selections*, 242–3.

19 This paragraph utilizes the 1960, 1962, 1964, 1965, 1967, and 1968 editions of *Come to Prince Edward Island Canada*.

20 See, for example, the photo in the 1960 guide of a girl photographing her parents, the caption reading, "A camera enthusiast at Wood Islands uses lobster traps as a background for her vacation 'shot.'" The caption returns in 1964, but this time with the picture of the family replaced by a more standard picture of a boat leaving a harbour, now identified as North Lake.

21 *"Here Is a Calm and Peaceful Land."*

22 Cited in 1990 *Visitors Guide*, no pagination.

23 There are exceptions. Perhaps because beach attire does not become dated quite as quickly as other clothes, a photo of a family walking along the shore of the national park lingered for an entire decade (see, for example the 2010 *Visitor's Guide*, 10).

24 MacDonald, "A Landscape ...with Figures," especially 84–5.

CHAPTER ELEVEN

1 Mumford, *Technics and Civilization*.

2 Wrigley, "Reflections on the History of Energy Supply," 3–21; Jones, *Routes of Power*.

3 Smil, *Energy at the Crossroads*, 1.

4 For more on this, see McNeill, *Something New under the Sun*.

5 White, *Science of Culture*, 368.

6 Carson, *Silent Spring*.

7 Nye, *Consuming Power*.

8 Saul, "Nature and Diffusion of Technology," 36–61.

9 Myllyntaus, *Electrifying Finland*, 5.

10 Ibid.

11 Sobey, *Early Descriptions of the Forests*, Part 1, 16–17; see also Clark, *Three Centuries and the Island*, 40.

12 See Wynn, *Canada and Arctic North America*, 113–38.
13 For more on railway development in Pictou County, Nova Scotia, see http://www.novascotiarailwayheritage.com/NOVA%20SCOTIA%20 RAILWAY%20BOOKS-1.htm, compiled by Jay Underwood, 8 August 2007.
14 See Holman, "A Lamp to Light Their Paths."
15 Stuart, "The Influence of Islandness."
16 MacEachern, *Institute of Man and Resources*.
17 Ibid.
18 *Lighting the Way.*
19 Sobey, *Early Descriptions*, Part 1, 5.
20 There was some abortive interest in the timber resources for naval construction. See Sobey, "Department of Marine," 10–18.
21 Ibid., 18–22; see also *Illustrated Historical Atlas*.
22 Clark, *Three Centuries*, 36.
23 Vass, "Early Island Roads," 19–26.
24 Clark, *Three Centuries*, 35.
25 *Illustrated Historical Atlas.*
26 Ibid., 69, 78-80.
27 Sobey, *Early Descriptions*, Part 1, 101. See also De Jong and Moore, *Shipbuilding on Prince Edward Island*; Bitterman, "From Wine to Wood."
28 Sobey, "Shipbuilding," 5. See also Martin, *View from the Bridge*, 58.
29 For a quick overview of the shipbuilding era, see Fischer, "Shipping Industry of Nineteenth Century Prince Edward Island," 15–21.
30 Bruce and Cran, *Working Together*, 48–56.
31 MacDonald, *If You're Stronghearted*, 56.
32 For a discussion of out-migration to 1900, see Brookes, "Islanders in the Boston States," 11–15.
33 MacIntyre, "Environmental Pre-History of Prince Edward Island."
34 MacKinnon, *Between Two Cultures*, 101.
35 Ibid., 115.
36 Sobey, "Shipbuilding," 6–7.
37 The idea of using railroads as a terrestrial connection between the ice-bound British North American colonies gained ground in the age of steam. Railways were promoted first for military purposes and later by Britain as a means to leverage Confederation. By the mid-1850s, the Nova Scotia Railway (NSR) brought coal from its mining areas to Halifax on the Atlantic and the ferry port of Pictou on the Northumberland Strait, important for steamships servicing Prince Edward Island. Similarly, the European and North American Railway (E&NAR) in New Brunswick first

connected Saint John with Shediac on the Strait in 1857. See Legget, *Railways of Canada*, 56.

38 MacDonald, *If You're Stronghearted*, 8.

39 Ibid., 9.

40 Clark, *Three Centuries*, 180. Of course, one of the reasons for this transition was practical. Without all-weather roads, autos were of limited utility in three of the Island's four seasons.

41 Ibid., 55; MacDonald, *If You're Stronghearted*, 117.

42 MacDonald, *If You're Stronghearted*, 241.

43 Ibid., 255.

44 See Mullally, "The Machine in the Garden," 16–25, which synthesizes a number of sources to give an account of the auto's reception and problems.

45 Cusack, *Magnificent Gift Declined*, 4.

46 Prince Edward Island, *38th Annual Statistical Review*.

47 Idem., *37th Annual Statistical Review*.

48 Idem., *Energy Framework and Renewable Energy Strategy*.

49 Holman, "A Lamp to Light their Paths," 139–40.

50 For a useful monograph for the history of electrification on PEI, see Bell, *Getting the Lights*.

51 Ibid., 8–9.

52 Ibid.

53 MacDonald, *If You're Stronghearted*, 151.

54 Bell, *Getting the Lights*, 15.

55 MacDonald, *If You're Stronghearted*, 247.

56 Ibid., 249.

57 Ibid., 22.

58 Maritime Electric Ltd is a wholly owned subsidiary of Fortis Inc., the largest investor-owned distribution utility in Canada. It is headquartered in Newfoundland & Labrador. See Maritime Electric Company Ltd, "Our Island Electricity," http://www.maritimeelectric.com.

59 Prince Edward Island, *38th Annual Statistical Review*.

60 Maritime Electric Ltd, http://www.maritimeelectric.com/about_us/ab_our_island_electricity.aspx

61 The proposal received approval after a lengthy and lively regulatory process in which responses to 76 requests for further information were filed. See *Report to IRAC on the Review of the MECL Proposal to Install a 50 MW Combustion Turbine at its Charlottetown Generation Station*, KnAP Energy Consultants, June 2004, accessed 11 September 2012, http://www.irac.pe.ca/publicnotices/documents/IRAC-UE20711-MECL-CT-2004.pdf

62 Information provided to this researcher during tour of new turbine facility, 2 November 2005.

63 Prince Edward Island, *Energy Framework.*

64 Idem., *37th Annual Statistical Review 2010.*

65 Fleming, *Power at Cost*, 74.

66 Dyck, "Farmers' Views of Rural Life," 134–9.

67 MacEachern, *Institute*, 41.

68 MacDonald, *If You're Stronghearted*, 67. See also Reddin, *Who We Are*, 5, documenting the history of home economics education which had an enormous influence on women, household modernization, public health, nutrition, family, and community in the twentieth century.

69 "UPEI receives BOMA BESt certification for 22 campus buildings," http://news.upei.ca/media/2011/08/03/upei-receives-boma-best-certification-22-campus-buildings.

70 See Samuelson, "Watermills of Prince Edward Island."

71 "Federal and Provincial Governments Support Wind Energy in PEI," Atlantic Canada Opportunities Agency press release, 25 April 2008, http://www.acoa-apeca.gc.ca/eng/Agency/mediaroom/NewsReleases/Pages/2372.aspx.

72 Prince Edward Island, *Energy Framework.*

73 Idem., *37th Annual Statistical Review.*

74 "$60M wind farm will lower power price: energy minister," CBC News Prince Edward Island, 15 January 2014, http://www.cbc.ca/news/canada/prince-edward-island/60m-wind-farm-will-lower-power-price-energy-minister-1.2498382.

75 Maritime Electric Ltd website, accessed 15 March 2015, http://www.maritimeelectric.com/customer_service/cust_green_power.aspx.

76 R. Estabrooks, "Power in the Wind," *Charlottetown Guardian*, 28 November 2002.

77 "P.E.I. Replacing License Plates," CBC News Prince Edward Island, 5 July 2013, http://www.cbc.ca/news/canada/prince-edward-island/p-e-i-replacing-licence-plates-1.1369174.

78 Wayne Thibodeau, "Island to Receive Big Power Upgrade," *Charlottetown Guardian*, 19 November 2005.

79 Ibid.

80 "Ottawa May Disconnect Support for Cable," CBC Prince Edward Island, 7 April 2006, accessed 21 May 2006, http://www.cbc.ca/pei/story/power-cable060407.html. One of the issues was apparently technical rather than political. It was unclear that the Confederation Bridge could safely carry a cable of the magnitude being contemplated.

81 Canada has the fourth highest ecological footprint per capita in the world
    (see www.footprintnetwork.org).
82 McNeill, *Something New*, 11.
83 MacKinnon, *Between Two Cultures*, 240.
84 Ibid., 238.
85 MacEachern, *The Institute*, 85.
86 Pratt, *Dictionary of Prince Edward Island English*, 10–11.
87 BERC, "In Prince Edward Island's Capital City, a Biomass Pioneer Just
    Keeps on Working," *Biomass Energy at Work: Case Studies of
    Community-Scale Systems in the US, Canada and Europe*, Biomass Energy
    Resource Centre, 2010.
88 http://www.climate.weatheroffice.ec.gc.ca/climate_normals/index_e.html.

EPILOGUE

1 Montgomery uses this phrase in *Anne's House of Dreams* and again in
   Further Chronicles of Avonlea.
2 Poole, *Earthrise*, 135–7.
3 "Bloomberg Backs Obama, Citing Fallout from the Storm," *New York
   Times*, 1 November 2012, http://www.nytimes.com/2012/11/02/nyregion/
   bloomberg-endorses-obama-saying-hurricane-sandy-affected-decision.
   html?pagewanted=all&_r=0.
4 Montgomery, *Jane of Lantern Hill*, 87–8.
5 I thank Heike Lotze for introducing me to this question; see, for example,
   Lotze et al., "Uncovering the Ocean's Past."
6 Prince Edward Island National Park is the most visited national park in
   Atlantic Canada, and the seventh most visited in Canada. (Apart from
   Saguenay–St Lawrence and Pacific Rim, the other most visited parks are all
   from the "Rocky Mountain Park bloc.") See http://www.pc.gc.ca/eng/docs/
   pc/attend/table3.aspx.
7 "Call for Bids Is Largest for Off-Shore Nova Scotia," media release,
   30 April 2012, http://novascotia.ca/news/release/?id=20120430001;
   see also http://energy.novascotia.ca/oil-and-gas/offshore; "BP, Shell
   Seal Largest Exploration Deals in Nova Scotia," *Financial Post*
   (16 November 2012); Canada-Nova Scotia Offshore Petroleum Board,
   http: //www.callforbids.ca/sites/default/files/node/ns151 full offshore
   map 1.jpg (2015) and Nova Scotia Department of Energy, http://
   energy.novascotia.ca/sites/default/files/files/onshore offshore May2015.
   pdf (2015).

APPENDIX

1 Academic analysis of the historical interaction between humans and the
   environment has been extremely limited on Prince Edward Island. This
   appendix is based on one of the first MA theses to utilize island studies
   research methodologies to examine Prince Edward Island as a case study in
   environmental history. See MacIntyre, "The Environmental Pre-History of
   Prince Edward Island, 1769–1970: A Reconnaissance in Force."

Bibliography

ARCHIVES

Acadia University Archives, Wolfville, Nova Scotia.
　Esther Clark Wright Collection, Robie W. Tufts Fonds, Vaughan Memorial
　　Library.
Archives Council of Prince Edward Island.
　Journal of the House of Assembly of Prince Edward Island.
Prince Edward Island Museum and Heritage Foundation, Charlottetown, PEI.
Prince Edward Island Collection, Robertson Library, University of Prince
　Edward Island, Charlottetown, PEI.
　"Fishery – Lobster." George Leard Papers (microfilm).
Public Archives and Records Office of Prince Edward Island (PARO).
　Colonial Office Correspondence, acc. 2324/8A.
　J.A. Mathieson Papers, RG 25.23.
　John MacEachern Diary, acc. 3192, item 1.
　Ledger of Roderick Munn, acc 4325.
　Smith-Alley Collection, acc. 2702, series 20, vol. 304 (1876).

PUBLISHED SOURCES

Abel, Kerry M. *Changing Places: History, Community, and Identity in
　Northeastern Ontario.* Montreal and Kingston: McGill-Queen's University
　Press 2006.
Acheson, Thomas William. "The National Policy and the Industrialization of
　the Maritimes, 1880–1910." *Acadiensis* 1, no. 2 (1972).
Acorn, Milton. *Dig Up My Heart: Selected Poems, 1952–83.* Toronto:
　McClelland & Stewart 1983.

Acts of the General Assembly of Prince Edward Island, 1773–1834. Charlottetown: James D. Haszard, King's Printer 1834.

Acts of the House of Assembly of Prince Edward Island. PEI Collection, Robertson Library, University of Prince Edward Island, Charlottetown, PEI. (Various compilations.)

Acts of the Legislative Assembly of Prince Edward Island. PEI Collection, Robertson Library, University of Prince Edward Island, Charlottetown, PEI. (Various compilations.)

Adler, Judith. "Tourism and Pastoral: A Decade of Debate." In *The Garden Transformed: Prince Edward Island, 1945–1980,* edited by Verner Smitheram, David Milne, and Satadal Dasgupta. Charlottetown: Ragweed Press 1982.

"Advanced Lobster Technology." PEI Collection, Robertson Library, University of Prince Edward Island, Charlottetown, PEI.

Agreement Covering Development Plan for Prince Edward Island. Ottawa: Queen's Printer, 1970.

Agricultural Crop Rotation Act, RSPEI 1988, A-8.01. http://www.gov.pe.ca/law/statutes/pdf/a-08_01.pdf.

Allen, P. "Final Report on Background Research and 2010 Archaeological Field Testing of Mount Stewart Historic Sites at Red Bank, Mount Stewart, Prince Edward Island." Manuscript on file, Aboriginal Affairs Secretariat, Government of Prince Edward Island, Charlottetown, 2010.

Anderson, David G. "Reindeer, Caribou, and 'Fairy Stories' of State Power." *Cultivating Arctic Landscapes: Knowing and Managing Animals in the Circumpolar North,* edited by David G. Anderson and Mark Nutall. Oxford: Berghahn Books 2003.

Anderson, N., E. Frenette, and G. Webster. "Global Village? Global Pillage: Irish Moss from PEI in the World Market." Unpublished report, PEI Collection, Robertson Library, University of Prince Edward Island, n.d.

Anderson, T.W. "Holocene Vegetation and Climatic History of Prince Edward Island." *Canadian Journal of Earth Sciences* 17 (1980).

Armstrong, David. *A Trumpet to Arms: Alternative Media in America.* Boston: South End Press 1981.

Arsenault, Georges. *L'agriculture chez les Acadiens de l'Ile-du-Prince-Edouard 1720-1980.* Summerside: Société de St. Thomas d'Aquin 1981.

– *The Island Acadians.* Charlottetown: Ragweed Press 1989.

– "The Settlement of Havre Saint-Pierre." *The Island Magazine* 53 (2003).

– "The Malpeque Bay Acadians, 1728–1758." *The Island Magazine* 66 (2009).

Arsenault, Sharon. "Packing Lobsters on the Beach: Cannery Life on Prince Edward Island." *The Island Magazine* 60 (2006).

Atlantic Geoscience Society. *The Last Billion Years: A Geological History of the Maritime Provinces of Canada.* Halifax: Nimbus 2001.

Atlantic Provinces Economic Council (APEC). "History of the Prince Edward Island Comprehensive Development Plan." PEI Collection, Robertson Library, University of Prince Edward Island.

Atwood, Margaret. *Survival: A Thematic Guide to Canadian Literature.* Toronto: House of Anansi Press 1972.

Bailey, A.G. *The Conflict of European and Eastern Algonkian Cultures, 1504–1700.* New Brunswick Museum, Monograph Series 2. Toronto: University of Toronto Press 1937. Reprinted in "The Use of Furbearers by Native North Americans after 1500," by Harold F. McGee Jr., in *Wild Furbearer Management and Conservation in North America,* edited by M. Novak et al. Toronto: Ontario Ministry of Natural Resources 1989.

Bain, Francis. *The Natural History of Prince Edward Island.* Charlottetown: G.H. Hazard 1890.

– "Every Lowly Tribe of the Deep Has Brought Its Tribute of the Store-House of Manurial Wealth." *Prince Edward Island Agriculturalist,* 11 March 1886.

Baldacchino, Godfrey. "The Coming of Age of Island Studies." *Tijdschrift voor Economische en Sociale Geografie* 95, no. 3 (2004).

– ed. *A World of Islands: An Island Studies Reader.* Charlottetown and Malta: Island Studies Press and Miller House 2007.

Baldacchino, Godfrey, and David Milne. *Lessons from the Political Economy of Small Islands: The Resourcefulness of Jurisdiction.* London: Palgrave Macmillan 2000.

Barrowclough, David A. "Expanding the Horizons of Island Archeology: Islandscapes Imaginary and Real." *Shima: The International Journal of Research into Island Cultures* 4, no. 1 (2010).

Bavington, Dean. *Managed Annihilation: An Unnatural History of the Newfoundland Cod Collapse.* Vancouver: UBC Press 2010.

Baye, P.R. "The Dynamics of Barrier Beach and Dune Systems: Great Britain and Canada." US Fish and Wildlife Service, Endangered Species Division 1982.

Beattie, Betsy. "The 'Boston States': Region, Gender, and Maritime Out-Migration, 1870–1930." In *New England and the Maritime Provinces: Connections and Comparisons,* edited by Stephen J. Hornsby and John G. Reid. Montreal: McGill-Queen's University Press 2005.

Beck, Boyde. *A Lobster Tale: The Lobster Fishery of Prince Edward Island.* Charlottetown: Prince Edward Island Museum and Heritage Foundation 2001.

Beer, Gillian. "The Island and the Aeroplane: The Case of Virginia Woolf." In *Nation and Narrative,* edited by Homi Bhabba. London: Routledge 1990.

Begley, Lorraine. "The Wave-Lined Edge of Home." *Atlantic Insight*, August
    1989.

Bell, A.K. *Getting the Lights: The Coming of Electricity to Prince Edward Island*.
    Charlottetown: Prince Edward Island Museum and Heritage Foundation
    1989.

Bell, H.P., and C.I. MacFarlane. "The Marine Algae of the Maritime Provinces
    of Canada I, List of Species with Their Distribution and Prevalence."
    Canadian Journal of Research 9 (1933).

– "The Marine Algae of the Maritime Provinces of Canada II, A Study of
    Their Ecology." *Canadian Journal of Research* 9 (1933).

Bell, Marilyn, ed. "Mr. Mann's Island: The Journal of an Absentee Proprietor,
    1840." *The Island Magazine* 33 (1993).

Bell, W. *Underwater World: Irish Moss*. Ottawa: DFO Communications Branch
    1981.

Belland, Réne J. "Mosses (Bryophyta) of the Atlantic Maritime Ecozone." In
    Assessment of Species Diversity in the Atlantic Maritime Ecozone, edited by
    D.F. McAlpine and I.M. Smith. Ottawa: NRC Research Press 2010.

Benoit et al. "State of the Ocean Report for the Gulf of St. Lawrence Integrated
    Management (GOSLIM) Area." Canadian Manuscript Reports of Fisheries
    and Aquatic Sciences 2012.

Berry, Wendell. *The Gift of Good Land: Further Essays Cultural and Agricul-
    tural*. San Francisco: North Point 1981.

– *The Unsettling of America: Culture as Agriculture*. San Franciso: Sierra Club
    1986.

Biard, P. "Missio canadensis epistola ex portu-regali in Acadia: transmissa [a]d
    praepositvm generalem Societatis Iesv a R. Petro Biardo ejvsdem." In *The
    Jesuit Relations and Allied Documents: Travels and Explorations of the
    Jesuit Missionaries in New France, 1610–1791*, vol. 2, edited by R.G.
    Thwaites. Cleveland: Burrows Brothers Co. 1896–1901.

Biggar, H.P., ed. *Voyages of Jacques Cartier*. Ottawa: King's Printer 1924.

Biomass Energy Resource Centre (BERC). "In Prince Edward Island's Capital
    City, a Biomass Pioneer Just Keeps on Working." In *Biomass Energy at
    Work: Case Studies of Community-Scale Systems in the US, Canada and
    Europe*, Biomass Energy Resource Centre 2010.

Birch, Cecil M. "The Fishing Industry of Prince Edward Island." Unpublished
    typescript, PEI Collection, Robertson Library, University of Prince Edward
    Island.

Bird, C.J., M.J. Dadswell, and D.W. Grund. "First Record of the Potential
    Nuisance Alga *Codium fragile* ssp. *tomentosoides* (Chlorophyta,

Caulerpales) in Atlantic Canada." *Proceedings of the Nova Scotia Institute of Science* 40 (1993).

Bird C.J., M. Greenwell, and J. McLachlan. "Benthic Marine Algal Flora of the North Shore of Prince Edward Island (Gulf of St. Lawrence), Canada." *Aquatic Botany* 16 (1983).

Bird, C.J., G.W. Saunders, and J. McLachlan. "Biology of *Furcellaria lumbricalis* (Hudson) Lamouroux (Rhodophyta: Gigartinales), a Commercial Carrageenophyte." *Journal of Applied Phycology* 3 (1991).

Bittermann, Rusty. "The Hierarchy of the Soil: Land and Labour in a Nineteenth-Century Cape Breton Community." *Acadiensis* 18, no. 1 (1988).

– *Rural Protest on Prince Edward Island: From British Colonization to the Escheat Movement.* Toronto: University of Toronto Press 2006.

– *Sailor's Hope: The Life and Times of William Cooper, Agrarian Radical in an Age of Revolutions.* Montreal and Kingston: McGill-Queen's University Press 2010.

– "From Wine to Wood: The Goslings of London and Prince Edward Island's Early Timber Trade." *The Island Magazine* 69 (2011).

Bittermann, Rusty, and Margaret E. McCallum. "The One That Got Away: Fishery Reserves in Prince Edward Island." *Dalhousie Law Review* 28, no. 2 (2005).

– "'One of the Finest Grass Countries I Have Met With': Prince Edward Island's Colonial Era Cattle Trade." *Agricultural History* (forthcoming).

Bleakney, J. Sherman. "A Zoogeographical Study of the Amphibians and Reptiles of Eastern Canada." National Museum of Canada Bulletin 155 (1958).

Bock, P.K. "Micmac." *Handbook of North American Indians*, edited by Bruce Trigger. Washington, DC: Smithsonian Institution 1978.

Bolger, F.W.P., ed. *Canada's Smallest Province: A History of Prince Edward Island.* Charlottetown: Prince Edward Island Centennial Committee 1973.

Bolster, W. Jeffrey. "Opportunities in Marine Environmental History." *Environmental History* 11 (2006).

– "Putting the Ocean in Atlantic History: Maritime Communities and Marine Ecology in the Northwest Atlantic, 1500–1800." *American Historical Review* 113, no. 1 (2008).

Bonnell, Jennifer, and Marcel Fortin eds. *Historical GIS Research in Canada.* Calgary: University of Calgary Press 2014.

Boomert, Arie, and Alistair J. Bright. "Island Archaeology: In Search of a New Horizon." *Island Studies Journal* 2, no. 1 (2007).

Botkin, Daniel.B. *Discordant Harmonies: A New Ecology for the Twenty-First Century.* New York: Oxford University Press 1990.

Bouck, G.B., and E. Morgan. "The Occurrence of *Codium* in Long Island Waters." *Bulletin Torrey Botany Club* 84 (1957).

Bousfield, E.L., and M.L.H. Thomas. "Postglacial Changes in Distribution of Littoral Marine Invertebrates in the Canadian Atlantic Region." *Proceedings of the Nova Scotia Institute of Science* 27, suppl. 3 (1975).

Boyd, M. "Of Price and Prices: Miminegash, Moss, and the Multinationals." *People, Resources, and Power: Critical Perspectives on Underdevelopment and Primary Industries in the Atlantic Region,* edited by G. Burrill and I. McKay. Fredericton: Acadiensis Press 1987.

Breeman, A.M. "Relative Importance of Temperature and Other Factors in Determining Geographic Boundaries of Seaweeds: Experimental and Phonological Evidence." *Helgolander Meerestuntersuchungen* 42 (1988).

– 1990. "Expected Effects of Changing Seawater Temperatures on the Geographic Distributions of Seaweed Species." In *Expected Effects of Climate Change on Marine Coastal Ecosystems,* edited by J.J. Beukema et al. Netherlands: Kluwer Academic 1990.

Brodie, J., M.D. Guiry, and M. Masuda. "Life History and Morphology of *Chondrus nipponicus* (Gigaartinales, Rhodophyta) from the North-Western Pacific." *Journal of Phycology* 28 (1991).

Broodbeck, Cyprian. "Insularity of Island Archaeologists: Comments on Rainbird's 'Islands out of Time.'" *Journal of Mediterranean Archaeology* 12, no. 2 (1999).

– *An Island Archaeology of the Early Cylade.* Cambridge: Cambridge University Press 2000.

Brookes, Alan A. "Islanders in the Boston States: 1850–1900." *The Island Magazine* 2 (1977).

Brown, Alfred Radcliffe. *The Andaman Islanders: A Study in Social Anthropology.* Cambridge, UK: Cambridge University Press 1922.

Brown, Jennifer A., Donald F. McAlpine, and Rosemary Curley. "Northern Long-Eared Bat, *Myotis septentrionalis,* (Chiroptera:Vespertilionidae) on Prince Edward Island: First Record of Occurrence and Over-Wintering." *Canadian Field-Naturalist* 121 (2007).

Bruce, Marian, and Emily Elizabeth Cran. *Working Together: Two Centuries of Co-operation on Prince Edward Island.* Charlottetown: Island Studies Press 2004.

Bumsted, J.M. "Sir James Montgomery and Prince Edward Island, 1767–1803." *Acadiensis* 7, no. 2 (1978).

- "British Colonial Policy and the Island of St. John." *Acadiensis* 9, no. 1 (1979).
- "'The Only Island There Is': The Writing of Prince Edward Island History." In *The Garden Transformed: Prince Edward Island, 1945–1980*, edited by Verner Smitheram, David Milne, and Satadal Dasgupta. Charlottetown: Ragweed Press 1982.
- *Land, Settlement and Politics on Eighteenth Century Prince Edward Island.* Kingston and Montreal: McGill-Queen's University Press 1987.
Burke, A.E. "Forestry in Prince Edward Island." *Journal of the Canadian Forestry Association* (1902).
Callbeck, Lorne C. *The Cradle of Confederation: A Brief History of Prince Edward Island from Its Discovery in 1534 to the Present Time.* Fredericton: Brunswick Press 1964.
- "Economic and Social Developments since Confederation." In *Canada's Smallest Province: A History of P.E.I.*, edited by Francis W.P. Bolger. Halifax: Nimbus 1991.
Cameron, Austin W. "Mammals of the Islands in the Gulf of St Lawrence." *National Museum of Canada Bulletin* 154 (1958).
Campbell, Claire, and Robert Summerby-Murray, eds. *Land and Sea: Environmental History in Atlantic Canada.* Fredericton: Acadiensis Press 2013.
Canada. Census Abstract. *Journal of the House of Assembly of Prince Edward Island, 1862.*
- *Annual Report of the Department of Marine and Fisheries.* Reports for 1876–1911. Sessional Papers of the Canadian Parliament, Ottawa, Canada, 1877–1912.
- *Sessional Papers of the Dominion of Canada.* Vol. 6, *Third Session of the Fourth Parliament, Session 1880–81.* 44 Victoria, Sessional Papers No. 11, A 1881.
- *Third Census of Canada, 1891.* Vol. 4, *Agriculture.* Ottawa: S.E. Dawson, 1897.
- *Report of the Canadian Lobster Commission, 1898.* Sessional Paper 11c, Parliament of Canada 1899.
- "Minutes of Meeting of Trade and Plantations, 8 July 1767." In "Land Grants in Prince Edward Island." *Report Concerning Canadian Archives for the Year 1905.* Ottawa 1906.
- "Lobster Fishing: Evidence …" Sessional Paper 21a, Parliament of Canada, 1910, vol. 13. Ottawa 1910.
- Introduction to *1961 Census of Canada: Agriculture, Bulletin 5.1-1.* Ottawa: Roger Duhamel, Queen's Printer, June 1963.

– Department of Regional Economic Expansion. *Development Plan for Prince Edward Island: A 15-Year Federal-Provincial Program for Social and Economic Advancement.* Ottawa: Queen's Printer 1969.

– "Canadian Biodiversity: Ecosystem Status and Trends 2010." Ottawa: Canadian Councils of Resource Ministers 2010.

"Canada's Terrestrial Protected Areas Status Report 2010: Number, Area and Naturalness. Edmonton: Global Forest Watch Canada 2011. http://www.globalforestwatch.ca/files/publications/20110629A_Canada_Protected_Areas_2010.pdf.

Canadian Committee for the International Biological Programme. *Ecological Reserves in the Maritimes.* Halifax 1974.

Canadian Science Advisory Secretariat (CSAS). "Canadian Marine Ecosystem Status and Trends Report." Department of Fisheries and Oceans (revised). July 2010.

Canadian Wildlife Service. *Wildlife Policy for Canada.* Environment Canada: Ottawa 1990.

Carson, Rachel. *The Sea around Us.* New York: Oxford University Press 1951.

– *Silent Spring.* Boston: Houghton Mifflin 1962.

– *The Edge of the Sea.* Boston: Houghton Mifflin 1998.

C.F.'s Diary, 1913–1952. Summerside: Annette M. Judge 1977.

Childe, V. Gordon. *Skara Brae: A Pictish Village in Orkney.* London: Kegan Paul, Trubner & Co. 1931.

Chopin, T. "The Red Alga *Chondrus crispus* Stackhouse (Irish Moss) and Carrageenans: A Review." *Canadian Technical Reports on Fisheries and Aquatic Sciences* (1986).

Chopin, T., and R. Ugarte. "The Seaweed Resource of Eastern Canada." In *World Seaweed Resources: An Authoritative Reference System*, edited by A.T. Critchley, M. Ohno, and D.B. Largo. DVD. Amsterdam: ETI BioInformatics 2006.

Chopin, T., J.D. Pringle, and R.E. Semple. "Impact of Drag Raking on the Reproductive Capacity of Southern Gulf of St. Lawrence Irish Moss *(Chondrus crispus).*" Canadian Atlantic Fisheries Science Advisory Committee Research Document, 87/90, 1987.

– "Impact of Harvesting on Frond Density and Biomass of Irish Moss (*Chondrus crispus* Stackhouse) Beds in the Southern Gulf of St. Lawrence." *Canadian Journal of Fisheries and Aquatic Sciences* 49 (1992).

Chouinard, Ghislain A., and Douglas P. Swain. "Predicted Extirpation of the Dominant Demersal Fish in a Large Marine Ecosystem: Atlantic Cod (*Gaddus morhua*) in the Southern Gulf of St. Lawrence." *Canadian Journal of Fisheries and Aquatic Science* 65 (2008).

Clark, A.H. "South Island, New Zealand, and Prince Edward Island, Canada: A Study of 'Insularity.'" *New Zealand Geographer* 3 (1947).

– *Three Centuries and the Island.* Toronto: University of Toronto Press 1959.

Clarke, David, and Patrick Maquire. *Skara Brae: Northern Europe's Best Preserved Neolithic Village.* Edinburgh: Historic Scotland 2000.

Clifford, James. *The Predicament of Culture: Twentieth-Century Ethnography, Literature, and Art.* Cambridge: Harvard University Press 1988.

Clifford, James, and George E. Marcus, eds. *Writing Culture: The Poetics and Politics of Ethnography.* Berkeley: University of California Press 1986.

Cobbett, William. *Rural Rides in the Counties of Surrey, Kent, Sussex, Hampshire* ... Original publication by Cobbett, 1830 and 1853.

Come to Prince Edward Island Canada. 1960, 1962, 1964, 1965, 1967, and 1968 editions. Charlottetown: Prince Edward Island Tourist Information/ Travel Bureau 1960–68.

Compton, Anne, ed. *The Edge of Home: Milton Acorn from the Island.* Charlottetown: Island Studies Press 2002.

Conkling, Philip. *Islands in Time: A Natural and Cultural History of the Islands of the Gulf of Maine.* Rockland, ME: Island Institute 2011.

Constance MacFarlane Seaplant Symposium. DVD. Charlottetown: Island Studies Press 2008.

Conzen, Michael P., Thomas A. Rumney, and Graeme Wynn. *A Scholar's Guide to Geographical Writing on the American and Canadian Past.* Chicago: University of Chicago Press 1993.

Cook, Francis R. "An Analysis of the Herpetofauna of Prince Edward Island." National Museum of Canada Bulletin 212 (1967).

Copes, Parzival. *The Development of the Fishing Industry in Prince Edward Island: Assessment of Progress since the Introduction of the Development Program of 1969.* Charlottetown: Department of Development 1973.

Council of Europe. *European Landscape Convention* 2004. http://conventions. coe.int/Treaty/en/Treaties/Html/176.htm.

Crawford, Michael A. "A Role for LIPs as Determinant of Evolution and Hominid Brain Development." In *Polyunsaturated Fatty Acids: Neural Function and Mental Health*, edited by Ole G. Mouritson and Michael A. Crawford. Copenhagen: Royal Danish Academy of Sciences and Letters 2007.

Croken, I.E. "Early Experiences of a Ranch Veterinary." *Rod and Gun and Canadian Silver Fox News* 31 (1929).

Cronk, Q.C.B. "Islands: Stability, Diversity, Conservation." *Biodiversity and Conservation* 6 (1997).

Cronon, William. *Changes in the Land: Indians, Colonists, and the Ecology of New England.* New York: Hill & Wang 1983.

– *Nature's Metropolis: Chicago and the Great West.* New York: Norton 1991.

Crosby, Alfred. *Ecological Imperialism.* Cambridge: Cambridge University Press 1986.

Crosskill, W.H. *Handbook of Prince Edward Island, The Garden Province of Canada.* 3rd ed. Charlottetown: Haszard & Moore 1906.

Croteau, J.T. *Cradled on the Waves.* Toronto: University of Toronto Press 1951.

Cunfer, Geoff. "Manure Matters on the Great Plains Frontier." *Journal of Interdisciplinary History* 34, no. 4 (2004).

Cunliffe, Barry. *Europe between the Oceans: Themes and Variations, 9000 BC–AD 1000.* New Haven: Yale University Press 2008.

Cunningham, Ann. "Limestone Study for Prince Edward Island: A Report Based on Information Obtained during Summer 1969." Charlottetown 1969.

Curley, Rosemary. "Population Dynamics and Morphological Variation of the Red Fox (*Vulpes vulpes rubricosa* Bangs) on Prince Edward Island." MSc thesis, Acadia University, 1983.

– "Introducing the Striped Skunk." *The Island Magazine* 17 (1985).

– "The Essential Salt Marsh." *The Island Magazine* 41 (1997).

Curran, M.L. "The Whipple Site and Paleo-Indian Tool Assemblage Variation: A Comparison of Intrasite Structuring." *Archaeology of Eastern North America* 12 (1984).

Cusack, Leonard. *A Magnificent Gift Declined: The Dalton Sanatorium of Prince Edward Island 1913–1923.* Charlottetown: Island Studies Press 2009.

Dale, M. "Phytosociological Structure of Seaweed Communities and the Invasion of *Fucus serratus* in Nova Scotia." *Canadian Journal of Botany* 60 (1982).

Daly, Whitman C. *Prince Edward Island – The Way It Was.* Pubished by the author, 1978.

D'Arcy, Paul. *The People of the Sea: Environment, Identity, and History in Oceania.* Honolulu: University of Hawaii Press 2006.

– "Maritime History in the Age of Sail from a Pacific Perspective." Paper delivered at Age of Sail Conference, Vancouver, BC, 2010.

Deal, M. "Prehistory of the Maritime Provinces." Memorial University of Newfoundland 2001. http://www.ucs.mun.ca/~mdeal/Anth3291/Anth3291sch.htm.

De Belle, Gail. *Roadside Erosion and Resource Implications in Prince Edward Island.* Ottawa: Department of Energy, Mines and Resources 1971.

DeGrace, John R. "Bathygnathus Comes Home." *The Island Magazine* 25 (1989).

– "In the Story of the Earth: The Page Called Prince Edward Island." *The Island Magazine* 46 (1999).

De Jong, N.J., and M.E. Moore. *Shipbuilding on Prince Edward Island: Enterprise in a Maritime Setting, 1787–1920*. Hull, PQ: Canadian Museum of Civilization 1994.

De la Pylaie, A.J.M. *Flore de l'Ile de Terre-Neuve et des Iles St. Pierre et Miclon*. Paris: A.F. Didot 1829.

Denys, N. *Histoire Naturelle des Peuples, des Animaux, des Arbre et Plantes de l'Amerique Septentrionale et de fes divers Climats*, edited by W. Ganong. Toronto: Champlain Society 1908 [1672].

Depraetre, Christian. "The Challenge of Nissology: A Global Outlook on the World Archipelago, Part 2: The Global and Scientific Vocation of Nissology." *Island Studies Journal* 3, no. 1 (2008).

Devor, Teresa. "The Explanatory Power of Climate History for the Nineteenth-Century Maritimes and Newfoundland: A Prospectus." *Acadiensis* 43, no. 2 (2014): 70–1.

Diamond, Jared. *Collapse: How Societies Choose to Fail or Succeed*. New York: Penguin 2005.

Dibblee, Randy. "The Beaver on Prince Edward Island: Seeking a Balance." *The Island Magazine* 35 (1994).

Dictionary of Creation Myths, edited by David and Margaret Leeming. Oxford: Oxford University Press 1994.

Dillehay, T.D., and J. Rosen. "Plant Food and Its Implications for the Peopling of the New World: A View from South America." In *The First Americans: The Pleistocene Colonization of the New World*, edited by N.G. Jablonski. San Francisco: California Academy of Sciences 2002.

Dillehay, T.D., C. Ramirez, M. Pino, M.B. Collins, J. Rossen and J.D. Navarro. "Monte Verde: Seaweed, Food, Medicine and the Peopling of South America." *Science* 320 (2008).

Dobyns, Henry F. "Estimating Aboriginal American Population: An Appraisal of Techniques with a New Hemispheric Estimate." *Current Anthropology* 7, no. 4 (1966).

Doern, G. Bruce, and Glen Toner. *The Politics of Energy: The Development and Implementation of the NEP*. Toronto: Methuen 1985.

Donahue, Brian. *The Great Meadow: Farmers and the Land in Colonial Concord*. New Haven: Yale University Press 2004.

Douglas, Thomas, Earl of Selkirk. Diary 1 (5 August–3 October, 1803, The Maritimes). *Lord Selkirk's Diary, 1803–1804: A Journal of His Travels in British North America and the North-Eastern United States*, edited by P.C.T. White. Toronto: Champlain Society 1958.

– "Settlement Formed in Prince Edward's Island / Its Difficulties / Progress / and Final Success." In *Observations on the Present State of the Highlands of*

Scotland ... Edinburgh, 1805. Reprinted in *The Writings and Papers of Thomas Douglas, Earl of Selkirk*, edited by J.M. Bumsted. Winnipeg: Manitoba Record Society 1984.

Duff, Roger. *The Moa-Hunter Period of Maori Culture*. Wellington, NZ: R.E. Owen, Government Printer 1950.

Dunn, A.M., G. Julien, W.R. Ernst, A. Cook, K.G. Doe, and P.M. Jackman. "Evaluation of Buffer Zone Effectiveness in Mitigating the Risks Associated with Agricultural Runoff in Prince Edward Island." *Science of the Total Environment* 409, no. 5 (2011).

Dupuis, Todd. "The Early History of Atlantic Salmon on Prince Edward Island." *The Island Magazine* 64 (2008).

Dyck, D. "Land Use and Farm Income in Prince Edward Island." *Economic Annalist* 31, no. 5 (1961).

– "Farmer's Views on Rural Life in Prince Edward Island." *Economic Annalist* 31, no. 6 (1961).

Dyke, Arthur S., Janis E. Dale, and Roger N. McNeely. "Marine Molluscs as Indicators of Environmental Change in Glaciated North America and Greenland during the Last 18,000 Years." *Géographie physique et Quaternaire* 50, no. 2 (1996).

Edelstein, T., M. Greenwell, C.J. Bird, and J. McLachlan. "Investigations of the Marine Algae of Nova Scotia, X. Distribution of *Fucus serratus* L. and Some Other Species of *Fucus* in the Maritime Provinces." *Proceedings of the Nova Scotia Institute of Science* 27 (1972).

Ellsworth, Alberta. "The Irish Moss Strike, October 1984." *New Maritimes* 3, no. 2 (1984).

"Endangered Spaces Progress Report No. 3." Toronto: World Wildlife Fund Canada 1992.

Environment Canada. "Canadian Biodiversity Strategy: Canada's Response to the Convention on Biological Diversity." 1995. http://www.biodivcanada. ca/560ED58E-0A7A-43D8-8754-C7DD12761EFA/CBS_e.pdf.

Erikson, T.H. "In Which Sense Do Cultural Islands Exist?" *Social Anthropology* 1 (1993).

Erskine, Anthony J. "The Great Cormorants of Eastern Canada." Canadian Wildlife Service Occasional Paper No.14. Environment Canada 1972.

– *Atlas of Breeding Birds of the Maritime Provinces*. Halifax: Nimbus Publishing and Nova Scotia Museum 1992.

Erskine, David S. *The Plants of Prince Edward Island*. Publication no. 1088, Canada Department of Agriculture, 1960. Reprinted as *The Plants of Prince Edward Island – with New Records, Nomenclatural Changes, and*

Corrections and Deletions by D.S. Erskine, with P.M. Catling and R.B. MacLaren. Publication no. 1798, Agriculture Canada 1985.

Evans, J. D. "Islands as Laboratories for the Study of Culture Process." In *The Explanation of Culture Change: Models in Prehistory*, edited by C.R. Renfrew. London: Duckworth 1973.

Farbotko, Carol. "Wishful Sinking: Disappearing Islands, Climate Refugees and Cosmopolitan Experimentation." *Asia Pacific Viewpoint* 51, no. 1 (2010).

Farlow, W.G. *The Marine Algae of New England*. Washington, DC: Report of the U.S. Fisheries Commission 1879.

Fischer, Lewis R. "The Shipping Industry of Nineteenth Century Prince Edward Island: A Brief History." *The Island Magazine* 4 (1978).

Fisheries and Oceans Canada. *State of the Ocean Report for the Gulf of St. Lawrence Integrated Management (GOSLIM) Area*, edited by H.P. Benoît, J.A. Gagné, C. Savenkoff, P. Ouellet, and M.-N. Bourassa. Canadian Manuscript Report of Fisheries and Aquatic Sciences 2986. Ottawa: Department of Fisheries and Oceans 2012.

Fisheries in the Atlantic Provinces. Background study no. 3. Ottawa: Atlantic Development Board 1969.

Fitton, J. H. "Fucoidans: Healthful Saccharides from the Sea." *Glycoscience and Nutrition* 6, no. 1 (2005).

Fleming, Keith R. *Power at Cost: Ontario Hydro and Rural Electrification, 1911–1958*. Montreal and Kingston: McGill-Queen's University Press 1991.

Flores, Dan. "Place: An Argument for Bioregional History." In *Northwest Lands, Northwest Peoples: Readings in Environmental History*, edited by Dale Goble and Paul Hirt, 31–50. Seattle: University of Washington Press 1999.

Forbes, E.R. "In Search of a Post-Confederation Maritime Historiography, 1900–1967." *Acadiensis* 8 (1978): 3–21.

– *The Maritime Rights Movement*. Montreal and Kingston: McGill-Queen's University Press 1979.

– *Challenging the Regional Stereotype: Essays on the Twentieth Century Maritimes*. Fredericton: Acadiensis Press 1989.

"Forget Report Bad News for Fishermen." *Cooper Report* 1, no. 1 (1987).

Forest, Stream and Seashore. Montreal: Intercolonial Railway and Prince Edward Island Railway of Canada 1905.

Forester, Joseph E., and Anne D. Forester. *Silver Fox Odyssey: The History of the Canadian Silver Fox Industry*. Charlottetown: Canadian Silver Fox Breeders Association and Prince Edward Island Department of Agriculture and Forestry 1980.

Fosberg, F.R., ed. *Man's Place in the Island Ecosystem*. Honolulu: Bishop Museum Press 1967.

Fralick, R.A., and A.C. Mathieson. "Ecological Studies of *Codium fragile* in New England, USA." *Marine Biology* 19 (1973).

Gallant, Cecile. *Histoire de la pêche chez les Acadiens de l'île-du-Prince-Edouard*. Summerside: La Societé Saint-Thomas d'Aquin 1980.

Gallant, D., L. Vasseur, M. Dumond, E. Tremblay, and C.H. Berube. "Habitat Selection by River Otters (*Lontra canadensis*) under Contrasting Land-Use Regimes." *Canadian Journal of Zoology* 87 (2009).

Gammel, Irene. "Embodied Landscape Aesthetics." *The Lion and the Unicorn* 34, no. 2 (2010).

Garbary, D.J., H. Vandermeulen, and K.Y. Kim. "*Codium fragile ssp. tomentosoides* (Chlorophyta) Invades the Gulf of St. Lawrence, Atlantic Canada." *Botanica Marina* 40 (1997).

Garron, Christine A., Kimberly C. Davis, and William R. Ernst. "Near-Field Air Concentrations of Pesticides in Potato Agriculture in Prince Edward Island." *Pest Management Science* 65, no. 6 (2009).

Gastner, Carol B. *Rachel Carson*. New York: Frederick Unger 1983.

Gaudet, J. Frank, *Forestry Past and Present on Prince Edward Island*. Charlottetown: Department of Agriculture and Forestry 1979.

Gesner, Abraham. Report on the Geological Survey of Prince Edward Island, 1846. Unpublished report, PARO, RG1, series 11, file 1.

Gilgan, M.W., B.G. Burns, and G.J. Landry. "Distribution and Magnitude of Domoic Acid Contamination of Shellfish in Atlantic Canada during 1988. In *Toxic marine phytoplankton*, edited by E. Granéli, B. Sundström, L. Edler, and D.M. Anderson. New York: Elsevier Science 1990.

Gilhooly, P.J., and A. Gosselin. "Farm Management Study of Prince Edward Island Potato Farms." *Economic Annalist*, May 1947.

Gilles Theriault & Associates. *Report on Consultations on Ecosystem Overview Report for the Northumberland Strait*. Moncton: Fisheries and Oceans Canada 2006.

Gillis, John. *Islands of the Mind: How the Human Imagination Created the Atlantic World*. New York: Palgrave/Macmillan 2004.

– *The Human Shore: Seacoasts in History*. Chicago: University of Chicago Press 2012.

Gillispie, Rosemary G., and David A. Clague, eds. *Encylopedia of Islands*. Berkeley: University of California Press 2009.

Girard, Michel F. *L'écologisme retrouvé: Essor et déclin de la Commission de la Conservation du Canada*. Ottawa: University of Ottawa Press 1994.

Glacken, C. "Changing Ideas of the Habitable World." In *Man's Role in Changing the Phase of the Earth*, edited by W.L. Thomas. Chicago: University of Illinois Press 1956.

Glen, William D. *Prince Edward Island Wildlife Legislation, 1780–1951.* Charlottetown: Prince Edward Island Department of Agriculture, Fisheries and Forestry 1995.

– "Prince Edward Island 1935/1936 Forest Cover Type Mapping." Charlottetown: Prince Edward Island Department of Agriculture, Fisheries and Forestry 1997.

Glen, William, and Douglas Sobey. "The Fall – and Rise? – of White Pine in the Forests of Prince Edward Island." *The Island Magazine* 65 (2009).

Gloin, Douglas. "Living Green before Their Time." *Toronto Star*, 20 May 2007.

Godfrey, W. Earl. "Birds of Prince Edward Island." National Museum of Canada Bulletin 132. Ottawa: Department of Northern Affairs and National Resources 1954.

Goin' to the Corner: A History of Elmsdale, Elmsdale West, and Brockton, Prince Edward Island. Vol. 1, *The Community.* Summerside: Crescent Isle 2006.

Goldman, Irving. "Variations in Polynesian Social Organization." *Journal of the Polynesian Society* 66 no. 4 (1957).

Goode, George Brown, Joseph W. Collins, H.E. Earll, and A. Howard Clark. *Materials for a History of the Mackerel Fishery.* Washington, DC: Government Printing Office 1883.

Goodenough, Ward. "Oceania and the Problem of Controls in the Study of Cultural and Human Evolution." *Journal of the Polynesian Society* 66, no. 2 (1957).

Gordon, H. Scott. *The Fishing Industry of Prince Edward Island.* Ottawa: Department of Fisheries 1952.

Gormley, K., D. Guignion, and K. Teather. "Distribution and Abundance of Slimy Sculpin (*Cottus cognatus*) on Prince Edward Island, Canada." *American Midland Naturalist* 1153, no. 1 (2005).

Gormley, Karen, Kevin L. Teather, and Daryl L. Guignion. "Changes in Salmonid Communities Associated with Pesticide Runoff Events." *Ecotoxicology* 14 (2005).

Gorveatt, Nancy. "'Polluted with Factories': Lobster Canning on Prince Edward Island." *The Island Magazine* 57 (2005).

Gosden, C., and C. Pavlides. "Are Islands Insular? Landscape vs. Seascape in the Case of the Arawe Islands, Papua New Guinea." *Archaeology in Oceania* 29 (1994).

Gould, Rebecca Kneale. *At Home in Nature: Modern Homesteading and Spiritual Practice in America*. Berkeley: University of California Press 2005.

Gower, John Gordon. "The Impact of Alternative Ideology on Landscape: The Back-to-the-Land Movement in the Slocan Valley." Master's thesis, University of British Columbia, 1990.

Graham, Allan. *A Photo History of the Prince Edward Island Railway*. Summerside: Allan Graham 2000.

Gramly, R.M. "The Vail Site: A Palaeo-Indian Encampment in Maine." *Bulletin of the Buffalo Society of Natural Sciences* (1982).

Greenhill, Basil. *The Evolution of the Wooden Ship*. London: R.T. Batsford 1988.

Greer, S., D. Strand, and P. Sias. "People, Caribou and Ice in the Dan History and Culture – Past Dimensions, Current Connections." In *Ta'n Wetapeksi'k: Understanding from Where We Come*, edited by T. Bernard, L. Rosenmeier, and S.L. Farrell. Proceedings of the 2005 Debert Research Workshop, Debert, Nova Scotia. Truro: Confederacy of Mainland Mi'kmaq 2011.

Griffin, Diane. "Prince Edward Island." In *Protecting Canada's Endangered Spaces, an Owner's Manual*, edited by M. Hummel. Toronto: Key Porter 1995.

Griffin, Watson. "Canada: The Land of Waterways." *Journal of the American Geographical Society of New York* 22 (1890).

Grove, Richard. *Green Imperialism: Colonial Expansion, Tropical Island Edens and the Origins of Environmentalism, 1600–1860*. Cambridge: Cambridge University Press 1995.

– "The Island and the History of Environmentalism: The Case of St Vincent." In *Nature and Society in Historical Context*, edited by Mikulas Teich, Roy Porter, and Bo Gustafsson. Cambridge: Cambridge University Press 1997.

– The Culture of Islands and the History of Environmental Concern. Harvard Seminar on Environmental Values, 18 April 2000. http://ecoethics.net/hsev/200004txt.htm.

Gurgel, C.F.D, S. Fredericq, and J.N. Norris. "Phylogeography of *Gracilaria tikvahiae* (Gracilariaceae, Rhodophyta): A Study of Genetic Discontinuity in a Continuously Distributed Species Based on Molecular Evidence." *Journal of Phycology* 40 (2004).

Gwyn, Julian. "Golden Age or Bronze Moment? Wealth and Poverty in Nova Scotia: The 1850s and 1860s." *Canadian Papers in Rural History* 8 (1992).

Haddon, A.C. "The Cambridge Anthropological Expedition to the Torres Straits and Sarawak." *Nature* (August 1899).

– ed. *Reports of the Cambridge Anthropological Expedition to Torres Strait*. Cambridge: Cambridge University Press 1901–31.

Hall, D.J. "The Commission of Conservation (1909–1921)." In *Clifford Sifton: A Lonely Eminence, 1901–1929*, edited by D.J. Hall. Vancouver: UBC Press 1985.

Halliday, W.E.D. *A Forest Classification for Canada*. Bulletin 89. Ottawa: Department of Mines and Resources, Forest Service 1937.

Hamell, G. "Strawberries, Floating Islands, and Rabbit Captains: Mythical Realities and European Contact in the Northeast during the Sixteenth and Seventeenth Centuries." *Journal of Canadian Studies* 21, no. 14 (1987).

Handbook of North American Indians, edited by Bruce Trigger. Washington, DC: Smithsonian Institution 1978.

Hanic, L. "Testing and Evaluation of the Genu Sea Plants Drag Cutter Harvester on PEI." Report to Prince Edward Island Department of Fisheries. Charlottetown 1975.

Hardin, G. "The Tragedy of the Commons." *Science* 162 (1968).

Harris, Julie, and Jennifer Mueller. "Making Science Beautiful: The Central Experimental Farm, 1886–1939." *Ontario History* 89, no. 2 (1997).

Harris, Marvin. *The Rise of Anthropological Theory: A History of Theories of Culture*. New York: Thomas Y. Crowell 1968.

Hartshorne, Richard. *The Nature of Geography: A Critical Survey of Current Thought in the Light of the Past*. Lancaster, PA: Association of American Geographers 1939.

– *Perspective on the Nature* of Geography. Chicago: Rand McNally & Co. 1959.

Harvey, D.C. *The French Regime in Prince Edward Island*. New Haven: Yale University Press 1926.

– ed. *Journeys to the Island of St. John or Prince Edward Island, 1775–1832*. Toronto: Macmillan 1955.

Harza of Canada. *Soil Conservation Program for the Atlantic Provinces: A Report Prepared for the Department of Forestry and Rural Development*. Moncton 1968.

Hatvany, Matthew. "Tenant, Landlord, and the New Middle Class." PhD diss., University of Maine, 1996.

– "Tenant, Landlord and Historian: A Thematic Review of the 'Polarization' Process in the Writing of 19th-Century Prince Edward Island History." *Acadiensis* 27, no. 1 (1997).

– "'Wedded to the Marshes': Salt Marshes and Socio-Economic Differentiation in Early Prince Edward Island." *Acadiensis* 30, no. 2 (2001).

Hay, G.U., and A.H. MacKay. "Marine Algae of New Brunswick." *Transactions of the Royal Society of Canada* 5 (1887).

Health Canada Pest Management Regulatory Agency. "Re-Evaluation Decision, RVD 2010-16, Carbofuran." Health Canada 2010.

Help Stop the Spread of Aquatic Invasive Species. Prince Edward Island Aquaculture Alliance, n.d.

Henderson, T. Stephen. "A Defensive Alliance: The Maritime Provinces and the Turgeon Commission on Transportation, 1948–1951." *Acadiensis* 35 (2006).

Henny, Charles J., Robert A. Grove, James L. Kaiser, and Branden L. Johnson. "North American Osprey Populations and Contaminants: Historic Overview and Contemporary Perspectives." *Journal of Toxicology and Environmental Health*, part B, 13 (2010).

Herrick, F.H. "The Protection of the Lobster Industry." Supplement to *25th Annual Report of the Department of Marine and Fisheries, 1893.* http://virtualology. com/virtualmuseumofnaturalhistory/aquatichall/lobsterpicture.com/.

Heyland, J.D. "The Decline of Gray Partridge, *Perdix perdix*, and Ring-Necked Pheasant, *Phasianus colchicus*, on Prince Edward Island, 1955–1961." Ottawa: Canadian Wildlife Service Report 1965.

"Here Is a Calm and Peaceful Land": Prince Edward Island. Charlottetown: Department of Tourism 1975.

Hill, N.M., and C.S. Blaney. "Exotic and Invasive Vascular Plants of the Atlantic Maritime Ecozone." In *Assessment of Species Diversity in the Atlantic Maritime Ecozone*, edited by D.F. McAlpine and I.M. Smith. Ottawa: NRC Research Press 2010.

Hill, Samuel Smith. *A Short Account of Prince Edward Island.* London: Madden & Co. 1839.

Hoarau, G., J.A. Coyer, J.H. Veldsink, W.T. Stam, and J.L. Olsen. "Glacial Refugia and Recolonization Pathways in the Brown Seaweed *Fucus serratus.*" *Molecular Ecology* 16 (2007).

Hoffman, B.G. "The Historical Ethnography of the Micmac of the Sixteenth and Seventeenth Centuries." PhD diss., Berkeley: University of California 1946.

Hoffmann, R.C., and Verena Winiwarter. "Making Land and Water Meet: The Cycling of Nutrients between Fields and Ponds in Pre-Modern Europe." *Agricultural History* 84, no. 3 (2010).

Hogan, Geoff. "Breeding Parameters of Great Cormorants (*Palacrocorax carbo carbo*) at Mixed Species Colonies on Prince Edward Island, Canada." MSc thesis, Brock University, St Catharines, ON, 1979.

– "An Infinite Number of Wood Pigeons." *The Island Magazine* 16 (1984).

– "'White Gold and Train Oil': The Walrus on P.E.I." *The Island Magazine* 20 (1987).

Holland, Samuel. Letter dated 4 March 1765 to Lord Hillsborough. Unpublished handwritten transcript, PARO, acc. 2324/8A.

– Letter dated 8 October 1765 to Richard Cumberland Esq., to accompany an annotated "Plan of the Island of St. John in the Province of Nova Scotia ..." Unpublished handwritten transcript, PARO, acc. 2324/8A.

– "Plan of the Island of St. John in the Province of Nova Scotia ... 19 September 1765." PARO, acc. 0617C. Photographic copy of a hand-drawn copy of the original plan at British National Archives, Kew (CO700/Prince Edward Island 3) made by C. Pettigrew of the Public Record Office in 1931, verified in the margin, dated 24 February 1932, by H.P. Biggar as "a correct copy."

Holloway, Emily. "'Give Us This Day Our Development Plan ...': The Politics of the Prince Edward Island Comprehensive Development Plan, 1969–1984." M.A. thesis, University of Guelph, 2005.

Holm, J. *Pidgins and Creoles.* Vol. 2, *Reference Survey.* Cambridge Language Surveys. New York: Cambridge University Press 1989.

Holman, H.T. "'A Lamp to Light Their Paths': Lighting the Streets of Charlottetown." In *Gaslights, Epidemics and Vagabond Cows: Charlottetown in the Victorian Era,* edited by D. Baldwin and T. Spira. Charlottetown: Ragweed Press 1988.

Holmes, William H. "Aboriginal Shell-Heaps of the Middle Atlantic Tidewater Region." *American Anthropologist* 9, no. 1 (1907).

Holmsgaard, J.E., M. Greenwell, and J. McLachlan. "Biomass and Vertical Distribution of *Furcellaria lumbricalis* and Associated Algae." *Proceedings of the International Seaweed Symposium* 10 (1981).

Hornby, Jim. "Bear Facts: The History and Folklore of Island Bears." *The Island Magazine* 22 (1987).

– "Bear Facts: The History and Folklore of Island Bears, Part 2." *The Island Magazine* 23 (1988).

Hough, Franklin. "Forestry of the Future." Speech delivered at American Forestry Congress, Cincinnati, April 1882.

Howatt, Betty King. "Farming Today: Use/Misuse of the Soil." *P.E.I. Environeer* 6 (1978).

HRH the Prince of Wales, with Tony Juniper and Ian Skelly. *Harmony: A New Way of Looking at Our World.* London: HarperCollins 2010.

Hudson, J. Arthur, and S. Jean Meggison. *Preserving the Past: A History of Cascumpec — Fortune Cove, 1779–1979.* Cascumpec-Fortune Cove Heritage Society 1979.

Hummel, M., and A. Hackman. Introduction to *Protecting Canada's Endangered Spaces, an Owner's Manual,* edited by M. Hummel. Toronto: Key Porter 1995.

Hutchings, J.S., and R.A. Myers. "The Biological Collapse of Atlantic Cod off Newfoundland and Labrador." In *The North Atlantic Fisheries*. Edited by Lawrence Felt and Ragnar Arnason. Charlottetown: Institute of Island Studies 1995.

Illustrated Historical Atlas of the Province of Prince Edward Island. Philadelphia: J.H. Meacham & Co. 1880. Reprint, Oshawa, ON: Maracle Press 1983.

Inwood, Kris E., ed. *Farm, Factory and Fortune: New Studies in the Economic History of the Maritime Provinces*. Fredericton: Acadiensis Press 1993.

Inwood, Kris, and Jim Irwin. "Land, Income and Regional Inequality: New Estimates of Provincial Incomes and Growth in Canada, 1871–1891." *Acadiensis* 31, no. 2 (2002).

Intercolonial Railway and Prince Edward Island Railway. *Forest, Stream and Seashore*. 1905. Reprint, Whitefish, MT: Kessinger Publishing 2010.

"Irish Moss Industry." *Cooper Report* 3, no. 3 (1987).

Jacob, Jeffrey. *New Pioneers: The Back-to-the-Land Movement and the Search for a Sustainable Future*. University Park, PA: Pennsylvania State University Press 1997.

Jacobsen, Rowan. *The Living Shore: Rediscovering a Lost World*. New York: Bloomsbury 2009.

Janssen, William. "Agriculture in Transition." In *The Garden Transformed: Prince Edward Island, 1945–1980*, edited by Werner Smitheram, David Milne, and Satadal Dasgupta. Charlottetown: Ragweed Press 1982.

Jay, Martin. "Scopic Regimes of Modernity." In *Vision and Visuality*, edited by Hal Foster. Seattle: Bay Press 1988.

Johnston, C.E., and J.C. Cheverie. "Repopulation of a Coastal Stream by Brook Trout and Rainbow Trout after Endosulfan Poisoning." *Progressive Fish-Culturist* 42, no. 2 (1980).

Johnstone, Kenneth. *The Aquatic Explorers: A History of the Fisheries Research Board of Canada*. Toronto: University of Toronto Press 1977.

Johnstone, Walter. *A Series of Letters Descriptive of Prince Edward Island in the Gulph of St. Lawrence*. Dumfries: J. Swan, 1822. Reprinted in *Journeys to the Island of St. John or Prince Edward Island*, edited by D.C. Harvey. Toronto: MacMillan 1955.

Jones, Christopher. *Routes of Power: Energy and Modern America*. Cambridge: Harvard University Press 2014.

Jones, J. Walter. *Fur-Farming in Canada*. 2nd ed. Commission of Conservation, Canada. Ottawa: Mortimer Company 1914.

Jørgensen, Dolly. "Not by Human Hands: Five Technological Tenets for Environmental History in the Anthropocene." *Environment and History* 20, no. 4 (2014).

Journal of the House of Assembly of Prince Edward Island. Charlottetown: George T. Haszard, 1830, 1851, 1856, 1861, 1866.

Judd, Richard W. *Second Nature: An Environmental History of New England.* Amherst: University of Massachusetts Press 2014.

Keenlyside, D.L. "Prehistory of the Gulf of St. Lawrence 'Southern Basin': Future Perspectives." In *Proceedings of the 1980 Conference on the Future of Archaeology in the Maritimes*, edited by D.M. Shimabuku. Halifax: Department of Anthropology Occasional Papers, Saint Mary's University, 1980.

– "In Search of the Island's First Peoples." *The Island Magazine* 13 (1983).

– "Ulus and Spearpoints: Two New Archaeological Finds from Prince Edward Island." *The Island Magazine* 16 (1984).

– "La periode Paleoindienne sur L'Île-du-Prince-Édouard." *Recherches amerindiennes au Quebec* 15, nos. 1–2 (1985).

– *An Archaeological Survey of the Upper Reaches of the Tracadie Estuary, New Brunswick.* Fredericton: Department of Municipalities, Culture and Housing 1990.

– "Palaeo-Indian Occupations of the Maritimes Region of Canada." In *Clovis: Origins and Adaptations*, edited by R. Bonnichsen and K. Turnmire. Orono, ME: Center for the Study of the First Americans 1991.

– "Progress Report Sutherland Site CcCp-7 Analysis, St Peter's Bay, PEI." Manuscript on file with Aboriginal Affairs Secretariat, Office of the Provincial Archaeologist, Charlottetown, 2002.

– "New Finds from the Island's Offshore." *The Island Magazine* 59 (2006).

– "Observations on Debert and the Late Palaeo/Early Archaic Transition." In *Ta'n Wetapeksi'k: Understanding from Where We Come*, edited by T. Bernard, L. Rosenmeier, and S.L. Farrell. Proceedings of the 2005 Debert Research Workshop, Debert, Nova Scotia. Truro: Confederacy of Mainland Mi'kmaq 2011.

Keenlyside, D.L., and C. Andreasen. "Indigenous Fishing in Northeast North America." In *A History of the North Atlantic Fisheries*, vol. 1, *From Early Times to the Mid-Nineteenth Century*, edited by D.J. Starkey, J. Thor, and I. Heidbrink. Bremen, Germany: Verlag H.M. Hauschild GmbH 2009.

Kemp, E. *Oyster Fisheries of Canada: A Survey and Practical Guide on Oyster Culture.* Ottawa: Government Printer 1899.

Kennett, Douglas J. *The Island Chumasch: Behavioral Ecology in a Maritime Society.* Berkeley: University of California Press 2005.

Keough, W.G. *The Slender Thread: Irish Women on the Southern Avalon, 1750–1860.* New York: Columbia University Press 2008.

Kirk, Andrew G. *Counterculture Green: The Whole Earth Catalog and American Environmentalism.* Lawrence: University of Kansas Press 2007.

Knight, A. *Official Report on Lobster Investigations, 1917, and Methods of Increasing the Lobster Supply in Canada*. Ottawa: King's Printer 1918.

Korneski, Kurt. "Development and Degradation: The Emergence and Collapse of the Lobster Fishery on Newfoundland's West Coast, 1856–1924." *Acadiensis* 41, no. 1 (2012).

Kranck, K. "Geomorphological Development and Post-Pleistocene Sea Level Changes, Northumberland Strait, Maritime Provinces." *Canadian Journal of Earth Sciences* 9 (1972).

Kristmanson, H. "The Ceramic Sequence for Southwestern Nova Scotia: A Refinement of the Petersen/Sanger Model." M.A. thesis, Memorial University of Newfoundland, 1992.

– "Taking Archaeology to Court: The Use of Archaeology in Aboriginal Rights and Title Litigation." PhD diss., Manchester, UK: University of Manchester, 2008.

– "Permit Report. Geophysical Survey. Pointe-Aux-Vieux Site (CdDx-5), Port Hill, PEI. Manuscript on file with Aboriginal Affairs Secretariat, Government of Prince Edward Island, Charlottetown, 2008.

– "Archaeology at Pointe-aux-Vieux." *The Island Magazine* 66 (2009).

– "Archaeological Investigations – Malpeque Bay Archeological Project. Pitawelkek Site, George's Island, PEI, October 7 and 9, 2009." Manuscript on file with Aboriginal Affairs Secretariat, Government of Prince Edward Island, Charlottetown, 2009.

– Malpeque Bay Archaeological Project. Excavations at Pointe-Aux-Vieux (CdCx-5). Manuscript on file with Aboriginal Affairs Secretariat, Government of Prince Edward Island, Charlottetown, 2012.

– Malpeque Bay Archaeological Project. Excavations at Pointe-Aux-Vieux (CdCx-5). Site Report in progress. Manuscript on file with Aboriginal Affairs Secretariat, Government of Prince Edward Island, Charlottetown, 2013.

– "Archaeology at Pointe-aux-Vieux, Part 1." *The Island Magazine* 78 (2015).

Kroeber, A.L. "Native American Population." *American Anthropologist* 36, no. 1 (1934).

Kuklick, H. "Islands in the Pacific: Darwinian Biogeography and British Anthropology." *American Ethnologist* 23, no. 3 (1996).

Lape, Peter V. "The Isolation Metaphor in Island Archaeology." *Voyages of Discovery: The Archaeology of Islands*, edited by Scott M. Fitzpatrick. Westport, CN: Praeger 2004.

Larkin, Maureen. "Our Way of Living: Survival Strategies in Lobster Fishing Households in Prince Edward Island." M.A. thesis, Memorial University of Newfoundland, 1990.

Larson, Edward J. *Evolution's Workshop: God and Science on the Galapagos Islands*. New York: Basic Books 2001.

Lattimer, J.E. *Economic Survey of Prince Edward Island*. Charlottetown: Department of Reconstruction 1944.

– *Taxation in Prince Edward Island, A Report*. Charlottetown: Department of Reconstruction 1945.

Lawrence, E., A.R.W. Jackson and J.M. Jackson. *Longman Dictionary of Environmental Science*. London: Addison Wesley Longman 1998.

Lawson, John. *Letters on Prince Edward Island*. Charlottetown: Haszard 1851.

Legget, Robert F. *Railways of Canada*. Vancouver: Douglas & McIntyre 1973.

Leonard, Kevin. "Mi'kmaq Culture during the Late Woodland and Early Historic Period." Ph.D. diss., Department of Anthropology, University of Toronto, 1996.

– "Archaeological Remains from a Mid-Eighteenth Century Acadian Well in Prince Edward Island National Park – Greenwich (15F2C)." Unpublished manuscript, revised 2010.

Levangie, D., and M. Soto Quenti. *Medicinal Seaplants of the Mi'kmaq and Williche*. Charlottetown: Island Studies Press 2008.

Lewellin, John L. *Emigration. Prince Edward Island: A Brief but Faithful Account of This Fine Colony*. Charlotte-Town [*sic*]: James D. Haszard, 1832. Reprinted in *Journeys to the Island of St. John or Prince Edward Island*, edited by D.C. Harvey. Toronto: Macmillan 1955.

Lewis, Henry T. "Reconstructing Patterns of Indian Burning in Southwestern Oregon." In *Living with the Land: The Indians of Southwest Oregon*, edited by Nan Hannon and Richard K. Olmo. Medford, OR: Southern Oregon Historical Society 1990.

Lewis, Martin W., and Karen Wigen. *Myth of Continents: A Critique of Metageography*. Berkeley: University of California Press 1997.

Lighting the Way: Knowledge Assessment in Prince Edward Island. National Research Council, co-published with National Academy Press and Island Studies Press, WA: National Academy Press 1999.

Lindstrom, S.C. "Possible Sister Groups and Phylogenetic Relationships among Selected North Pacific and North Atlantic Rhodophyta." *Helgolander Meerestuntersuchungen* 41 (1987).

Lockerby, Earle. "The Comte de Saint-Pierre and Île Saint-Jean." *The Island Magazine* 61 (2007).

Loefgren, Orvar. "From Peasant Fishing to Industrial Trawling: A Comparative Discussion of Modernization Processes in Some Northern Atlantic Regions."

In *Modernization and Marine Fisheries Policy*, edited by John Maolo and Michael Orban. Ann Arbor, MI: Ann Arbor Science 1982.

Losos, Jonathan B., and Robert E. Ricklefs. "Adaptation and Diversification on Islands." *Nature* 457 (February 2009).

Lotze, Heike, et al. "Uncovering the Ocean's Past." *Shifting Baselines: The Past and the Future of Ocean Fisheries*, edited by Jeremy B.C. Jackson, Karen E. Alexander, and Enric Sala. Washington, DC: Island Press 2011.

Lotze, Heike K., H.S. Lenihan, and B. Bourke et al. "Depletion, Degradation, and Recovery Potential of Estuaries and Coastal Seas." *Science Reprint* 312 (June 2006).

Loucks, O.L. "A Forest Classification for the Maritime Provinces." *Proceedings of the Nova Scotia Institute of Science* 25, part 2, 1961.

Lowenthal, David. *George Perkins Marsh: Prophet of Conservation*. Seattle: University of Washington Press 2000.

Lower, A.R.M. *Settlement and the Forest Frontier in Eastern Canada*. Toronto: Macmillan 1936.

– *Great Britain's Woodyard: British America and the Timber Trade, 1763–1867*. Montreal: McGill-Queen's University Press 1973.

Luning, K. *Seaweeds, Their Environment, Biogeography and Ecophysiology*. John Wiley & Sons 1990.

Luning, K., M.D. Guiry, and M. Masuda. "Upper Temperature Tolerance of North Atlantic and North Pacific Geographic Isolates of Chondrus Species (Rhodophyta)." *Helgolander Meerestuntersuchungen* 41 (1987).

MacArthur, Robert H., and Edward O. Wilson. *The Theory of Island Biogeography*. New Jersey: Princeton University Press 1967.

Macdonald, Archibald John. "Father's Memoirs, Written in 1909 in His 76th Year." Unpublished manuscript, copy in possession of Edward MacDonald.

MacDonald, Edward. "Running the Lines." *The Island Magazine* 19 (1986).

– "The Yankee Gale." *The Island Magazine* 38 (1995).

– *If You're Stronghearted: Prince Edward Island in the Twentieth Century*. Charlottetown: Prince Edward Island Museum and Heritage Foundation 2000.

– "A Landscape … with Figures: Tourism and Environment on Prince Edward Island." *Land and Sea: Environmental History in Atlantic Canada*, edited by Claire Campbell and Robert Summerby-Murray. Fredericton: Acadiensis Press 2013.

MacDonald, George. *Debert: A Palaeo-Indian Site in Central Nova Scotia*. Ottawa: National Museum of Man 1968.

MacDougall, Gerald. "The Return of the Bald Eagle." *The Island Magazine* 61 (2007).

MacDougall, J.I., C. Veer, and F. Wilson. *Soils of Prince Edward Island: Prince Edward Island Soil Survey*. Agriculture Canada, Research Branch 1988.

MacDowell, Laurel Sefton. *An Environmental History of Canada*. Toronto: University of British Columbia Press 2012.

MacEachern, Alan. "No Island Is an Island: A History of Tourism on Prince Edward Island, 1870–1939." M.A. thesis, Queen's University, 1991.

– *Natural Selections: National Parks in Atlantic Canada*. Kingston and Montreal: McGill-Queen's University Press 2001.

– *The Institute of Man and Resources: An Environmental Fable*. Charlottetown: Island Studies Press 2003.

– "What Can This Place Teach Us?" Program for Time and a Place: Environmental Histories, Environmental Futures, and Prince Edward Island Conference, Institute of Island Studies, University of Prince Edward Island, 2010.

MacEachern, Alan, and Ryan O'Connor. "Back to the Island: The Back-to-the-Land Movement on PEI." http://niche-canada.org/member-projects/backto-theisland/narrative2.html.

MacEachern, Alan, and William J. Turkel. *Method and Meaning in Canadian Environmental History*. Toronto: Nelson Education 2009.

MacFadyen, Joshua. "Drawing Lines in the Ice: Regulating Mussel Mud Digging in the Southern Gulf of St. Lawrence." In *Land and Sea: Environmental Histories of Atlantic Canada*, edited by Claire Campbell and Robert Summerby-Murray. Fredericton: Acadiensis Press 2013.

MacFadyen, Joshua, and William Glen. "Top-Down History: Delimiting Forests, Farms, and the Agricultural Census on Prince Edward Island Using Aerial Photography, c.1900–2000." *Historical Geographic Information Systems in Canada*, edited by Jennifer Bonnell and Marcel Fortin. Canadian History and Environment Series. Calgary: University of Calgary Press 2013.

MacFarlane, C.I. *Irish Moss in the Maritime Provinces*. Halifax: Nova Scotia Research Foundation 1956.

– "The Seaweed Industry of the Maritimes Provinces." *Proceedings of the International Seaweed Symposium* 4 (1964).

– "Ecological Observations on Two Marine Algae in Nova Scotia – *Furcellaria fastigiata* and *Polyides rotundus*." In *Botanica Gothburgensia* 3, edited by T. Levring. Proceedings of the 5th Marine Biological Symposium, 1964. Halifax: Nova Scotia Research Foundation 1965.

MacGregor, John. *Historical and Descriptive Sketches of the Maritime Colonies of British North America*. London: Longman, Rees, Orme, Brown & Green, 1828. Reprint, Wakefield, UK: S.R. Publishers; New York: Johnson Reprint 1968.

– *British America*. Vol. 1. Edinburgh: Blackwood 1832.

MacIntyre, Colin A. "The Environmental Pre-History of Prince Edward Island, 1769–1970: A Reconnaissance in Force." Master's thesis, University of Prince Edward Island, 2010.

Mack, John. *The Sea: A Cultural History*. London: Reaktion 2011.

MacKinnon, D.A. "Fisheries." In *Past and Present of Prince Edward Island*, edited by D.A. MacKinnon and A.B. Warburton. Charlottetown: B.F. Bowen [1906].

MacKinnon, Robert A., and Ronald H. Walder. "Agriculture in Atlantic Canada, 1851." *The Historical Atlas of Canada*, vol. 1. Toronto: University of Toronto Press 1993.

MacKinnon, Robert, and Graeme Wynn. "Nova Scotian Agriculture in the 'Golden Age': A New Look." *Geographical Perspectives on the Maritime Provinces*, edited by Douglas Day. Halifax: Saint Mary's University 1988.

MacKinnon, Wayne. *Between Two Cultures: The Alex Campbell Years*. Stratford, PEI: Tea Hill Press 2005.

MacKinnon, Wayne, and Elinor Vass. *The Best of the Past: Traditional Sustainable Agriculture in Prince Edward Island*. Prepared for the Prince Edward Island Department of Agriculture. Charlottetown: Institute of Island Studies, March 1989.

MacNeil, Alan R. "The Acadian Legacy and Agricultural Development in Nova Scotia, 1760–1861." In *Farm Factory and Fortune: New Studies in the Economic History of the Maritime Provinces*, edited by K. Inwood, 1–16. Fredericton: Acadiensis Press 1993.

Macphail, Andrew. "Discoloration in Canned Lobsters." Supplement to the *29th Annual Report of the Department of Marine and Fisheries*. Ottawa: 1897.

– *The Master's Wife*. Toronto: McClelland & Stewart 1977.

MacQuarrie, Ian. *Soil Erosion on Prince Edward Island: A Report to Executive Council*. Charlottetown: Environmental Associates 1979.

– *Bonshaw Hills*. Charlottetown: Island Studies Press 1989.

– "The Case of the Unsatisfactory Collection." *The Island Magazine* 36 (1994).

MacQuarrie, Ian, and Daryl Guignion. "Hunting for Money: Market Gunning on Prince Edward Island." *The Island Magazine* 19 (1986).

Majka, Christopher. "Sugar Shack Bugs." *The Island Magazine* 68 (2010).

Malinowski, Bronislaw. *Argonauts of the Western Pacific*. London: Routledge & Kegan Paul 1922.

Mancke, Elizabeth. "Spaces of Power in the Early Modern Northeast." In *New England and the Maritime Provinces*, edited by Stephen J. Hornsby and John G. Reid. Montreal: McGill-Queen's University Press 2005.

Mandelbrot, Benoit. "How Long Is the Coast of Britain? Statistical Self-Similarity and Fractional Dimension." *Science*, New Series, 156, no. 3775 (1967).

Marean, Curtis W., Miryam Bar-Matthews, Jocelyn Bernatchez, et al. "Early Human Use of Marine Resources and Pigment in South Africa during the Middle Peistocene." *Nature* 449 (2007).

Marris, Emma. "Reconstituted Edens." *Nature* 472 (2011).

Marsh, George Perkins. *Man and Nature; or, Physical Geography as Modified by Human Action.* New York: Charles Scribner 1864.

Martin, C. "The European Impact on the Culture of a Northeastern Algonquian Tribe: An Ecological Interpretation." *William and Mary Quarterly* 31, no. 1 (1974).

– "The Four Lives of a Micmac Copper Pot." *Ethnohistory* 22, no. 2 (1975).

– *Keepers of the Game.* Berkeley: University of California Press 1978.

Martin, Finley. *A View from the Bridge: Montague, P.E.I.* Montague, Prince Edward Island: Garden of the Gulf Museum 2005.

Martin, Kathy. "Francis Bain, Farmer Naturalist." *The Island Magazine* 6 (1979).

– *Watershed Red: The Life of the Dunk River, Prince Edward Island.* Charlottetown: Ragweed Press 1981.

Martin, Kenneth R., and Nathan Lipfert. *Lobstering and the Maine Coast.* Bath, ME: Maine Maritime Museum 1985.

McAlpine, Donald F., Robert W. Harding, and Rosemary Curley. "Occurrence and Biogeographic Significance of the Pickerel Frog (*Rana palustris*) on Prince Edward Island, Canada." *Herpetological Natural History* 10, no. 1 (2006).

McAskill, J. Dan. "The People's Forest." *The Island Magazine* 22 (1987): 20–8.

McCaffery, M. "Aboriginal Occupations of the Magdalen Islands." *Info GéoGraphes* 1 (1992).

McCalla, Douglas. "Upper Canadians and Their Guns: An Exploration via Country Store Accounts (1808–61)." *Ontario History* 97 (2005).

McCann, Larry. "Living a Double Life: Town and Country in the Industrialization of the Maritimes." In *Geographical Perspectives on the Maritime Provinces*, edited by Douglas Day. Halifax: Saint Mary's University 1988.

McClellan, John. "Changing Patterns of Land Use." In *The Garden Transformed: Prince Edward Island 1945–1980*, edited by. V. Smitheram, D. Milne, and S. Dasgupta. Charlottetown: Ragweed Press 1982.

McCready, J.E.B. *Prince Edward Island: A Summer Paradise.* Charlottetown: Government of Prince Edward Island 1913.

McDaniel, Gillian. "Homesteading in Maine: Going Back to the Land on a Shoestring Budget." *Mother Earth News* (January/February 1977).

McDonald, S.M., and W.M. Glen. *1958 Forest Inventory of Prince Edward Island*. Charlottetown: PEI Department of Environment, Energy and Forestry 2006.

McGee, Harold F., Jr. "The Use of Furbearers by Native North Americans after 1500." In *Wild Furbearer Management and Conservation in North America*, edited by M. Novak et al. Toronto: Ontario Ministry of Natural Resources 1987.

McKenna, Ryan. "Marooned in the Past: A Glimpse into the Shore Fishery off Cable Head during the 1960s." *The Island Magazine* 60 (2006).

McKenzie, Matthew. *Clearing the Coastline: The Nineteenth Century Ecological and Cultural Transformation of Cape Cod*. Hanover, NH: University Press of New England 2010.

McNabb, Debra. "The Role of the Land in the Development of Horton Township 1760–1775." *They Planted Well: New England Planters in Maritime Canada*, edited by Margaret Conrad. Fredericton: Acadiensis Press 1988.

McNeill, John. "Report of the Superintendent of the Census Returns." *Abstract of the Census of the Population, and Other Statistical Returns of Prince Edward Island, Taken in the Year 1871*. Charlottetown: Reilly & Co. 1871.

McNeill, J.R. "Of Rats and Men: A Synoptic Environmental History of the Island Pacific." *Journal of World History* 5 (1994).

– *Something New under the Sun: An Environmental History of the Twentieth-Century World*. New York: Norton 2000.

McRae, Matthew John. "Manufacturing Paradise: Tourism, Development and Mythmaking on Prince Edward Island, 1939–1973." M.A. thesis, Carleton University, 2004.

McRobie, George. *Small Is Possible*. London: Abacus 1982.

Mead, Margaret. *Coming of Age in Samoa: A Psychological Study of Primitive Youth for Western Civilization*. 1928. Reprint, New York: HarperCollins 2001.

– *Growing Up in New Guinea: A Comparative Study of Primitive Education*. New York: Blue Ribbon Books 1930.

– "Introduction to Polynesia as a Laboratory for the Development of Models in the Study of Cultural Evolution." *Journal of the Polynesian Society* 66 (1957).

Melquist, W.E., and A.E. Dronkert. "River Otter." In *Wild Furbearer Management and Conservation in North America*, edited by M. Novak et al. Toronto: Ontario Ministry of Natural Resources 1987.

Miller, C.L., and G.R. Hamell. "A New Perspective on Indian-White Contact: Cultural Symbols and Colonial Trade." *Journal of American History* 73 (1987).

Miller, R.F. "Environmental History of the Atlantic Maritime Ecozone." In *Assessment of Species Diversity in the Atlantic Maritime Ecozone*, edited by D.F. McAlpine and I.M. Smith. Ottawa: NRC Research Press 2010.

– "Late Glacial and Post-Glacial Fauna: Fossil Evidence from the Maritimes from the Last Glacial Maximum to the Holocene." In *Ta'n Wetapeksi'k: Understanding from Where We Come*, edited by T. Bernard, L. Rosenmeier, and S.L. Farrell. Proceedings of the 2005 Debert Research Workshop, Debert, Nova Scotia. Truro: Confederacy of Mainland Mi'kmaq 2011.

Miller, V. "Aboriginal Micmac Population: A Review of the Evidence." *Ethnohistory* 23, no. 2 (1976).

Miles, E. Introduction to *Voyages to New France, 1599–1603* by Samuel De Champlain, translated by M. Macklem. Ottawa: Oberon Press 1971.

Mineau, Pierre. "Birds and Pesticides: Is the Threat of a Silent Spring Really behind Us?" Rachel Carson Memorial Lecture. *Pesticides News* 86 (2009).

Montgomery, L.M. *Anne of Green Gables*. Boston: L.C. Page 1908.

– *Anne's House of Dreams*. Toronto: McClelland, Goodchild & Stewart 1917.

– *Further Chronicles of Avonlea*. Toronto: McClelland & Stewart 1920.

– *Jane of Lantern Hill*. Toronto: McClelland & Stewart 1937.

– *Selected Journals*. Edited by Mary Rubio and Elizabeth Waterston. 5 vols. Toronto: Oxford University Press 1985.

Mooney, J. "The Aboriginal Population of America North of Mexico." *Smithsonian Miscellaneous Collections* 80, no. 7 (1928).

Moore, Barrington, Jr. *Social Origins of Dictatorship and Democracy: Lord and Peasant in the Making of the Modern World*. 1966. Reprint, Boston: Beacon Press 1993.

Moore, David R. *The Torres Strait Collections of A.C. Haddon: A Descriptive Catalogue*. London: British Museum Publications 1984.

Morgan, L.H. *Systems of Consanguinity and Affinity of the Human Family*. Smithsonian Contributions to Knowledge 17. Washington: Smithsonian Institution 1871.

Morton, John Chalmers ed. *A Cyclopedia of Agriculture, Practical and Scientific*. Vol. 2 London: Blackie & Sons 1875.

Mott, R.J. "Palaeoecology and Chronology of Nova Scotia Relating to the Debert Archaeological Site." In *Ta'n Wetapeksi'k: Understanding from Where We Come*, edited by T. Bernard, L. Rosenmeier, and S.L. Farrell. Proceedings of the 2005 Debert Research Workshop, Debert, Nova Scotia. Truro: Confederacy of Mainland Mi'kmaq 2011.

Mullally, Sasha. "The Machine in the Garden: A Glimpse at Early Automobile Ownership on Prince Edward Island, 1917." *The Island Magazine* 54 (2003).

Mumford, Lewis. *Technics and Civilization*. London: Routledge & Kegan Paul 1934.

Murchison, J.N., and J.D. Murchison. "Quantity Survey of *Gracilaria* in the Malpeque and Cascumpec Bays of PEI." PEI Department of Fisheries Technical Report, 1974.

Mutch, J.P., M.A Savard, G.R.J Julien, B. MacLean, B.G. Raymond, and J. Doull. "Pesticide Monitoring and Fish Kill Investigations on Prince Edward Island, 1994–1999." In *Effects of Land Use Practices on Fish, Shellfish, and Their Habitats on Prince Edward Island*, edited by D.K. Cairns. Canadian Technical Report of Fisheries and Aquatic Sciences no. 2408. Charlottetown: Oceans and Science Branch, Department of Fisheries and Oceans 2002.

Myllyntaus, Timo. *Electrifying Finland: The Transfer of a New Technology into a Late Industrializing Economy*. London: Macmillan Academic/ Helsinki: ETLA 1991.

Nance, R.D., T.R. Worsley, and J.R. Moody. "The Supercontinent Cycle." *Scientific American* 256, no. 7 (1988).

Nash, Roderick. *Wilderness and the American Mind*. New Haven: Yale University Press 1973.

National Film Board of Canada. "Room for a Co-op," Directed by Ralph Holt. 1977.

Nebel, S., A. Mills, J.D. McCracken, and P.D. Taylor. "Declines of Aerial Insectivores in North America Follow a Geographic Gradient." *Avian Conservation and Ecology* 5, no. 2 (2010).

Needler, A.W.H. "Irish Moss Industry in the Maritime Provinces." *Fisheries Research Board of Canada*, General Series 10, 1947.

Neill, Robin. *A History of Canadian Economic Thought*. London: Routledge 2003.

Neushul, M. *Method for the Treatment of AIDS Virus and Other Retroviruses*. U.S. Patent No. 4,783,466, 1988.

Nicosia, Frank, and Kari Lavalli. "Homarid Lobster Hatcheries: Their History and Role in Research, Management, and Aquaculture." *Marine Fisheries Review* 61, no. 2 (1999).

North American Waterfowl Management Plan. "A Strategy for Cooperation." Ottawa: Canadian Wildlife Service 1986.

Novaczek, I. "Response of *Ecklonia radiata* (Laminariales) to Light at 15 C with Reference to the Field Light Budget at Goat Island Bay, New Zealand." *Marine Biology* 80 (1984).

- "Response of Gametophytes of *Ecklonia radiata* (Laminariales) to Temperature in Saturating Light." *Marine Biology* 82 (1984).
- "Exercising Community Control in the Marketplace." *Alternatives Journal* 21, no. 1 (1995).
- "Macroalgal Invasions in Atlantic Canada: The Story of *Codium, Furcellaria* and *Fucus*. In *Marine Biological Invasions: A Perspective on Atlantic Canada and New England*," edited by A.R.O. Chapman. Proceedings of a workshop in Halifax, NS, May 2001. Marine Issues Committee Special Publication 11. Halifax: Ecology Action Centre 2001.

Novaczek, I., and J. McLachlan. "Investigations of the Marine Algae of Nova Scotia XVII: Vertical and Geographic Distributions of Marine Algae on Rocky Shores of the Maritime Provinces." *Proceedings of the Nova Scotia Institute of Science* 38 (1989).

Novaczek, I., R. Angus, and N. Lewis. "Evolution of Post-Colonial Indigenous Peoples' Fisheries Management Systems: Fiji and Prince Edward Island." In *Remote Control: Governance Lessons for and from Small, Insular, and Remote Regions*, edited by G. Baldacchino, L. Felt, and R. Greenwood. St. John's: ISER Books 2009.

Novaczek, I., C.J. Bird, and J. McLachlan. "Phenology and Temperature Tolerance of the Red Algae *Chondria baileyana, Lomentaria baileyana, Griffithsia globifera*, and *Dasya baillouviana* in Nova Scotia." *Canadian Journal of Botany* 65 (1987).

Novaczek, I., S. Fitzpatrick, S. Roach-Lewis, and J. Mitchell. *At the Table: Exploring Women's Roles in the PEI Fishery*. Charlottetown: Institute of Island Studies 2009.

Novak, Milan. "Beaver." In *Wild Furbearer Management and Conservation in North America*, edited by M. Novak, A. Baker, M.E. Obbard and B. Malloch. Toronto: Ontario Ministry of Natural Resources 1987.

Nunn, Patrick D. "Environmental Catastrophe in the Pacific Islands, AD 1300." *Geoarchaeology* 15, no. 7 (2000).
- "Island Origins and Environments." In *A World of Islands: An Island Studies Reader*, edited by Godfrey Baldacchino. Charlottetown: Institute of Island Studies 2007.
- *Vanished Islands and Hidden Continents of the Pacific*. Honolulu: University of Hawai'i Press 2009.
- "The AD 1300 Event in the Pacific Basin." *Geographical Review* 97, no. 1 (2010).

Nye, David E. *Consuming Power: A Social History of American Energies*. Cambridge, MA: MIT Press 1998.

O'Grady, M.A. "In the Footsteps of Jesse Walter Fewkes: Early Archaeology of Rustico Island." *The Island Magazine* 33 (1993).

Olmstead, Alan L., and Paul Webb Rhode. *Creating Abundance: Biological Innovation and American Agricultural Development*. Cambridge: Cambridge University Press 2008.

Ontario Ministry of Agriculture and Food. "Factsheet on Universal Soil Loss Equation." Agdex no. 572/751. May 2000.

"Osprey Helped by Man." *Prince Edward Island Environeer* 3, no. 4 (1975).

Owens, E.H. "The Effects of Ice on the Littoral Zone at Richibucto Head Eastern New Brunswick." *Revue de Géographie de Montréal* 30, nos. 1–2 (1976).

Parenteau, Bill. "Care, Control and Supervision: Native People in the Canadian Atlantic Fishery, 1867–1900." *Canadian Historical Review* 79, no. 1 (1998).

– "A 'Very Determined Opposition to the Law': Conservation, Angling Leases, and Social Conflict in the Canadian Atlantic Salmon Fishery, 1867–1914." *Environmental History* 9, no. 3 (2004).

Parks Canada. "Green Gables Area Plan Concept, 27." Ottawa: Parks Canada 1981.

Parks Canada Agency. "*Unimpaired for Future Generations?' Protecting Ecological Integrity with Canada's National Parks*. Vol. 2, *Setting a New Direction for Canada's National Parks*. Report of the Panel on Ecological Integrity of Canada's National Parks, 2000.

Pastor, J., and D.J. Mladenoff. "The Southern Boreal – Northern Hardwood Border." In *A Systems Analysis of the Global Boreal Forest*, edited by H.H. Shugart, R. Leemans, and G.B. Bonan. Cambridge: Cambridge University Press 1992.

Patton, Mark. *Islands in Time: Island Sociogeography and Mediterranean Prehistory*. London: Routledge 1996.

Pearce-Pratt, R., and D.M. Phillips. "Sulfated Polysaccharides Inhibit Lymphocyte-to-Epithelial Transmission of Human Immunodeficiency Virus-1." *Biology of Reproduction* 54 (1996).

Peters, Robert L., and Thomas E. Lovejoy. "Terrestrial Fauna." In *The Earth as Transformed by Human Action: Global and Regional Changes in the Biosphere over the Past 300 Years*, edited by B.L. Turner et al. Cambridge: Cambridge University Press 1990.

Philpotts, L.E. "Aerial Photo Interpretation of Land Use Changes in Fourteen Lots in Prince Edward Island." Unpublished report 64-9. Ottawa: Canada Department of Agriculture, Economics Division 1958.

Pilkey, Orrin H., and Rob Young. *The Rising Sea*. Washington, DC: Island Press 2009.

Pimental, David. "Soil Erosion and Agricultural Productivity." *World Soil Erosion and Conservation*, edited by David Pimental et al. Cambridge: Cambridge University Press 1993.

Pintal, Jean-Ives. "Aux Frontieres de la Mer: La Prehistoire de Blanc Sablon." Dossiers no. 102, *Les Publications du Québec*. Collections patrimonies et Municipalite de Blanc-Sablon, Quebec, 1998.

Piper, Liza. "Colloquial Meteorology." In *Method and Meaning in Canadian Environmental History*, edited by Alan MacEachern and William Turkel, 102–23. Toronto: Nelson Education 2009.

Poole, Robert K. *Earthrise: How Man First Saw the Earth*. New Haven: Yale University Press 2008.

Pope, Peter. *Fish into Wine: The Newfoundland Plantation in the Seventeenth Century*. Chapel Hill: University of North Carolina Press 2004.

Porter, Dianne. "Women in Fishing Households in Prince Edward Island, 1998." Master's thesis, Carleton University, 1999.

Pratt, Terry Kenneth. *Dictionary of Prince Edward Island English*. Toronto: University of Toronto Press 1996.

Prichard, J.C. *Researches into the Physical History of Man*. London: Sherwood, Gilbert and Piper 1813.

Prince Edward Island. *Abstract of the Census of the Population, and Other Statistical Returns of Prince Edward Island, Taken in the Year 1861*. Charlottetown: John Ings, Queen's Printer 1861.

– Land Commissioners' Court – 1862. *Abstract of the Proceedings before the Land Commissioners' Court, Held during the Summer of 1860, to Inquire into the Differences Relative to the Rights of Landowners and Tenants in Prince Edward Island* ("The Protestant" Office, 1862. Charlottetown: John Ings, Queen's Printer 1862.

– *Commission under Land Purchase Act, 1875*. Charlottetown: Queen's Printer 1875.

– *Current and Proposed Programs in Soil Conservation*. Charlottetown: PEI Department of Agriculture and Forestry, Soil and Crops Division 1973.

– *And So Goes the Soil: A Case for Better of Management on Prince Edward Island*. Charlottetown: PEI Department of Agriculture and Forestry 1979.

– *Royal Commission on the Future of the Potato Industry on Prince Edward Island*. Charlottetown: Government of Prince Edward Island 1987.

– *Everything before Us*. Report of the Royal Commission on the Land. Charlottetown: Government of Prince Edward Island 1990.

– "Impact of Land Based Activities on Fish and Marine Water and the Products They Generate." Discussion paper prepared for the Round Table on Resource Land Use and Stewardship. Charlottetown: PEI Department of Environmental Resources, Water Resources Section 1996.

– *Water on Prince Edward Island: Understanding the Resource, Knowing the Issues*. Charlottetown: PEI Department of Fisheries and Environment, and Environment Canada 1996.

- *Cultivating Island Solutions: Round Table on Resource Land Use and Stewardship*. Charlottetown: Government of Prince Edward Island 1997.
- *Wildlife Conservation Act*. RS Prince Edward Island Cap W-4.1 1998.
- "Creating a Vision for the Future." Discussion Paper, Prince Edward Island Forest Policy. Charlottetown: Government of Prince Edward Island 2004.
- *Prince Edward Island Energy Framework and Renewable Energy Strategy, 2004*. Charlottetown: PEI Department of Environment and Energy 2004.
- *Restoring a Balance in Island Forests*. Prince Edward Island Forest Policy. Charlottetown: Government of Prince Edward Island 2006.
- *We Are All Downstream, We Are All Upstream, We Are All Part of the Watershed*. A Report on the Public Consultations on Managing Land and Water on a Watershed Basis. Charlottetown: Environmental Advisory Council of Prince Edward Island 2007.
- *Report of the Commission on Nitrates in Groundwater*. Charlottetown: Government of Prince Edward Island 2008.
- *Growing the Island Way*. Report of the Commission on the Future of Agriculture and Agri-Food on Prince Edward Island, 2009.
- *New Foundations*. Commission on Land and Local Governance. Charlottetown: Government of Prince Edward Island 2010.
- *2010 State of the Environment*. Charlottetown: PEI Department of Energy and Forestry 2011.
- *Province of Prince Edward Island 36th Annual Statistical Review, 2009*. Charlottetown: PEI Department of Finance and Municipal Affairs 2010.
- *Province of Prince Edward Island 37th Annual Statistical Review, 2010*. Charlottetown: PEI Department of Finance and Municipal Affairs 2011.
- *Province of Prince Edward Island 38th Annual Statistical Review, 2011*. Charlottetown: PEI Department of Finance and Municipal Affairs 2012.
- *Watercourse and Wetland Protection Regulations*, RSPEI 1988, E-9. 2012. http://www.gov.pe.ca/law/regulations/pdf/E&o9-16.pdf.
Prince Edward Island: Canada's Garden Province. Charlottetown: Prince Edward Island Travel Bureau 1954.
"Prince Edward Island Conservation Strategy." Coordinating Committee for Conservation. Government of Prince Edward Island 1987.
"Prince Edward Island Dam Inventory." Department of Regional Economic Expansion. Unpublished project 961.2.1.69, Amherst, Nova Scotia 1969.
"Prince Edward Island Forest Inventory 1990/1992: Summary." Charlottetown: PEI Department of Energy and Forestry, Forestry Branch 1992.
Prince Edward Island: Its Resources and Opportunities. Ottawa: Department of the Interior 1926–27.

Prince Edward Island Land Use Commission. Written decision, Boughton Island Appeal Hearing, 12 May 1989.

"Prince Edward Island Natural Areas Survey." Unpublished manuscript, Biology Department, University of Prince Edward Island, Charlottetown, 1982.

Prince Edward Island: The England of Canada. Charlottetown, 1941.

Pringle, J.D. "Structure of Certain North American Fishery Agencies and Effective Resource Management." *Ocean Management* 10 (1986).

Pringle, J.D., and R.E. Semple. "Dragrake Harvesting Intensity in Irish moss (*Chondrus crispus* Stackhouse) Beds in the Southern Gulf of St. Lawrence." *Proceedings of the International Seaweed Symposium* 11 (1984).

Pringle, J.D., and G.J. Sharp. "Multispecies Resource Management of Economically Important Marine Plant Communities of Eastern Canada." *Helgolander Meerestuntersuchungen* 33 (1980).

Proskie, John. "Costs and Earnings of Dragger Fishing Enterprises, Prince Edward Island, 1952–1967." Report prepared for the PEI Department of Fisheries and Department of Fisheries and Oceans, July 1968.

Public Consultations on the PEI Museum System. Charlottetown: Institute of Island Studies 2007.

Putz, George. "A Singular Community." *The Best of Islands Journal, 1984–2004,* edited by Philip Conkling and David Platt. Rockland: Island Institute 2004.

Pyne, Stephen J. *Fire in America: A Cultural History of Wildland and Rural Fire.* Princeton, NJ: Princeton University Press 1982.

– "Indian Fires: The Fire Practices of North American Indians Transformed Large Areas from Forest to Grassland." *Natural History* 92, no. 3 (1983).

Quammen, David. *Song of the Dodo: Island Biogeography in an Age of Extinction.* New York: Scribner 1996.

Raban, Jonathan. *Coasting: A Private Voyage.* New York: Penguin 1988.

Rackham, Oliver. *Ancient Woodland – Its History, Vegetation and Uses in England.* Dalbeattie, Kirkcudbrightshire: Castlepoint Press 2003.

Rainbird, P. "Islands out of Time: Towards a Critique of Island Archaeology." *Journal of Mediterranean Archaeology* 12, no. 2 (1999).

Ramankutty, N., and J.A. Foley. "Estimating Historical Changes in Land Cover: North American Croplands from 1850 to 1992." *Global Ecology and Biogeography* 8, no. 5 (1999).

Ramankutty, N., Elizabeth Heller, and Jeanine Rhemtulla. "Prevailing Myths about Agricultural Abandonment and Forest Regrowth in the United States." *Annals of the Association of American Geographers* 100, no. 3 (2010).

Rand, S.T. *Micmac Place-Names in the Maritime Provinces and Gaspé Peninsula.* Ottawa: Surveyor General's Office 1919.

Ray, A.J. "The Fur Trade in North America: An Overview from a Historical Geographic Perspective." *Wild Furbearer Management and Conservation in North America*, edited by M. Novak et al. Toronto: Ontario Ministry of Natural Resources 1987.

Raymond, C.W., and J.A. Rayburn. "Land Abandonment in Prince Edward Island." *Geographical Bulletin* 19 (1963).

Reddin, J.E., ed. *Who We Are: Home Economics in Prince Edward Island.* Charlottetown: Home Economics Publishing Collective, University of Prince Edward Island 2006.

Rees, W.E., and Mathis Wackernagel. *Our Ecological Footprint: Reducing Human Impact on Earth.* Gabriola Island: New Society Publishing 1995.

Reich, Charles A. *The Greening of America.* New York: Random House 1970.

Rhatigan, P. *Prannie Rhatigan's Irish Seaweed Kitchen: The Comprehensive Guide to Healthy Everyday Cooking with Seaweeds.* Holywood, Ireland: Booklink 2009.

Richards, John F. *The Unending Frontier: An Environmental History of the Early Modern World.* Berkeley: University of California Press 2005.

Roberts, Callum. *The Unnatural History of the Sea.* Washington, DC: Island Press 2007.

Robertson, Ian Ross. *Sir Andrew Macphail: The Life and Legacy of a Canadian Man of Letters.* Montreal: McGill-Queen's University Press 2008.

– "Sir Andrew Macphail and Orwell." *The Island Magazine* 1 (1976).

– *The Tenant League Movement of Prince Edward Island, 1864–1867.* Toronto: University of Toronto Press 1996.

Robin, Libby. "No Island Is an Island." *Aeon Magazine* (18 December 2014). aeon.co/magazine/science/no-island-is-an-island-in-a-cosmopolitan-age/.

Robinson, C.B. "The Distribution of *Fucus serratus* in North America." *Torreya* 3 (1903).

Robinson, John. "Squaring the Circle? Some Thoughts on the Idea of Sustainable Development." *Ecological Economics* 48, no. 4 (2004).

Rockström, Johan, Will Steffen, Kevin Noone, et al. "A Safe Operating Space for Humanity." *Nature* 461 (2009).

Rollins Epperly, Elizabeth. *The Fragrance of Sweet-Grass: L.M. Montgomery's Heroines and the Pursuit of Romance.* Toronto: University of Toronto Press 1992.

Rosling, Hans, and Zhongxing Zhang. "Health Advocacy with Gapminder Animated Statistics." *Journal of Epidemiology and Global Health* 1, no. 1 (2011).

Roszak, Theodore. *The Making of a Counter Culture: Reflections on the Technocratic Society and Its Youthful Opposition.* Garden City, NY: Doubleday 1969.

Rowe, J.S. *Forest Regions of Canada*. Department of Northern Affairs and Natural Resources, Bulletin 123, Forestry Branch. Ottawa 1959.

Rozwadowki, Helen. *Fathoming the Ocean: The Discovery and Exploration of the Deep Sea*. Cambridge: Harvard University Press 2005.

Russell, Peter A. *How Agriculture Made Canada: Farming in the Nineteenth Century*. Kingston and Montreal: McGill-Queen's University Press 2012.

Rutherford, Wilder, and H.C. Frick. *An Economic Appraisal of the Canadian Lobster Fishery*. Ottawa: Queen's Printer 1967.

Sager, E.W., and L.R. Fischer. *Shipping and Shipbuilding in Atlantic Canada, 1820–1914*. Canadian Historical Association booklet no. 42. Ottawa: Canadian Historical Association 1986.

Sager, E.W., and Gerald E. Panting. *Maritime Capital: The Shipping Industry in Atlantic Canada, 1820–1914*. Kingston and Montreal: McGill-Queen's University Press 1990.

Sahlins, Marshall. "Differentiation by Adaptation in Polynesian Societies." *Journal of the Polynesian Society* 66, no. 3 (1957).

Samuelson, JoDee. "The Watermills of Prince Edward Island, Canada and Gotland Island, Sweden: An Historical Survey." Master's thesis, University of Prince Edward Island, 2013.

Sandwell, R.W. "Mapping Fuel Use in Canada: Exploring the Social History of Canadians' Great Fuel Transformation." In *Historical GIS Research in Canada*, edited by Jennifer Bonnell and Marcel Fortin. Calgary: University of Calgary Press 2014.

Sanger, David. *The Carson Site and the Late Ceramic Period in Passamaquoddy Bay, New Brunswick*. Mercury Series No. 135. Ottawa: National Museum of Man 1987.

Sauer, Carl O. "Seashore: Primitive Home of Man." In *Land and Life: A Section from the Writings of Carl Otwin Sauer*, edited by John Leighly. Berkeley: University of California Press 1963.

Saul, S.B. "The Nature and Diffusion of Technology." In *Economic Development in the Long Run*, edited by A.J. Youngson. London: Allen & Unwin 1972.

Saunders, Albert C. "The Rapid Progress of Prince Edward Island." *Industrial Canada* 30, no. 2 (June 1929): 56–9.

Scarratt, David. *A Handbook of Northern Mussel Culture*. Montague: Island Press 1993.

Schei, Liv, and Gunnie Moberg. *The Orkney Story*. London: Hippocreme Books 1985.

Schumacher, E.F. *Small Is Beautiful: Economics as If People Mattered*. New York: Harper & Row 1973.

Scott, G.A.J. *Canada's Vegetation: A World Perspective*. Montreal and Kingston: McGill-Queen's University Press 1995.

Scudder, G.G.E, and V.R.Vickery. "Grasshoppers (Orthoptera) and Allied Insects of the Atlantic Maritime Ecozone." In *Assessment of Species Diversity in the Atlantic Maritime Ecozone*, edited by D.F. McAlpine and I.M. Smith. Ottawa: NRC Research Press 2010.

Setchell, W.A. "The Law of Temperature Connected with the Distribution of Marine Algae. *Annals of the Missouri Botanical Garden* 2 (1915).

– "The Temperature Interval in the Geographical Distribution of Marine Algae." *Science* 52 (1920).

Sharp, G.J., C. Têtu, R. Semple, and D. Jones. "Recent Changes in the Seaweed Community of Western Prince Edward Island: Implications for the Seaweed Industry." *Hydrobiologia* 260-1 (1993).

Sharpe, Errol. *A People's History of Prince Edward Island*. Charlottetown: Steel Rail 1976.

Shaw, J. "Geomorphic Evidence of Postglacial Terrestrial Environments on Atlantic Canadian Continental Shelves." *Geographie physique et Quaternaire* 59, nos. 2–3 (2005).

– "Palaeogeography of Atlantic Canadian Continental Shelves from the Last Glacial Maximum to the Present, with an Emphasis on Flemish Cap." *Journal of Northwest Atlantic Fishery Science* 37 (2006).

Shaw, J., and D.L. Forbes. "Short- and Long-Term Relative Sea-Level Trends in Atlantic Canada." Proceedings, Canadian Coastal Conference, 1990, Kingston, ON. Ottawa: National Research Council Canada 1990.

Sheridan, Richard C. "Chemical Fertilizers in Southern Agriculture." *Agricultural History* 53, no. 1 (1979).

Sherman, Rexford B. "Daniel Webster, Gentleman Farmer." *Agricultural History* 53, no. 2 (1979).

Shi, David E. *The Simple Life: Plain Living and High Thinking in American Culture*. Athens, GA: University of Georgia Press 1985.

Shortt, S.E.D. *The Search for an Ideal: Six Canadian Intellectuals and Their Convictions in an Age of Transition, 1890–1930*. Toronto: University of Toronto Press 1976.

Shutt, F.T., and L.E. Wright. *Peat, Muck, and Mud Deposits, Their Nature and Composition and Agricultural Uses*. Charlottetown: PEI Department of Agriculture 1933.

Simmons, Terry Allen. "But We Must Cultivate Our Garden: Twentieth Century Pioneering in Rural British Columbia." PhD diss., University of Minnesota, 1979.

Smethurst, Gamaliel. *A Narrative of an Extraordinary Escape out of the Hands of the Indians in the Gulph of St. Lawrence; ... Also a Providential Escape after a Shipwreck in Coming from the Island St. John, in Said Gulph; with an Account of the Fisheries Round That Island.* ... London: J. Bews, A. Grant 1774.

Smil, Vaclav. *Energy at the Crossroads: Global Perspectives and Uncertainties.* Cambridge, MA: MIT Press 2005.

Smit, A.J. "Medicinal and Pharmaceutical Uses of Seaweed Natural Products: A Review." *Journal of Applied Phycology* 16 (2004).

Smith, A.D., and R.W. Fyfe. "A Proposal for the Acquisition of Land in the Vicinity of Deroche Point, Prince Edward Island, for a National Wildlife Area." Unpublished manuscript. Sackville, NB: Canadian Wildlife Service 1968.

Smith, Alisa, and J.B. Mackinnon. *The 100-Mile Diet: A Year of Local Eating.* Toronto: Vintage Canada 2007.

Smith, M.W. "Prince Edward Island Trout Fishery." Fisheries Research Board of Canada Report 574. Originally published in the *Charlottetown Guardian*, 1 April 1958.

Snow, D.R. *The Archaeology of New England.* London: Academic Press 1980.

Sobey, Douglas G. "Analysis of the Ground Flora and Other Data Collected during the 1991 Prince Edward Island Forest Inventory." Plant Community Analysis. Charlottetown: PEI Department of Agriculture, Fisheries and Forestry 1995.

– "The Department of Marine and the Search for Masts on Ile Saint-Jean." *The Island Magazine* 50 (2001).

– *Early Descriptions of the Forests of Prince Edward Island.* Part 1, *The French Period, 1534–1758.* Charlottetown: PEI Department of Agriculture and Forestry 2002.

– "The Forests of Prince Edward Island: A Classification and Ordination Using Multivariate Methods." *Canadian Field-Naturalist* 116, no. 4 (2002).

– "The Department of Marine and the Search for Masts on Ile Saint-Jean," *The Northern Mariner* 13, no. 1 (2003).

– *Early Descriptions of the Forests of Prince Edward Island.* Part 2, *The British and Post-Confederation Periods – 1758–c. 1900.* Section A, The Analyses, and Section B, The Extracts. Charlottetown: PEI Department of Environment, Energy and Forestry 2006.

– "An Analysis of the Historical Records for the Mammalian Fauna of Prince Edward Island." *Canadian Field-Naturalist* 121 (2007).

– *Early Descriptions of the Forests of Prince Edward Island.* Part 3, *The Early Twentieth Century.* Charlottetown: PEI Department of Environment, Energy and Forestry 2008.

– "Shipbuilding and the Forests of Prince Edward Island: An Analysis of the Types and Amounts of Wood Used in Island Ships – Based on the Surveyors'

Reports of the Lloyd's Register of British and Foreign Shipping."
Charlottetown: PEI Department of Environment, Energy and Forestry 2011.

Sobey, Douglas, and William M. Glen. *Analysis of the Ground Flora and Other Data Collected during the 1990–1992 Prince Edward Island Forest Biomass Inventory*. Part 4, *The Distribution of Forest-Types on Prince Edward Island*. Charlottetown: PEI Department of Agriculture and Forestry 1999.

– "Forests of Prince Edward Island: A Classification and Ordination Using Multivariate Methods. *Canadian Field-Naturalist* 116 (2002).

– "A Mapping of the Present and Past Forest-Types of Prince Edward Island. *Canadian Field-Naturalist* 118, no. 4 (2004).

– *Mapping the Pre-Settlement Forests of Prince Edward Island*. Charlottetown: Department of Agriculture and Forestry 2014.

Somers, George, Bruce Raymond, and William Uhlman. *Water Quality Interpretive Report*. Charlottetown: Prince Edward Island Department of Technology and Environment and Environment Canada 1999.

South, G.R. *A Guide to the Common Seaweeds of Atlantic Canada*. St John's, NFLD: Breakwater/Memorial University 1981.

– "A Checklist of Marine Algae of Eastern Canada, Second Revision." *Canadian Journal of Botany* 62 (1984).

Spate, O.H.K. "Islands and Men." In *Man's Place in the Island Ecosystem: A Symposium*, edited by F.R. Fosberg. Hawaii: Bishop Museum Press 1963.

Speth, J.G. "Environmental Failure: A Case for a New Green Politics." *Guardian*, 21 October 2008. http://www.guardian.co.uk/environment/2008/oct/21/network.

Spierenburg, H.A. *Historical Statistics of Prince Edward Island*, 2007. Charlottetown: Government of Prince Edward Island 2007.

Spriggs, Matthew. "Are Islands Islands?" In *Islands of Inquiry: Colonisation, Seafaring and the Archaeology of Maritime Landscapes*, edited by Geoffrey Clark, Foss Leach, and Sue O'Connor. Terra Australis 29. Canberra: ANU E-Press 2008.

Squire, Shelagh J. "Literary Tourism and Sustainable Tourism: Promoting *Anne of Green Gables* in Prince Edward Island." *Journal of Sustainable Tourism* 4, no. 3 (1996).

Stea, R. "Geology and Palaeoenvironmental Reconstruction of the Debert-Belmont Site." In *Ta'n Wetapeksi'k: Understanding from Where We Come*, edited by T. Bernard, L. Rosenmeier, and S.L. Farrell. Proceedings of the 2005 Debert Research Workshop, Debert, Nova Scotia. Truro: Confederacy of Mainland Mi'kmaq 2011.

Stephens, Henry, and J.S. Skinner. *Book of the Farm: Detailing the Labors of the Farmer, Steward, Plowman, Hedger, Cattle-Man, Shepherd, Field-Worker, and Dairymaid*. Vol. 2. New York: C.M. Saxton 1851.

Steward, J. *Theory of Culture Change: The Methodology of Multilinear Evolution*. Urbana, IL: University of Illinois Press 1995.

Stewart, F.L.S. Faunal Remains from the Sandhills Region, Malpeque Bay, PEI, Excavated in 2007 by Helen Kristmanson. Manuscript on file with Aboriginal Affairs Secretariat, Government of Prince Edward Island, Charlottetown, 2008.

Stewart, John. *An Account of Prince Edward Island in the Gulf of St Lawrence, North America*. London: Winchester & Sons 1806. Reprint, Wakefield, UK: S.R. Publishers; New York: Johnson Reprint 1967.

Stilgenbauer, F.A. "The Geography of Prince Edward Island." PhD diss., University of Michigan, Ann Arbor, 1929.

Stilgoe, John. *Alongshore*. New Haven: Yale University Press 1994.

Stoll, Steven. "Farm against Forest." *American Wilderness: A New History*, edited by Michael Lewis. Oxford: Oxford University Press 2007.

Stott, Philip. "A Magical Process." *Nature* 468, no. 7325 (2010): 764.

Stratford, Elaine, Godfrey Baldacchino, Elizabeth McMahon, and Andrew Hardwood. "Envisioning the Archipelago." *Island Studies Journal* 6, no. 2 (2011).

Strommel, Henry. *Lost Islands: The Story of Islands That Have Vanished from Nautical Charts*. Vancouver: University of British Columbia Press 1984.

Stuart, Kathleen. "The Influence of Islandness on Energy Policy and Electricity Supply." Master's thesis, University of Prince Edward Island, 2006.

Submission by the Province of Prince Edward Island to the Royal Commission on Transportation, July 1949. Charlottetown: Irwin Printing, 1949.

Sue, Nelly, Dian, Carol, and Billie. *Country Lesbians: The Story of the WomanShare Collective*. Grants Pass, OR: Womanshare Books 1976.

Sullivan, Kevin. Foreword to *Anne of Green Gables, Centennial Edition*. Toronto: Davenport Press 2008.

Sutherland, George. *Manual of the Geography and Natural and Civil History of Prince Edward Island*. Charlottetown: John Ross 1861.

Taussig, Michael. *Shamanism, Colonialism and the Wild Man: A Study in Terror and Healing*. Chicago: University of Chicago Press 1986.

Taverner, P.A. *Birds of Eastern Canada*. 2nd ed. Biological Series no. 3, Department of Mines, Geological Survey Memoir 104. Ottawa: Kings Printer 1922.

Taylor, W.R. *Marine Algae of the Northeast Coast of North America*. Ann Arbor, MI: University Michigan Press 1957.

Terrasson, F., and G. Tendron. "The Case for Hedgerows." *The Ecologist* 11, no. 5 (1981).

Theroux, Paul. *Fresh Air Fiend*. Boston: Houghton Mifflin 2000.

Thomas, Howard H., and Randall L. Dibblee. "A Coyote, *Canis latrans*, on Prince Edward Island." *Canadian Field-Naturalist* 107 (1985).

Thompson, Ian D. *Sportfishing in Prince Edward Island: A Survey of Anglers.* Ottawa: Environment Canada 1976.

Thomson, Don W. *Skyview Canada: A Story of Aerial Photography in Canada.* Ottawa: Energy, Mines and Resources Canada 1975.

"Travel Intentions Survey 2009." Charlottetown: Tourism Research Centre, School of Business UPEI 2009.

Tubbs, C.H., and D.R. Houston. "*Fagus grandifolia*, American Beech." In *Silvics of North America*, vol. 2, *Hardwoods*, edited by R.M. Burns and B.H. Honkala. Washington, DC: U.S. Department of Agriculture, Forest Service 1990.

Tufts, R.W. *The Birds of Nova Scotia.* Halifax: Nova Scotia Museum 1961.

Turnbull, Chris, and Pat Allen. "More Palaeo-Indian Points from New Brunswick." *Man in the Northeast* 15–16 (1978).

Turner, B.L., William C. Clark, Robert W. Kates, John F. Richards, Jessica T. Mathews, and William B. Meyer, eds. *The Earth as Transformed by Human Action: Global and Regional Changes in the Biosphere over the Past 300 Years.* Cambridge: Cambridge University Press 1990.

United Nations World Commission on Environment and Development. *Our Common Future* (Brundtland Report). Oxford: Oxford University Press 1987.

Upton, L.F.S. *Micmacs and Colonists: Indian-White Relations in the Maritimes, 1713–1867.* Vancouver: University of British Columbia Press 1979.

Van den Hoek, C. "Phytogeographic Distribution Groups of Benthic Marine Algae in the North Atlantic Ocean: A Review of Experimental Evidence from Life Histories." *Helgolander Meerestuntersuchungen* 35 (1982).

– "World-Wide Latitudinal and Longitudinal Seaweed Distribution Patterns and Their Possible Causes, as Illustrated by the Distribution of Rhodophytan Genera." *Helgolander Meerestuntersuchungen* 38 (1984).

Van den Hoek, C., and A.M. Breeman. "Seaweed Biogeography of the North Atlantic: Where Are We Now?" In *Evolutionary Biogeograhy of the Marine Algae of the North Atlantic*, edited by D.J. Garbary and G.R. South. Berlin: Springer Verlag 1990.

Van den Hoek, C., A.M. Breeman. and W.T. Stam. "The Geographic Distribution of Seaweed Species in Relation to Temperature: Past and Present." In *Expected Effects of Climate Change on Marine Coastal Ecosystems*, edited by J.J. Beukema et al. Netherlands: Kluwer Academic Publishers 1990.

Van Wey, Leah K., Gilvan R. Guedes, and Álvaro O. D'Antona. "Out-Migration and Land-Use Change in Agricultural Frontiers: Insights from Altamira Settlement Project." *Population and Environment* 34, no. 1 (2012).

"Variety of Crops Grown in Maritime Provinces." *The Busy East of Canada* 7, February 1917. Saint John, NB: Busy East Press.

Vass, Elinor. "The Agricultural Societies of Prince Edward Island." *The Island Magazine* 7 (1979).

– "Early Island Roads." *The Island Magazine* 19 (1986).

– "Mrs. Haviland's Plants." *The Island Magazine* 36 (1994).

Vass, Elinor, and Wayne MacKinnon. *The Best of the Past: Traditional Sustainable Agriculture in Prince Edward Island.* Charlottetown: Institute of Island Studies 1989.

Vass, Stan. "The Black Bear on Prince Edward Island: A Natural History." *The Island Magazine* 22 (1987).

Vaugelade, P., C. Hoebler, F. Bernard, F. Guillon, M. Lahaye, P.H. Dree, and B. Darcy-Vrillion. "Non-Starch Polysaccharides Extracted from Seaweed Can Modulate Intestinal Absorption of Glucose and Insulin Response in the Pig." *Reproduction Nutrition Development* 40, no. 1 (2000).

Vayda, A.P., and R.A. Rappoport. "Island Cultures." In *Man's Place in the Island Ecosystem*, edited by F.R. Fosberg. Honolulu: Bishop Museum Press 1963.

Vining, Daniel R., and Anne Strauss. "A Demonstration That the Current Deconcentration of Population in the United States Is a Clean Break with the Past." *Environment and Planning* 9, no. 7 (1977).

Visitors Guide. 1990 and 2010 editions. Charlottetown: PEI Department of Tourism. 1990–2014.

Vonnegut, Mark. *The Eden Express.* New York: Praeger 1975.

Wake, Winifred. "Prince Edward Island's Early Natural History Society." *The Island Magazine* 37 (1995).

Wallace Ferguson, Birgitta. "Selective Exploitation of Shellfish at Rustico Island, Prince Edward Island." Paper presented to Meeting of Canadian Archaeological Association, Fredericton, NB, 10–14 May 1989.

Wallis, W.D., and R.S. Wallace. *The Micmac Indians of Eastern Canada.* Minneapolis: University of Minnesota Press 1955.

Way, Albert. "'A Cosmopolitan Weed of the World': Following Bermudagrass." *Agricultural History* 88, no. 3 (2014).

Weale, David. "The Mud Diggers." *The Island Magazine* 5 (1978).

– "The Shell-Mud Diggers of Prince Edward Island." *Canadian Papers in Rural History* 2 (1980).

– *Them Times.* Charlottetown: Institute of Island Studies 1992.

– *Chasing the Shore: Little Stories about Spirit and Landscape.* Charlottetown: Tangle Lane 2007.

Weale, David, and Harry Baglole. *Prince Edward Island and Confederation.* Summerside: Williams & Crue 1973.

Weaver, Sharon. "First Encounters: 1970s Back-to-the-Land Cape Breton, N.S., and Denman, Hornby and Lasqueti Islands, BC," Special Issue, "Talking Green: Oral History and Environmental History." *Oral History Forum d'histoire orale* 30 (2010).

Weeks, Blair. *Minding the House: A Biographical Guide to Prince Edward Island MLAs, 1873–1993.* Charlottetown: Acorn Press and Association of Former Members of the Legislative Assembly of Prince Edward Island 2000.

Weir, John A. "Rural Reconstruction on Prince Edward Island: An Evaluation." PhD diss., Notre Dame University, South Bend, IL, 1964.

Wells, Kennedy. *The Fishery of Prince Edward Island.* Charlottetown: Ragweed Press 1986.

– "An Extinct Breed? Whatever Became of Our 'Farmer-Fishermen'?" *Rural Delivery* 15, no. 1 (1990).

White, H.C. "Some Observations on the Eastern Brook Trout (*Salvelinus fontinalis*) of Prince Edward Island." *Transactions of the American Fisheries Society* 60 (1930): 100–8.

White, Leslie A. *The Science of Culture.* New York: Grove Press 1949.

White, R. *The Middle Ground: Indians, Empires and Republics in the Great Lakes Region, 1650–1815.* Cambridge: Cambridge University Press 1991.

Whitehead, R.H. "The Proto-Historic Period in the Maritime Provinces." In *Prehistoric Archaeology in the Maritime Provinces*, edited by S. Blair and M. Deal. Past and Present Research Reports in Archaeology 8. Fredericton: New Brunswick Council of Maritime Premiers 1991.

– "Nova Scotia: The Protohistoric Period, 1500–1630." *Curatorial Report* 75. Halifax: Nova Scotia Museum 1993.

– *Stories from the Six Worlds: Micmac Legends.* Halifax: Nimbus 1988.

Whiteside, G.B. *Soil Survey of Prince Edward Island.* 2nd ed. Ottawa: Queen's Printer 1965.

Wightman, F.A. "The Shell-Mines of Prince Edward Island." *The Canadian Magazine* (1913).

Williams, Judith. *Clam Gardens: Aboriginal Mariculture on Canada's West Coast.* Vancouver: New Star 2006.

Willis, Nancy. *Report on the Comparative Study of Regimes for Soil Restoration and Fertility Maintenance.* Souris, PEI: Institute of Man and Resources, 1978.

Wilson, Catharine Anne. *Tenants in Time: Family Strategies, Land, and Liberalism in Upper Canada, 1799–1871.* Kingston: McGill-Queen's University Press 2008.

Wilson, Edward O. *The Future of Life.* New York: Vintage Books 2002.

Wilson, E.O., and R.H. MacArthur. *The Theory of Island Biogeography*. Princeton: Princeton University Press 1967.

Wilson, J. Tuzo. "Did the Atlantic Close and Then Re-Open?" *Nature* 211(1966).

Woods, Michael. *Rural Geography: Processes, Responses and Experiences in Rural Restructuring*. London: Sage 2005.

Worster, Donald, ed. *The Ends of the Earth: Perspectives on Modern Environmental History*, Cambridge, UK: Cambridge University Press 1988.

Wrigley, E.A. "Reflections on the History of Energy Supply, Living Standards and Economic Growth." *Australian Economic History Review* 33, no. 1 (1993).

Wynn, Graeme. "Administration in Adversity: The Deputy Surveyors and Control of the New Brunswick Crown Forest before 1844." *Acadiensis* 7 (1977).

– *Timber Colony: A Historical Geography of Early Nineteenth Century New Brunswick*. Toronto: University of Toronto Press 1981.

– "1800–1810: Turning the Century." In *The Atlantic Region to Confederation: A History*, edited by P.A. Buckner and J.G. Reid. Toronto: University of Toronto Press/Fredericton: Acadiensis Press 1994.

– "Remapping Tutira: Contours in the Environmental History of New Zealand." *Journal of Historical Geography* 23, no. 4 (1997).

– *Canada and Arctic North America: An Environmental History*. Nature and Human Societies Series. Santa Barbara, CA: ABC-CLIO 2007.

– "A 'Deep History' of the American Environment." *Journal of Historical Geography* 43 (2014).

Wynn, Graeme, Craig Colten, Robert M. Wilson, Martin V. Melosi, Mark Fiege, and Diana Davis. "Reflections on the American Environment: A Roundtable." *Journal of Historical Geography* 43 (January 2014).

Contributors

JEAN-PAUL ARSENAULT served for over twenty years with the Government of Prince Edward Island in a number of capacities, including as director of forestry and director of planning and development for the Department of Agriculture and executive secretary of both the Round Table on Resource Land Use and Stewardship and the Commission on Land and Local Governance. In 1995 he chaired the National Task Force on the federal Feed Freight Assistance Program. He holds a bachelor of Science in forestry from the University of New Brunswick and an MBA from Université Laval.

BOYDE BECK is curator of history for the Prince Edward Island Museum and Heritage Foundation and editor of its popular history journal, *The Island Magazine*. His formal training includes a master's degree in history from Queen's University and an MA in museum studies from the University of Toronto. He has worked as director of the Fishery Museum at Basin Head, PEI, and has curated several exhibits on various aspects of the fishery on Prince Edward Island.

CLAIRE CAMPBELL is an associate professor at Bucknell University, where she teaches Canadian, North American, and environmental history. She is the author of *Shaped by the West Wind: Nature and History in Georgian Bay*, the editor of *A Century of Parks Canada, 1911–2011*, and the co-editor, with Robert Summerby-Murray, of *Environmental Histories of Atlantic Canada* (Acadiensis Press 2013). As an historian, she is interested in exploring the environmental dimensions of designated historic sites, how these places nurture Canada's national and regional identities, and how they might be used to enhance public education about environmental issues.

ROSEMARY CURLEY recently retired from her position as natural areas biologist with the Province of Prince Edward Island. Her duties included membership on the Committee on the Status of Endangered Wildlife in Canada and conserving species-at-risk on PEI. While participating in the General Status of Species in Canada program, she coordinated coarse status assessments of more than 1,500 PEI species from mosquitoes to mammals. She has also participated in plant collections that will lead to a new book on the flora of Prince Edward Island. She is currently editor of the Atlantic Society of Fish and Wildlife Biologists newsletter, *The Biolink*, and is a member of the editorial committee of *The Island Magazine*.

JOHN R. GILLIS, professor emeritus, Rutgers University, is now actively involved with the Island Institute at Rockland, Maine. He has also taught at Stanford, Princeton, and the University of California, and is a life member of Clare Hall, Cambridge. He is the author of *Islands of the Mind: How the Human Imagination Created the Atlantic World* (2004) and the co-editor of *Becoming Historians* (2009). His *The Human Shore: Seacoasts in Human History* (2013) traces coastal migrations around the world. He is concerned not only with the material conditions of coasts but with their cultural meanings. He challenges the conventions of both maritime and territorial history that have treated coasts as belonging either to water or to land by showing they are ecotones, combining both elements in a unique environment that has produced a distinctive culture now threatened with extinction.

DAVID KEENLYSIDE is executive director of the Prince Edward Island Museum and Heritage Foundation. An archaeologist by profession, he worked at the National Museum of Man in Ottawa and later the Canadian Museum of Civilization for thirty-five years as Atlantic provinces archaeologist. He has been conducting fieldwork in Prince Edward Island and the Maritimes since 1978, investigating Aboriginal archaeological sites, and has served on professional and volunteer heritage organizations in Alberta, Ontario, New Brunswick, and Nova Scotia for many years. Most recently he is co-author of *The Landscapes of Confederation* (2010), a compendium of historical materials relating to the Charlottetown Conference of 1864.

HELEN KRISTMANSON is the director of Aboriginal Affairs and Archaeology with the government of Prince Edward Island. Kristmanson's career in Maritime Provinces archaeology spans more than two decades. After completing a master of Arts degree in archaeology at the Memorial University of Newfoundland, Kristmanson earned a PhD from the University of Manchester (UK). Her doctoral research examined the utility of archaeological knowledge to Aboriginal rights litigation. She began her doctoral studies while working as consultant for the Conne River Mi'kmaq Band in Newfoundland and subsequently served as ethno-archaeologist at Parks Canada Agency. Helen became PEI's first provincial archaeologist in 2009; in 2014, she curated the award-winning exhibit *Digging into the Past: An Archaeological Discovery at Malpeque Bay.*

EDWARD MACDONALD is an associate professor in the Department of History at the University of Prince Edward Island where he teaches Prince Edward Island, Atlantic Canadian, Canadian, and public history. He is the author of *If You're Stronghearted: Prince Edward Island in the Twentieth Century* (2000) and co-author of *The Landscapes of Confederation* (2010), as well as three museum catalogues and more than forty articles dealing primarily with the social and cultural history of Prince Edward Island.

ALAN MACEACHERN is a professor in the Department of History at the University of Western Ontario. His research gravitates to topics involving humans' past relations with nature: environmental history, a field too pertinent to present-day concerns (and too interesting) to stay within the academic domain. He is the director of NICHE (Network in Canadian History and Environment), which assists Canadian environmental history researchers in developing their projects and works to make the field better known to governments, public history organizations, environmental groups, and the public. His first book, *Natural Selections: National Parks in Atlantic Canada, 1935–1970*, received an honourable mention for the Sir John A. Macdonald Prize.

JOSHUA MACFADYEN is assistant professor in the School of Historical, Philosophical and Religious Studies and the School of Sustainability at Arizona State University. His PhD was in rural and environmental history at the University of Guelph, and his postdoctoral work establishes a new estimate of forest disturbance for domestic energy requirements in Eastern Canada after 1850.

COLIN MACINTYRE graduated from the University of Prince Edward Island with a bachelor's degree in history in 2007 and a master's degree in Island Studies in 2011. His MA thesis, "An Environmental Pre-History of Prince Edward Island: A Reconnaissance in Force, 1769–1970," examined two hundred years of environment-related legislation. Works in progress include two articles for *The Island Magazine*, "The Prince Edward Island Potato Bug Plague," and "Albert E. Morrison: Pioneer Environmentalist."

IRENÉ NOVACZEK was born in Scotland but spent her formative years in the Maritime provinces and Quebec. She gained a BSc in biology, geology, and chemistry at Kings College/Dalhousie University, studied marine botany at the University of British Columbia, and then gained a PhD in marine ecology at the University of Auckland, New Zealand. Her postdoctoral studies focused on biogeography and shellfish toxicology. A long-time activist for social and environmental justice, she works with NGOs and rural communities on coastal fisheries and community development. She also worked on small islands of the Caribbean, Indonesia, Southeast Asia, and the South Pacific before becoming director of the Institute of Island Studies at University of Prince Edward Island, a post she occupied from 2004 to 2013. She owns a rural microenterprise, Oceanna Seaplants, which manufactures health and beauty products from seaweeds and organic herbs, while continuing to act as an adjunct professor and graduate faculty member in Island Studies at UPEI.

DOUGLAS SOBEY taught environmental biology at universities in Northern Ireland from 1979 until his retirement in 2004. Over the past eighteen years he has been researching the history of the forests of Prince Edward Island. He is especially interested in the composition and structure of the pre-European-settlement forest, in the processes that led to its alteration and destruction, and in the attitudes of Islanders to the forest from the arrival of the first settlers to the end of the nineteenth century. He is currently examining early manuscript maps and field survey books in the Prince Edward Island Public Archives for their information on the forest. He is also carrying out a study of the woods used in Island shipbuilding in the nineteenth century, based on the survey reports of the Lloyd's Register of Shipping. He is the co-author of *Samuel Holland: His*

Work and Legacy on Prince Edward Island (2015), published by Island Studies Press.

KATHLEEN STUART received her MA in island studies from the University of Prince Edward Island, completing research on the influence of "islandness" on energy policy and electricity supply in Prince Edward Island. She has taught island studies as a sessional lecturer at UPEI and presented papers to international conferences in the Åland Islands, Bornholm, Curaçao, Hong Kong, Malta, Maui, the Shetland Islands, and the Turku Archipelago. She is a contributor to *Pulling Strings*, an edited book about policy and governance in sub-national island jurisdictions including Prince Edward Island. Her articles have also appeared in *Sustainable Development, Journal of Small Business & Entrepreneurship*, and *Island Studies Journal*.

GRAEME WYNN, a professor of environmental and historical geography at the University of British Columbia, has studied human transformations of the earth for four decades. The core of his work has always been interdisciplinary, rooted in geography and history and engaged with the environmental sciences. His research contributes to debate on and understanding of the development of European settlements overseas, the history of migration, the connections between environment and empire, and the developing field of environmental history. His most recent books are *Canada and Arctic North America: An Environmental History* (2007) and *Culture and Agriculture on the Tantramar Marshes* (2012). He held the Brenda and David McLean Chair in Canadian Studies at UBC from July 2011 to June 2013.

Index

Page numbers in italics refer to illustrations.